Using the *Teach Yourself in 24 Hours* Series

Welcome to the *Teach Yourself in 24 Hours* series! You're probably thinking, "What, they want me to stay up all night and learn this stuff?" Well, no, not exactly. This series introduces a new way to teach you about exciting new products: 24 one-hour lessons, designed to keep your interest and keep you learning. Because the learning process is broken into small units, you will not be overwhelmed by the complexity of some of the new technologies that are emerging in today's market. Each hourly lesson has a number of special items, some old, some new, to help you along.

10 Minutes

The first 10 minutes of each hour lists the topics and skills that you will learn about by the time you finish the hour. You will know exactly what the hour will bring with no surprises.

20 Minutes

Twenty minutes into the lesson, you will have been introduced to many of the newest features of the software application. In the constantly evolving computer arena, knowing everything a program can do will aid you enormously now and in the future.

30 Minutes

Before 30 minutes have passed, you will have learned at least one useful task. Many of these tasks take advantage of the newest features of the application. These tasks use a hands-on approach, telling you exactly which menus and commands you need to use to accomplish the goal. This approach is found in each lesson of the *24 Hours* series.

40 Minutes

You will see after 40 minutes that many of the tools you have come to expect from the *Teach Yourself* series are found in the *24 Hours* series as well. Notes and Tips offer special tricks of the trade to make your work faster and more productive. Warnings help you avoid those nasty time-consuming errors.

50 Minutes

By the time you're 50 minutes in, you'll probably run across terms you haven't seen before. Never before has technology thrown so many new words and acronyms into the language, and the New Terms elements found in this series will carefully explain each and every one of them.

60 Minutes

At the end of the hour, you may still have questions that need answered. You know the kind—questions on skills or tasks that come up every day for you, but that weren't directly addressed during the lesson. That's where the Q&A section can help. By answering the most frequently asked questions about the topics discussed in the hour, Q&A not only answers your specific question, it provides a succinct review of all that you have learned in the hour.

Navigating in PowerPoint 97

Standard

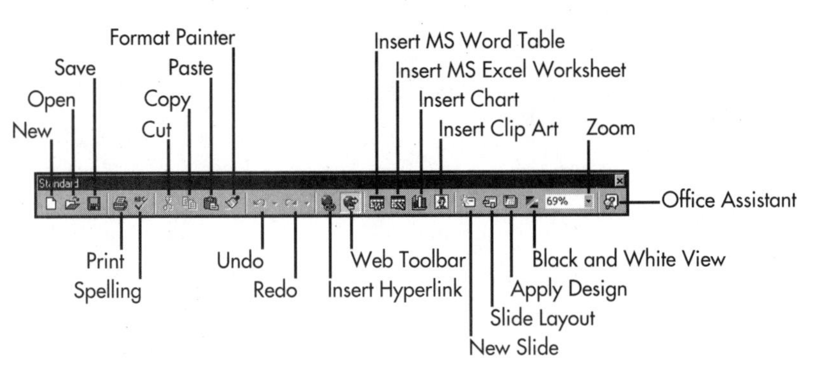

Formatting

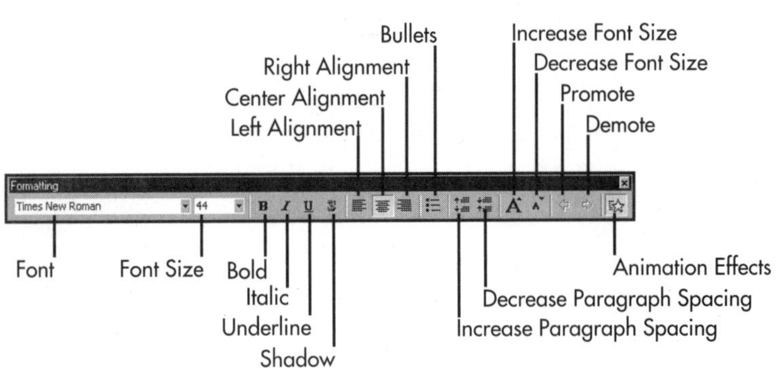

Drawing

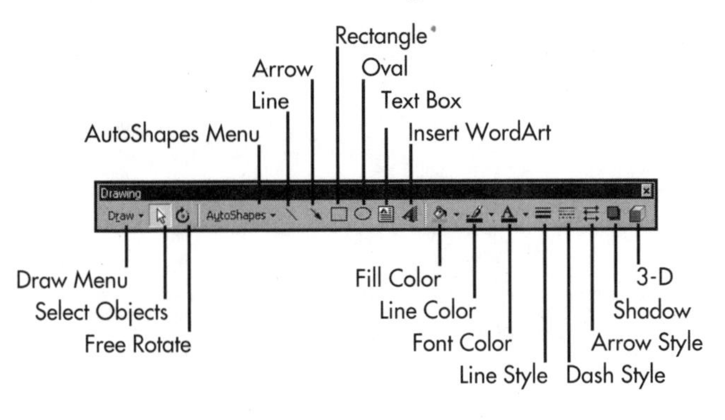

How to Use This Book

This book is designed to teach you topics in one-hour sessions. All the books in the Sams *Teach Yourself* series allow the reader to start working and become productive with the product as quickly as possible. This book will definitely do that for you!

Each hour, or session, starts with an overview of the topic, so you know what to expect in each lesson. The overviews help you determine the nature of the lesson and whether it's relevant to your needs.

The book is divided into six sections that can be reviewed independently, or you can read the whole book cover to cover. Each chapter should take about one hour to cover, and we have included a workshop at the end of each chapter with a "Test What You've Learned" section to help reinforce the material covered during that hour.

How to Use This Book

Teach Yourself PowerPoint 97 in 24 Hours

Teach Yourself
PowerPoint 97
in 24 Hours

Alexandria and
Christopher Haddad

SAMS
PUBLISHING
201 West 103rd Street
Indianapolis, Indiana 46290

FIRST EDITION

International Standard Book Number: 0-672-31117-8

Library of Congress Catalog Card Number: 97-6669

2000 99 4 3

Interpretation of the printing code: the rightmost double-digit number is the year of the book's printing; the rightmost single-digit, the number of the book's printing. For example, a printing code of 97-1 shows that the first printing of the book occurred in 1997.

Composed in AGaramond and MCPdigital by Macmillan Computer Publishing

Printed in the United States of America

Trademarks

Publisher and President Richard K. Swadley
Publishing Manager Dean Miller
Director of Editorial Services Cindy Morrow
Director of Marketing Kelli S. Spencer
Product Marketing Manager Wendy Gilbride
Assistant Marketing Manager Rachel Wolfe

Acquisitions Editor
Cari Skaggs

Development Editor
Brian-Kent Proffitt

Production and Copy Editor
Lisa M. Lord

Indexer
Tim Wright

Technical Reviewer
Jim Grey

Editorial Coordinator
Katie Wise

Technical Edit Coordinator
Lynette Quinn

Resource Coordinators
Deborah Frisby
Tonya Simpson

Editorial Assistants
Carol Ackerman
Andi Richter
Rhonda Tinch-Mize

Cover Designer
Tim Amrhein

Book Designer
Gary Adair

Copy Writer
David Reichwein

Production Team Supervisors
Brad Chinn
Charlotte Clapp

Production
Georgiana Briggs
Michael Dietsch
Lana Dominguez
Tim Osborn

Overview

Contents

Dedication

We would like to dedicate this book to little Anastasia. Ana has shown us, since she was five (she is now nine), how much fun PowerPoint could be. PowerPoint was the first "real" application she was taught, and she has since come up with hours of drawing and slide fun to show to Mommy and Daddy. If a five-year-old can do it, so can you. (Don't be afraid—pretend you're in kindergarten.)

Acknowledgments

Alexandria and Christopher would like to thank the following individuals and groups who have contributed to this book:

- Lynn and Holly at Softek Services, Inc. (`http://www.ssitraining.com`) for showing Alex how to professionally teach and write about software she already knew how to use. Alex thinks Softek is the best company she has ever worked for because everyone there strives for excellence and complete customer satisfaction.
- Ruel Hernandez, who wrote Hour 21, "Multimedia." He took the time to learn our writing style and has produced a quality chapter, packed full of some great information.
- Our great friend Kimberley Taylor who came to our rescue many, many times. Seemed like the baby always picked deadline days (and nights) to want Mommy and Daddy's undivided attention. Anthony accepted Kimberley as an appropriate substitute; without her help, we would have never, ever finished.
- The excellent team at Sams Publishing who made significant contributions to the production of this book. In part, we would like to personally thank Cari Skaggs, Brian-Kent Proffitt, Lisa Lord, Jim Grey, Tonya Simpson, and those individuals who worked behind the scenes.
- And last, but certainly not least, the Microsoft PowerPoint 97 team (most often referred to as "those nice folks at Microsoft"). Without them, this book couldn't have been written.

About the Authors

Alexandria and Christopher Haddad live in Arlington, Virginia with their daughter Anastasia and new baby Anthony. They have the best of all worlds, as best friends and business partners. They both love good music and motorcycles and enjoy working with computer hardware and software.

Alexandria

Alexandria has been hacking at computer software applications for over 10 years and has been a software consultant/instructor for the last three. She currently works out of their home creating Web sites and writing training manuals for Softek Services, Inc. (`http://www.ssitraining.com/`). In addition to teaching Anastasia and Anthony everything they never wanted to know about PowerPoint 97, she finds time to write for Sams.

Christopher

Christopher has been coding computer software for the last 20 years (starting in the fifth grade). He is currently an equity partner of Rock Creek Technologies (`http://www.rockcreek.com/`), a software and consulting company in Washington, DC. He has authored and co-authored several books for Sams Publishing, including portions of *The Web Programming Resource Library* and *JavaScript Unleashed.*

Tell Us What You Think!

As a reader, you are the most important critic and commentator of our books. We value your opinion and want to know what we're doing right, what we could do better, what areas you'd like to see us publish in, and any other words of wisdom you're willing to pass our way. You can help us make strong books that meet your needs and give you the computer guidance you require.

Do you have access to CompuServe or the World Wide Web? Then check out our CompuServe forum by typing `GO SAMS` at any prompt. If you prefer the World Wide Web, check out our site at `http://www.mcp.com`.

> If you have a technical question about this book, call the technical support line at 317-581-4669.

As the publishing manager of the group that created this book, I welcome your comments. You can fax, e-mail, or write me directly to let me know what you did or didn't like about this book—as well as what we can do to make our books stronger. Here's the information:

Fax: 317-581-4669

E-mail: Dean Miller, `opsys_mgr@sams.mcp.com`

Mail: Dean Miller
201 W. 103rd Street
Indianapolis, IN 46290

Introduction

Have you ever had to (or do you anticipate having to) stand in front of a group of people and tell them about something? Maybe you need to prepare presentations for someone else to use? Are you thinking of putting together some information and making it all available on the World Wide Web? Or do you have Microsoft PowerPoint 97 available because it was included with Microsoft Office 97, and want to know how and what you could use it for? (After all, you did pay for it.) If you answered yes to any of these questions, then you need this book.

For those of you who don't give presentations (and will never give a presentation), you too might want to thumb through this book. The nice folks at Microsoft have packed a lot of great stuff into PowerPoint 97. You can create attractive drawings, graphs, and organizational charts. The possibilities are endless when you let your imagination run free.

This book is written for anyone who wants to create dynamic presentations. If you want to put together a few simple pages to hand out for the upcoming PTA budget meeting or maybe create a drawing or company logo, PowerPoint 97, used with this book as a resource, will have you on the road to infamy before you know it.

Because Alex has been a successful software instructor for several years, we have incorporated her teaching style into the pages of this book. She has taught people from all walks of life, from grandmothers to professionals, and believes that whether you're a beginner or an old pro, you will find this book extremely helpful. Her goal has always been to have each student walk out of her class learning at least one thing.

Our easy-to-follow, step-by-step instructions leave no questions about what you're supposed to do next. We have thrown in lots of tips, tricks, and cautions for good measure, and the questions, in the "Q&A" sections at the end of each hour, come from real people.

PowerPoint basics are covered in Parts I, II, and III. Parts IV, V, and VI cover everything else, from creating cool drawings to posting presentations on the World Wide Web. So don't just sit there—it's time to get going:

1. Pay the nice person at the counter.
2. Go home.
3. Turn on your machine.
4. Set your clock and get ready to rock. (Just a small bit of humor. ☺)

Main Sections

Each lesson has a main section that covers the lesson topic clearly and concisely by breaking it down into logical component parts and explaining each component clearly.

Embedded into each lesson are Time Saver, Caution, and Just a Minute boxes, which give you additional information.

TIME SAVER

Time Savers inform you of tricks or elements that are easily missed by most computer users. You can skip them, but often Time Savers show you an easier way to perform a task.

CAUTION

A Caution deserves at least as much attention as a Time Saver because it points out a troublesome element of the operating system. Ignoring the information in the Caution could have adverse effects on your computer's stability. These are the most important informational boxes in this book.

JUST A MINUTE

Just a Minutes are designed to clarify the concept that's being discussed. They elaborate on the subject, but if you're comfortable with your understanding of the subject, you can bypass them without danger.

Additional Sections

The "Test What You've Learned" section of each lesson consists of exercises that reinforce concepts you've learned and helps you apply them in new situations. You can skip this section, but it's better for you to go through the exercises to see how the concepts can be applied to other common tasks.

The "Q&A" sections give you the answers to PowerPoint users' most frequently asked questions.

Other Conventions Used in This Book

This book uses the following conventions:

- Menu names are separated from menu options by a vertical bar (|). For example, "File|Open" means "Select the File menu and choose the Open option."
- New terms, in addition to appearing in *italic*, usually follow a "New Term" icon. Italics are sometimes used for emphasis, too.
- Some computer terms and all the text that you type in appear in `monospace` font.

PART I

Getting Started

Hour

Part I

Hour 1

PowerPoint 97 Basics

Welcome to the wonderful world of presentations. A *presentation* is a structured delivery of information. Teachers, professors, politicians, and sales representatives make a living delivering informative presentations. If you want to quickly create powerful multimedia presentations, then reading this book will be a great investment. Eventually, you will probably have to provide an oral or written report to your boss, client, or colleagues. Knowing the ins and outs of PowerPoint 97 will help you make sure the message is properly presented, well received, and remembered long after you've left the room.

PowerPoint 97 helps you structure the ideas and information that should be conveyed to the audience. With it, you can add visual images, animation, supporting documents, and audio recordings to enhance your message, and you can transform your message into a captivating experience. For example, you can easily do the following:

- Turbocharge that tired old training speech with animation and sound clips
- Visually demonstrate the importance of the yearly budget numbers by incorporating charts, tables, and high-impact graphics

- Impose structure on a presentation so the audience grasps the message
- Post the presentation on the World Wide Web so others can review it
- Generate an outline for your presentation
- Create audience handouts and speaker's notes

NEW TERM *Multimedia*: A format that involves more than one media type, such as a document that contains sound, images, and text.

You have picked an excellent product to help you prepare your presentation. PowerPoint 97 includes several templates that supply a presentation framework for many common topics. The task of building multimedia slides isn't a chore with PowerPoint 97 because it has many of the formatting and content creation tools built into other Office 97 products. It also includes a rich library of clip art and sound files to jazz up the text. PowerPoint 97 has drawing capabilities and can help you create a dynamic presentation by including animation and action buttons in the presentation. In addition to slide creation tools and navigation features, different slide perspectives are available to help you structure your ideas into a coherent presentation.

After you have reviewed your presentation and are ready to publish the content, PowerPoint 97 supports a variety of display mediums. You can deliver your presentation with overhead projections (black and white or color), with 35mm slides, on the Internet, or simply onscreen. You can configure onscreen presentations to run in several display modes, depending on the target audience. By combining PowerPoint 97 with your favorite presentation topic and this book, I hope you have as much fun as I had learning to use PowerPoint 97 to create fantastic presentations.

Before you get started, I want to take a few moments and cover the basics. This hour gives you a solid foundation to make sure you get the most out of PowerPoint 97. Before you create a presentation, you should check to make sure the application has been properly installed. You also should become familiar with what PowerPoint 97 has to offer in terms of documentation and help desk tools. This first hour covers the following:

- What's new and improved in PowerPoint 97 (for those who have used previous versions of PowerPoint)
- What options you should choose to install in PowerPoint 97
- The channels that Microsoft provides for getting more information and help, either online or through mechanisms built into PowerPoint 97
- The all-important technical support contact numbers

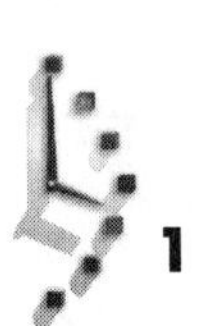

What's New and Improved

If you've used previous versions of PowerPoint, you're in for some wonderful surprises. Many old features have been enhanced to make PowerPoint 97 an even better application. To make the upgrade to PowerPoint 97 even more exciting, Microsoft has added some really cool new features. Table 1.1 lists just some of the new presentation features to whet your appetite.

Table 1.1. New features in PowerPoint 97.

Feature	Description
The Office Assistant	Interactive computer guides that make your computer act almost like HAL 9000
PowerPoint Central	An online magazine with many helpful tips, tricks, and links to other sites that provide useful information for creating better presentations
Custom Shows	The ability to create several mini-presentations in a single PowerPoint file
Automatically Expand Slides	Turn a single crowded slide with multiple bullets into several more concise and effective slides
Create a Summary Slide	Automatically create an informative summary slide from your presentation content
Insert Duplicate Slides	The ability to copy the text and formatting from one slide to another
Slide Finder	Quickly preview slides from existing presentations on your hard disk and import the content into a new presentation
Clip Gallery Live	Access the Microsoft Clip Gallery Web site to choose from over 1,000 new images, sounds, and movie files
ScreenTips in Charts	Holding the mouse over a chart element displays the item's name and value
Chart Data Tables	Include supporting data in tabular format next to the corresponding chart
Animated Charts	Animate chart data for more emphasis
Action Buttons	Add easily recognizable buttons to a presentation and configure them to provide slide navigation or custom actions
Voice Narration	Create a self-running slide show with a narrative soundtrack

continues

Table 1.1. continued

Feature	Description
Play CD Soundtrack	Configure PowerPoint slides to play a background musical soundtrack during the presentation
View on Two Screens	Display separate and different screens for the presenter and the audience
Hyperlinks in Online Presentations	Links to other slides, documents, and intranet pages can be accessed through hyperlinks
Save As PowerPoint Show	Save the slide show so that it automatically opens up in Slide Show View
Browse Mode	Save the presentation so that onscreen navigation controls are displayed when the audience sees the presentation
Kiosk Mode	Specify that PowerPoint should display only a linear slide show suitable for marketing kiosks
Support for ActiveX Macros	Add custom user-interface components to a presentation

Important and familiar features have been improved in PowerPoint 97, making the application even easier to use and more powerful. Table 1.2 highlights improvements in the core product.

Table 1.2. Improved features in PowerPoint 97.

Feature	Description
Meeting Minder	Enter and save notes while viewing a presentation
AutoContent Wizard	New and improved content templates to supply a framework for common presentation topics
Design Templates	More than 30 new design templates that can be applied to slides
Clip Gallery	Organizes images, sounds, and movies so that resources can be found easily
New Chart Types	Even more 3-D and 2-D chart types
Animation Effects	Captivating animation effects to apply to text, graphics, and slides
Custom Animation	An easier interface to help you organize and review animated effects

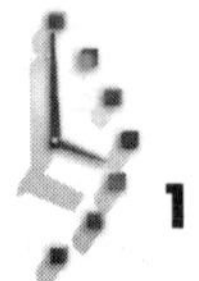

Feature	Description
Action Settings	Better control over the connection of other slides and Office documents in a presentation
Slide Master View	See a miniature of the current slide while working in Slide Master View
Pack and Go Wizard	An improved wizard that compresses and packs into a single file all the files needed to view a PowerPoint presentation
Add-Ins	Improved facilities to create and install custom functions and features and modify the entire PowerPoint user interface

You can easily create dynamic presentations by experimenting with the tools in PowerPoint 97. Many of the new features help the designer work more efficiently and create more robust presentations. Microsoft has also expanded the scope of the application to embrace Internet technology and access to online resources. If you want to get the most out of PowerPoint 97, I recommend installing all the available options.

Installing PowerPoint 97

If you have already installed PowerPoint 97, you might want to skip this section. You can always run the setup program again in the future if you need to install a previously overlooked component. However, to fully tap into the power of the application and use this book effectively, you might want to make sure that all PowerPoint 97 components have been installed.

Just a Minute

This book makes the assumption that you have a basic working knowledge of how to use standard Windows applications. Experience in controlling the pesky mouse pointer, selecting menu commands, and double-clicking buttons is a prerequisite.

If you're new to the Windows PC environment, or are installing the complete Microsoft Office 97 suite for the first time, you will probably want to start with basic information about all the excellent features available in Windows 95 and Office 97. I recommend that you start with Greg Perry's *Teach Yourself Microsoft Office 97 in 24 Hours*, published by Sams Publishing. You will find that learning PowerPoint 97 is much easier when you understand how Windows 95 and the Office 97 suite interact as a team.

Before installing PowerPoint 97, make sure your computer has the necessary equipment. If you install and start PowerPoint 97 on top of the recommended computer platform, you won't be frustrated later when you try to build that blockbuster presentation.

The Hardware and Software You Need

As the most advanced application for creating presentations available today, PowerPoint 97 runs best when it operates in the recommended environment. If you want to take full advantage of all the goodies PowerPoint 97 has to offer, you should make sure your machine has the correct hardware and software combination.

Hardware is the machine or computer and all its components. Basically, it's anything on your computer that you can touch.

Software is the application you load into your machine from CD-ROMs or floppy disks. Software supplies the intelligence to an otherwise useless construction made of silicon and steel.

The Hardware

A software application can operate properly only if the underlying hardware matches the program's requirements. Here are the minimum requirements for successfully installing and operating PowerPoint 97:

- A PC with an 80486 or higher microprocessor

Just a Minute

The 80486 microprocessor is the formal computer "geek" name for what we common folks call a 486 computer. The "or higher" phrase refers to either a Pentium or Pentium Pro computer. I would recommend that you operate PowerPoint 97 on at least a 100MHz Pentium computer. When you're working with PowerPoint's exotic graphic capabilities, you might find a 486 too slow.

- A minimum of 8M of RAM (random access memory)

Time Saver

I recommend that your machine have at least 16M of RAM installed. Ideally, more memory is better. I have 32M on my machine, and even that's frequently not enough to concurrently execute all the applications used to write this book.

To determine how much memory is available in your machine, open Explorer, click Help from the main menu, and then select the About Windows 95 or About Windows NT menu item. The amount of physical RAM installed in your machine should be displayed under the license information.

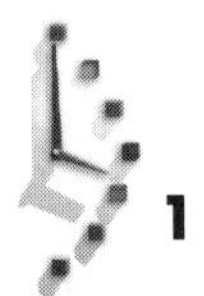

- At least 200M of available hard disk space

TIME SAVER

> The 200M amount designates the space required for installing Office 97 Standard Edition, which includes PowerPoint 97. If you want to install every component of PowerPoint 97 without installing other Office applications, you need to have 34M of hard disk space available. To take full advantage of PowerPoint 97, I recommend installing the entire Office 97 suite. You will then have all the tools you need to create charts, tables, and documents that can be embedded into PowerPoint presentations.

- 3.5-inch high-density (1.44) disk drive or CD-ROM player (recommended)
- VGA, SVGA (recommended), or XGA video adapter
- Any Microsoft-compatible mouse, track ball, or other pointing device

The Software

Unlike the hardware checklist, there's only one software requirement. PowerPoint 97 is tuned to operate on only the most advanced and updated Microsoft operating systems, so check to make sure you have either Microsoft Windows 95, Windows NT 3.51 with Service pack 5 or higher, or an even newer operating system, such as Windows NT 4.0.

CAUTION

> PowerPoint 97 will not run on earlier versions of Windows. Machines that run Windows 3.1 or Windows for Workgroups don't have the required functionality. Users should migrate their systems to the more advanced, 32-bit architectures of Windows 95 or Windows NT to take advantage of the advanced features built into the new Office suite.

How to Install PowerPoint 97

Proper installation of the Office 97 suite or PowerPoint application is a quick, but important, process. This section gives you some useful tips and advice so you can get the most out of PowerPoint 97 when you're working on concepts presented in later chapters.

When you look in the box that contains PowerPoint 97 (or Office 97), you will see a copious amount of reading material. If you have never installed a software application or Microsoft product before, you should take the time to read through all the material. Also, you should keep all the documentation in an easily accessible location; a file folder or a box on a shelf is ideal. I keep all my application documentation in the original box on my bookshelf. If I ever need to refer back to some hard copy, I'll have it handy.

After opening the box and finding the installation disks or CD-ROM, all you need to do is turn on your computer (if it's not already on), close any active applications that might be open on the machine, and go through the following instructions. Steps 1 through 7 start the installation program. If your computer is set to AutoPlay installation CD-ROMs, the computer will automatically launch the installation program when the CD-ROM is inserted into the drive. You can then go ahead from step 8. These are the steps to install PowerPoint 97 (or Office 97, depending on the CD-ROM you have):

1. Insert the CD-ROM.
2. Click Start.
3. Choose Settings | Control Panel.
4. Double-click the Add/Remove Programs icon.
5. Click Install.
6. Click Next.
7. After Setup locates the SETUP.EXE file, click Finish.
8. The installation program starts and asks you a few questions. Follow the instructions and answer the questions that appear onscreen.
9. First, choose the type of installation you want to execute. The options vary based on the type of installation you choose.

A PowerPoint 97 installation sequence can follow one of three installation types, listed in Table 1.3. The fastest way to install all components of PowerPoint 97 is to choose the Custom installation option and then click Select All, which means that every feature available for the application should be loaded into your computer.

Table 1.3. PowerPoint 97 installation types.

Name	Description
Typical	This option is usually just fine for most people, but does leave out some of the more advanced components.
Custom	This option allows you to choose which components you want installed. I usually choose a Custom installation just to make sure I'm getting everything.
Run from CD-ROM	This is a good option if you don't have a lot of hard disk space available (as on a laptop computer). However, you must always place the CD into the CD-ROM drive when you run PowerPoint 97. Also, you might notice that PowerPoint 97 operates much slower.

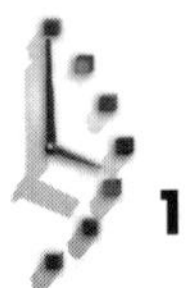

Starting PowerPoint 97

After you have PowerPoint 97 properly installed on your computer, you will probably want to skip any additional marketing fluff or technical disclaimers (the legendary readme file) and start your first PowerPoint 97 session. Although there are several methods available to start any application in the Windows 95 environment, the easiest by far is to find and use the Start button in the lower-left corner. To start PowerPoint 97 from the Start button, do the following:

1. Click Start.
2. Highlight the Programs menu item.
3. Click Microsoft PowerPoint, as shown in Figure 1.1.

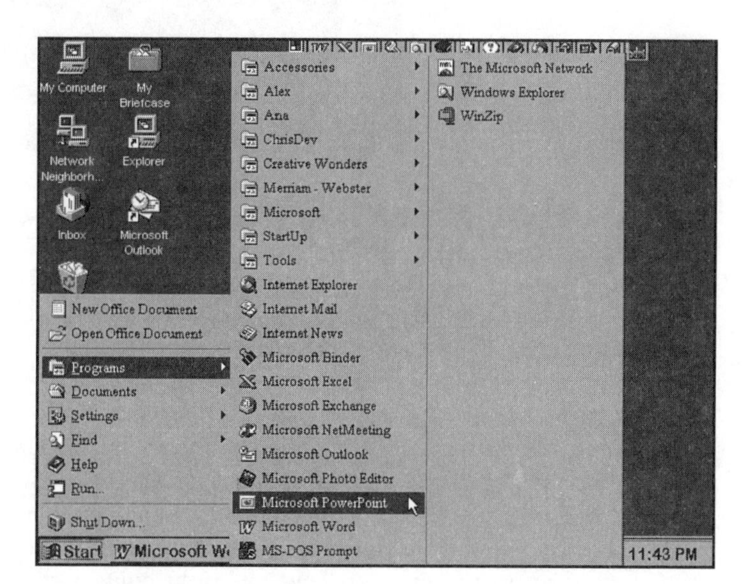

Figure 1.1.
Starting PowerPoint 97 from the desktop.

If you previously installed the complete Microsoft Office 97 suite, you can also start the PowerPoint 97 application by clicking the Microsoft PowerPoint button. The button is located on the Microsoft Office Shortcut Bar, as shown in Figure 1.2.

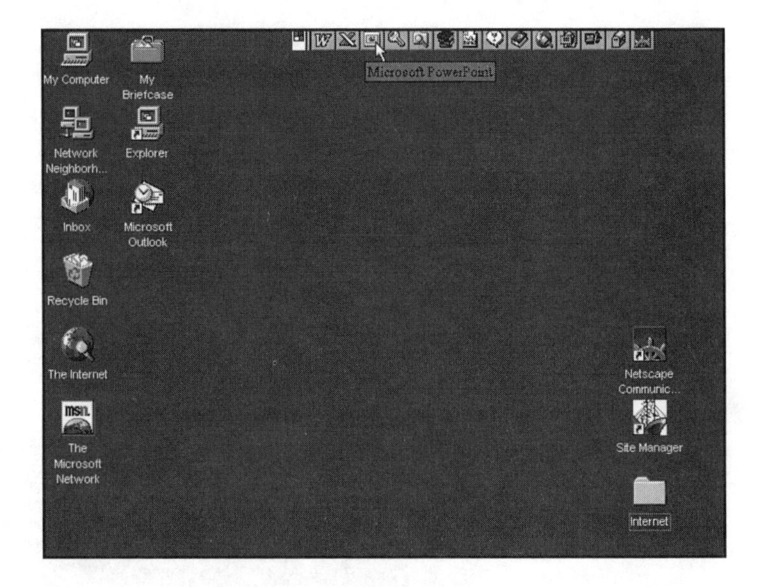

Figure 1.2.
Starting PowerPoint 97 from the Microsoft Office Shortcut Bar.

Using the *Getting Results* Book

The Office 97 suite comes with an easy-to-use electronic book called *Getting Results*. To open it, just click the Getting Results button on the Office 97 toolbar. The book is formatted just like traditional World Wide Web pages or Windows Help files. To navigate through the documents, simply click the colored "links" that change the view to a specific chapter or page. Although there are some helpful facts in *Getting Results*, *Teach Yourself PowerPoint 97 in 24 Hours* has all the standard information and much, much more. If you want to get as much information as possible, go ahead and take a quick peek at the *Getting Results* material. I'm a voracious reader of every fragment of information on PowerPoint I can find and firmly believe that reviewing written material reinforces your knowledge. Another important store of information that might prove helpful is the online Office 97 Resource Kit at `http://www.microsoft.com/office/ork/`.

Using PowerPoint Central

PowerPoint Central is Microsoft's online magazine for PowerPoint 97. The magazine site is actually an online PowerPoint 97 presentation with links to the Internet that allow you to find all the latest tips and tricks for PowerPoint 97 applications. The material includes resources for tutorials, additional PowerPoint templates, and files containing clip art, pictures, music, sound, video clips, and animation.

To open the *PowerPoint Central* magazine, choose Tools | PowerPoint Central from the menu. If you have Internet access, you can connect to the Microsoft Web site that hosts

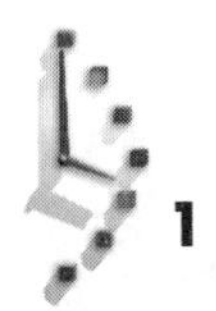

PowerPoint Central. The *PowerPoint Central* Web site is an interactive site that automatically customizes itself to your presence. For example, the site indicates how long it has been since you last checked for updates. The site also lets you know if there's a newer version available for download. You can then download the newer version or wait until after that important presentation deadline has passed.

You should check into *PowerPoint Central* occasionally to keep yourself abreast of all the newest developments and additions to PowerPoint 97.

TIME SAVER

If you have access to the Internet and also have a Usenet newsreader, you might want to check out the PowerPoint newsgroup at `microsoft.public.powerpoint`. The newsgroup provides a forum to read and post messages with other PowerPoint users. Microsoft's Internet News is an excellent newsreader that can read Usenet sites.

Usenet: A public discussion area where people can correspond through publicly displayed e-mail, much like a community bulletin board.

Getting Help

When you know what you want to accomplish, but don't know how to get there, who are you going to call? Even if you don't have a 24×7 (24 hours a day, 7 days a week) world-class help desk, PowerPoint 97 has several different options for getting help when you need it. It offers the Office Assistant, online help files, a What's This option, and access to Microsoft on the Web for those users with Internet connectivity. I have often found that the help options are very useful in solving my question without a call to the resident human PowerPoint wizard. When you have mastered using the help systems, you will have found the framework that can help you become a PowerPoint expert.

Internet connectivity: A computer industry term that means the ability to access the Internet from your computer.

The Office Assistant

The first time PowerPoint 97 starts on your machine, the friendly, helpful Office Assistant greets you. This animated paper-clip fellow, called Clipit, hangs around to give you help and advice while you work with PowerPoint 97 (or any of the Office 97 applications). Unlike your other real-world office assistants, you can fully customize the Office Assistant in many ways. For example, you can change its persona or character; imagine trying *that* one out on Bob next door. Also, you can customize other Office Assistant attributes, such as whether the character responds to the F1 (help) key, is noisy, or displays keyboard shortcuts, and set many other options.

Just a Minute

If you have used previous versions of PowerPoint, the Office Assistant takes the place of the Answer Wizard. You will find the Office Assistant to be much more knowledgeable.

Using the Office Assistant

Any time you need help with a feature, the Office Assistant is there to calmly and politely help. You can type your questions in plain English, and the Office Assistant finds the appropriate help file and gives you an answer. To start the Office Assistant, press the F1 function key or choose Microsoft Word Help from the Help menu. To use the Office Assistant, follow these steps:

1. Click the Office Assistant.
2. Type your question.
3. Click Search.
4. Select an option item from the help list. If you don't see the item in the help list, click See More, if available, to view additional relevant topics, or enter a new question and click Search.

The help file for your question should now be displayed. Figure 1.3 shows an Office Assistant answering a simple question.

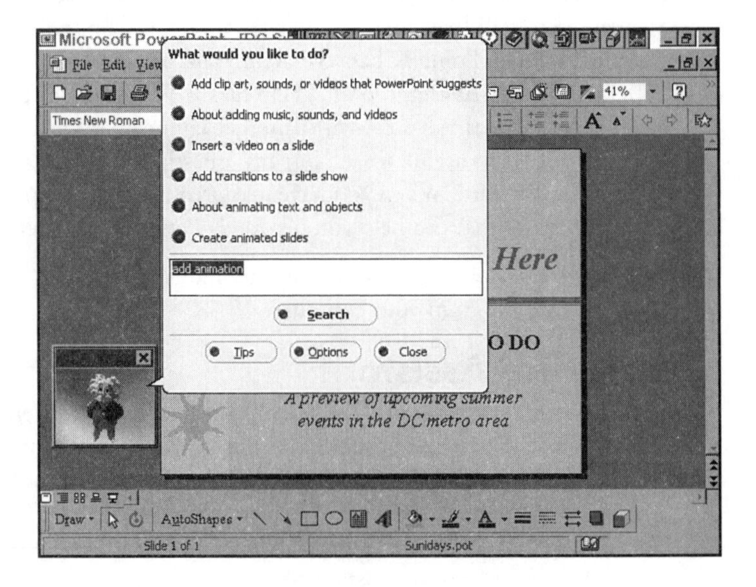

Figure 1.3.
The Office Assistant answering a question.

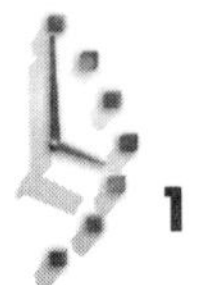

Changing the Office Assistant Character

After a while, you might decide that you don't like to correspond with Clipit, the standard paper-clip character, anymore. However, you can change the Office Assistant's character at any time. Each of the nine characters from which you can choose has its own unique personality and traits. The entire cast with my favorite, Scribble the cat, is described in Table 1.4.

JUST A MINUTE

> You have all nine characters available only if you bought the entire Office 97 suite. If you bought PowerPoint 97 on its own, just the Clipit and the Office Logo characters are available.

Table 1.4. Office Assistant characters with descriptions.

Character	Description
	Genius: A wise assistant with powerful thoughts
	Clipit: A helpful paper clip
	Dot: A friendly guide to the electronic frontier
	HoverBot: A smart computer robot
	Office Logo: The no-nonsense business partner
	Mother Nature: For creators who are more in tune with the earth
	Power Pup: Your dynamic help champion
	Scribble: A cat that follows your commands
	Will: An assistant with dramatic flair

CAUTION

Changing the Office Assistant in PowerPoint 97 changes the Office Assistant for all the other Office 97 applications.

To switch your Office Assistant companion, follow these steps:

1. Click on the Office Assistant.
2. Click Options.
3. Click the Gallery tab.
4. Click the Next and Back buttons to view the different assistants.
5. When you find one you like, click OK.

JUST A MINUTE

You must have the Office 97 CD-ROM to change the Office Assistant for the first time.

Changing Office Assistant Options

Several customization options are available for defining the Office Assistant's personality. Do you want sound? How about keyboard shortcuts? Do you want the Office Assistant to move out of the way? All these items, and more, can be customized to your liking by following these steps:

1. Click the Office Assistant.
2. Click Options.
3. Click the Options tab.
4. Select the options you want, shown in Figure 1.4.
5. Click OK.

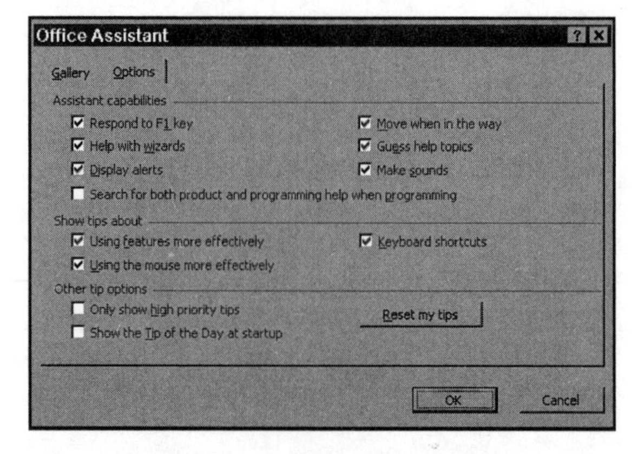

Figure 1.4.
Office Assistant options.

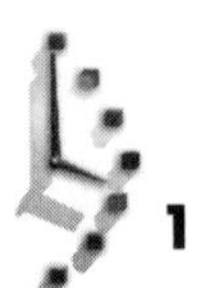

Using the Online Help

PowerPoint 97 includes excellent online help files. With a little patience, you should be able to quickly find answers to your questions. The key to successfully using the online help is to understand when to choose the Contents, Index, or Find options.

Help Contents

You should refer to the Contents section of the help file when you want to find information about a general topic. If you aren't familiar with presentation terms or are new to Office applications, the Contents section is a good place to start. Figure 1.5 shows a help window with some relevant topics that correspond to this lesson. To find the predefined help topics, follow these steps:

1. Choose Help | Contents and Index from the menu.
2. Click the Contents tab.
3. Double-click any book icon. The icons indicate chapters in the file, as shown in Figure 1.5.
4. Double-click the topic title of interest to read the documentation.

Figure 1.5.
The Help window with expanded topics.

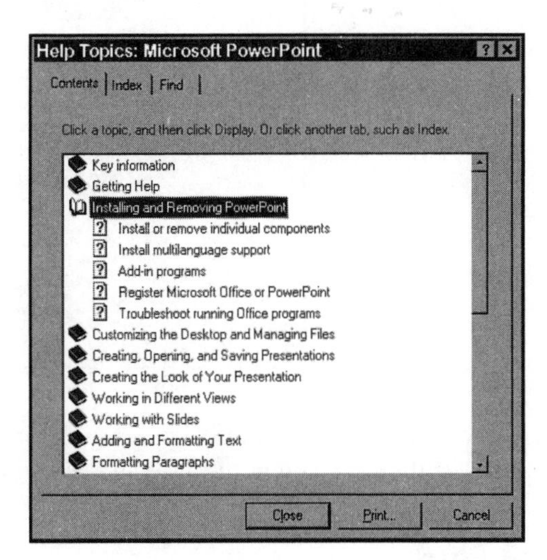

When you have finished reading about a topic, you have a few more choices. You can click the Help Topics button to look up another topic or the Close button to exit the help system. Another option is to return to a previous help topic by clicking the Back button.

Help Index

The help Index is useful when you need to find help on a very specific topic and don't have time to review every option available in the topic listing. The Index option can quickly advise you on how to perform a specific task because it does a limited context-sensitive search. To use the help Index, follow these steps:

1. Choose Help | Contents and Index from the menu.
2. Click the Index tab to display the help Index.
3. To indicate the search topic, enter a keyword.
4. Click the Display button to search the documentation and open the Topics Found dialog box that display the matches. (See Figure 1.6.)
5. Select the appropriate topic.
6. Click the Display button to display the documentation.

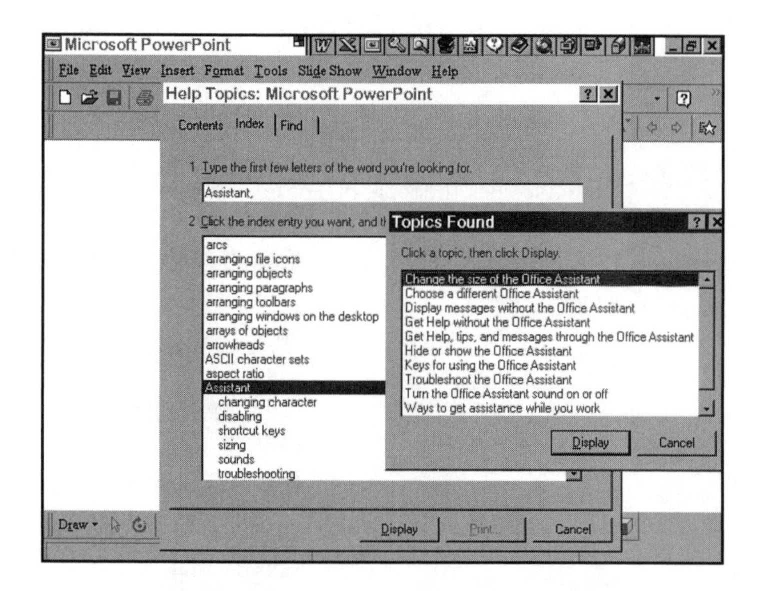

Figure 1.6.
Using the Index option to search topics.

The Topics Found dialog box can display more than one topic match from which to choose. Simply select the topic you want to see and click the Display button. PowerPoint 97 then displays the help topic.

Help Find

The Find option lets you perform a full text search across the entire help file. If the keyword is anywhere in the help file, you'll find it. The first time you start a Find search, PowerPoint prompts you for the size of the keyword database. Choose "Maximize search capabilities" to make sure you get the most accurate search results. After you have entered the keyword and performed the search, the help interface conventions are the same as for the Contents and Index options.

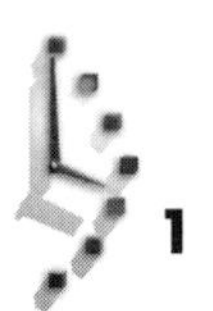

JUST A MINUTE

Find can sometimes give you too many matches. This help feature works best when you can't "find" the right answer from any of the previously discussed options.

Printing Help Topics

Although the help window stays onscreen so you can read the help file, it can be distracting. Sometimes it's better to quickly scan and then print out the help topic documentation. No matter how you access a help topic—using the Office Assistant, Contents, Index, or Find—you can print out the topic quite easily. Printing the documentation contents takes only two quick steps:

1. With the help topic displayed onscreen, click the Options button.
2. Choose Print Topics from the menu.

That's all there is to it. You can now close the help window and continue with the entire monitor screen devoted to just PowerPoint.

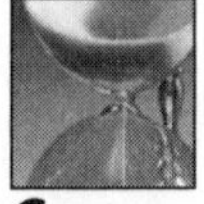

CAUTION

It has been my experience that when I can't locate help by using the Index or Find option, it's usually because I haven't typed the keyword correctly. Spelling is important when you use help.

Using ScreenTips

You can use the ScreenTips option to display information about any toolbar button on the screen. To activate the ScreenTip, hold the mouse pointer over the button in question to display a pop-up information box. Figure 1.7 demonstrates how to get ScreenTip information for the Print button.

JUST A MINUTE

If you have previously used any Microsoft Office application, ScreenTips have taken the place of ToolTips. They still work pretty much the same way.

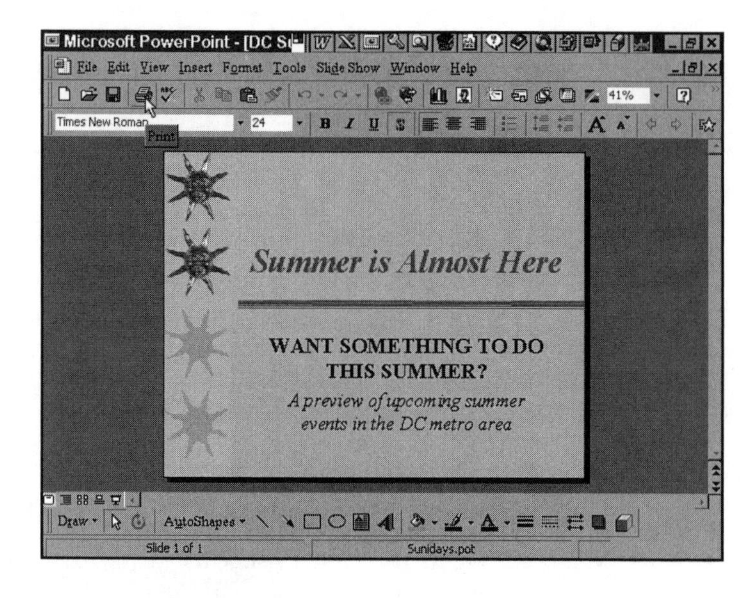

Figure 1.7.
ScreenTip help.

Using Microsoft on the Web

Another new feature included in PowerPoint 97 is the Microsoft on the Web option, available from the Help menu. If you have Internet access, this is a great option for finding free stuff, getting up-to-date product news, reading frequently asked questions, getting online support, and more. To use Microsoft on the Web, follow these easy steps:

1. Make sure your modem is on.
2. Choose Help | Microsoft on the Web from the main menu.
3. Select any option displayed in the submenu, such as Free Stuff.
4. PowerPoint 97 connects you to the Microsoft site you selected.

Time Saver

The Free Stuff option is a great place to get add-in programs for enhancing PowerPoint 97. The site offers the latest template designs, clip art, sound files, and links to third-party software vendors. If you are going to be using PowerPoint 97 extensively, visit the site often to find excellent resources that make creating presentations easier, faster, and more fun.

Technical Support

When it comes to technical support, Microsoft has given you many options. Before you call, make sure you have your product ID number ready, which you can find by choosing

Help | About Microsoft PowerPoint from the menu. Table 1.5 lists important technical support numbers.

Table 1.5. Microsoft technical support.

Option Name	Number	Times Available	Notes
Microsoft PowerPoint AnswerPoint	(206) 635-7145	Weekdays 6 a.m.–6 p.m. Pacific time	
Standard support	(206) 635-7145	6:00 a.m.–6:00 p.m. Pacific time, Monday through Friday, excluding holidays	If you bought the Microsoft Office Standard Edition, you have unlimited, no-charge, support on this line. You are also entitled to two free calls for assistance with custom solutions. If you bought the Microsoft Office Professional Edition, you have two more (for a total of four) free calls for assistance with custom solutions.
Priority support	(900) 555-2000	24 hours a day, 7 days a week, except holidays	Calls are $35 each and charges appear on your telephone bill.
Text telephone	(206) 635-4948	6:00 a.m.–6:00 p.m. Pacific time, Monday through Friday, excluding holidays	TT/TDD services are available for the deaf or hard-of-hearing.

In addition to the technical support options listed in Table 1.5, there are many more options available to you. To see even more technical support options, follow these steps:

1. Choose Help | About Microsoft PowerPoint from the main menu.
2. Click the Tech Support button.
3. From the contents listing, select the support option you want.

Summary

PowerPoint 97 should now be properly installed, and you know where to find the answers for any questions you might have. Microsoft has built many help options into PowerPoint 97. The Office Assistant establishes a helpful dialog box and asks questions before any confusion arises. ScreenTips display informative phrases, and Microsoft on the Web gives you round-the-clock access to the latest information. In the next hour, you're introduced to the AutoContent Wizard, a helpful tool for automatically creating and structuring your presentation.

Workshop

Welcome to the PowerPoint 97 Workshop. In this final section (there will be one each hour), you have an opportunity to test what you've learned. Based on the contents of each chapter, a step-by-step exercise helps reinforce the concepts discussed. Each Workshop section also has some common questions and answers about the subject matter of each particular hour.

Test What You've Learned

In all the years I have been teaching, I have found that nothing compares with hands-on experience. So take a seat, buckle up, and start your engine.

1. Install PowerPoint 97 (if it hasn't been previously installed).
2. Start PowerPoint 97.
3. Click Cancel on the PowerPoint dialog box (you learn about the PowerPoint dialog box in Hour 2, "Quick Start: Creating Your First Presentation").
4. Change the Office Assistant character, as shown in Figure 1.8.
5. Using your mouse, point (don't click) to buttons on the standard, formatting, and drawing toolbars to see the ScreenTips and familiarize yourself with the buttons.
6. Choose Help | About Microsoft PowerPoint from the menu to find those all-important technical support numbers to the nice people at Microsoft. (See Figure 1.9.)
7. Exit PowerPoint by using one of the following methods:
    - Choose File | Exit from the menu, as shown in Figure 1.10.
    - Click the application Close button (the little × in the upper-right corner of the window).

Figure 1.8.
Using HoverBot as the Office Assistant character.

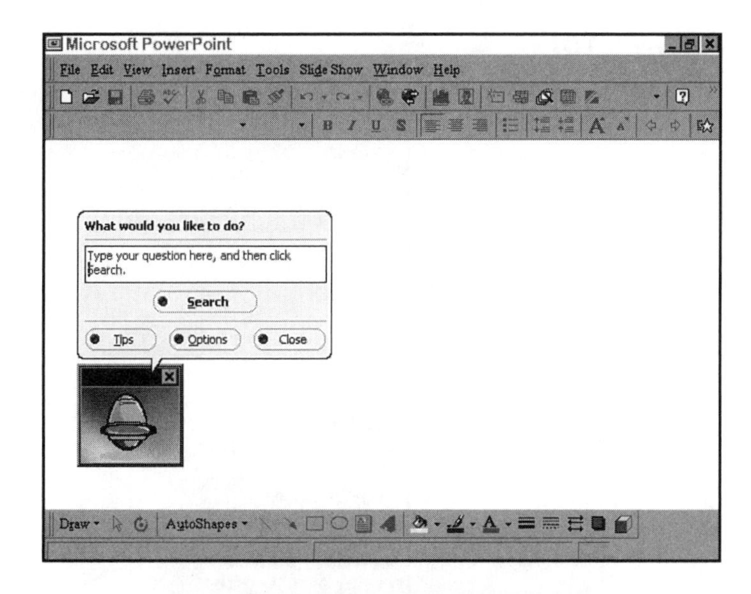

Figure 1.9.
The About Microsoft PowerPoint dialog box.

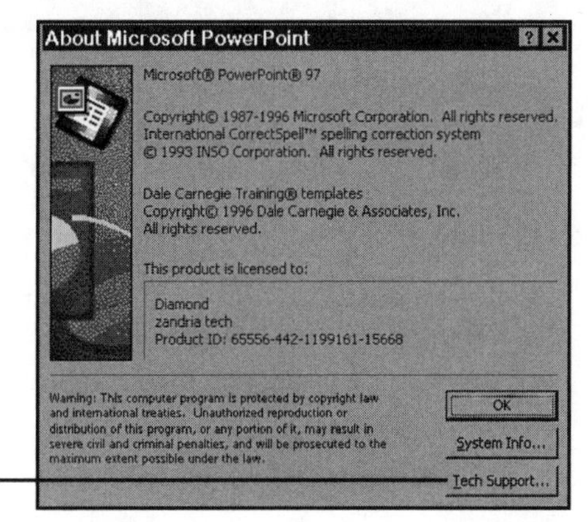

Figure 1.10.
Exiting PowerPoint.

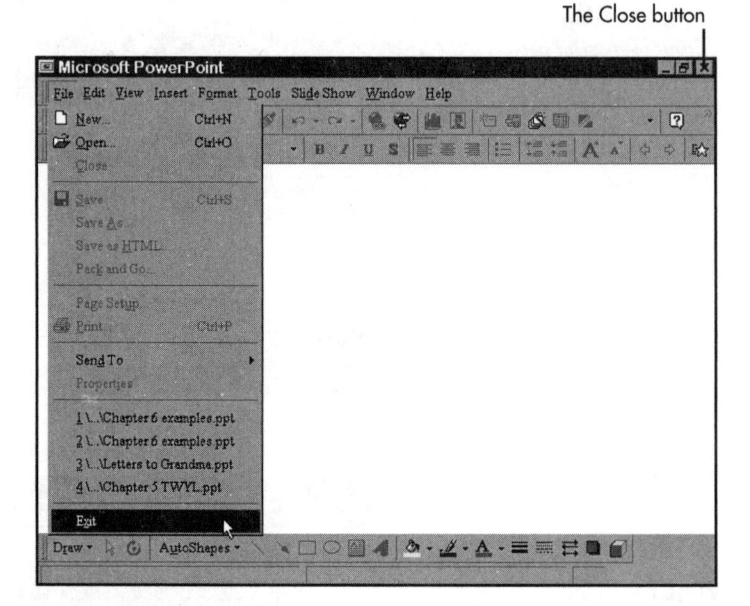

Q&A

Q What if I find out later that I really don't need or want all the components I have previously installed?

A You can always uninstall any portion of PowerPoint or Office. To remove a component, first follow the steps listed in this lesson for installing PowerPoint 97. When the Setup dialog box opens, follow these steps:

1. Click the Add/Remove button.
2. Click Microsoft PowerPoint.
3. Click the Change Option button.
4. Click on any option you want to deselect. An option is selected if it has a checkmark next to it; if there's no checkmark, it's deselected.
5. Click OK (you might need to click more than one OK button).
6. Click Continue.
7. Setup then deletes any options you previously deselected.

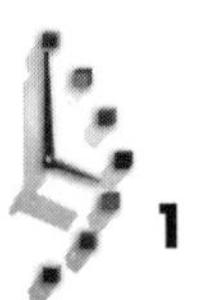

Q I don't have a Usenet newsreader. Can I still read the messages posted to the newsgroup?

A Not in the traditional way, but you have a couple of options available. One option is performing a search of the Usenet newsgroups through an Internet search engine (I use Alta Vista). However, the best option is to get a newsreader. Microsoft's Internet News is a good choice. At the time of this book's writing, you can download Internet Mail & News for no charge from the Internet Explorer site at `http://www.microsoft.com/ie/download/`.

PART

I

Hour 2

Quick Start: Creating Your First Presentation

Congratulations! You made it through the first hour on background information and installing PowerPoint 97. The rest of this book gives you the information you need to actually start using PowerPoint 97. Hour 2 is designed to help you quickly create presentations using the powerful but simple tools built into PowerPoint 97. In tandem with Hour 3, "Basic PowerPoint File Management: Saving, Opening, and Creating Presentations," you learn the basics of producing decent-looking, coherent presentations. If you cover only the next two hours, you could put this book on the shelf and still be able to create basic presentations. However, if you want to learn about all the cool features of PowerPoint 97 that will impress your audience, you'll read the entire book twice. In this hour, you will learn the following:

- How to use the AutoContent Wizard
- The correct names for all the PowerPoint screen elements and what they do for you

- How to view your presentation in different ways
- How to spellcheck and print your presentation

Starting the AutoContent Wizard

Every time you start PowerPoint 97, the PowerPoint dialog box is displayed, as shown in Figure 2.1. You can use it to choose the method for starting your PowerPoint 97 session. The main choices are creating a new presentation or opening an existing presentation. More information about the dialog box options is given in Hour 3.

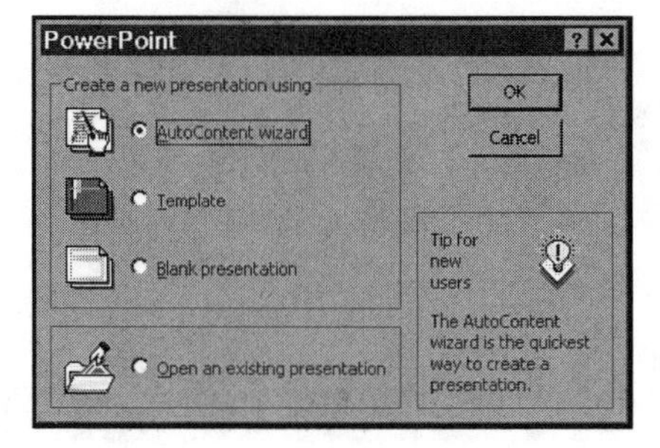

Figure 2.1.
The PowerPoint dialog box.

JUST A MINUTE

The PowerPoint dialog box shows up only when you first start a PowerPoint 97 session. After its first appearance, it disappears. You don't see it again until you exit PowerPoint 97 and start a new session. Maybe in the next version, potentially PowerPoint 2000, Microsoft programmers will allow you to open the PowerPoint dialog box at any time.

The first option in the PowerPoint dialog box list is the AutoContent Wizard, the best method for starting a presentation if you're new to PowerPoint. It's also a great tool to use if you need to create a presentation quickly. The AutoContent Wizard is a guide composed of several screens that help you create professional presentations. It leads you through a series of questions so you can choose the best layout for your presentation. You can select from several predefined content templates. The AutoContent Wizard supplies not only the design for your presentation, but also ideas, starter text, formatting, and organization. It's an excellent tool to use if you don't know where to start.

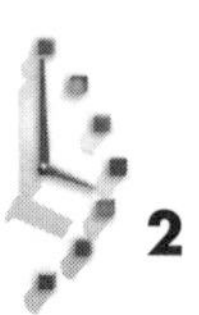

If you have used previous versions of PowerPoint, you will notice that the AutoContent Wizard has been greatly enhanced in PowerPoint 97. The wizard contains many professionally designed templates, some of which include tips on how to become a better presenter.

When the AutoContent Wizard starts, the first screen displayed is the start screen, shown in Figure 2.2. It provides explanatory text that introduces you to the AutoContent Wizard. You can read it if you want, and then click Next.

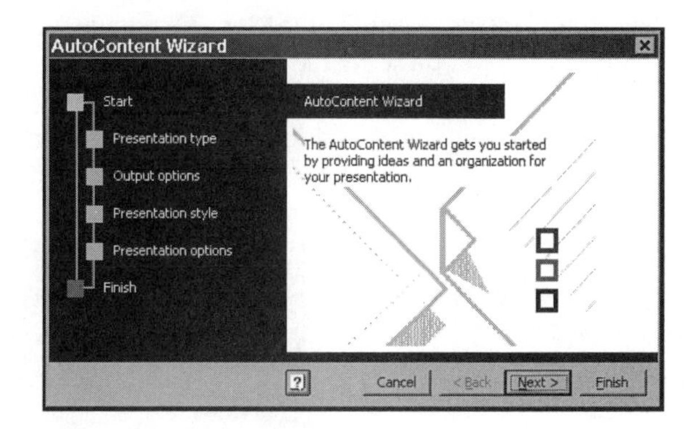

Figure 2.2.
The start screen of the AutoContent Wizard.

The second screen in the wizard defines the presentation type. You use this screen to select the type of presentation you're going to create. You can scroll through the list of all the available types or click a category button to narrow the list of choices. If you don't see a presentation type to fit your needs, just click the General button and select the Generic presentation type. For example, if you were going to create a presentation on computer training, an unsupported topic, click the General button, as shown in Figure 2.3. After you have selected a presentation type, click Next.

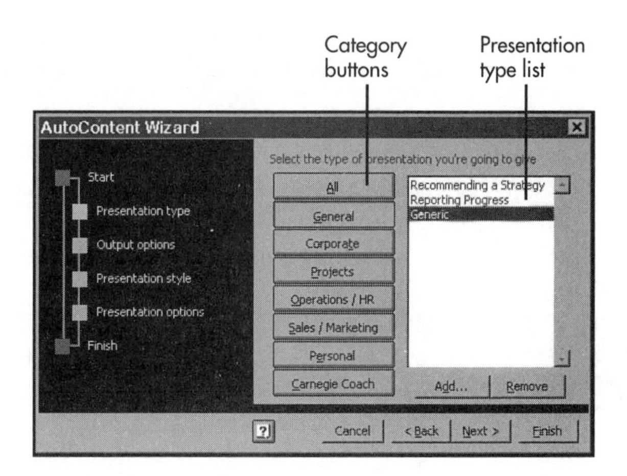

Figure 2.3.
The AutoContent Wizard's presentation type screen with the Generic presentation type selected.

TIME SAVER

You can add your own presentation types to the AutoContent Wizard by selecting a category and then clicking the Add button. This feature is especially helpful if you have downloaded new presentation designs from the Microsoft site mentioned in Hour 1, "PowerPoint 97 Basics," and want those designs available when you use the AutoContent Wizard.

The AutoContent Wizard's third screen contains the output options section, shown in Figure 2.4, where you select the target output format for your presentation. You have two choices: The first radio button is used for selecting formats for presentations, informal meetings, and handouts; the second format is for Internet or kiosk presentations. After you have set the output option for your presentation, click Next.

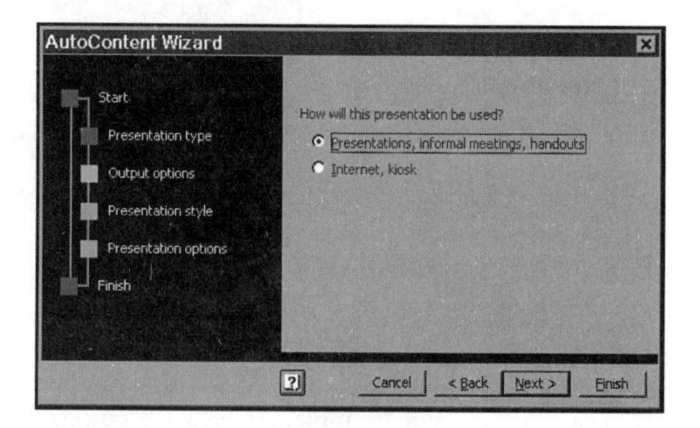

Figure 2.4.
The output options screen of the AutoContent Wizard.

Choose the option for presentations, informal meetings, and handouts if you will have physical control of how the individual slides advance during your presentation. If your presentation will be available for people to automatically view on their own without a speaker present, then choose the option for an Internet or a kiosk presentation.

When you choose the option for presentations, informal meetings, and handouts, the AutoContent Wizard displays the presentation style screen, as shown in Figure 2.5. The AutoContent Wizard needs to be told how you will publish the presentation: onscreen, overhead projection (color or black and white), or 35mm slides. You also need to indicate whether you want handouts generated. After you have made your selections, click Next.

You won't see the screen in Figure 2.5 if you chose the option for Internet or kiosk presentations in the output options screen.

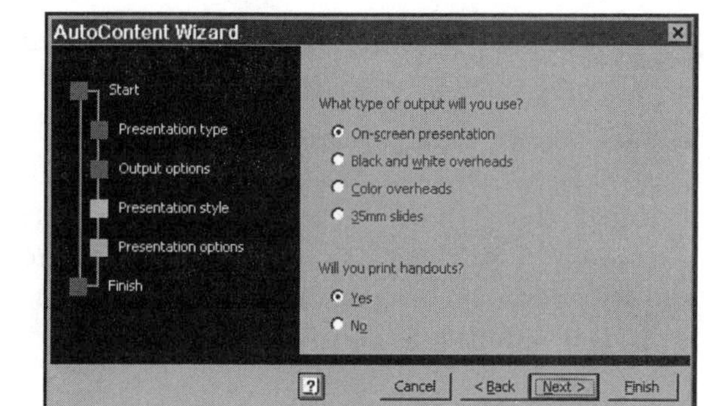

Figure 2.5.
The presentation style screen of the AutoContent Wizard.

The presentation options screen is the fifth and final AutoContent Wizard section in which you enter information. (See Figure 2.6.) In this screen, enter any information that should appear on your title slide. At the very least, you should type a title for your presentation. You can also make your name and other additional information appear on the title slide. When you have entered all the your information, click Next.

Just a Minute

Don't put too much additional information on the title slide. The additional information box is designed for topics such as the company name, address, and telephone number.

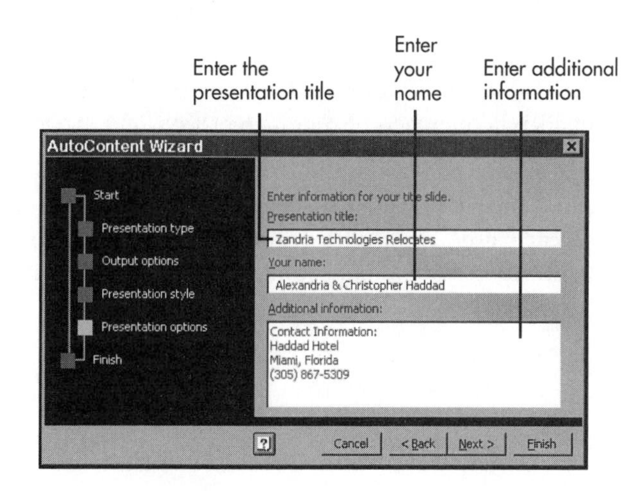

Figure 2.6.
The presentation options screen of the AutoContent Wizard with information entered.

NEW TERM The *title slide* is the first slide in your presentation.

The last AutoContent Wizard screen is the finish screen, shown in Figure 2.7. The AutoContent Wizard has finished its question and answer session, so it's time to generate the presentation file. If you need to change any previously set options, now would be a good time. You can use the Back button to go backward through the wizard screen-by-screen and change any option you want. You can also just cancel the whole darn thing and go to lunch. If you've decided to take the plunge, all you need to do is click the Finish button to view your generated presentation.

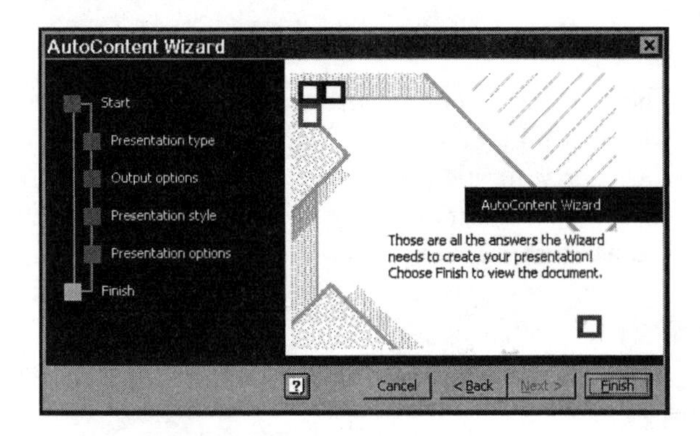

Figure 2.7.
The AutoContent Wizard finish screen.

What You See Onscreen

Now that you have finished with the AutoContent Wizard, you can see your presentation in the Outline View displayed in Figure 2.8. The PowerPoint 97 screen also displays several toolbars, a color view of your presentation, and the helpful Office Assistant.

The presentation outline is made up of sample slides that have been generated by the AutoContent Wizard. The slides have suggestions that indicate the type of information to be entered on each slide. Before you begin to customize the presentation with specific information, you should become familiar with the PowerPoint screen elements and what they can do for you.

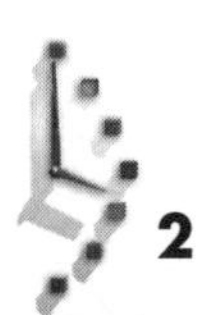

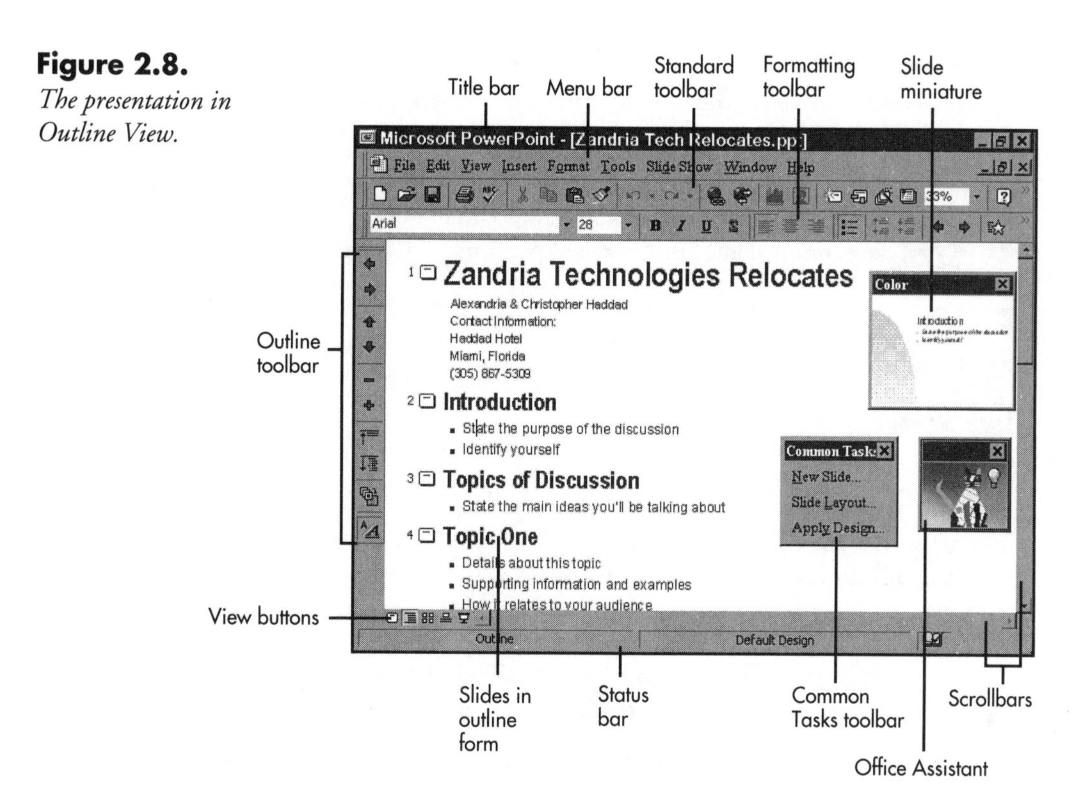

Figure 2.8.
The presentation in Outline View.

The Bars

There are several bars on your screen, and they all have a different job to do (but they don't serve any stiff drinks). The following sections give you a brief description of each bar type, starting from the top of the screen and working down.

Title Bar

The *title bar* sits at the top of your screen. Its job is to display the title of the application you're using and your presentation's name. If you haven't yet saved your presentation and given it a name (that step comes in Hour 3), the title is a generic name. The default name, Presentation1, is often seen on the title bar. The title bar also holds the application's control menu on the far left and the Minimize, Restore/Maximize, and Close buttons on the far right.

Menu Bar

The *menu bar* is where you should go to choose PowerPoint 97 commands. The menu bar also holds the current presentation's control menu on the far left and the Minimize, Restore/ Maximize, and Close buttons on the far right.

A *command* is a task that you want to do in PowerPoint. There are commands to save, print, change the font, and perform many other operations.

TIME SAVER

I like to think of the Close button as the Exit button. I associate the graphical × with Exit, because that's exactly what happens when you click the button.

Toolbars

Toolbars are the catchy bars that contain little buttons with graphical images on them; you click the buttons to perform certain tasks. PowerPoint 97 comes with several predesigned toolbars. You can customize any toolbar or even create your own; PowerPoint gives you total flexibility. You learn more about customization in Hour 24, "PowerPoint Power Hour." The three main toolbars are the standard, formatting, and drawing toolbars. If you're in Outline View, you automatically see the outline toolbar, too.

You can turn the display of any toolbar off or on. To do so, follow these steps:

1. Choose View | Toolbars from the menu to display the Toolbar dialog box.
2. Click the checkbox next to the toolbar you want to turn off (or on). A checkmark indicates that a toolbar display is activated.

TIME SAVER

There's another method for changing the display attributes for the toolbars. You can position the mouse pointer on any toolbar and right-click, and then select the toolbar you want to turn off (or on).

The standard toolbar, shown in Figure 2.9, has buttons for the most common tasks you perform in PowerPoint 97, such as saving, printing, or spellchecking a presentation.

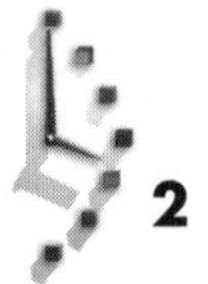

Figure 2.9.
The PowerPoint 97 standard toolbar.

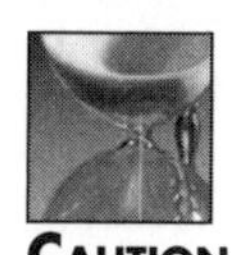

CAUTION

I don't recommend using the Print button to print your presentations. When you use the Print button, PowerPoint prints the entire presentation using the default print settings, so you don't get an opportunity to change any print options. All the Print buttons in the Microsoft Office products operate in this manner. The button is usually a great shortcut, but with PowerPoint, you often don't want to print the entire presentation in full color.

2

The formatting toolbar has buttons that make formatting a snap. You use most of the buttons to format text, such as changing the font type or size, making your text bold or italic, turning bullets off, and many other options. Figure 2.10 illustrates a standard formatting toolbar.

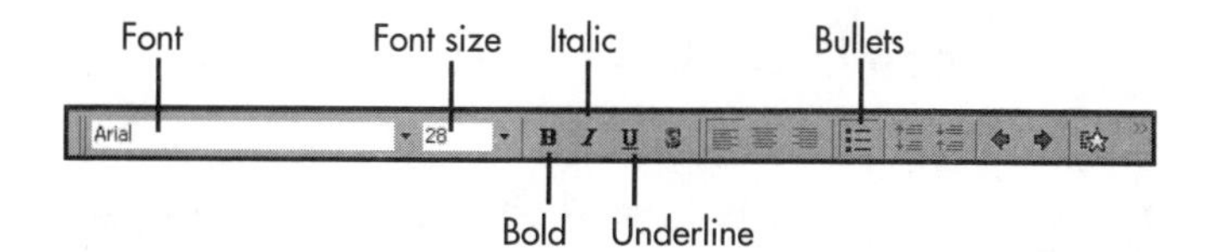

Figure 2.10.
The PowerPoint 97 formatting toolbar.

The outline toolbar sits on the left side of your screen when you're in Outline View (more about views in the section "Presentation Perspectives"). If you have used Microsoft Word's outline feature, you'll recognize this toolbar, although it has fewer buttons in PowerPoint. Figure 2.11 is a graphical view of the outline toolbar's buttons. The outline toolbar is handy when you need to promote or demote large blocks of text.

NEW TERM When you *promote* text, PowerPoint moves the text up to the next higher level, for example, from a second-level bullet to a first-level bullet. To *demote* text is to move text to the next lower level, as you would if you were moving text from a second-level bullet to a third-level bullet.

Figure 2.11.
The PowerPoint 97 outlining toolbar.

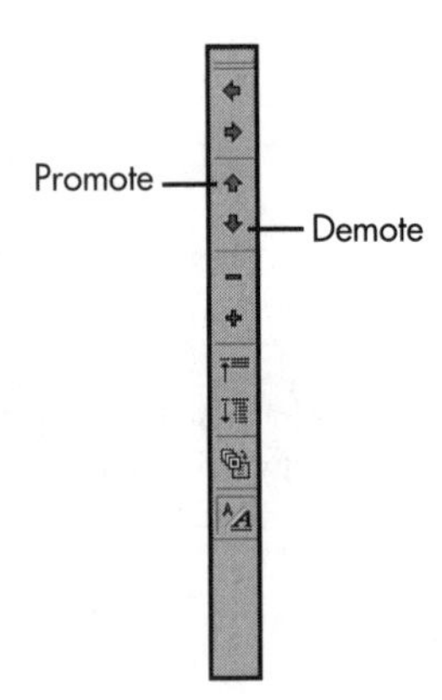

The Common Tasks toolbar (refer to Figure 2.8) is initially a floating toolbar. There are only three options on this toolbar, but they are important:

- **New Slide:** Used to create a new slide in a presentation.
- **Slide Layout:** Used to change the layout of a slide.
- **Apply Design:** Used to change the presentation's design.

TIME SAVER

The PowerPoint 97 menu bar and all the toolbars can be moved (or *docked*) to any side of your screen. They can also be converted into floating toolbars. To move the menu bar or any other toolbar, follow these steps:

1. On a docked bar, place your mouse pointer on the move handle (the dim gray lines on the left or top of the bar) or the title bar of a floating toolbar.
2. Drag the bar to the new location.
3. To dock the bar, drag it to the edge of the window.

A bar is docked if you see the move handle, and it's floating if you see a title bar. In Figure 2.12, the toolbar positions have been radically customized. You'll rarely move the bars around this much, but the figure does make a point.

JUST A MINUTE

If you're familiar with PowerPoint 4.0 or PowerPoint 95, you might remember that the common tasks buttons used to be on the lower-right portion of the PowerPoint window.

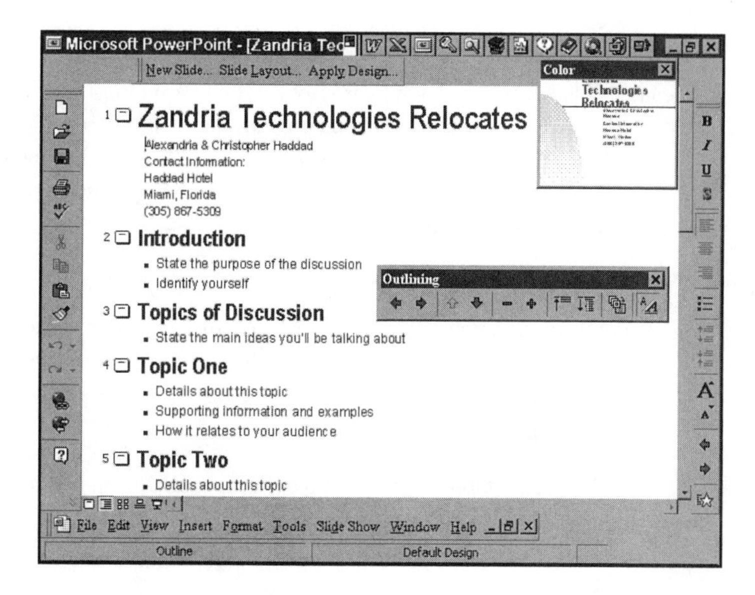

Figure 2.12.
PowerPoint 97 with the menu bar and toolbars moved.

Scrollbars

Scrollbars are used to scroll through the current presentation. When you drag the scroll button on the vertical scrollbar, PowerPoint 97 displays a ScreenTip that indicates which slide you're going to display.

Status Bar

The PowerPoint 97 *status bar* is the bar at the bottom of the PowerPoint window. It tells you two pieces of information. If you're in Outline or Slide Sorter View, PowerPoint 97 indicates that you're in the respective mode. If you're in Slide or Notes Pages View, PowerPoint 97 displays the slide (page) you're currently working on and indicates how many slides you have in the entire presentation. The second piece of information that the PowerPoint 97 status bar displays is the name of the current presentation design for the active presentation.

JUST A MINUTE

Slide views are discussed in this hour's section "Presentation Perspectives." Presentation design is covered in Hour 4, "Working with Slides."

TIME SAVER

To choose a new design for your presentation, you can double-click the design area of the status bar. You can then apply a different presentation design to the presentation.

Slide Miniature

The Slide Miniature View is exactly what its name implies: a miniature view of your slides. This view, typically used with the Outline View, lets you actually see what the slide text will look like on the slide. You can close the Slide Miniature View by clicking its Close button. If you want to display the slide miniatures after closing the view, choose View | Slide Miniature from the menu.

The Office Assistant

As mentioned in Hour 1, the Office Assistant is available to help you with sage advice. If you would rather not have the Office Assistant hanging around, just click its Close button. To bring the Office Assistant back if you need help, you have two choices:

- Press F1.
- Choose Help | Microsoft PowerPoint Help from the menu.

Click the Office Assistant button on the standard toolbar.

For information on using the Office Assistant, refer to the section in Hour 1 called "Using the Office Assistant."

Presentation Perspectives

After you have finished answering the questions posed by the AutoContent Wizard, you see the sample presentation displayed in Outline View, but other views are available. PowerPoint 97 has five different ways to view your presentation:

Slide View

Outline View

Slide Sorter View

Notes Pages View

Slide Show View

Each view has a different function, described in the following sections. To switch views, you can use either the View menu or the view buttons in the lower-left corner of the PowerPoint window.

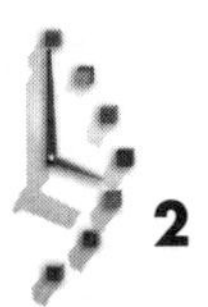

Slide View

In Slide View, you view only one slide at a time. The slides are displayed in almost the same manner they appear in your presentation. (See Figure 2.13.) You can add text, graphics, or any other PowerPoint object to slides while you're in Slide View. In fact, most of your work can be performed in Slide View so you can get instant, visual feedback about how the changes affect the slide's presentation.

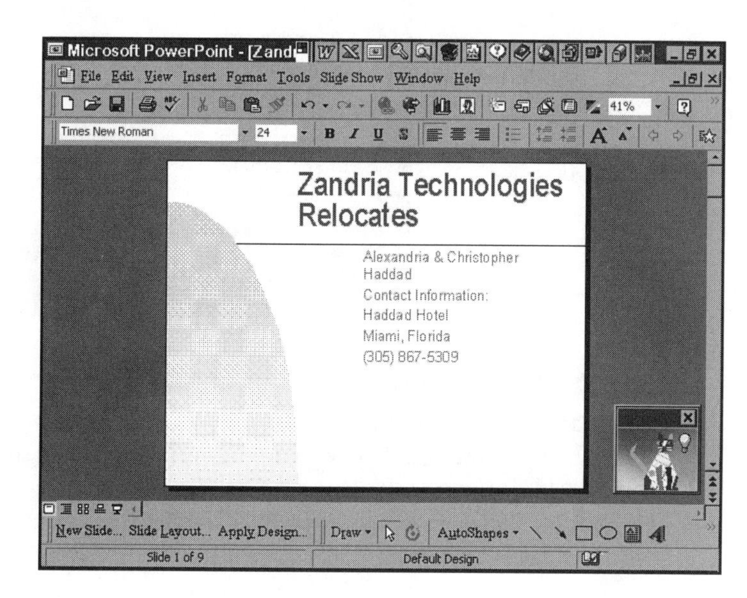

Figure 2.13.
The Zandria Technologies Relocation presentation in Slide View.

NEW TERM A *PowerPoint object* is any graphic, text, button, or other element on your slide. Everything you work with in PowerPoint can be defined as an object. For example, the title of the slide is the title object, the text in your slide is a text object, and a piece of clip art is a clip art object. Basically, if an element has handles when you click it in Slide View, it's an object. You work more with objects in Hour 5, "Working with PowerPoint Text Objects," and Hour 6, "Working with Clip Art and Pictures."

Outline View

Outline View is the perfect place to organize the ideas and concepts to display in your presentation. Use Outline View to make sure the presentation has smooth transitions and a coherent conceptual flow. While in Outline View, you can see the full presentation text that's in the slides. Figure 2.14 portrays the sample presentation in Outline View. You can easily rearrange the order of your presentation by either using the move buttons on the outlining toolbar or dragging the little slide icon to a different presentation location. The slide icon has a picture if the slide contains an object that's not a text object, such as clip art, graphs, or WordArt.

Figure 2.14.
The presentation in Outline View.

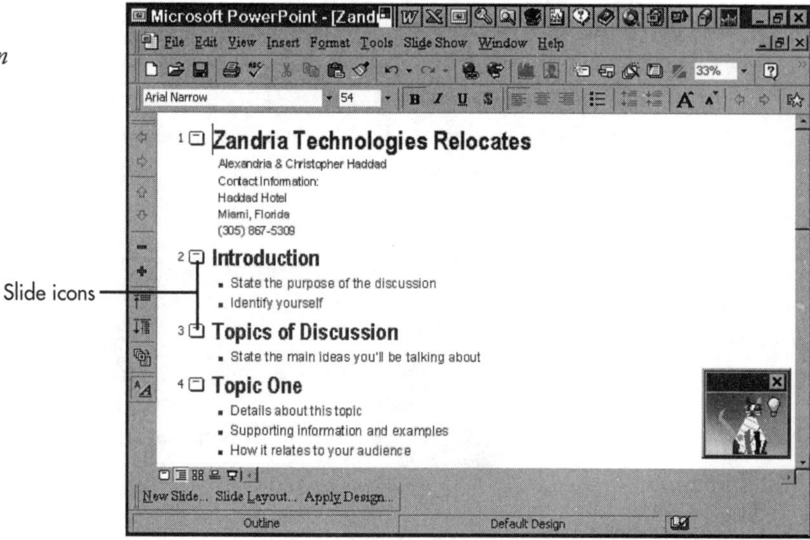

Slide Sorter View

The Slide Sorter View displays a miniature of each slide in your presentation, as shown in Figure 2.15. Use the Slide Sorter View when you want to add some polish to a presentation. You can add transitions to your presentation (see Hour 9, "Basics of Slide Shows," and Hour 10, "Adding Pizzazz to a Slide Show"), or use the Slide Sorter View to easily move, delete, and copy slides.

Figure 2.15.
The presentation in Slide Sorter View.

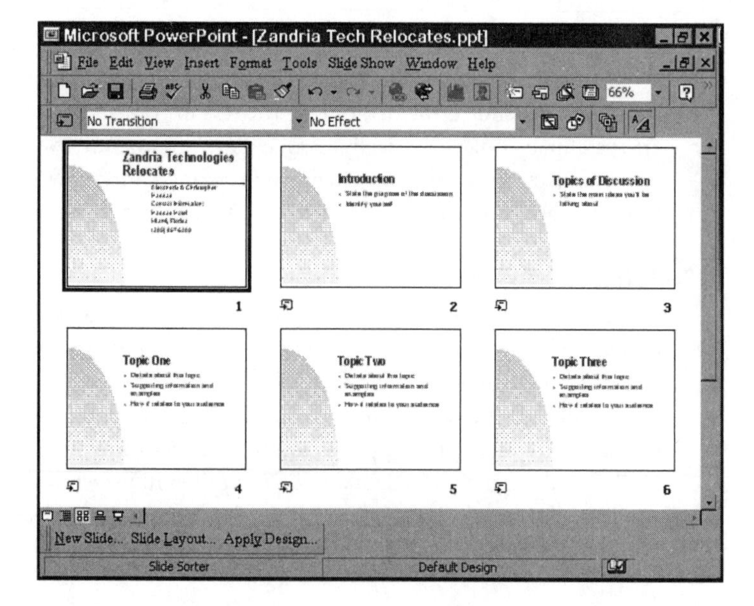

Notes Pages View

Notes Pages View is the perspective to use when you want to create your speaker's notes. (See Figure 2.16.) The Notes Pages View displays a page with the slide in the upper half of the screen and a text object, for notes, in the lower half. Because the notes region is so small, zoom (refer to the section "Zooming" later in this chapter) into the notes text object before you type the speaker notes.

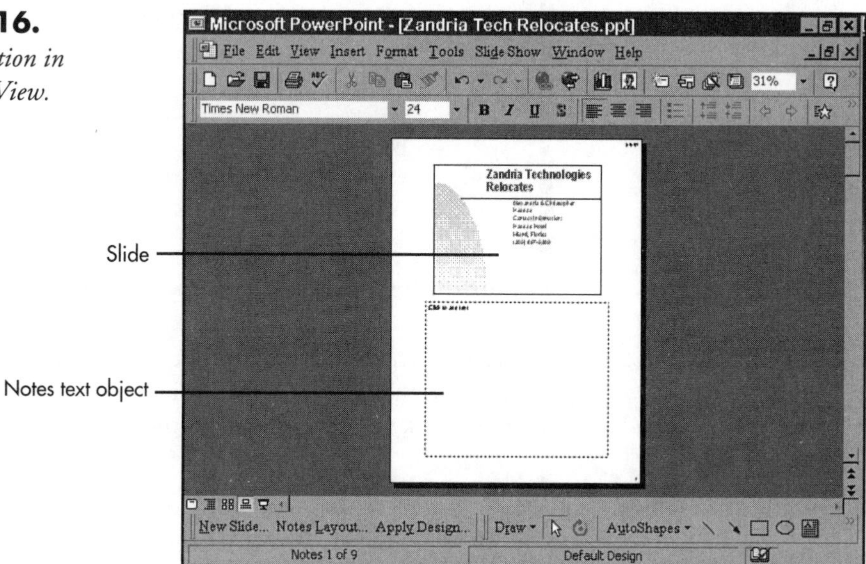

Figure 2.16.
The presentation in Notes Pages View.

Slide Show View

Slide Show View is the mode to operate in if you want to display your presentation as an onscreen presentation while you edit the material. (See Figure 2.17.) To move from slide to slide, simply click the mouse until you reach the end of your presentation. You can always cancel the presentation and end early by pressing the Esc key on your keyboard.

CAUTION

If you want to see the entire presentation from slide one to the end of the presentation or want to use show timings, choose View | Slide Show from the menu. If you click the Slide Show button, your presentation begins from the current slide and continues without timings.

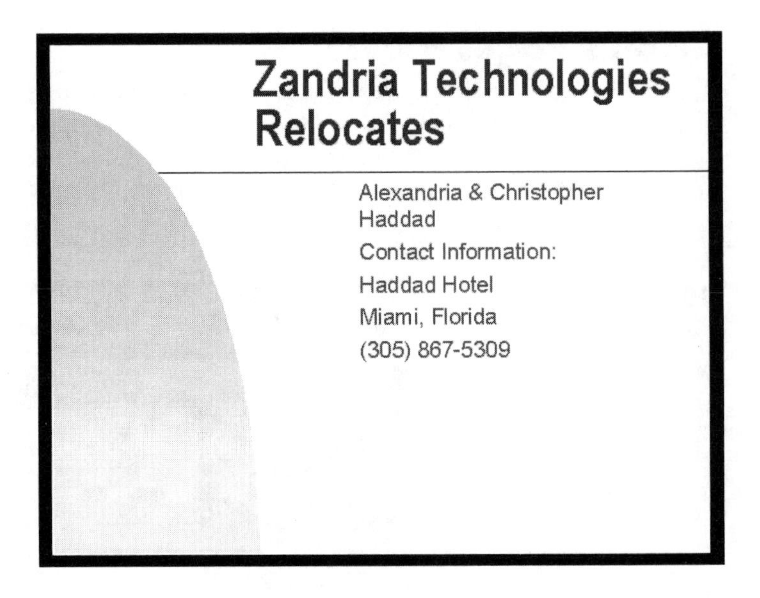

Figure 2.17.
The presentation in Slide Show View.

Show timings allow you to set a specific display time (in seconds) for each slide so you can give your presentation without having to manually advance from slide to slide. Refer to Hour 9 for more on setting and using show timings.

Displaying Slides

There are several ways to move from slide to slide when you're editing your presentation. The method you choose depends on what view mode is currently active and whether you prefer the keyboard or the mouse.

Using the Keyboard

Table 2.1 lists navigation keys you can use to display different slides in your presentation.

Table 2.1. Common PowerPoint 97 navigation keys.

Key Combination	Movement
Pg Up	In Slide and Notes Pages Views, moves you back one slide at a time. In Outline and Slide Sorter Views, moves you up one screen at a time.
Pg Dn	In Slide and Notes Pages Views, moves you forward one slide at a time. In Outline and Slide Sorter Views, moves you down one screen at a time.

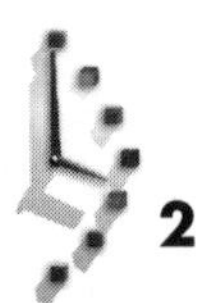

Key Combination	Movement
Ctrl+Home	In all views, moves you to the beginning of the presentation.
Ctrl+End	In all views, moves you to the end of the presentation.

Using the Mouse

You also can use the mouse to scroll through your presentation. In Slide and Notes Pages Views, the vertical scrollbar also contains Previous Slide and Next Slide buttons. You can click the buttons to move to the previous or next slide.

TIME SAVER

In all the views, using the keyboard is the easiest way to navigate through the presentation. Most of the time, I avoid the scrollbars and buttons.

Zooming

At times, you might find that you need to change the onscreen magnification for a slide. Magnification is commonly referred to as *zoom*. When you start working with the drawing tools or want to create speaker notes, the ability to zoom in and out of a slide is extremely important.

To change the zoom options, follow these steps:

1. Choose View | Zoom from the menu to open the Zoom dialog box.
2. Select the appropriate zoom percentage, as shown in Figure 2.18.
3. Click OK.

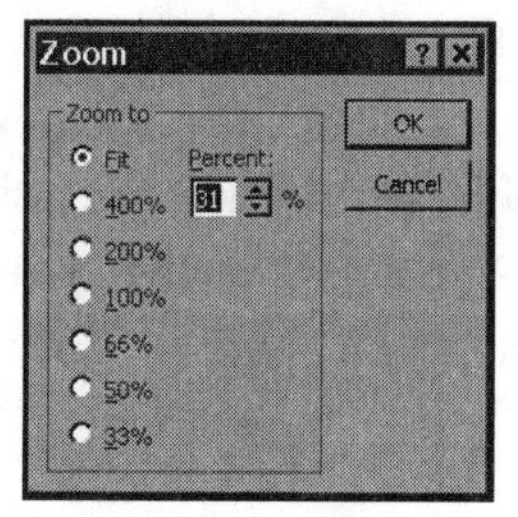

Figure 2.18.
Selecting the zoom percentage in the Zoom dialog box.

TIME SAVER

You also can use the Zoom button on the standard toolbar to quickly zoom in or out of a slide.

Customizing the Sample Slides

You now should be familiar with all the PowerPoint screen elements and know how to move between your presentation slides, so you're ready to learn how to customize the generic presentation. The standard sample text previously generated by the AutoContent Wizard needs to be replaced with your specific information. Figures 2.19 and 2.20 illustrate a generic slide and the customized content that was added. You can edit the presentation in either Outline or Slide View. Editing in Outline View is probably the easiest for now, but later you might find that you perform most of your editing in Slide View.

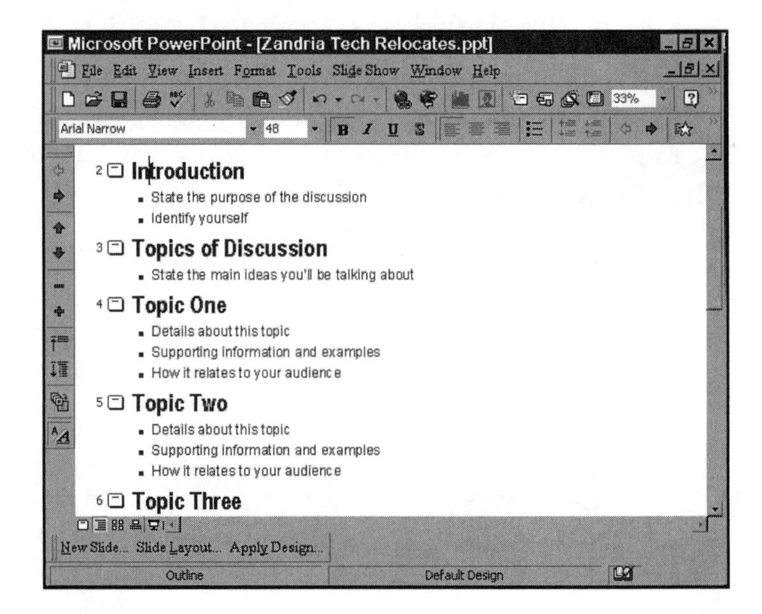

Figure 2.19.
The Zandria Technologies presentation with the AutoContent Wizard sample text.

Editing in Outline View

The AutoContent Wizard's sample text serves as a guide that gives you an idea of what content should be displayed on each slide. These are only suggestions, however; you can display any message you want in your presentation. PowerPoint's Outline View makes editing slide content very easy. Simply type your own words into the presentation outline and delete the sample text created by the AutoContent Wizard. The modified text automatically

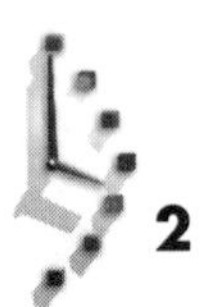

appears on the appropriate slide. You often use the Outline View when you have a lot of text to edit. It's also appropriate to use when you're initially designing your presentation's structure.

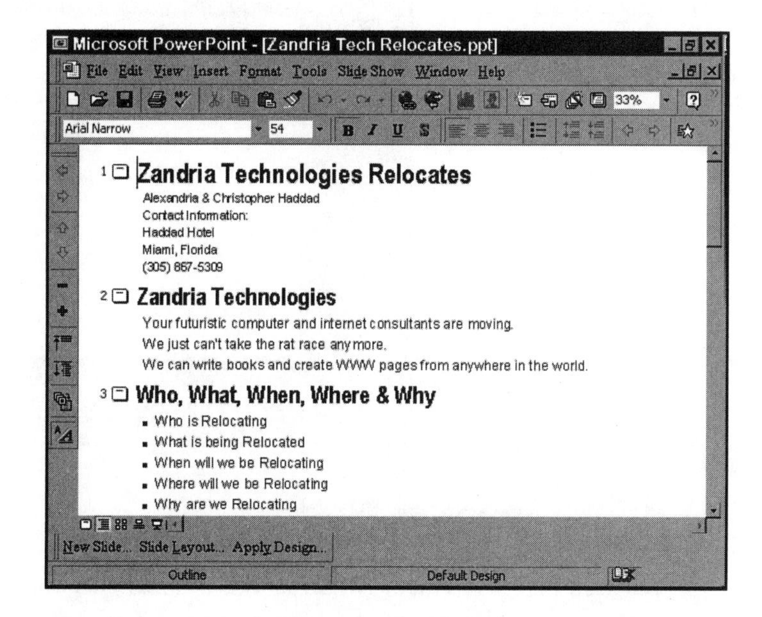

Figure 2.20.
The presentation after entering specific information.

Time Saver

To get the project done fast so you can take Friday off, PowerPoint lets you skip a step. You can select the sample text and then just type in your replacement text. This method saves time by not having to delete the generic text first. Hour 5 covers different ways to select text.

Editing in Slide View

Editing in Slide View is easy when you understand the basics of working with text objects. To edit a text object, just click the text string you want to edit and start typing. PowerPoint displays a cursor, shown in Figure 2.21, that shows you where to add and delete text. You might need to move the cursor to the correct position before you edit the text. Using the arrow keys on the keyboard is usually the easiest way to do that.

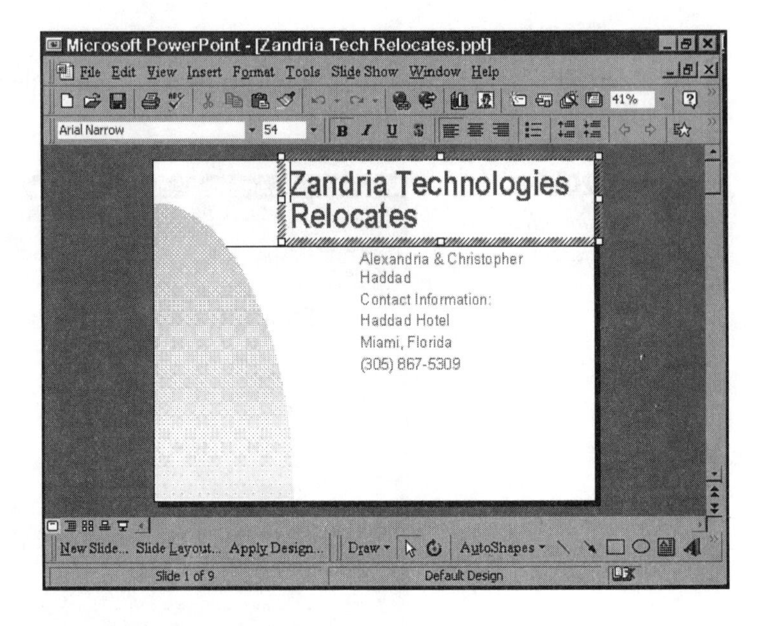

Figure 2.21.
Slide one of the Zandria Technologies presentation with the title object selected.

Adding Speaker Notes

PowerPoint 97 not only creates your presentation, but also helps you create *speaker's notes*, which are paragraphs that serve as your reference material when you give your presentation. You type speaker's notes into your presentation while it's in Notes Pages View. The only time the notes are displayed is if you print the notes pages or if you're in Notes Pages View. (See Figure 2.22.) To add speaker's notes, follow these steps:

1. Switch to Notes Pages View.
2. Click the text object box under the picture of the slide.
3. Type your notes.
4. Click any area outside the slide (any gray area) to deselect the text object.

TIME SAVER

You might want to zoom in so that you can see what you're typing. Usually, a zoom percentage of 75 percent or 100 percent is ideal.

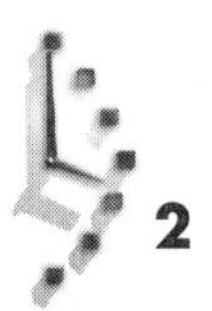

Figure 2.22.
The presentation in Notes Pages View, with speaker's notes added.

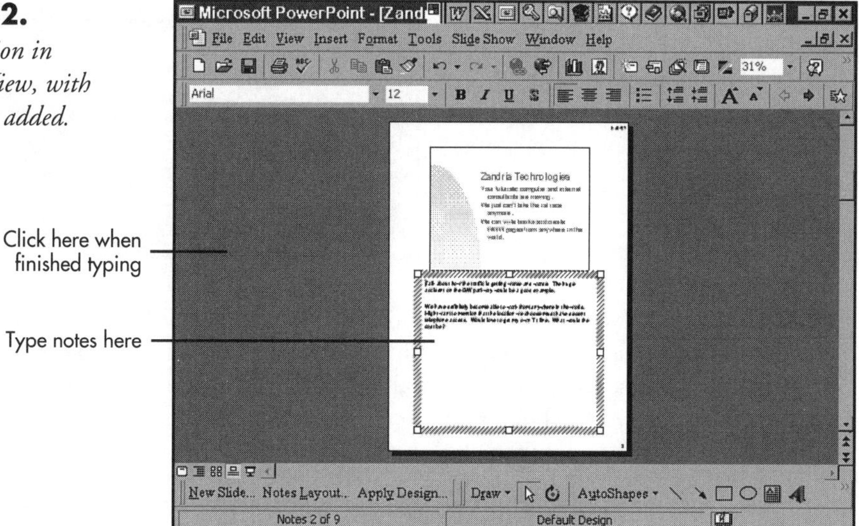

Spellchecking the Presentation

While you have been busy typing all the important information for your presentation, PowerPoint has been making sure you're spelling the words correctly. You might have noticed the automatic spellcheck at work when a red wavy underline is displayed beneath a misspelled word. This line appears every time you misspell a word. You can fix your spelling immediately when PowerPoint tells you a mistake has been made, or you can wait until you have finished typing and run a complete spellcheck. If you've used Microsoft Word before, you will recognize the spellchecker in PowerPoint 97. You can spellcheck your presentation in one of two ways:

- Choose Tools | Spelling from the menu.
- Click the Spelling button on the standard toolbar.

With either method, the Spelling dialog box, shown in Figure 2.23, opens and your spellcheck begins.

Figure 2.23.
The PowerPoint 97 Spelling dialog box with a misspelled word.

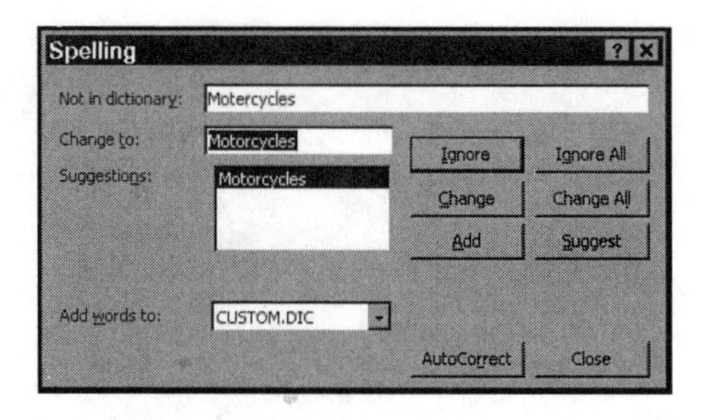

Every misspelled word or word that's not recognized by the spellchecker is highlighted in the "Not in dictionary" box. PowerPoint usually makes an appropriate suggestion in the "Change to" box about how the spelling of the word should be changed. PowerPoint sometimes gives you a whole list of suggestions to choose from in the Suggestions listbox. To modify the spelling, simply click the correct word, and then click the Change button.

If the word is spelled correctly, but PowerPoint just doesn't recognize it as a "real" word, you can tell PowerPoint to ignore the word by clicking the Ignore button. You have a few other options when you run the spellchecker. Table 2.2 covers each option and the operation it performs.

Table 2.2. PowerPoint spellcheck options.

Option	What It Does
Ignore	Ignores the word for that one time.
Ignore All	Ignores every occurrence of this word (only in this presentation).
Change	Changes the misspelled word to the word displayed in the "Change to" box.
Change All	Changes every occurrence of a misspelled word to the word displayed in the "Change to" box.
Add	Adds the word to the open dictionary file. The default file is CUSTOM.DIC. This is the option you want for words like your name and your company name.
Suggest	Looks for a similar word in the dictionary.
AutoCorrect	Does the same thing the Change button does with the added bonus of adding the misspelled word and the correctly spelled word to your AutoCorrect dictionary.
Close	Closes the spellchecker.

Time Saver

You can correct a misspelled word without running the spellchecker on the entire document. To immediately correct a misspelled word that has a red wavy underline, right-click the word and select an option from the shortcut menu. (See Figure 2.24.)

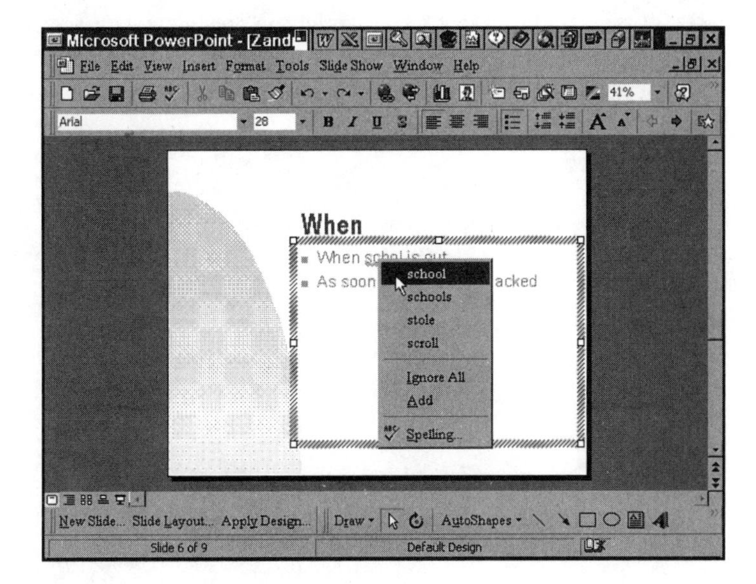

Figure 2.24.
The spellchecker's shortcut menu.

Previewing the Slides in Black and White

If you have created a color onscreen presentation, but must print it on a black-and-white printer, you can preview your presentation in black and white first. You would want to preview the presentation in black and white on the screen to check the presentation's quality when it's printed. There are two ways to preview your presentation in black and white:

- Choose View | Black and White from the menu.
- Click the Black and White View button.

Printing the Presentation

When you have finished editing the presentation contents, you can print your presentation. As you can see in Figure 2.25, you have access to many print options. In the PowerPoint Print dialog box, you can select what pages to print, what slide content to print, and how many copies to print. You can also choose to print all the presentation's slides, just the current slide, or a specific combination of slides. You have even more options for determining the contents to be printed. For example, you can print the slides, speaker's notes, handouts, or the presentation's outline.

JUST A MINUTE

Although PowerPoint can print more than one copy of your presentation, it's better to just use a copying machine if you need multiple copies.

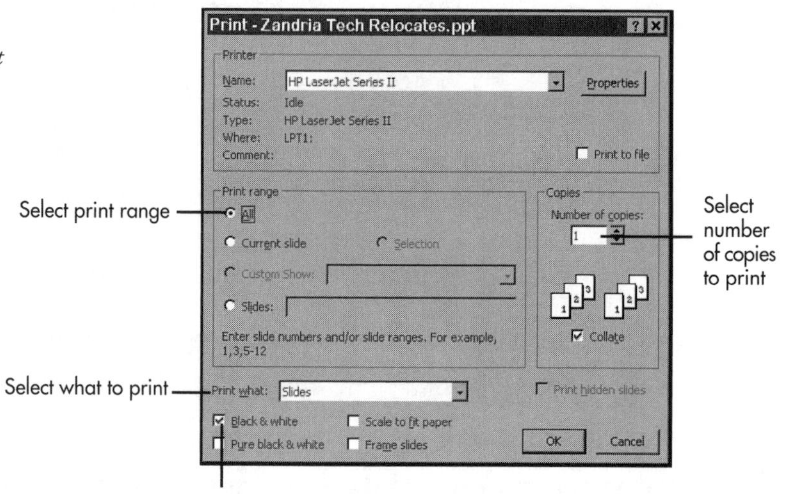

Figure 2.25.
The PowerPoint Print dialog box.

To print your presentation, you can either click the Print button or follow these steps:

1. Choose File | Print from the menu.
2. Change any settings you want.

CAUTION

Although clicking the Print button is an option, resist the urge to use it. All the Microsoft Office applications use the Print button as a super shortcut to print the current document with no questions asked. I have found that in PowerPoint, more than any other application, you should select print options before you print. I once had a client who didn't realize that the print button doesn't display the Print dialog box until Windows informed her that her printer was out of paper (her printer was in an adjoining room). Also, if you're printing to a black-and-white printer, make sure the Black & white checkbox is checked, or you might find yourself with some very dark printouts.

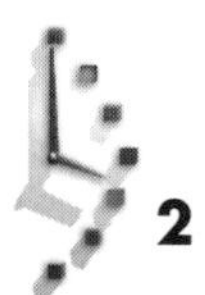

Summary

This hour has been jam-packed with information. You have learned how to create a presentation by using the powerful AutoContent Wizard. You've also learned about all the screen elements, how to use them, and how they can help you get your work done a little quicker. PowerPoint has five different views for you to display your slides, and each view helps you perform different tasks.

You can quickly move to another slide in your presentation by using the mouse or the keyboard, and zooming allows you to view a slide either close up or from a distance, depending on your needs. After you have created an initial presentation using the AutoContent Wizard, you can edit the content of the sample slide with either Outline View or Slide View.

PowerPoint also makes it easy to create and print speaker's notes. If you're not a great speller, no need to fear; with PowerPoint's handy spellchecker, you'll look like a spelling bee champion. If you need to print your presentation on a black-and-white printer, PowerPoint lets you view the presentation with the Black & White View. And printing has never been easier—you can simply click a button to print the entire presentation quickly, or use the menu command to select which slides and what view to print.

Hold on to your hats! Next up is Hour 3, "Basic PowerPoint File Management: Saving, Opening, and Creating Presentations."

Workshop

Once again, you've made it to the "Workshop" section. In this hour's "Test What You've Learned," you start a new presentation with the AutoContent Wizard and practice all the skills you've learned. You will be printing the presentation you create, so make sure your printer is armed and running.

Don't forget to read over the "Q&A" section, too. You never know what tricks you might learn.

Test What You've Learned

JUST A MINUTE

The "Test What You've Learned" sections in Hours 2 and 3 work best when practiced together, so if you have time, read Hour 3 first, and then do the "Test What You've Learned" sections from both hours at the same time.

1. Start PowerPoint.
2. Create a new presentation using the AutoContent Wizard.

3. Dock the Common Tasks toolbar on the bottom of the screen.
4. Close the slide miniature and open it.
5. Close the Office Assistant and open it.
6. Practice switching between the different views: Slide, Outline, Slide Sorter, Notes Pages, and Slide Show.
7. View different slides using the keyboard and the mouse.
8. Switch to Slide View and zoom to 100%. Now use the Zoom To Fit option to see the difference.
9. Change the sample information in the slides while using Slide View and Outline View.
10. Add speaker's notes to any slide.
11. Spellcheck the presentation.
12. Preview the presentation in black and white.
13. Print the presentation.

Q&A

The following are more questions and helpful answers. They just might answer the question poised on the tip of your tongue.

Q What do all these buttons on all these toolbars do?

A They all do different things, but if you position your mouse pointer on any button (don't click), you get a little ScreenTip that pops up and tells you what a particular button does if you click it.

Q Why don't I see any ScreenTips?

A For some reason, this option has been turned off. To turn it back on, follow these steps:

1. Choose View | Toolbars | Customize from the menu.
2. Click the Options tab.
3. Click Show ScreenTips On Toolbars.
4. Click OK.

Refer to Hour 24 for more information about customizing the toolbars.

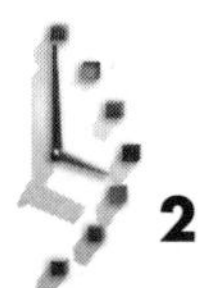

Q I like to check my spelling after I have finished typing the text for my entire presentation. I find the automatic spellchecking to be very distracting. Can I turn it off?

A Yes. To turn the automatic spellcheck off, follow these steps:

1. Choose Tools | Options from the menu to open the Options dialog box.
2. Click the Spelling tab.
3. Uncheck the Spelling checkbox.
4. Click OK.

Q I create a lot of presentations for overseas clients, so I use many foreign words and phrases. Does PowerPoint recognize words from other languages, or do I have to explicitly add each word to the dictionary?

A PowerPoint 97 has a new language feature that lets your computer check the spelling of text written in a foreign language. You must do two things to configure foreign language support. First, you must have multilanguage support installed with Windows. Second, you must select all the text that contains foreign words and mark it as belonging to another language. To mark text as another language, follow these steps:

1. Select the text.
2. Choose Tools | Language from the menu.
3. Select the appropriate language from the "Mark selected text as" list.
4. Click OK.

Q I want to print only slides 4, 5, 6, and 10, but every time I click the Print button, the printer prints all 30 slides of my presentation. How can I print only the slides I need?

A First, don't click the Print button. This is a habit learned from using the other Office applications, but it's usually not a very useful option when you're working in PowerPoint. Instead, use the File | Print menu option, and select the Slides option under Print range. The range you would enter for the sample question would be `4-6, 10`.

PART I

Hour 3

Basic PowerPoint File Management: Saving, Opening, and Creating Presentations

Welcome to Hour 3. Now that you have created your first presentation, you need to save it and know the steps for reopening it later. After you save your presentation document, you can give it to colleagues so they can add some final comments or modifications. Here are a few questions that can come up when you're working with files:

- Where is my presentation file located on my computer?
- How do you open the file?
- What concepts and tasks make up file management?

These questions and other intriguing issues are answered in this hour. You might also be at the point where you're thinking, "The AutoContent Wizard is great, but I have my own ideas for my presentation." This hour also covers how to create a new presentation in your own unique format. In this hour, you learn how to do the following:

- How to save or open an existing presentation or start a new presentation
- How to select a different disk drive or folder in which to store or retrieve a presentation file
- How to check a file for a bad or dangerous macro before you open it
- How to search for and locate a specific file
- How to work on more than one file at a time (multitask)

A Few Words on How a PC Stores Presentations

A computer's scariest attribute is the intangible aspect of its contents. As humans, we're used to touching objects before we believe they're real. When they first start working with computers, most people initially have a hard time understanding exactly where all their hard work is actually stored in the "boxes" that sit on (or under) their desks.

Computers store presentation files on a storage medium called a *disk drive*. The information is stored on the drive as thousands of little magnetic fields that are either on or off. However, you really don't need to concern yourself with all the technical aspects of data storage; it's all handled by Windows and the hardware. You do need to understand the operations required to save and retrieve your work in an organized fashion. PowerPoint 97 builds on Windows to present easy-to-use dialog boxes that allow you to organize your presentation files.

The best way to visualize the physical and logical storage of files is to correlate computer concepts with real-world objects, which makes Windows file management much easier to understand. The Windows interface uses disk drives, folders, subfolders, and documents for file management.

A *disk drive* is analogous to an office filing cabinet. Like a filing cabinet, a disk drive is used to store documents that can contain presentations, spreadsheets, or databases. Each disk drive has a unique name. Typically, you access drives by referring to a corresponding letter, such as A, B, C, D, and so on. Each letter represents a distinct container—a separate filing cabinet—that's used to store information in your computer. Usually, the A: or B: drive is reserved for removable media, such as floppy disks. The C: drive letter designates your computer's hard drive. Other letters commonly represent additional drives—the D: drive can be assigned to the CD-ROM drive, and any letter higher in the alphabet is probably a remote networked drive.

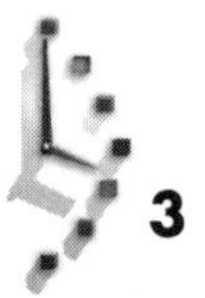

You can understand the *folder* and *subfolder* components by expanding the filing cabinet analogy. A filing cabinet has drawers with green hanging file folders in them; these file folders can contain smaller manila folders used to store paper documents. The folder and subfolder concepts correspond to the green hanging folders and manila folders, respectively. As in the real world, you can store document files in either folders or subfolders. In Figure 3.1, the document path C:\My Documents\PowerPoint\ZT Relocates.ppt has been broken down to correlate it with real-world objects.

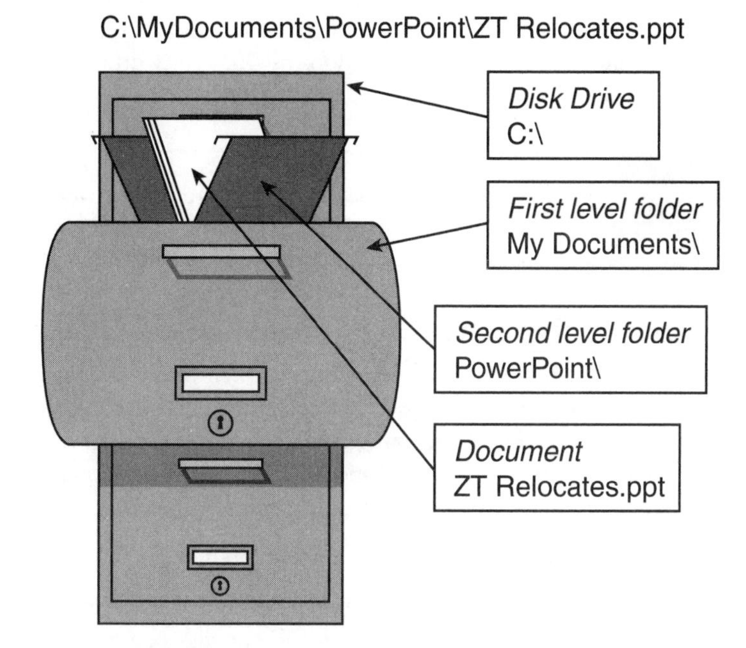

Figure 3.1.
The relationship of a computer document to physical file objects.

Saving a Presentation

Saving your work might be the most important task you do when you work with PowerPoint. Until you save your work, it doesn't exist in a permanent form. Saving is extremely easy, and you should do it often. When you save a presentation, you must provide a filename for the document that should indicate the presentation's contents. By using an easy-to-remember filename, you can readily locate the presentation in future PowerPoint sessions.

PowerPoint 97 also includes options for saving your presentation in other formats. For example, you can save a presentation to the HTML format so the presentation can be viewed through a standard Web browser. You can post the presentation on the Internet so it's accessible for anyone who can reach your Web site. For more information about formatting a presentation for the World Wide Web, see Part VI, "Multimedia, the World Wide Web, and Other Cool Stuff." You also can save a presentation with information about its runtime characteristics. If you want to distribute the electronic presentation document to an audience, save it in Slide Show View (which is explained in more detail in Hour 9, "Basics of Slide Shows").

There are two types of save operations: Save As or Save. For an unnamed presentation that hasn't been previously saved, both options work in exactly the same way. However, after a presentation has been given a document name, the options work a little differently. Save As lets you specify a new document name or folder to hold the presentation contents. The Save operation simply saves the presentation under the current name into the current folder, with no questions asked. These options might seem a little difficult to understand at first, but they'll make sense after you use them a few times.

Just a Minute

The Save button on the standard toolbar works much like the Print button. You won't see anything happen, but your file will be saved.

Using the Save As Command

You should use the Save As command when you save a file for the first time. Save As is also used when you want to give a presentation a new name or you want to save it in a different location or folder. You can quickly save a presentation to a floppy disk with the Save As operation by specifying the appropriate drive letter. To save your presentation for the first time or to give a presentation a new name, follow these steps:

1. Choose File | Save As from the main menu.
2. In the File Name box, enter a name for your presentation.
3. To save the presentation to a floppy disk or a different folder, select the appropriate location from the Save In drop-down list.
4. Click Save.

Just a Minute

Your filename can have up to 255 alphanumeric characters and can also contain the space character, as shown in Figure 3.2.

After you save your presentation, the filename appears in the PowerPoint application's title bar instead of the generic Presentation*X* moniker. PowerPoint also automatically assigns the .PPT extension to the end of your filename.

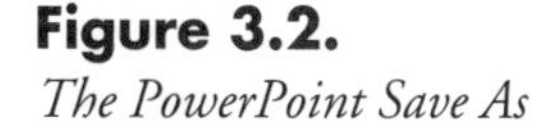

Figure 3.2.
The PowerPoint Save As dialog box.

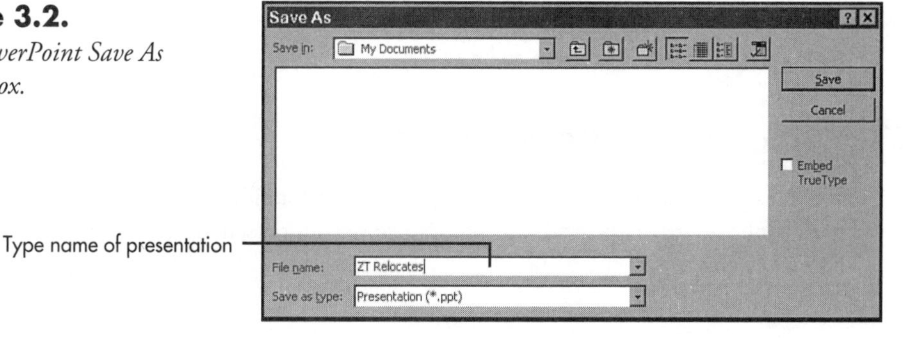

JUST A MINUTE

The .PPT extension at the end of the filename tells Windows 95 that your file is a PowerPoint presentation.

JUST A MINUTE

You might not see the .PPT extension, depending on the system options that have been initialized for your operating system (Windows 95 or Windows NT).

Changing the Drive or Folders

By default, PowerPoint saves all your presentations on the C:\ disk drive in the My Documents folder. The correct path is C:\My Documents\. If you want to save a presentation on a different disk drive (such as a floppy disk) or in a different folder, you must indicate a different presentation destination by selecting an alternative disk drive and folder from the Save In list box. For example, to save the presentation to the A:\ drive, click the down triangle next to the Save In list box and select the 3 1/2 Floppy (A:) option from the list.

If you want to save a presentation in a different folder on your C:\ drive, you must first select the (C:) option from the Save In list box. You can then open a folder and subsequent subfolders by double-clicking the appropriate folder icon until you reach the appropriate location to store the presentation.

Using the Save Command

To quickly protect your work, use the Save command to periodically update your presentation document. A good rule of thumb is to save every 10 minutes or to save after every major modification. Saving takes only a moment, so do it often. If your computer inadvertently crashes between saves, you have a better chance of retrieving all your hard work. You can save and update your presentation in one of two ways:

- Choose File|Save from the menu.
- Click the Save button on the toolbar.

Closing a Presentation

Closing a presentation takes it out of sight and mind. Before you go to lunch, walk to the water cooler, or leave for the day, it's best to close your presentation. You can do this in one of two ways:

- Choose File|Close from the menu.
- Click the document Close button on the menu bar.

After you have closed a presentation, you have three options available:

- Open an existing presentation
- Start a new presentation
- Exit from PowerPoint 97

Each of these options is covered in the following sections.

Opening an Existing Presentation

You can open any PowerPoint presentation that has been previously created and saved. If you want to review or modify the presentation, you first must open the presentation document. Opening a presentation is a simple process. In fact, it's almost the same as the steps you use to save a presentation. The only requirement to open a presentation is to supply the saved presentation's location. In PowerPoint, you can see a preview of the presentation file before it's officially opened. Figure 3.3 shows the Open dialog box with the Preview option. Use the following step to open a PowerPoint presentation:

1. Choose File|Open from the menu.

Or, do the following:

1. Click the Open button on the standard toolbar.
2. Select the correct drive or folder.

JUST A MINUTE

> To open a presentation document that's in a different location, select the drive or folder from the Look In drop-down list.

3. Select from the file list the file you want to open.
4. Click Open.

Figure 3.3.
The Open dialog box, previewing the ZT Relocation presentation.

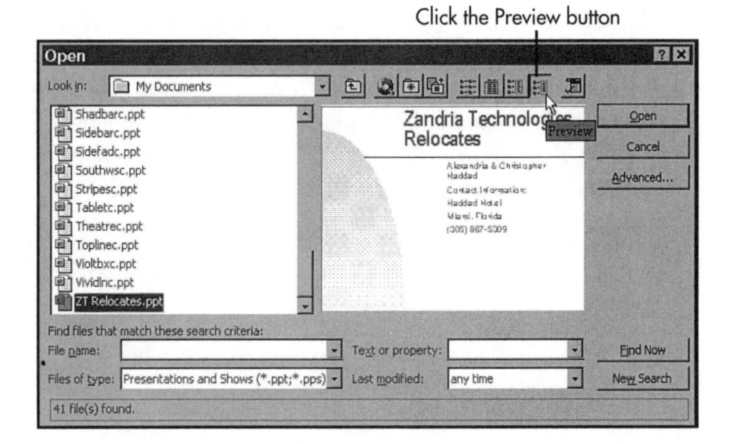

TIME SAVER

PowerPoint remembers the last four files you have worked on. A quick way to open a presentation you have been working on recently is to select the filename from the bottom of the File menu.

Checking for Bad Macros

Good macros, bad macros...what *is* a macro? A *macro* can be considered a little program. In its simplest and most rudimentary form, a macro contains a recording of keystrokes. Having keystroke macros in your toolbox can be very useful. You can activate the macro in one keystroke to reproduce an operation that has several complicated keystroke combinations. If you frequently perform the operation, the time you save with the macro can be substantial.

As the Microsoft Office suite has become more popular, less friendly macros have surfaced. Some people who have way too much time on their hands and very little ethical integrity entertain themselves by writing small but dangerous macros that are attached to documents. When the files are opened, they can infect other files. The migration of a dangerous macro is analogous to passing a cold from one person to the next. Sharing a macro-infested document is just like sharing a tissue with someone who has a bad cold. Most macro viruses are harmless, but a few can perform very dangerous and subversive operations. A bad macro could even destroy all the files on your hard drive.

Your computer can activate and replicate a macro virus when you simply open a document containing the virus program. The document file might be one you got from an offbeat or strange location, or it could have come from Bob next door. These little macro guys are pesky, however, and might have attached their program code to colleagues' files, unknown to them or you.

Unfortunately, PowerPoint can't warn you that a macro is bad, but it does contain a rudimentary warning system. PowerPoint's macro virus protection feature can warn you when you're opening a file that contains a macro. You can then decide whether to open the presentation with all the macros disabled (off) or enabled (on). If you're unsure, the safest course of action is to disable the macros. When macro programs are disabled, they can't perform any "terrorist" acts. Therefore, make sure you have the macro virus protection enabled. To do so, follow these steps:

1. Choose Tools|Options from the menu to open the Options dialog box.
2. Click the General tab.
3. Make sure the "Macro virus protection" checkbox is checked, as shown in Figure 3.4.
4. Click OK.

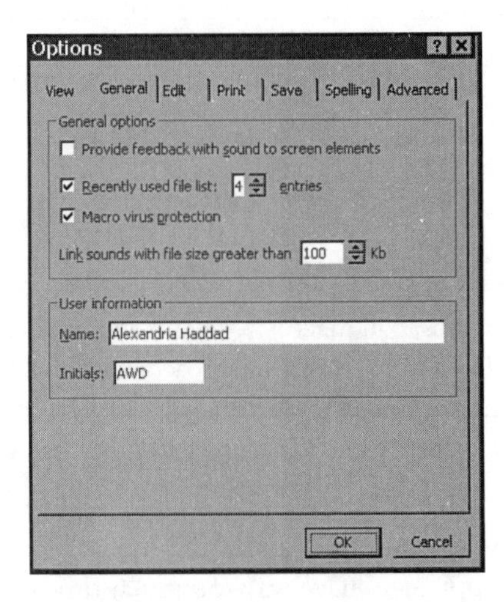

Figure 3.4.
The Options dialog box with macro virus protection on.

JUST A MINUTE

You can download the latest virus protection information from Microsoft's Web site at `http://www.microsoft.com/office/msofc/work_virus.htm`.

Selecting and Opening Multiple Files

With PowerPoint, you can work on one presentation at a time or open several concurrent sessions. To open several presentations at once, follow these steps:

1. Choose File|Open from the menu to display the Open dialog box.
2. From the displayed list of files, select the files you want to open.

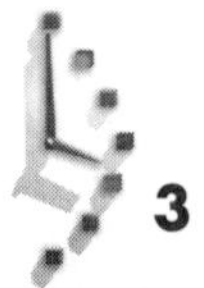

JUST A MINUTE

To select multiple contiguous files, click the first file, hold down the Shift key, and click the last file.

To select multiple non-contiguous files, click the first file, and then hold down the Ctrl key while you click each subsequent file.

3. Click the Open button to load and activate the presentations.

When you have multiple presentations open, you should use the Window menu item to switch between presentation documents. See the "Navigating Open Presentations" section of this lesson for more information.

Starting a New Presentation

Starting a new presentation when you first open the PowerPoint application is an easy technique to grasp. Figure 3.5 shows the window you see with each new session of PowerPoint. From the "Create a new presentation using" area of the PowerPoint dialog box, select one of the following three options:

- AutoContent wizard
- Template
- Blank presentation

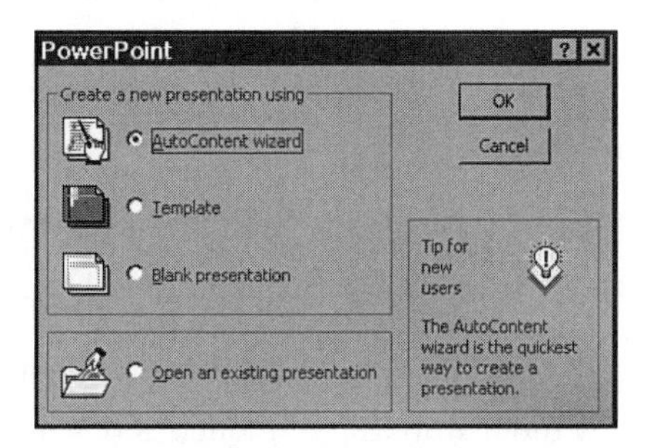

Figure 3.5.
The PowerPoint dialog box.

When you want to create a new presentation in the middle of an active PowerPoint session, the steps are a little different. You still have the same three options for your new presentation, but they are found in different places and are activated with different commands. The following sections explain where to find each of the options that are initially displayed in the PowerPoint dialog box.

AutoContent Wizard

During your PowerPoint session, the friendly AutoContent Wizard has gone into hiding. But don't worry—you can still find it in the New Presentation dialog box. To start a new presentation using the AutoContent Wizard, follow these steps:

1. Choose File|New from the menu to open the New Presentation dialog box.
2. Click the Presentations tab.
3. Click the AutoContent Wizard, as shown in Figure 3.6.
4. Finally, click OK to start the wizard.

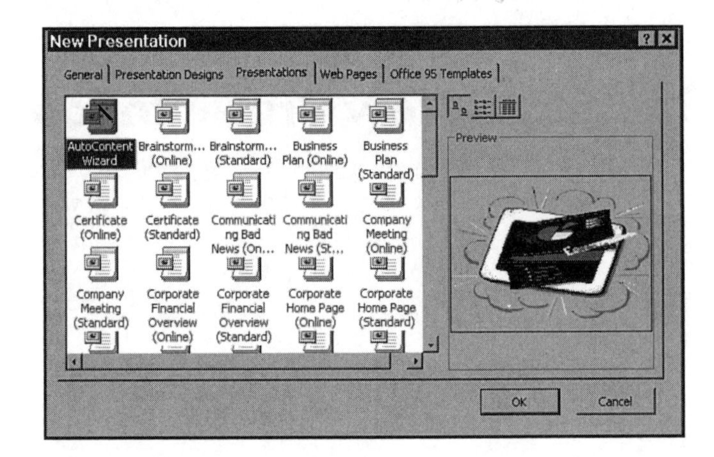

Figure 3.6.
The New Presentation dialog box with the AutoContent Wizard selected.

Using the AutoContent Wizard was explained in Hour 2, "Quick Start: Creating Your First Presentation."

Presentation Design (or Template)

When you first create a presentation, choosing the Template option is appropriate if you don't need any help with the logical flow of the ideas in the presentation. You already know the content each slide will contain. Templates allow you to focus on creating the presentation message without worrying too much about the presentation's overall style. The *template*, which can also be called a *presentation design*, supplies the artistic theme or style for the slides. The template you choose defines the choice of colors, background graphics, and fonts. I use this option quite a bit because some excellent designs have already been created by professional commercial artists. As much as I love to play with PowerPoint, I often don't have the time to create the entire content for a presentation and worry about the design elements, too.

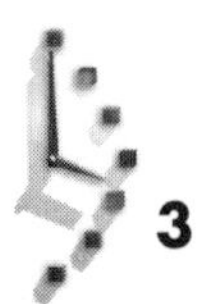

Follow these steps to select an appropriate presentation design for your message:

1. Choose File | New from the menu to open the New Presentation dialog box.
2. Click the Presentation Designs tab. (See Figure 3.7.)
3. Select an applicable design theme.
4. Click OK.

JUST A MINUTE

The first few times you select a presentation design, it's a good idea to preview all the designs you have available. You can preview a presentation design template either by clicking once on each design name or by using the arrow keys on your keyboard to highlight each design. You should also realize that the number of designs available on a computer varies. For example, Bob might have downloaded some extra design sets from the Microsoft Web site.

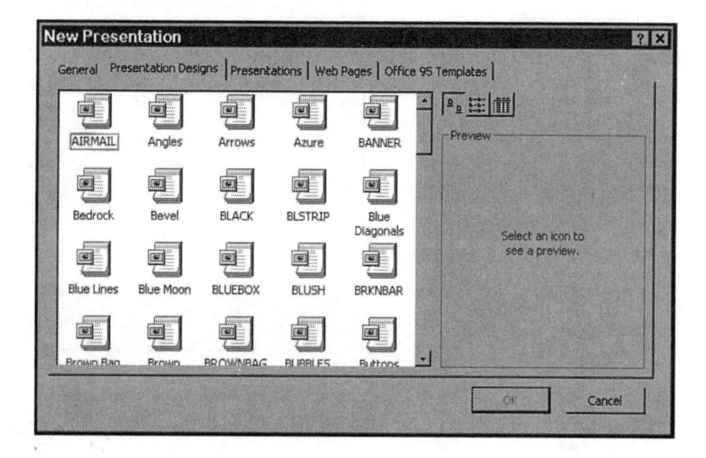

Figure 3.7.
The Presentation Designs tab of the New Presentation dialog.

Blank Presentation

The last option available for creating a new presentation is to start a blank presentation. A blank presentation has no color, no design, and not a shred of fancy stuff. PowerPoint leaves all the slide formatting up to you. Unless you need to design a very specialized presentation—for example, when you're using your company's colors, logo, and font choices—I don't recommend using this option. If you need to create a presentation design for your company's use, then use the blank presentation option. In general, though, when you start from a blank presentation, you could find yourself putting much more work into a presentation than what's really necessary. Choose the AutoContent Wizard or a premade presentation design, if possible. However, when you need a blank canvas to create an exceptionally unique slide, follow these steps to start a new blank presentation:

1. Choose File | New from the menu to open the New Presentation dialog box.
3. Click the General tab, as shown in Figure 3.8.
4. Select Blank Presentation.
5. Click OK.

JUST A MINUTE

When you want to start a new blank presentation, you can also just click the New button. However, if you want to select a presentation design or use the AutoContent Wizard, you must use the File | New menu command.

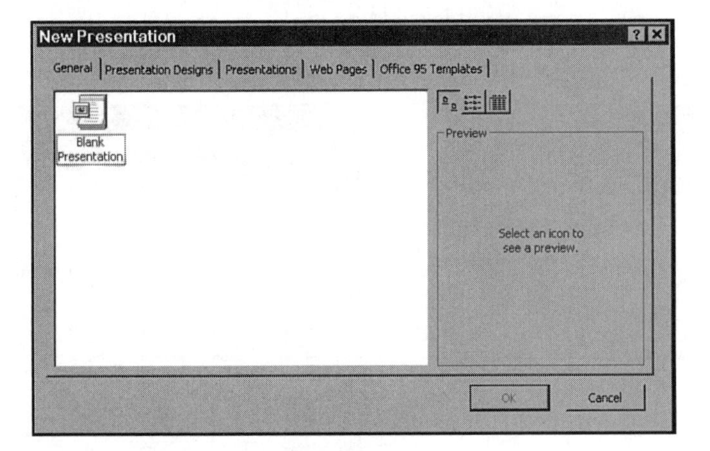

Figure 3.8.
The New Presentation dialog box with the Blank Presentation option.

Navigating Open Presentations

You can start a new presentation without closing the currently active presentation. Having several presentations open at once in PowerPoint 97 is acceptable; however, you need to know how to switch between the presentations. At first, having several presentations open is a little confusing—it's like having many stacks of paper on a desk. Even though most people can work on only one thing at a time, it doesn't keep them from having many documents on their desktop. Just like switching from one stack of papers to another on an actual desk, PowerPoint lets you do the same thing with presentation documents. You just use your mouse instead of your hand, and instead of having paper documents on your desk, you have document windows.

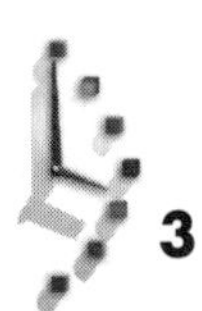

All the presentations you currently have open are listed in the Window menu, which has several options for navigating between open presentations. The easiest method is to just select the actual presentation name from the list. As you can see in Figure 3.9, the example contains three open presentations. The presentation your attention is currently focused on is called the *active presentation*, which has a checkmark by its name. To switch presentations, simply select the presentation by name and presto—you're now billing some other client for the work! Here are the steps for switching between open presentations:

1. Select the Window menu.
2. Click the presentation you want to switch to.

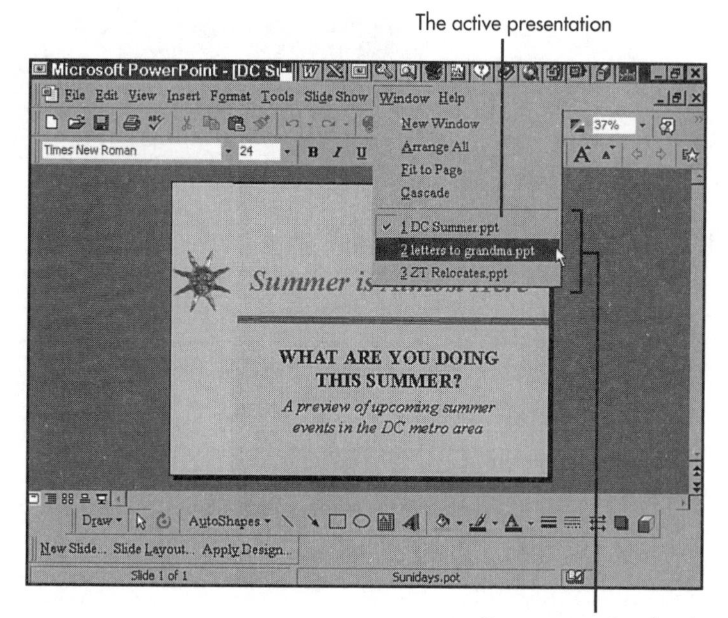

Figure 3.9.
The Window menu with three presentations currently open.

The Window menu has a few other options worth mentioning here. The New Window, Arrange All, Fit to Page, and Cascade items all play important roles in the quest for seamless presentation navigation.

New Window

The New Window option simply copies and opens your current, active presentation in another window. You can use New Window to move or drag an object, such as a picture, from one slide into another, as shown in Figure 3.10. You can also use it to compare the black-and-white view and the color view.

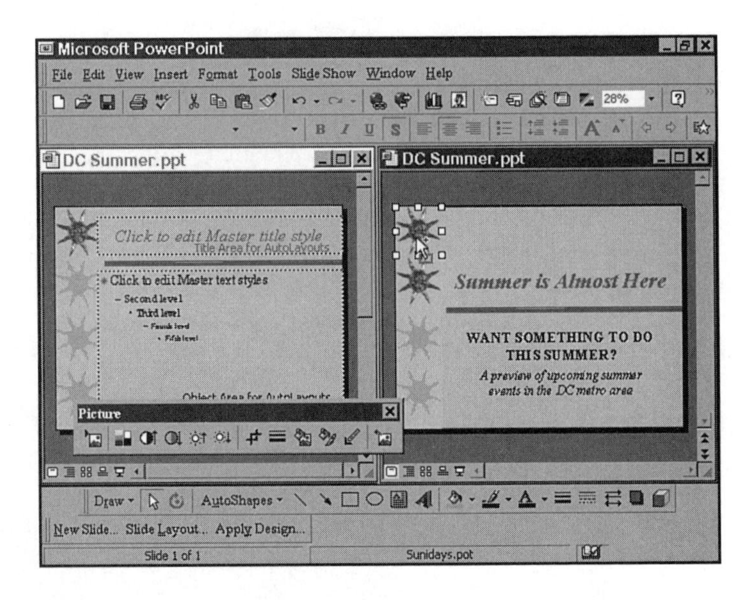

Figure 3.10.
The same presentation open in two different windows for comparison.

JUST A MINUTE

You can also arrange the two windows in Figure 3.10 by using the Arrange All feature.

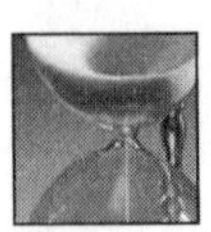

CAUTION

New Window doesn't create another copy of the presentation on the disk; it just creates one in memory. Also, any content changes you make in one window are made in any other windows you opened with the New Window command.

Arrange All

The Arrange All option in the Window menu arranges any open presentation windows to fit on the screen. This feature is very useful when you want to compare two or more presentations, such as those shown in Figure 3.11.

Fit to Page

The Fit to Page option is vital if you commonly use floating toolbars. The command resizes the active slide window so that it properly fits the boundaries of your screen. Figure 3.12 shows a window resized with the Fit to Page option.

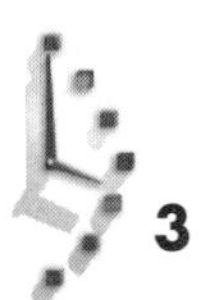

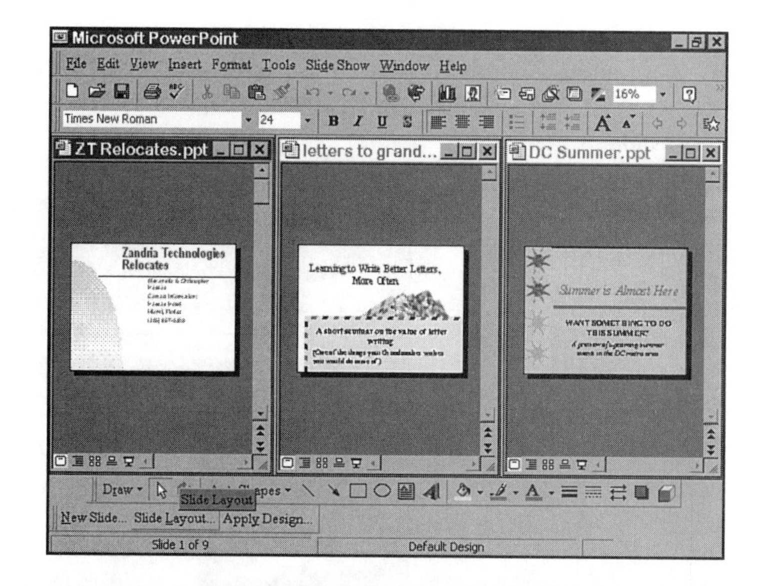

Figure 3.11.
Open presentation windows arranged onscreen with the Arrange All command.

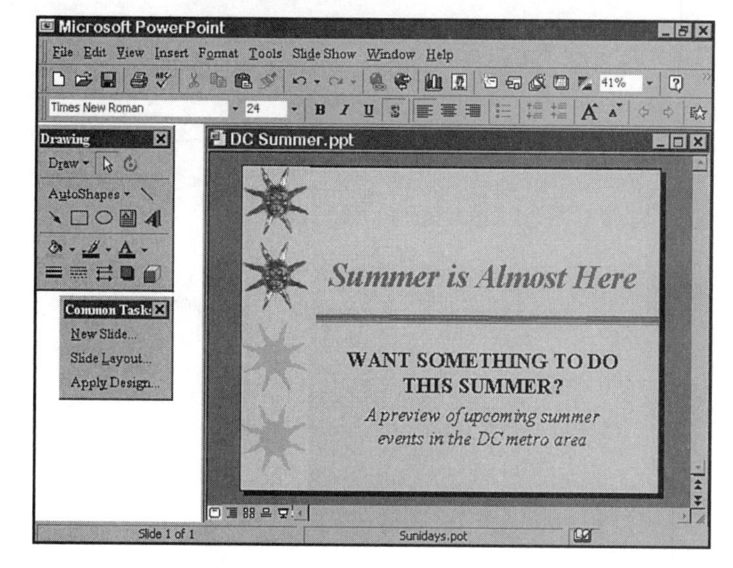

Figure 3.12.
A presentation window after using the Fit to Page option.

Cascade

The final option in the Window menu is Cascade, which arranges all open presentation windows in a stack so you can view the title bar of each. I once knew an army colonel who would arrange all the papers on his desk in this manner. He was a very organized person, and every time I cascade my windows, it reminds me of his desk. See Figure 3.13 for a "declassified" view. Why would you cascade windows? Because it makes switching between the different presentations easier. Simply click the title bar of the presentation you want to work on and watch the window move to the front (just like a paper document on that colonel's desk).

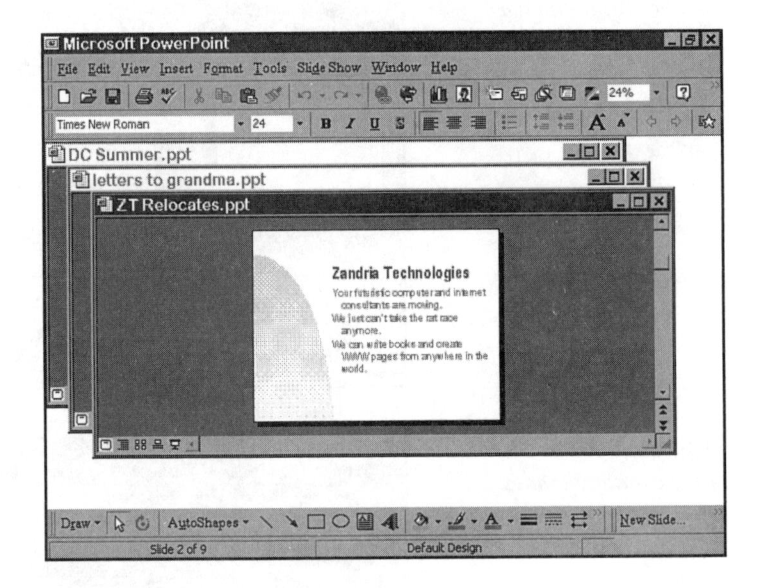

Figure 3.13.
Open presentations that have been cascaded.

Exiting PowerPoint

The last item covered this hour is how to exit PowerPoint so you can go home at the end of the day. I know, you're having so much fun, you just hate to go. But the time will come when you need to quit. To exit PowerPoint, you have two options:

- Choose File | Exit from the menu.
- Click the application Close button.

Summary

You now know the fundamentals that allow you to create, print, show, and save a basic presentation. You could put this book down now if that was all you needed to know, but the fun has just begun. You wouldn't really be happy just knowing the basics; the real excitement of PowerPoint starts after learning how to change colors, insert clip art, and add word art and animation to a presentation. Also, you haven't yet explored the features that will make Bob actually want to give you that raise in salary, so don't stop now!

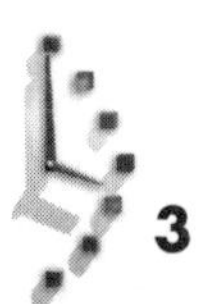

Workshop

This hour's "Workshop" covers how to save, close, and open presentation files. In "Test What You've Learned," you get to practice three different ways to start a new file and learn how to multitask. The questions and answers relate to material covered in this lesson. PowerPoint wizards are people who can answer even the most obscure queries.

Test What You've Learned

Just a Minute

If you're following from Hour 2's "Test What You've Learned" section, you can skip Step 1.

1. Start PowerPoint and go through the AutoContent Wizard to create a new presentation.
2. Save the presentation as `TWYL Hour 3a`.
3. Close the presentation.
4. Next, open the presentation.
5. Start a new presentation by using the AutoContent Wizard.
6. Save the presentation as `TWYL Hour 3b`.
7. Start a new presentation by using a presentation design (template).
8. Save the presentation as `TWYL Hour 3c`.
9. Start a new blank presentation.
10. Save the presentation as `TWYL Hour 3d`.
11. Switch to `TWYL Hour 3a`.
12. Arrange all the open presentation windows.
13. Cascade all the open presentation windows.
14. Exit PowerPoint.

Q&A

The first question is for those who think UPS is only a package delivery service.

UPS: Another industry acronym that makes you seem "in the know." It stands for *Universal Power Supply*, which is a device with batteries used to operate and shut down your computer during a power failure.

Q If the power goes out, do I lose all my work?

A Not necessarily. PowerPoint has an AutoRecover feature you can set for just this purpose. Usually, AutoRecover is set to do a backup every 10 minutes. To view your current AutoRecover settings, follow these steps:

1. Choose Tools | Options from the menu to display the Options window.
2. Click the Save tab.
3. Change any settings you want.
4. Click OK.

Q I always save my files to my A: drive. Can I change the default drive and folder in which PowerPoint automatically saves?

A Yes. You can change the default file location to be any drive or folder. If you change the default file location to the A: drive, you need to always have a floppy disk in the disk drive to open a file or save a file, even if you plan on switching to the C: drive, because PowerPoint attempts to look in the default file location first. This is OK if you always work from your A: drive, but if you don't, you might find it annoying to have to constantly stop and put a disk in the computer. To change the default file location for PowerPoint, follow these steps:

1. Choose Tools | Options from the menu to display the Options window.
2. Click the Advanced tab.
3. In the "Default file location" box, type the new file location. For example, type `A:\` for the A: drive.
4. Click OK.

Now, every time you want to open or save a presentation, PowerPoint goes to the new location you specified.

Q Can I control the order in which my presentation windows cascade?

A Not really. Even though the files are listed in the Window menu in alphabetical order, they cascade in the order you opened (or created) them. If you want them to cascade in a certain order, close all presentations, and then open them in the order that should control the display.

Part II

Slides and PowerPoint Objects

Hour

Part II

Hour 4

Working with Slides

In the next three hours, you will be creating and formatting a complete presentation from the first slide to the last. During this hour, you learn how to work with the building blocks of a presentation: the slides. After reading this chapter, you will know how to do the following:

- Select the best layout for a slide using the AutoLayout feature
- Create and work with a title slide
- Add, delete, and move slides within a presentation
- Create and work with bullet slides
- Expand a single crowded slide into many clearer slides
- Change the layout of a slide or modify the design of the presentation

Using AutoLayout

After you start a new presentation using either the presentation design or blank presentation option, the first screen you see is the New Slide dialog box. (See Figure 4.1.) You should also see it every time you insert a new slide. The box asks you to select an *AutoLayout*, which is a preliminary draft layout for your presentation's slides. All the AutoLayout formats except Blank have placeholders for different types of PowerPoint objects. PowerPoint has 24 AutoLayout designs you can choose from, and these presentation designs typically start with a title slide.

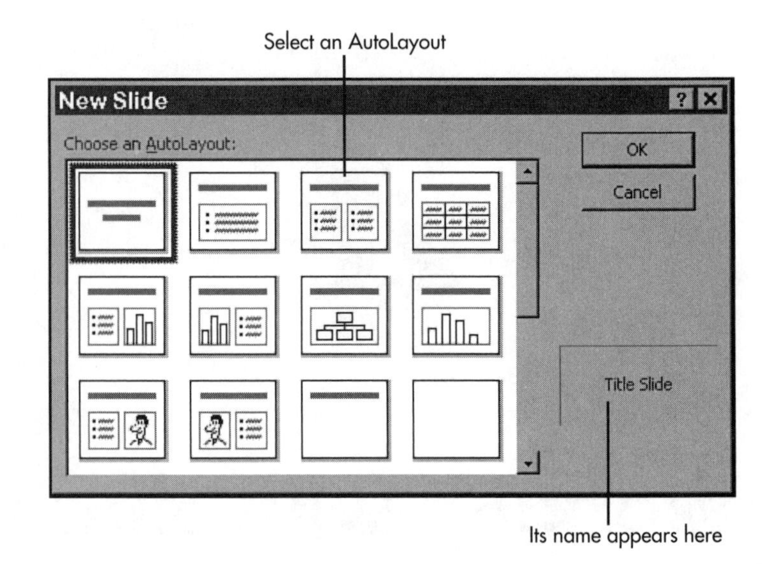

Figure 4.1.
The New Slide dialog box.

TIME SAVER

If you're going to be adding text to your slide, you probably want the information included in the presentation outline. It's best to start with some sort of layout format rather than start with a blank slide. Although you can add text to a blank presentation, it won't be included in the outline because the text you add to the slide is considered a type of drawing object. Text that's displayed in the Outline View must be entered in a text box object. If you don't have an AutoLayout that fits your needs exactly, pick the one that's closest to the final format you want. You can always change things around later.

Creating a Title Slide

The *title slide* is the very first presentation slide your audience sees, so it sets the tone for the rest of the presentation. When you use the AutoContent Wizard, it prompts you for a presentation title, the presenter's name, and any additional information. You can enter this same information on any title slide you create with an AutoLayout. After adding a title slide, switch to Slide View and change the title slide information. To do this, just select the title or subtitle object and enter the appropriate text.

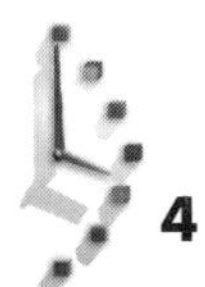

NEW TERM An *object* is a building block of the slide, which is, in turn, a building block of the presentation. In PowerPoint, every item you work with is considered an object. This model is unlike a word processor, where you work with mostly text. You work with text in PowerPoint, too, but the text is contained as an object, so the text information is contained in a text object. There are other objects, too, such as clip art objects and drawing objects. Figure 4.2 shows a title slide that has a title and subtitle object placeholder. PowerPoint even tells you, right on the slide, what to do: "Click to add title."

Figure 4.2.
A PowerPoint title slide with the title entered and the subtitle object selected.

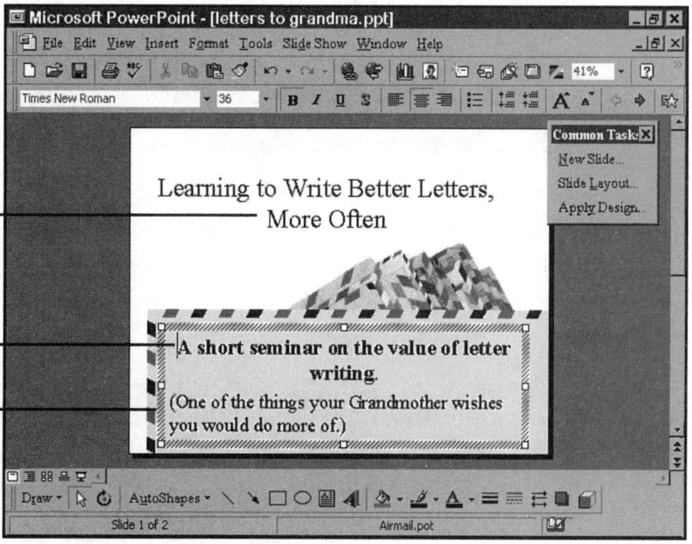

Title object

Subtitle object

Selection box

Undoing Your Mistakes

If an operation doesn't give you the effect you want, you can reverse it. The Undo feature can always be used to erase the last command, and sometimes can go back even further to undo operations you've performed. PowerPoint stores your previous commands in a buffer until you save the presentation. To go back one step, you can either choose Edit | Undo from the menu or click the Undo button on the standard toolbar.

PowerPoint is initially set to remember the last 20 actions you have performed, so you could click the Undo button 20 times if necessary. The Undo button also has a small down-pointing triangle next to it that displays, when clicked, a complete history of your most recent actions. To undo several commands at one fell click, simply click the last command you want in the list.

Just a Minute

Right next to the Undo button is the Redo button. Redo undoes your undo (for all of us who get trigger happy).

Adding New Slides

Unlike working with a word processing application, in PowerPoint you have to explicitly add each new page (slide) you want to include in your presentation. PowerPoint doesn't do the addition for you automatically. You have several different methods for adding a new slide, which are illustrated in Figure 4.3. To create a new slide, simply select the method you prefer. Or, to add a bit of variety, use different methods on different days:

- Choose Insert | New Slide from the menu.
- Press the Ctrl+M key combination.
- Click the New Slide button on the standard toolbar.
- Click the New Slide button on the Common Tasks toolbar.

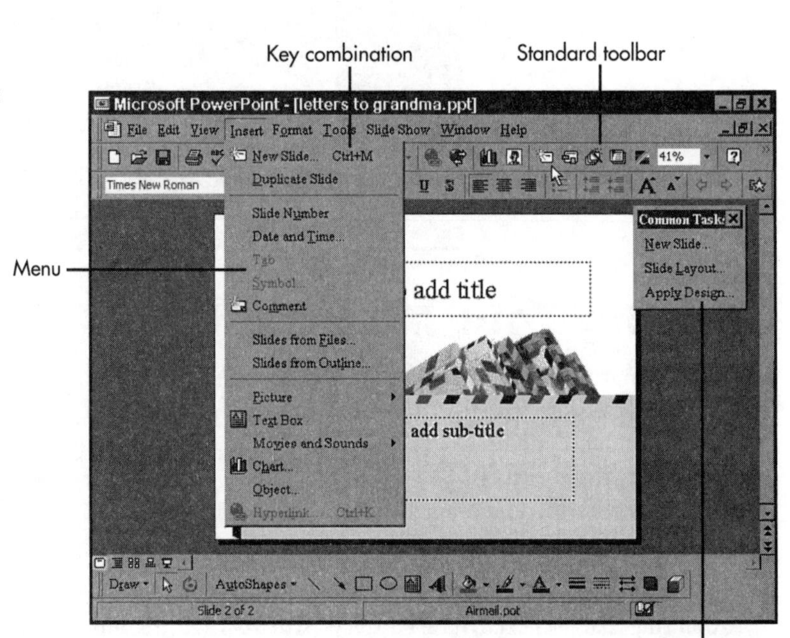

Figure 4.3.
Methods for creating a new slide.

Just a Minute

PowerPoint adds a new slide *after* the current slide, as opposed to the standard convention of adding a slide to the end of the presentation. Suppose you have five slides in the presentation and are currently editing slide two; a new slide added to the presentation is then slide three. Don't worry too much about the insertion location because you can always move slides around later. For example, if you want to add a new slide at the beginning of your presentation, you must add the slide first and then move it to the beginning of the show. Refer to the section "Moving Slides" later in this chapter for more in-depth information.

Creating and Using Bullet Slides

Most presentations you create contain at least one list of key points. The bullet list presents this information in a manner your audience can easily understand. The slide in Figure 4.4 shows a simple bullet slide in my "Letters to Grandma" presentation.

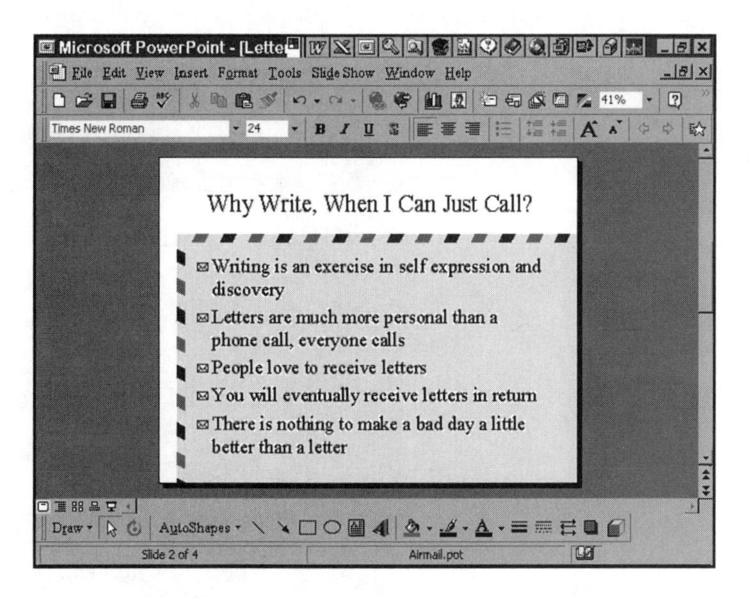

Figure 4.4.
A bullet slide with one bullet level.

Just a Minute

Although PowerPoint allows a bullet slide to have up to five levels, I don't recommend five levels of detail on a single slide. You want to get your point across to your audience, not lose them in too much crowded text. If you have that much to say, spread the material over several separate slides.

You can enter text in a bullet slide while you're using either the Slide or Outline View. I use both Slide View and Outline View to create bullet lists; it really depends on the bullet content for the specific slide. One- or two-level lists are usually easier to create in Slide View. Also, if I know the flow of my presentation and just need to get it quickly created, I generally use Slide View. If I'm structuring and developing my thoughts as I create the presentation, I use Outline View.

Entering Bullet Text in Slide View

It's very simple to enter and modify bullet text while you're in Slide View. You can quickly *promote* (move up in the hierarchy) or *demote* (move down in the hierarchy) bullet items.

Follow these steps to enter text in Slide View:

1. Click on the body of the slide's text object.
2. Type your message text.

Each paragraph is identified by a unique bullet. To move the bullet item down one level (demote), press the Tab key. To move text one bullet level higher (promote), press the Shift+Tab key combination. Figure 4.5 shows a bullet slide in Slide View.

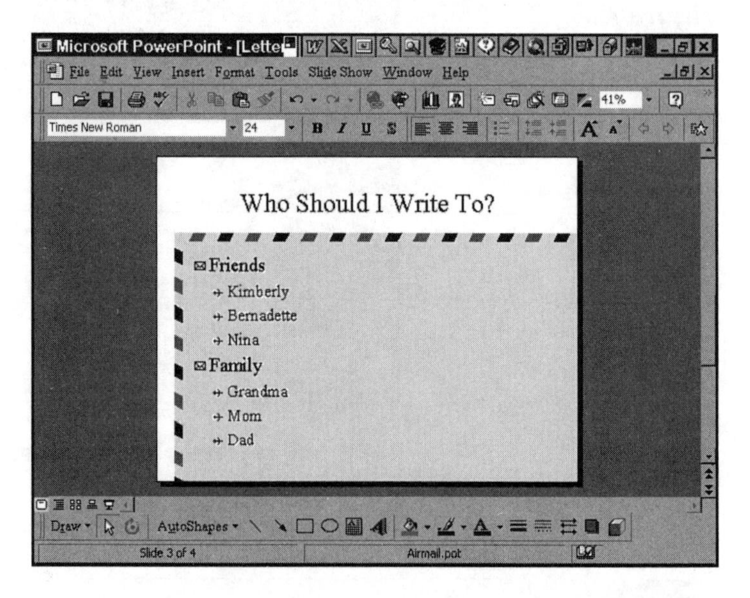

Figure 4.5.
Bullet slide with multiple bullet levels in Slide View.

JUST A MINUTE

The type of bullet character you see for each level depends on the presentation design you chose when you first started the presentation. You can change the bullet style, color, and size, if you want. Hour 5, "Working with PowerPoint Text Objects," explains the steps for customizing bullet characteristics.

Entering Text in Outline View

You can also easily enter bullet text in Outline View, almost as easily as you can in Slide View. To enter text in Outline View, just use the following steps:

1. Press the Enter key after the title of the slide. PowerPoint then adds a new slide.
2. Press the Tab key or click the Demote button on the outlining toolbar to convert the new slide to a text object that's designated as a first-level bullet. Figure 4.6 shows the bullet slide in Outline View.
3. Type your text and press Enter.

Repeat steps 2 and 3 for each bullet point you want to add. Use the Tab key to demote text and the Shift+Tab key combination to promote text. You can also change the level of the bullet text by clicking the Demote or Promote button.

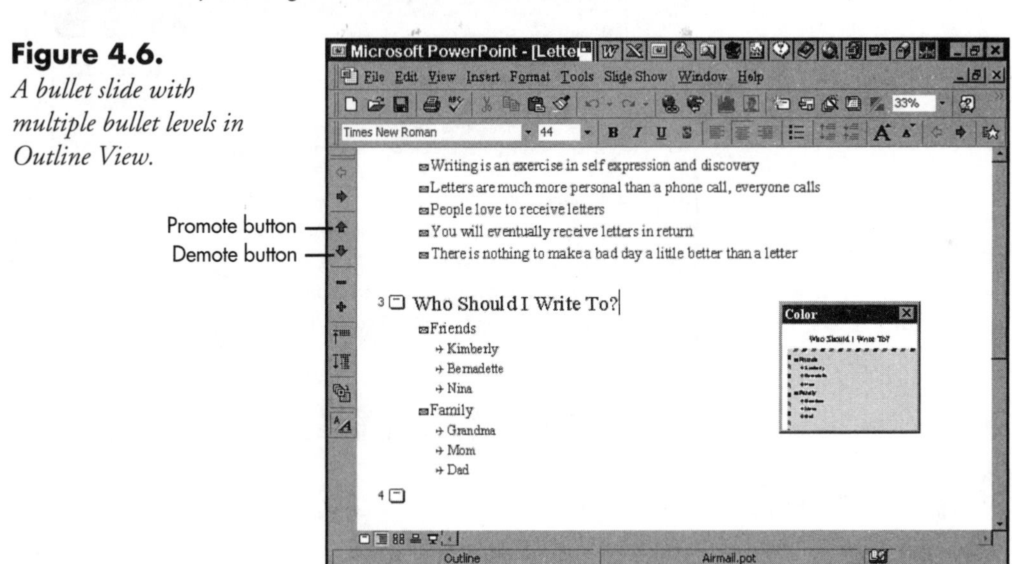

Figure 4.6.
A bullet slide with multiple bullet levels in Outline View.

Expanding a Slide

PowerPoint 97 makes it easy to expand on your thoughts by giving you the ability to easily expand a bullet slide. It takes each first-level bullet and moves the information to a new slide. The bullet text then becomes the title of the new slide. To expand a slide, follow these steps:

1. If you're in Slide View, display the slide to be expanded. If you're in Outline View, click anywhere on the slide you want to expand.
2. Choose Tools|Expand Slide from the menu.

After a few seconds, PowerPoint generates a new set of slides for your presentation. Figure 4.7 shows an expanded set of slides.

JUST A MINUTE

The new slides are inserted after the original slide marked for expansion. If you're in Slide View and choose to expand a slide, PowerPoint prompts you for the correct view mode after performing the expansion. The view choices are Outline or Slide Sorter View. I prefer to see the slides in Slide Sorter View so that it's clear how the expansion turned out. You can decide whether Slide Sorter View works better for you.

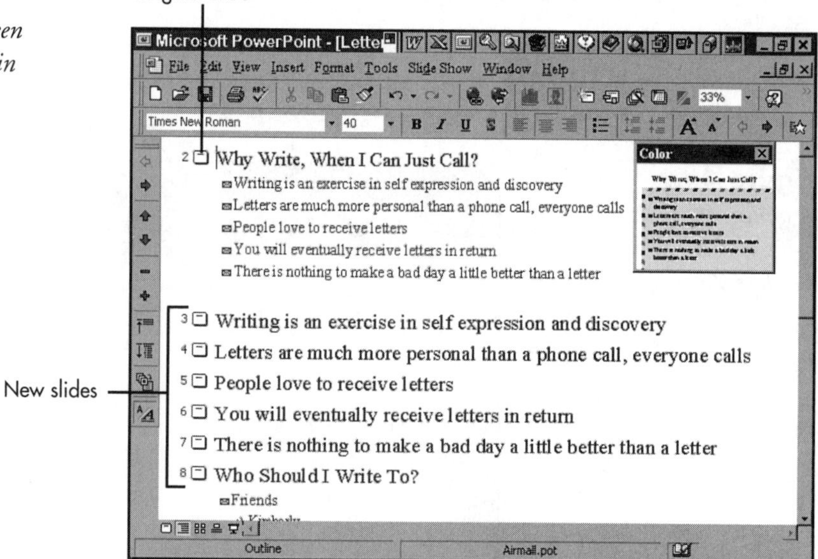

Figure 4.7.
A slide that has been expanded, shown in Outline View.

Duplicating a Slide

A new feature of PowerPoint 97 is the ability to duplicate a slide. This time-saving feature allows you to replicate a slide that has information that should be reused in another slide. I don't want to retype any information that's already available, and I'm sure you don't, either. To duplicate a presentation slide, follow these steps:

1. If you're in Slide View, display the slide. If you're in Outline View, click anywhere on the slide you want to duplicate.
2. Choose Insert | Duplicate Slide from the menu.

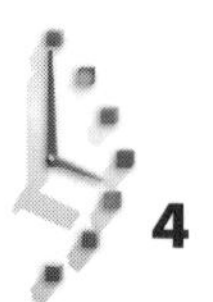

JUST A MINUTE

The duplicate slide is inserted after the original. Don't worry—you can always move the slide to a different location, if you want.

Moving Slides

Constantly inserting and duplicating slides means the order of your presentation can become a royal mess. Never fear, though; there's a way to quickly and easily move your slides around. You can't move slides while you're in Slide View, however. You need to use the Outline View. To move a slide, follow these steps:

1. Place your mouse pointer on the slide icon for the slide you want to move. The mouse pointer looks like a four-headed arrow when it's over the slide icon.
2. Drag the slide icon to the new location and release the mouse.

PowerPoint displays a horizontal line, shown in Figure 4.8, that indicates the final destination for the moved slide. It couldn't be easier to rearrange your thoughts or your slides, so move those slides, baby.

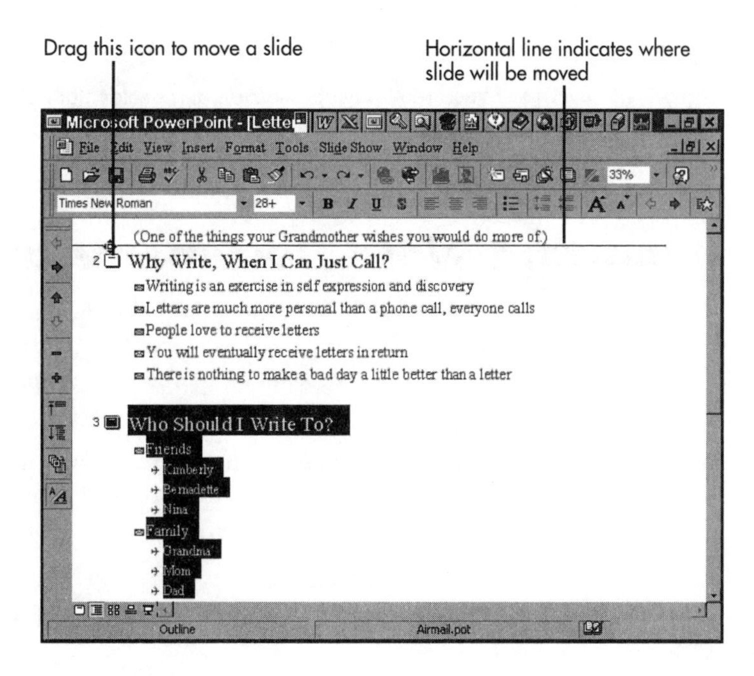

Figure 4.8.
Moving a slide in Outline View.

TIME SAVER

You can also move slides while you're in Slide Sorter View, which is my preferred method. Simply switch to Slide Sorter View and drag the slide to the new location.

Deleting Slides

I know that most of us never make a mistake, but just pretend for a moment that you do. You're going through your presentation and realize you don't really need a particular slide. For example, the slide that covers the reasons you don't write to your mother (she can't cook, she didn't let you date the really cute guy who lived down the street but was 10 years older than you, and so on). How do you make the slide disappear? Why, you can just delete it with these two simple steps:

1. If you're in Slide View, display the slide. If you're in Outline View, click anywhere on the slide you want to delete.
2. Choose Edit | Delete Slide from the menu. The slide you previously selected will be deleted.

TIME SAVER

If you aren't paying attention and accidentally delete the wrong slide, just click the Undo button or choose Edit | Undo from the menu.

Importing Word Documents as Slides

If the information for your slide presentation is already entered into a Word document, there's no need to type it again. You have several methods you can use to import the document; which one you use depends on how the document is structured.

If the Word document is already in outline format, it can be imported by using the Open dialog box. A document in outline format is created with the outline feature, contains multilevel bullets, or has a logical outline structure. To import a Word document that's in outline format and have PowerPoint convert it into a presentation, follow these steps:

1. Choose File | Open from the menu.
2. Change the "Files of type" drop-down listbox to select All Files (*.*), as shown in Figure 4.9.

JUST A MINUTE

Your Word documents aren't displayed in the File list if you don't select the All Files option.

3. Select your document filename from the list.
4. Click the Open button.

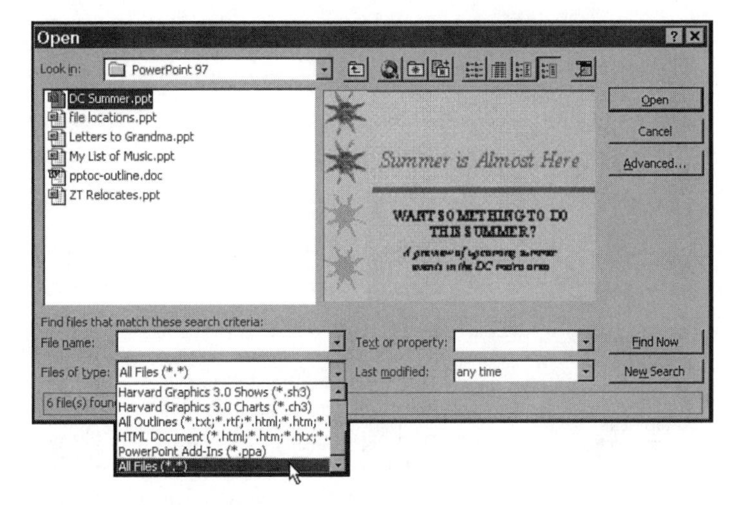

Figure 4.9.
The Open dialog box showing the All Files (.*) option.*

If your Word document is a text document, you can use the preceding method, but you will probably have a lot of reformatting to do in PowerPoint. The best method to bring in multiple blocks of text is to copy the text from Word, and then paste the text into a PowerPoint slide with the following steps:

1. Start Word (if you don't already have it started) and open the document with the text you need for your presentation.
2. Select the text.

JUST A MINUTE

The easiest way to select text is to position the mouse pointer at the beginning of the text, hold the mouse button down, and drag the mouse over the text. The text to be copied is then highlighted in black. If you mess up the highlight operation, just click on any non-selected area of the document and try again.

3. Choose Edit | Copy item from the menu (or click the Copy button on the standard toolbar).
4. Switch to PowerPoint.

JUST A MINUTE

To switch to PowerPoint, the application must be running. If it's already active, you should see a button on the taskbar at the bottom of the screen for Microsoft PowerPoint. If PowerPoint isn't running, you need to start it, but there's no need to exit from Word; just minimize it. You can also press the Alt+Tab key combination to switch between the two open applications.

5. Click on the slide where you want to insert the text.

JUST A MINUTE

You can have either Slide View or Outline View active.

6. Choose Edit | Paste from the menu (or click the Paste button on the standard toolbar).

JUST A MINUTE

There are many different methods for copying information from one application into another. The method I described is the easiest to understand and explain. If you know how to tile windows, you can also use the drag-and-drop method, which is probably the fastest method, but it's best explained through a hands-on demonstration. If you have a computer guru available in your office, ask him or her to show you the steps.

Determining Page Setup

Use the Page Setup dialog box to set the size, orientation, and type of presentation slides you're creating. By default, your slides are sized for an On-screen Show and set to print in Landscape orientation. You can change any page settings, but it's usually best to make changes before you start entering information in your presentation. To change the page setup, follow these steps:

1. Choose File | Page Setup from the menu to open the Page Setup dialog box shown in Figure 4.10.
2. From the "Slides sized for" drop-down list, select the appropriate slide format.

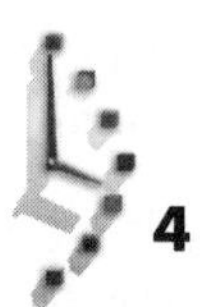

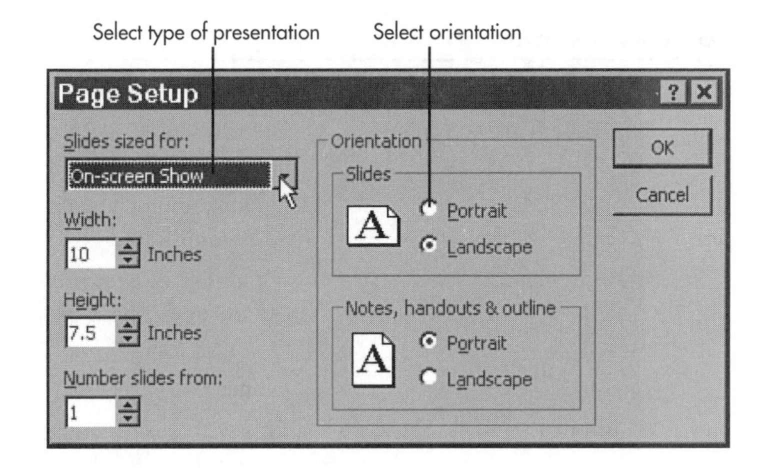

Figure 4.10.
The Page Setup dialog box.

Just a Minute

Table 4.1 lists the seven different formats you can choose from. If you select a custom format, you need to specify the presentation's width and height.

3. Select the orientation for the slides.

Just a Minute

Portrait is tall (vertical orientation), and Landscape is wide (horizontal orientation). The picture to the left of the radio button demonstrates the difference.

4. Select the orientation for your notes, handouts, and outline.
5. Select the slide number to start with in the "Number slides from" box.
6. Click the OK button.

Table 4.1. Page setup formats.

Slide Type	Description
On-screen Show	Use this format when you're giving your presentation as an onscreen slide show with a computer, television, projector, or another similar device.
Letter Paper (8.5 × 11 in)	Use this setting when the presentation is printed as handouts on standard U.S. letter paper.

Table 4.1. continued

Slide Type	Description
A4 Paper (210 × 297 mm)	Use this setting when the presentation is printed as handouts on International A4 paper.
35mm Slides	Use this setting when the presentation is published on 35mm slides.
Overhead	Use this setting for presentations that use transparencies on an overhead projector.
Banner	Use this setting for designing an 8-inch × 1-inch banner.
Custom	This setting is for any other type of presentation that doesn't fit one of the preceding options. You will need to supply the page measurements.

Changing a Slide's Layout

With PowerPoint, you can change a slide's layout template anytime. This feature is especially useful if you have just expanded a slide but want to use a different layout for some of the newly created slides. To change the layout of a slide, follow these steps:

1. If you're in Slide View, display the slide. If you're in Outline View, click anywhere on the slide you want to change.
2. Choose Format | Slide Layout from the menu, or click the Slide Layout button on the standard toolbar, or click the Slide Layout button on the Common Tasks toolbar. Any of these choices opens the Slide Layout dialog box.
3. Select a new layout.
4. Click the Reapply button, shown in Figure 4.11.

CAUTION

When you change a slide's layout, you're actually reapplying the layout's specific formatting to the slide. Although you won't lose any presentation information previously typed into a slide (or any objects that have been previously added), you might lose formatting modifications to the text.

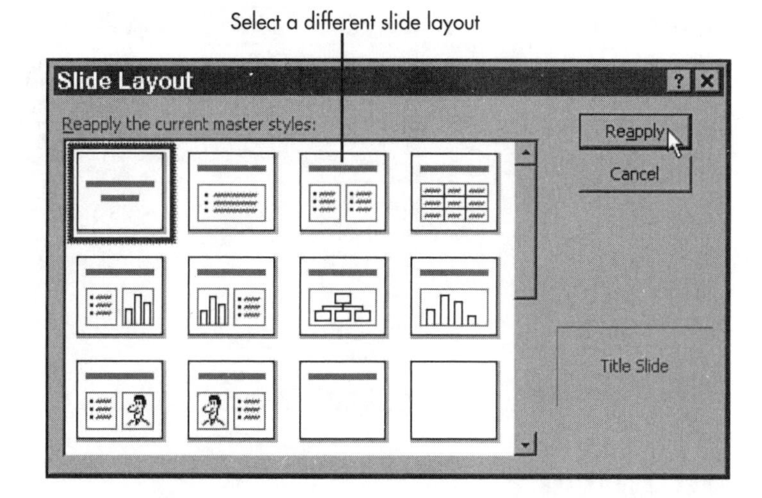

Figure 4.11.
The Slide Layout dialog box.

Changing the Presentation's Design

This hypothetical situation just might come true: You've been working on a presentation for many hours and believe you have the ultimate delivery for it. However, you show it to your colleagues, and they all unanimously agree that they hate the background design. They want a totally different tone for the entire presentation, which is over 30 slides. What to do, what to do.... Fortunately, you can simply change the presentation's design by following these steps:

1. Choose Format | Apply Design from the menu, or click the Apply Design button on the standard toolbar, or click the Apply Design button on the common tasks toolbar. Any of these choices opens the Apply Design dialog box.
2. Select a new design for the presentation, as shown in Figure 4.12.
3. Click the Apply button. The new design is then applied to every slide in your presentation.

CAUTION

Changing the document's presentation design is similar to changing the layout of an individual slide. When you apply the presentation design's formatting to your presentation, your slides won't lose any text you have typed or any objects you have previously added. Changing a presentation design can, however, reverse any custom text formatting.

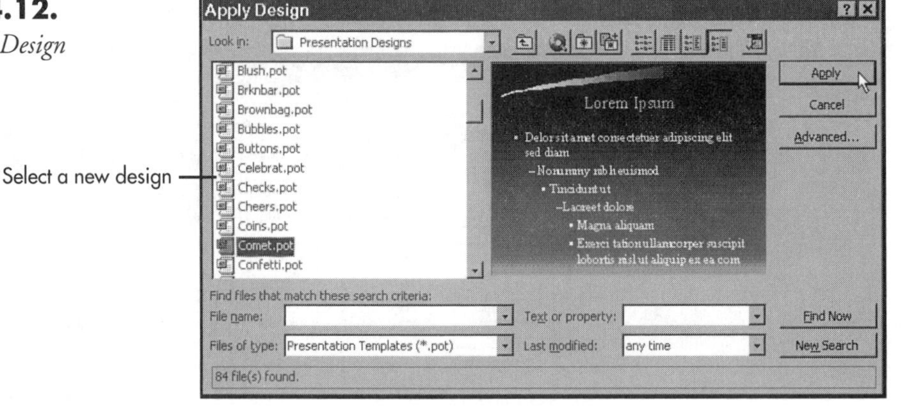

Figure 4.12.
The Apply Design dialog box.

Summary

In this hour, you have covered everthing you need to know when working with slides, from selecting the proper layout for an individual slide to changing the overall design for the whole presentation. You should now be familiar with creating a new presentation and a title slide. You know how to add new slides to your presentation and create, edit, and expand a bullet slide, and duplicating, moving, and deleting slides should now be easy tasks.

Workshop

Are you ready to play follow the leader? The following exercise in "Test What You've Learned" covers some of the skills you've learned in the past four hours and creates a fun presentation.

After you're done with the exercise, you should still have some time left for an informative question-and-answer session. The questions in "Q&A" relate to topics covered during the past hour.

Test What You've Learned

You might want to follow the steps listed below, then branch off on your own. If you don't know how to perform an operation, refer back to previous hours.

1. Start a new presentation with the Presentation Designs option.
2. Select your favorite design.
3. Select the title slide from the New Slide dialog box.
4. Select the title object and type a title, such as this example:

```
SUMMER IS JUST AROUND THE CORNER
```

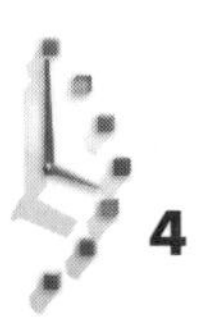

5. Select the subtitle object and type a subtitle, as shown:

```
A Presentation of Summer Activities
By [Your Name]
[Your Company]
[Telephone Number]
```

6. Start a new slide.
7. Select the Bulleted List layout.
8. Select the title object for the second slide and type a title:

```
SUMMER ACTIVITIES IN DC
```

9. Select the body area and type four activities:

```
Visit the Monuments
Visit the Smithsonian
Watch the Fireworks on the 4th of July
Do the Bar Crawl
```

10. Expand the slide.
11. Duplicate the slide.
12. Go to Slide Sorter or Outline View and move the duplicate slide to the end of your presentation.
13. Delete the slide.
14. Change the layout of the four new slides to the Text and Clipart options.

TIME SAVER

You can quickly change the slides' layout while you're in Slide Sorter View. Just select all four slides at once, and then change the layout. To select multiple slides, hold down the Shift key and click on each slide.

15. Change the presentation's design. Click Undo if you decide you don't like the modification to the slides.
16. Save the presentation as `Hour 4 TWYL`.

Q&A

Q I want one slide to be displayed in Portrait orientation and all the other slides to be displayed in Landscape orientation. How can I do this?

A You can't do this on slides within the same presentation. The Page Setup options apply to all the slides in a single presentation. If you really need to display slides with different orientations or other Page Setup options, you must create separate presentation documents. In older versions of PowerPoint, having content in different presentations didn't allow for a seamless onscreen show. However, with PowerPoint 97, you can branch to another presentation. Hour 24, "PowerPoint Power Hour," explains branching between presentations in detail.

Q I've created my presentation and want it to be printed on 35mm slides. How do I print them?

A To print the slides out in 35mm format, you need access to a piece of equipment called a *film recorder*. Basically, you print the slides to the film recorder instead of a printer. The film recorder photographs your slides and produces undeveloped film, which you can then take to any photo-processing store to have it developed into slides.

If you don't have a film recorder, you can always send your presentation (after formatting it for 35mm slides) to a service bureau that does all the hard work of properly transferring the presentation. Check the Yellow Pages under "Computer Graphics" for local firms.

Q I have a presentation that was created in Harvard Graphics. Can I use it in PowerPoint?

A Most likely. PowerPoint can import most files that have been created in other presentation software packages, such as Harvard Graphics. Just follow these steps:

JUST A MINUTE

Before you import a presentation, you must either open an existing presentation or start a new one.

1. Start a new presentation.
2. Choose Insert|Slides from Files from the menu to open the Slide Finder dialog box.
3. Click the Find Presentation tab.
4. Click the Browse button and select the file you want to import.

TIME SAVER

You can type the full path and name of the file in the File text box, if you like.

5. Click the Display button to view the presentation's slides.
6. Click the Insert All button to insert all the slides from the presentation.

JUST A MINUTE

You can also select individual slides and click the Insert button to insert one slide at a time.

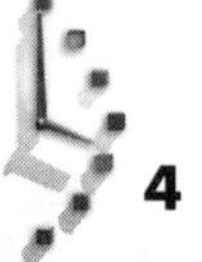

7. Click the Close button.

CAUTION

PowerPoint 97 can't import or open a Corel Presentations file.

Part II

Hour 5

Working with PowerPoint Text Objects

In the next hour, you will learn all the different methods available in PowerPoint 97 to edit and control text. If you're familiar with operating a word processing program, such as Microsoft Word, you have probably noticed that PowerPoint deals with text in a manner that's slightly different. When you enter text in PowerPoint, you're not only entering the text on a slide, but you're also entering the text into a text object. It's very important to understand that you're not only working with text, but also the underlying object. This next hour covers most of the options available when working with text and text objects. You will learn how to do the following:

- Tell the difference between text objects and text boxes
- Move and copy a text object
- Select text in a text object
- Change font properties, such as font type, size, and color

- Work with bulleted text
- Change text object attributes
- Use the Find and Replace commands
- Set tabs

Text Objects Versus Text Boxes

Text is text, isn't it? In PowerPoint, however, this isn't always entirely accurate. You have two different methods for entering message text on a presentation slide. You can insert text by clicking a placeholder object and typing the text; in Outline View, you just type the text next to the slide icon. Another method is explicitly inserting a text box on the slide and typing your text in the box.

Text object or text box—does it matter? It depends on your particular needs. If you want the text to show up in the outline of your presentation, you have two choices. You can enter the text using a text object placeholder (if you're in Slide View), or you can type the text directly into the Outline View document.

JUST A MINUTE

When you enter text in Outline View, PowerPoint automatically creates the text object placeholder and enters the text information into the placeholder object. When you enter text in Slide View, you need to have a placeholder already created. If you don't have a text placeholder available, you need to either enter text in the presentation's Outline View or change the slide's layout.

If displaying the text information in the presentation outline isn't required, you can skip creating a text object. While in Slide View, create a text box and type your text. Text boxes are useful for graphics captions or callouts. Hour 11, "Drawing Text-Type Objects," goes into more detail on text boxes.

Selecting Text and Text Objects

Before you can move text or change any of the text attributes, you need to know how to select text. Most of the objects and elements that have been selected up to this point have been triggered by simply clicking once on the item you want. When working with text information, the process is slightly different. Typically, you need to modify or replace only a portion of the text, and the selected text segment indicates the portion that will be changed. By first selecting only the text you want to enhance or change, you tell PowerPoint what text will be affected by the change. Text is selected when it's highlighted in black.

There are several ways to select text and text objects. In Hour 4, "Working with Slides," you learned about the simplest way to select text: dragging the mouse. Table 5.1 describes a few other quick ways to select blocks of text in PowerPoint.

Just a Minute

If you want to affect all the text in a text object, then you should select the entire object. If you select too much text, press the Esc key to reverse the selection and start over.

Table 5.1. Selecting text in PowerPoint.

What to Select	How to Select
Any amount of text	Place the mouse pointer at the beginning of the text; the pointer should be shaped like an I-beam. Hold the mouse button down and drag the pointer over the text you want to select.
Single word	Place the mouse pointer (shaped like an I-beam) anywhere on the word and double-click.
Single sentence	Hold down the Ctrl key and click anywhere on the sentence.
Single paragraph	Place the mouse pointer (shaped like an I-beam) anywhere on the paragraph and triple-click.
All text in an object	Click once in the text. Choose Edit | Select All from the menu.
Entire text object	Click once on the text object. You will see the gray placeholder border and a blinking cursor in the text. Position the mouse on the placeholder border and click a second time (you should still see the placeholder border, but not the blinking cursor).

Just a Minute

You have probably noticed that the mouse pointer changes shape. The shape of the mouse pointer tells you what you can do. Table 5.2 illustrates the most common mouse pointer shapes and describes what the different pointer symbols represent.

Table 5.2. Pointer shape basics.

Pointer Shape	What It Does
	When the mouse pointer looks like a white or black arrow (the most commonly seen pointer), you can select any object by clicking on it.
	When the mouse pointer looks like an I-beam, you can select text.
	When the mouse pointer looks like a double arrow (usually when it's placed on a resize handle), you can resize an object by dragging the handle to a new location.
	When the mouse pointer looks like a four-headed arrow, you can move an object by dragging it to a new location.
	When the mouse pointer looks like an hourglass, Windows is asking you to be patient and wait for a few seconds. Although sometimes you can perform another task when you see the hourglass, it's usually a good idea to let Windows finish the operation it's working on first.

Moving or Copying Text and Text Objects

Now that you know how to select text, you can start moving and copying it. It's very easy to do in PowerPoint. You can rearrange snippets of text, or you can relocate an entire text object. Being able to copy and move text is a feature that makes MS Office applications so much more productive than pen and paper.

Moving or Copying Snippets of Text

If you have ever moved or copied text in a Windows application, you already know how to move or copy text in PowerPoint. You can move or copy text when you're in Slide or Outline

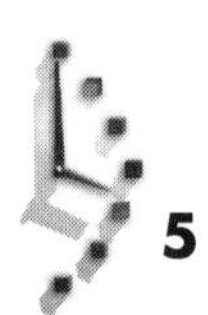

View. There are four basic steps involved, but one step differs depending on whether you want to move or copy the text. To move or copy text, follow this sequence of steps:

1. Select the text you want to move or copy.
2. To move text, choose Edit | Cut from the menu or click the Cut button on the standard toolbar.

   or

2. To copy text, choose Edit | Copy from the menu or click the Copy button on the standard toolbar.
3. Position the blinking cursor where you want to move the text.
4. Choose Edit | Paste from the menu or click the Paste button on the standard toolbar.

TIME SAVER

> You have several methods for moving or copying text. If you have been using Windows applications for a while, you're probably familiar with the drag-and-drop method. Once you have the text selected, place the mouse pointer in the selected (highlighted) area, click the mouse button and hold it down, and then drag the text to the new location. To copy text, just hold the Ctrl key while dragging. You can also use the shortcut menus that are just a right-click away.

Moving or Copying Text Objects

In many cases, you want to move an entire text object instead of just a text fragment. In Figure 5.1, for example, the slide's title would look better if it was moved up just a bit.

To move or copy text objects, you must have the Slide View active. The cut-and-paste methods commonly used to move a text fragment won't work, so you must drag the object if the location is going to be changed. To move a text object, follow these steps:

1. Click once on the text object to select it; you should see a gray outline border around the text object.
2. Place the mouse pointer on any part of the border for the text object. The pointer should change shape and become a move pointer (the four-headed arrow).
3. Drag the object to the location you want. (See Figure 5.2.)

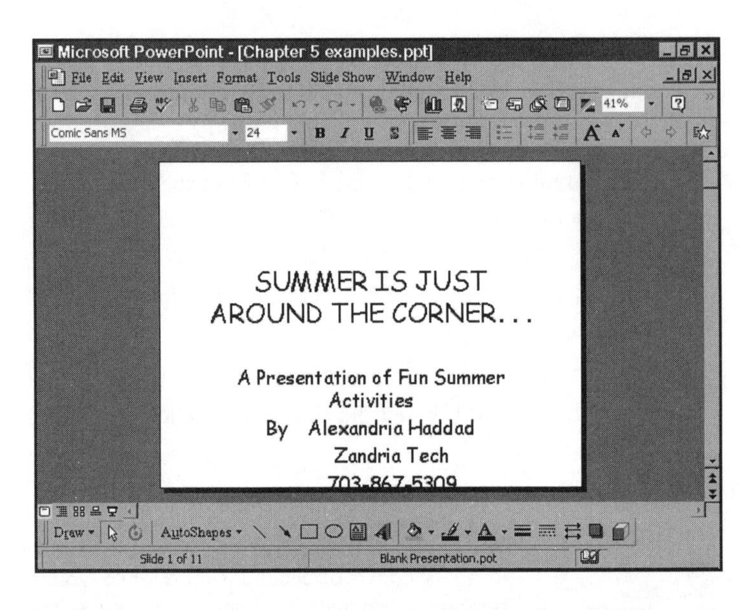

Figure 5.1.
A slide with the title text placed too low.

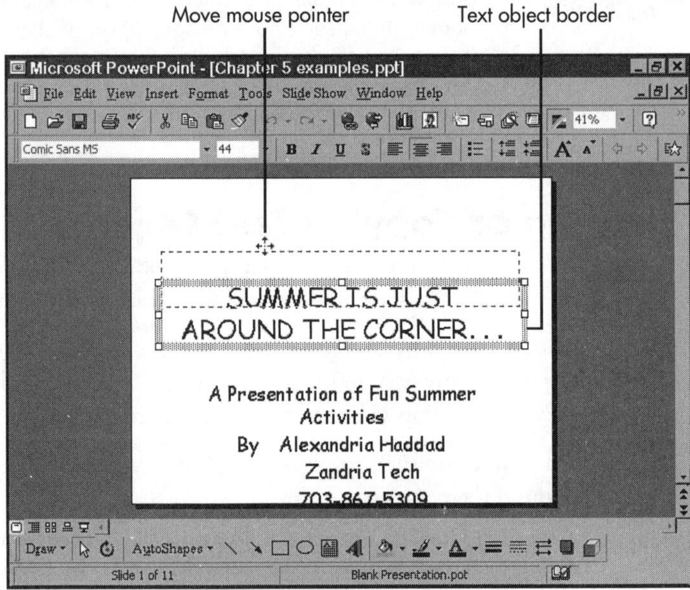

Figure 5.2.
Dragging a text object.

JUST A MINUTE

You must have the mouse pointer on the border of a text object to move it. The pointer looks like a four-headed arrow when PowerPoint can move the text. If the mouse pointer looks like a double-headed arrow, you can't move anything. The double-headed arrow means PowerPoint thinks you want to resize the text object.

You can copy an object in the same manner; just hold down the Ctrl key while the object is dragged (notice the plus sign next to the mouse pointer in Figure 5.3). You can also use the copy-and-paste method discussed previously to copy an object. Once you paste the object, you then have to move the text object to the location you want.

Figure 5.3.
Copying a text object.

Changing Text Properties

Now the real fun starts—changing fonts for intense graphical impact. Fonts are one of my favorite things to fool around with. You can change the mood of a whole presentation just by changing the font type. Windows and Office 97 offer several dozen font types for use in your PowerPoint presentation. Go ahead—be daring and put a little pizzazz in your presentation.

The *font face* (also called the typeface) is a description of what the font looks like. Sample descriptors include script type fonts, such as Brush Script; sans serif fonts, such as Arial; or serif fonts, such as Times Roman.

Time Saver

If you have Internet access, there are thousands of sites with fonts for you to download. Some of the fonts are free, but most sites charge a fee. Here are two free sites:

```
http://www.torget.se/users/d/dezoe/4fonts/index.htm
http://www.microsoft.com/truetype/
```

The easiest way to find fonts available on the Internet is to do a search on the basic keyword word "font." I used Yahoo!, which returned dozens of sites. Be prepared to spend some time finding just the right font.

CAUTION

Although I love really cool fonts, just a word of advice: Keep your audience in mind when choosing a font type. I wouldn't advise using a really "pretty" script font for a board of directors' presentation (unless it was the board of directors for Mary Kay, and even then I would think twice). Remember, you can change the mood of the whole presentation with fonts, for better or worse.

Before you change any font attributes, you must first select the text that will be affected by the change. To change the font for a portion of text—for example, just the one word you want in bold—select just that one word. To change the font for an entire text object—if you want the entire title a bit bigger, for instance—select the text object.

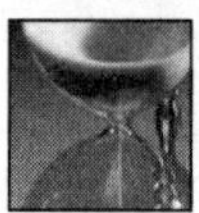

CAUTION

Again, you shouldn't select text when you want the font change to affect the entire object. Select the object instead. If you don't, you might notice later that new text added to the slide isn't displayed with the new font attributes.

JUST A MINUTE

If you want to change the font attributes for every slide in your presentation, you could change each slide one by one, but that's a lot of work if you have 50 slides. The best method for changing slides globally is to change the font in the Slide or Title Master. Hour 8, "Working with the Masters," covers how to do this. Any changes to the master affect your whole presentation, and you have to make the change only once.

Face, Size, Color, Style, and Effects

You can find most font attributes in the Font dialog box. The ones you can change include face, size, color, style, and effects. Figure 5.4 shows three text boxes with different font attributes applied. Remember, if you want to change the font attributes for the entire object, first select the object; if you want to change the attributes for just a portion of text, select only the text that should change.

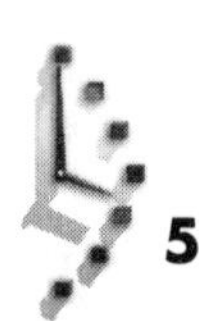

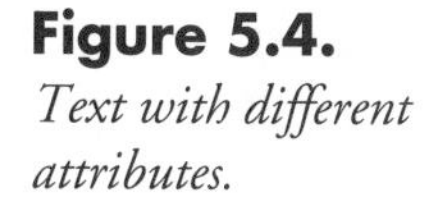

Figure 5.4.
Text with different attributes.

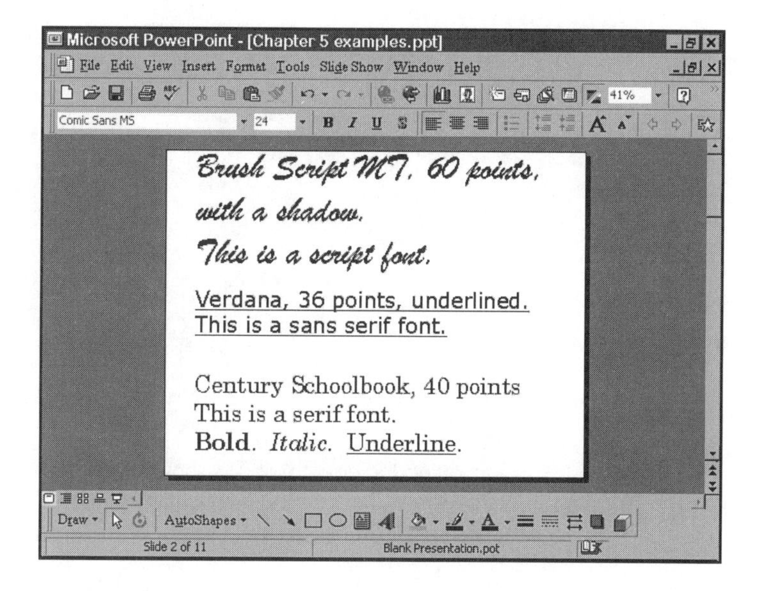

The Font dialog box, shown in Figure 5.5, has the entire set of font attributes in one location, so you don't have to click around to find different attributes, and includes a Preview button so you can preview the font modifications before clicking OK to finalize the modification.

To change font attributes, follow these steps:

1. Select the text or text object that will have the new font attributes.
2. Choose Format | Font from the menu.
3. Select the font attributes you want.
4. Click the Preview button to see a preview.

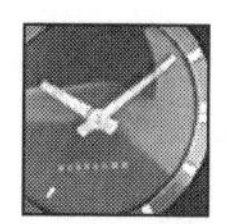

Just a Minute

When you click the Preview button to see what the change looks like, you should be aware of two things. First, the change is displayed on the actual slide. Don't be afraid—the change isn't permanent until you click the OK button. Second, most of the time when you choose to preview a change, you need to move the dialog box out of the way to see the slide. To do that, just place the mouse pointer in the title bar of the dialog box, click and hold down the mouse button, drag the box to the location you want, and release the mouse button.

5. Click the "Default for new objects" checkbox to change the default font for all new objects (text and drawing).
6. Click the OK button to accept your changes.

Figure 5.5.
The Font dialog box.

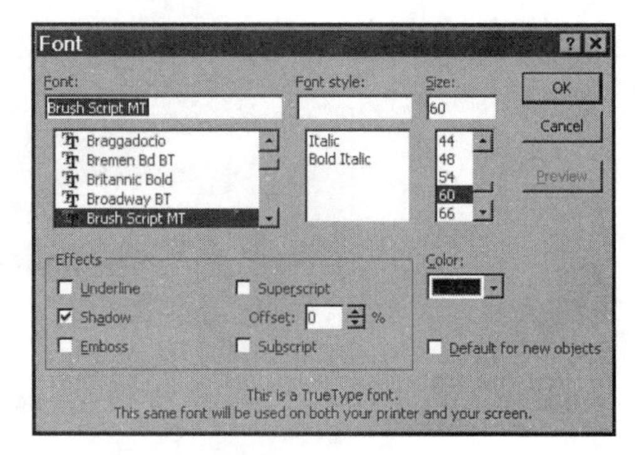

JUST A MINUTE

> You can also change most font attributes by selecting items on the formatting toolbar. Table 5.3 shows the different buttons on the formatting toolbar and their corresponding attributes.

Table 5.3. The formatting toolbar.

Toolbar Button	Attribute
Comic Sans MS	Font face
24	Font size
B I U S	Bold, italic, underline, and shadow
A	Font color (on the drawing toolbar)

Alignment

The alignment of the text on the slide is based on the placeholder bounding box. Figure 5.6 displays three text objects that are affected by different alignment options. Notice that the text isn't aligned with the slide boundaries; it's placed in relation to the placeholder bounding box. If you want an object aligned within the edges of the entire slide, simply resize the bounding box to match the width of the slide.

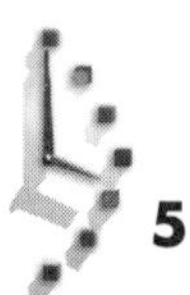

Figure 5.6.
Different text alignment options.

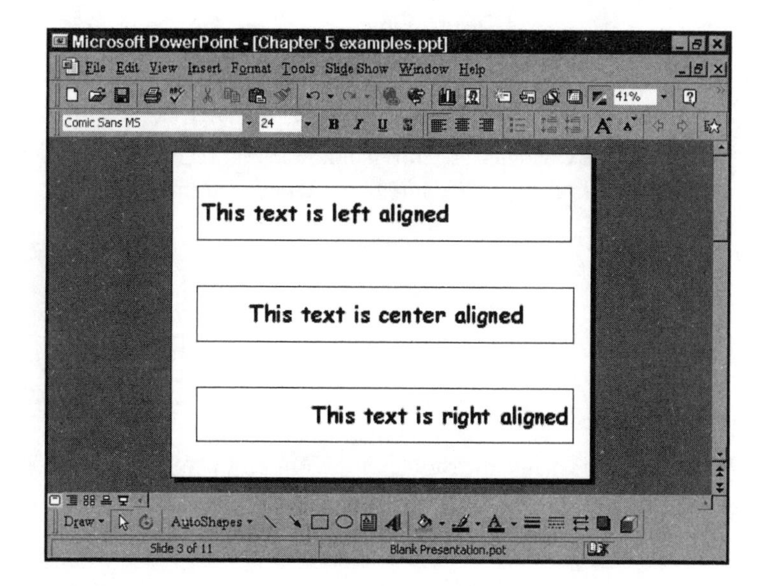

Follow these steps to change the text alignment:

1. Select the object you want to change the alignment for.
2. Choose Format | Alignment from the menu.
3. Select the Left, Right, Center, or Justify menu item.

JUST A MINUTE

You can also click the alignment buttons on the formatting toolbar. Table 5.4 illustrates the buttons and their corresponding alignment attributes. Notice, however, that there's no Justify button for aligning text.

Table 5.4. Alignment buttons.

Toolbar Button	Alignment
	Left
	Center
	Right

Changing Text Case

hAVE YOU EVER LEFT THE cAPS lOCK KEY ON BY ACCIDENT, ONLY TO LOOK UP AT THE SCREEN AND SEE SOMETHING LIKE THIS? PowerPoint saves the day with the Change Case command. (See Figure 5.7.) There are five capitalization options to choose from, so one is sure to match your needs.

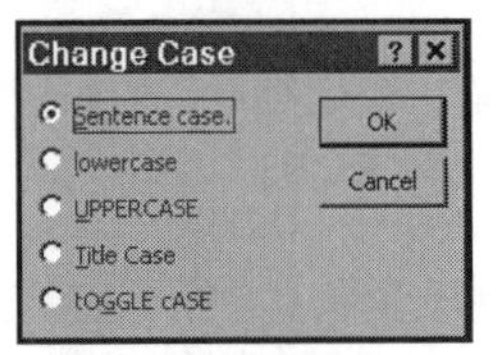

Figure 5.7.
The Change Case dialog box.

You can change the capitalization option by following these steps:

1. Select the text you want to change.
2. Choose Format | Change Case from the menu.
3. Select one of the five capitalization options.
4. Click OK to change the text.

Replacing Font

PowerPoint has a great tool that allows you to change a particular font face throughout the entire presentation. Usually, you globally replace fonts for the entire presentation after importing pre-existing documents. To replace a font, follow these steps:

1. Choose Format | Replace Font from the menu.
2. Select the font you want to replace from the Replace drop-down list, shown in Figure 5.8.
3. Select the font you want as the replacement from the With drop-down list.
4. Click the Replace button.

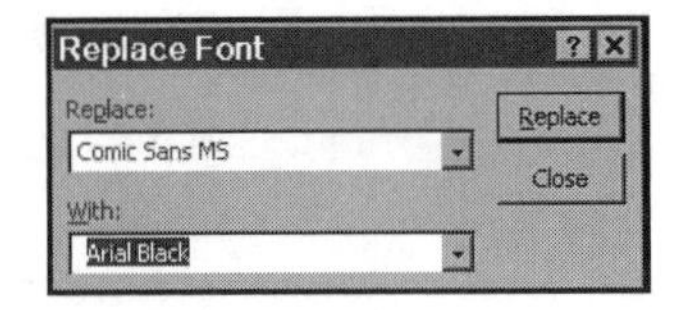

Figure 5.8.
The Replace Font dialog box.

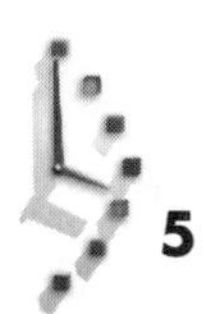

Working with Bulleted Text

When you have slides with bulleted text, there are a few tricks you can use to get a professional text presentation. In PowerPoint, your slides can have up to five bullet levels. Each level can have a different bullet character, and each descending level is automatically defined with a font size smaller than the preceding bullet level. The two most common operations people want to perform with bulleted text are to modify the bullet symbols (Bob wants checkmarks instead of smiley faces, for example) and to change the relative font size.

Changing Bullet Symbols

Changing the style of a bullet is fairly simple. The biggest hurdle to overcome is trying not to get overwhelmed by all the different symbols to choose from. Keep your audience and presentation subject in mind when choosing bullet symbols. The bullets in Figure 5.9, for example, are congruent with the computer theme for this book.

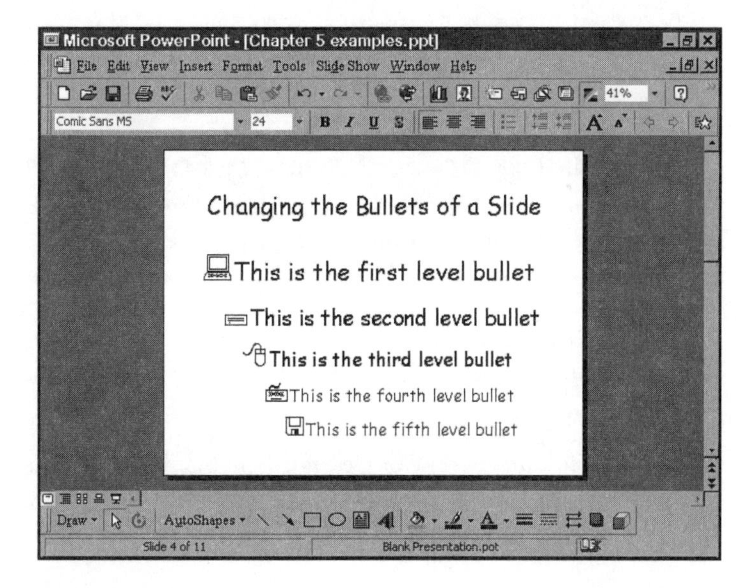

Figure 5.9.
A slide with different bullet styles.

To change the bullet style, follow these simple steps:

1. Click on the line where you want the bullet symbol changed.
2. Choose Format | Bullet from the menu.
3. Select a font from the "Bullets from" drop-down list.
4. Click a symbol from the symbol grid.

TIME SAVER

The first time you see the Bullet dialog box, it's a bit overwhelming (I told you so). So many symbols, so little time. However, here's a little trick you can use: Click on the first symbol in the grid (the symbol "pops up" so you can see it better) and use the arrow keys on the keyboard to review each symbol. If you can't find just the right symbol, try a different font. The two most popular symbol fonts are Monotype Sorts and Wingdings.

5. Change the color or size of the bullet symbol, if you want.
6. Click the OK button.

Repeat these steps for each bullet item you want to change, or you can select all the bullet items to make a global change.

JUST A MINUTE

If you want to change the bullet symbol for every slide in your presentation, you should use the Slide Master, which is covered in Hour 8.

Increasing or Decreasing Font Size

As mentioned earlier, each descending bullet level is displayed with a slightly smaller font size than the one before it. If you need to change the font size for a bulleted list, you could select the text object and make the whole object the same size. Although this will work, it becomes much harder for your audience to visually distinguish between the different levels. A better option is to change the relative size of the text object, which results in an increase or decrease of each bullet level. To increase or decrease the font size, follow these steps:

1. Select the text object.
2. Click the Increase or Decrease Font Size button on the formatting toolbar.

Line Spacing

When you want to create more distance between lines of text or bullet points, don't press the Enter key an extra time. PowerPoint gives you a much simpler option for changing the line spacing that also gives you much more control than pressing Enter and adding an extra blank line. The Line Spacing option affects any lines of text you have previously selected. You can set the measurement for line spacing in number of lines or by points. Figure 5.10 shows the Line Spacing dialog box.

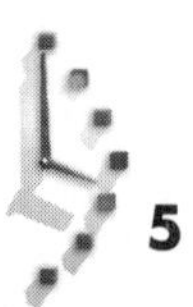

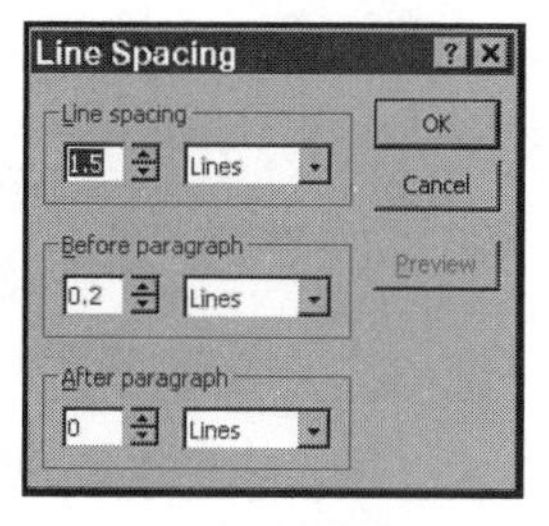

Figure 5.10.
The Line Spacing dialog box.

Point size is the unit of measurement typically used for fonts. One point is 1/72 inch. Therefore, 72 points is 1 inch, 36 points is 1/2 inch, 18 points is 1/4 inch, 9 points is...well, you get the picture.

Follow these steps to change the line spacing for selected text:

1. First, select the lines to modify.
2. Choose Format | Line Spacing from the menu.
3. Select the amount of space you want between lines of text.
4. Select the unit of measure for the line spacing.
5. Click the OK button.

JUST A MINUTE

You can also use the Decrease or Increase Paragraph Spacing buttons on the standard toolbar to get the same effect. They change the line spacing, not the space between paragraphs, as their names might lead you to think.

CAUTION

If you have bulleted paragraphs that contain more than one line, the Line Spacing option changes the space between all lines of text. To change the spacing between each bulleted item, use the Before Paragraph or After Paragraph options in the Line Spacing dialog box.

Changing Text Object Attributes

In the first part of this hour, you have learned about different ways to change or enhance the text on your slides. This next section covers how the text object affects the text contained in it and how to control the text object itself. The features explained in this section are all options you can find in the Format AutoShapes dialog box. Although most people would never think of using this option for a text object (AutoShapes are covered in Hour 12, "Drawing Shapes in PowerPoint"), it's possible to use it for that purpose. Each of the following sections explains a different option, and the title object is used as the sample object.

Adding a Border or Fill

The first feature is adding a border or *fill* (shading) to your text object, which is a great way to make text stand out from the crowd. Figure 5.11 shows how a text object can be formatted with borders and shading.

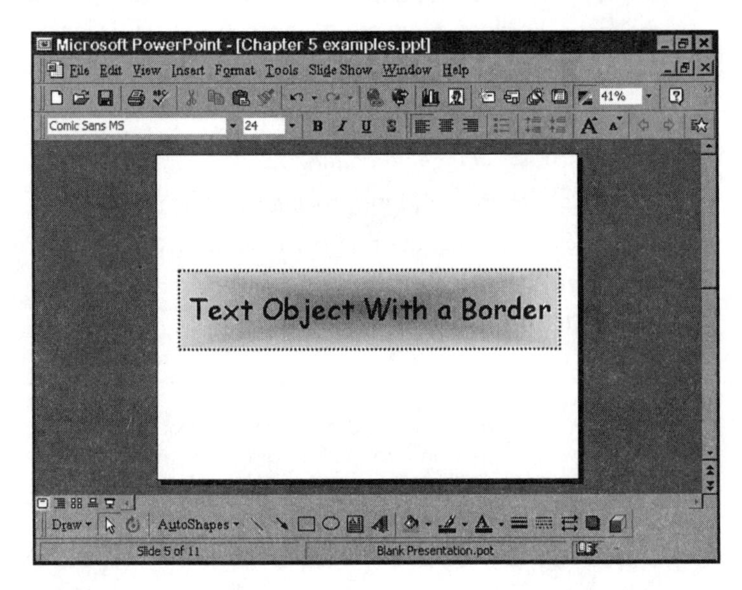

Figure 5.11.
A text object with a border and a gradient fill.

NEW TERM *Gradient fill* is a very cool special effect that you can use with almost every PowerPoint object. With a gradient fill effect, one color gradually fades into black, white, or another color. PowerPoint 97 also has several preset color schemes you can choose from.

To add a border or fill to a text object, follow these steps:

1. Select the object you want to border or fill.
2. Choose Format | AutoShape from the menu.
3. Select the Colors and Lines tab. (See Figure 5.12.)
4. If you want to add a fill, select an option from the Color drop-down list in the Fill section.

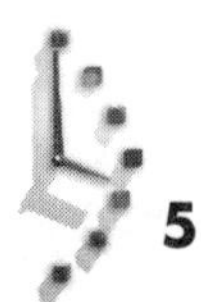

JUST A MINUTE

Use the Fill Effects option from the Color drop-down list to apply a gradient effect or any other fill effect to your text object. There are several effects to choose from; just remember that your audience must be able to read the message text.

5. If you want a border, select a line color from the Color drop-down list in the Line section of the dialog box.
6. Change the Style, Dashed, and Weight options for the border, if you want.
7. Click the Preview button to preview your changes before accepting them.
8. Click the OK button when you're finished.

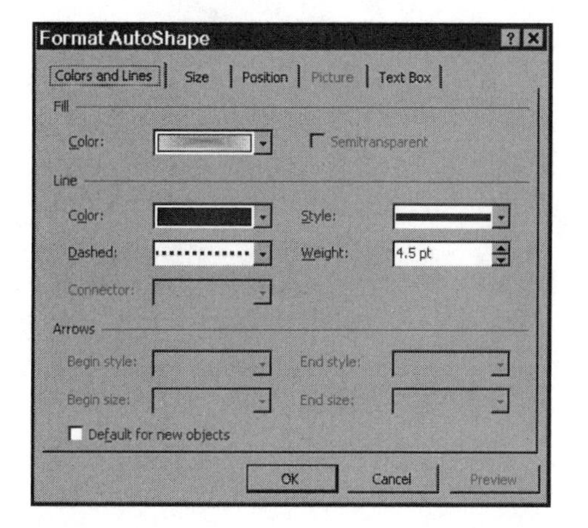

Figure 5.12.
The Colors and Lines tab of the Format AutoShape dialog box.

5

Changing the Size and Rotation of a Text Object

Changing the size of a text object is *not* the same as modifying the size of the text. When you change the size of a text object, you're changing the size of the placeholder bounding box that contains the text. Usually, you want the bounding box to be the same size as the text it holds. This rule of thumb is especially true if you're adding a border or fill option to the text object. As you can see in Figure 5.13, when the bounding box is smaller than the text within it, it creates a problem when you add a border to the text object.

You can also rotate text objects in varying degrees from horizontal, all the way from 0 to 359 degrees. The text object is always rotated in a clockwise direction. To change the size of the text object or rotate its orientation, follow these steps:

1. Click once on the text object to select it.
2. Choose Format | AutoShape from the menu.

3. Select the Size tab.
4. Enter an exact height and/or width for the bounding box.

Figure 5.13.
The bounding box is too small.

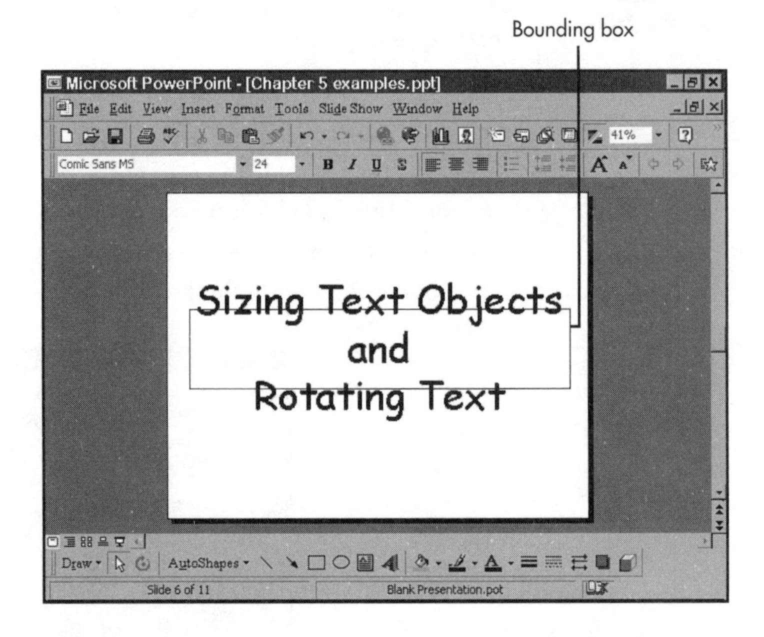

JUST A MINUTE

You can also scale the text object by entering a percentage for height and width in the Scale section of the dialog box. (See Figure 5.14.)

5. Enter the amount of rotation you want for the text object.
6. Click the Preview button to review your changes before accepting them.
7. Click the OK button when you're finished.

TIME SAVER

The method described in these steps is great when you know the exact size for the text object. A much quicker method that's often used is to position the mouse pointer on any object sizing handle and drag the bounding box to a different size.

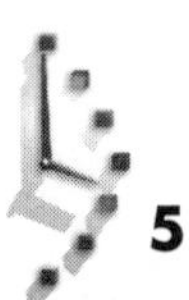

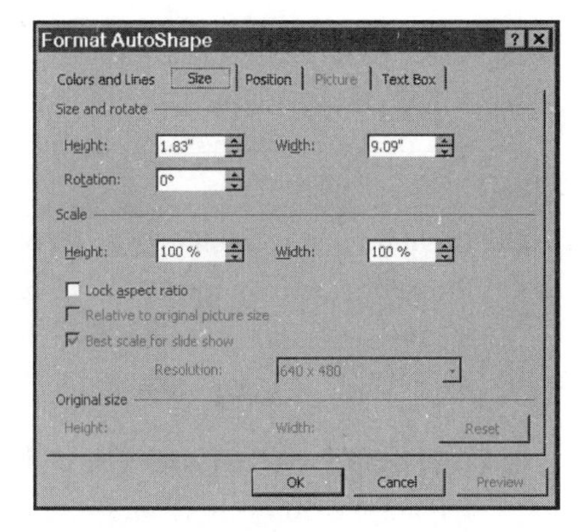

Figure 5.14.
The Size tab of the Format AutoShape dialog box.

Just a Minute

> With PowerPoint, you can also free-rotate or flip any object. These options are covered in Hour 13, "Bringing Drawing Objects Together."

Positioning in an Exact Location

To move a text object, the drag method explained earlier works fine in most situations. However, in some situations you need a text object placed in an exact location. When that's the case, you should use the position option in the Format AutoShapes dialog box. Figure 5.15 shows a text object that has been positioned at an offset exactly 1/2 inch horizontally and 1/2 inch vertically from the upper-left corner of the slide.

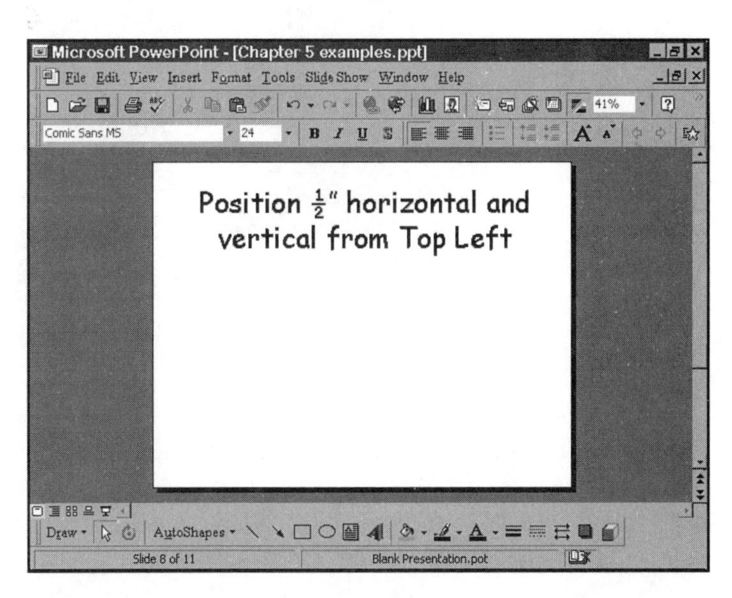

Figure 5.15.
Positioning a text object in an exact location.

Follow these seven steps to position a text object in an exact location:

1. Select the text object you want to position.
2. Choose Format | AutoShape from the menu.
3. Select the Position tab.
4. Enter the horizontal position for the text object.
5. Enter the vertical position for the text object.
6. Click the Preview button to review your changes before accepting them.
7. Click the OK button when you're finished.

Setting the Text Anchor Point

When you're trying to get the best look for your presentation, you can control how the text is anchored within a text object, especially when you have used a border or fill option. The *text anchor point* is the point where the text sits in the object. Text can be anchored to an object position at the top, middle, bottom, top center, middle center, or bottom center. Figure 5.16 shows two text objects, each with a different anchor point.

Figure 5.16.
Message text anchored to the middle and bottom of the text box.

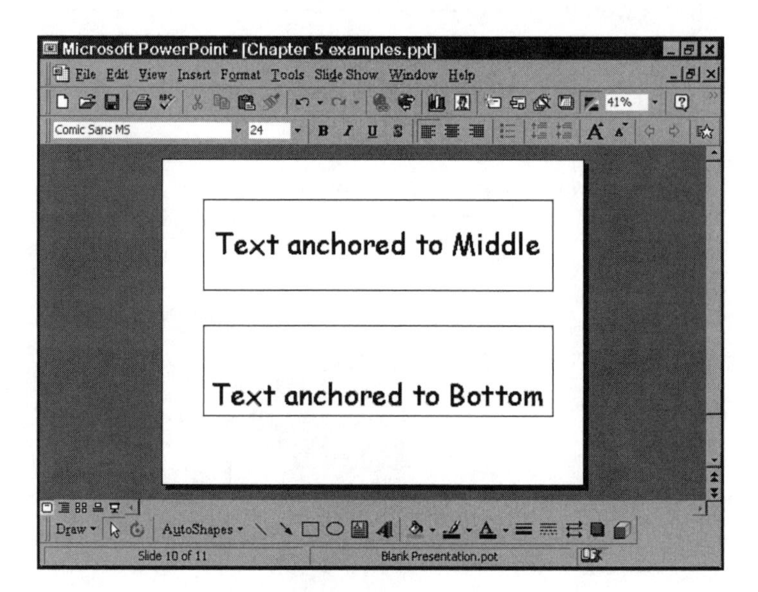

If you need to change the anchor point, follow these steps:

1. Select the text object.
2. Choose Format | AutoShape from the menu.
3. Select the Text Box tab, shown in Figure 5.17.

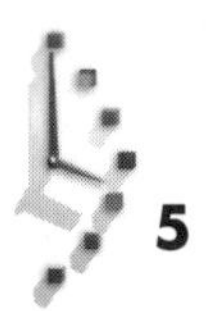

4. Select a new anchor point from the "Text anchor point" drop-down list.
5. Click the Preview button to see a preview of your change.
6. Click the OK button.

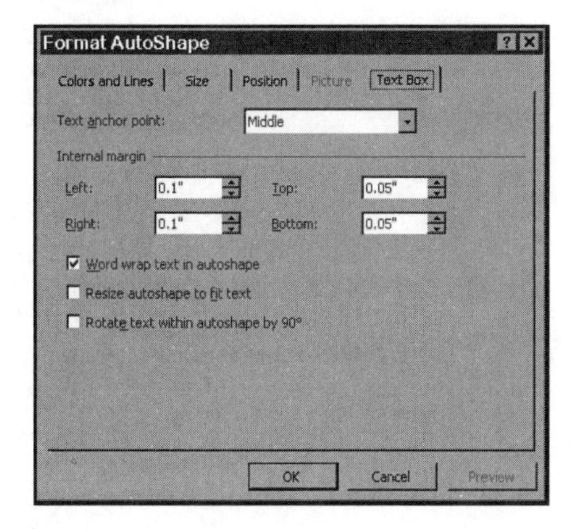

Figure 5.17.
The Format AutoShape dialog box displaying the Text Box tab.

JUST A MINUTE

You have a rotate option, too, in the Text Box tab. This option rotates the text one 90-degree turn to the right. When you choose this option, you should turn off the word-wrapping feature and have PowerPoint automatically resize the text object to fit around the text.

Using Find and Replace

You can use the PowerPoint Find option to quickly locate a phrase or word in your presentation. PowerPoint searches all the text objects—including all slides and speaker's notes—in your presentation for the text you specify.

JUST A MINUTE

Although you can use the Find or Replace option in Slide Sorter View, it's not recommended.

To find text, follow these simple steps:

1. Choose Edit | Find from the menu.
2. Type the text you want to find in the "Find what" box, as shown in Figure 5.18.

3. Select "Match case" to match the case of the text exactly.
4. Select "Find whole words only" to find only whole words.

Figure 5.18.
The Find dialog box.

JUST A MINUTE

Use the "Find whole words only" option when you want to replace words, such as *form*, that might appear within another word, such as *in**forma**tion*. In this example, if you wanted to replace *form* with *screen*, you wouldn't want to end up with the word *in**screen**ation*. Using the "Find whole words only" option can save you a lot of time.

5. Click the Find Next button to start the search.

TIME SAVER

The Find dialog box has a Replace button you can use to quickly switch to the Replace dialog box.

If you want to not only find specific text, but also replace it with other text, use the Replace option to quickly substitute a phrase or word in your presentation. You can choose to approve (or disapprove) each replacement or have PowerPoint replace all instances of the text you're searching for (sometimes called a *global replace*). To replace text, follow these steps:

1. Choose Edit | Replace from the menu.
2. Type the text you want to find in the "Find what" box, as shown in Figure 5.19.
3. Type the text you're substituting in the "Replace with" box.
4. Select the "Match case" checkbox to match the case of the text exactly.
5. Select the "Find whole words only" checkbox to find only whole words.
6. Click the Find Next button to start the find.
7. Click the Replace button to replace the selection with the text in the "Replace with" box and find the next occurrence of the text.

   or

7. Click the Replace All button to replace all occurrences of the text in your document.

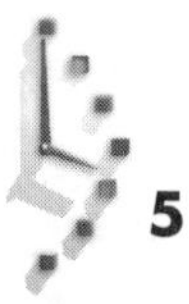

Figure 5.19.
The Replace dialog box.

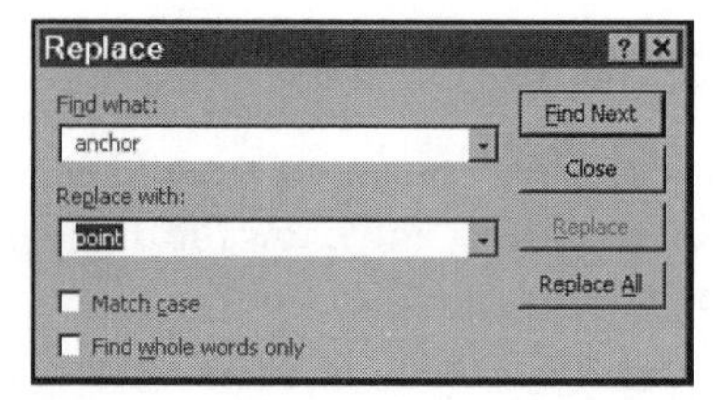

Setting Tabs and Indenting Paragraphs

Although you won't need to set tab stops or indent paragraphs very often in PowerPoint, these options can also be changed if needed. To set tabs or indents in PowerPoint, you use the ruler shown in Figure 5.20.

Figure 5.20.
The ruler with tab stops.

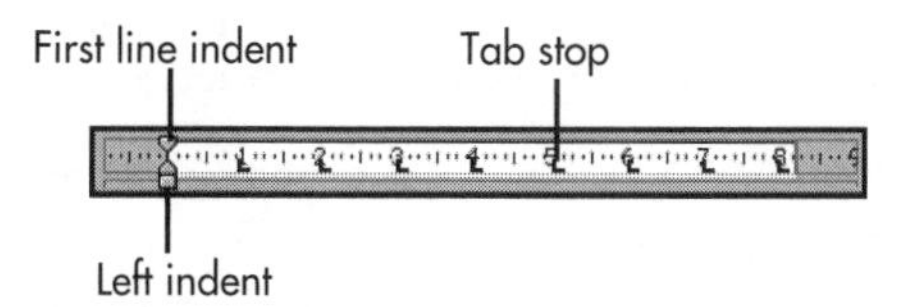

When setting a tab stop, follow these steps:

1. Select the text or text object where you want to set the tab stops.
2. Switch to Slide View (if you're not already there).
3. Choose View | Ruler from the menu.
4. Click on the ruler at the point where you want to set the tab stop.

TIME SAVER

To delete a tab stop, drag it off the ruler.

After you set the tabs—or instead of setting tabs—you might want to set paragraph indents. When you indent a paragraph in PowerPoint, you can indent the first line of text (much like pressing the Tab key) or indent the entire paragraph. To indent text, follow these steps:

1. Select the text or text object where you want to indent.
2. Choose View | Ruler from the menu.
3. Drag the indent marker to the desired location.

Summary

You've had a good hour—you should now be comfortable working with any type of PowerPoint text object and know the difference between a text object and a text box. Once you select a text object or just a snippet of text, you can move or copy it to any location. You have seen how to enhance your presentation by changing any text properties you want, but don't get carried away. Although you have a ton of font options available to you, most presentations look best when they're kept simple.

When you make a mistake, such as leaving the Caps Lock key on or using the wrong word, PowerPoint is there to make corrections as simple as can be. PowerPoint also makes it easy to modify bulleted text with a host of tools and options available to you. You can change the bullet symbol used for each level of text, increase or decrease the font size in proportion to the rest of the text, and change the line spacing, if needed. And setting tab stops or indenting paragraphs is easy when you use the ruler.

PowerPoint makes enhancing text objects fun and easy—you can add a border or a fill with a few simple clicks; resize, rotate, and reposition the text object by using the mouse or a dialog box, or align text with just the click of a button.

Workshop

Grab another cup of joe, and run through another nifty Workshop. After you finish the exercise in this hour's "Test What You've Learned" section, you will be competent with the skills you've learned in this hour. There are also a couple of questions, and of course the answers are provided for you.

Test What You've Learned

1. Open the Hour 4 TWYL presentation you saved from Hour 4, "Working with Slides."

JUST A MINUTE

> If you're "clicking around" this book and didn't do the "Test What You've Learned" section for Hour 4, just start a new presentation using the AutoContent Wizard, answer the questions, and save the file as `Hour 4 TWYL`.

2. Move the title or subtitle to fit the slide better (if you don't think that either needs to be moved, just do this for practice; you can always undo it).
3. Select the title object and change the font face, size, and color.

4. Select the text `By [your name]`, `[your company]`, and `[phone]` in the subtitle; make it bold and italic and decrease the font size.
5. Change the alignment of the title and/or subtitle.
6. Replace the original title font with the new title font for the whole presentation (undo it if you don't like the change).
7. Go to slide two.
8. Change the bullet symbol for each bullet item (make each one different).
9. Increase the font size.
10. Change the spacing between the bullet items.
11. Add a border and fill option to the bullet list.
12. If necessary, fix the indenting for the bullet list.
13. Save the file as `Hour 5 TWYL`.

Q&A

Q When I try to center a text object in the presentation slide using the exact positioning method, the text is askew. How do I center my text exactly?

A PowerPoint positions the text object by using the upper-left edge of the object. If you want to center a text object, setting the horizontal and vertical positions at 0 inches from the center won't center the text object. If you want to center a text object, I suggest turning on the guides by choosing View | Guides from the menu and dragging the object to the center of the window. The object should snap to the guides and automatically center.

Q When I convert a Word outline into a PowerPoint presentation, how do the headings appear on the slides?

A The Word document's Level 1 headings become slides, and lower-level headings are displayed as multilevel bullets.

Part II

Hour 6

Working with Clip Art and Pictures

Enhancing text by making it bold or big is great, but, as the old saying goes, "A picture is worth a thousand words." Enter clip art and pictures. In this hour, you will learn all you ever wanted to know about adding clip art and pictures to your presentation. This chapter explains how to do the following:

- Have PowerPoint suggest an image to use for your slide
- Insert a clip art image or a picture
- Move, copy, and resize images
- Ungroup clip art to use just a portion of the picture
- Enhance image objects with options such as borders, fill, color, brightness, and shadows
- Animate images
- Add images to the Clip Gallery

TIME SAVER

Go online! PowerPoint comes with over 1,100 clip art images and pictures. If you still can't find just the right image from the CD-ROM, use the Web. You can use the site `http://www.Webplaces.com/search/` to search for all kinds of images, including clip art. Some of the images are for sale, and some are free.

The image used for the slide in Figure 6.1 came from just such a search; I found it at `http://milkman.cac.psu.edu/~cooper/TourOfDC/monuments/washington-monument.html`. If you do use an image found on the Web, a word of advice: You should ask permission before using any art you've downloaded. Almost everything published on the Web is copyrighted. Most Webmasters don't mind personal or commercial use of their pictures and will give you permission if you ask. Just dash off an e-mail requesting permission to use the image and wait for a reply.

CAUTION

If you're going to publish the clip art in a for-profit project, I'd suggest getting an actual letter of permission and consider having the corporate legal department scrutinize the language for holes.

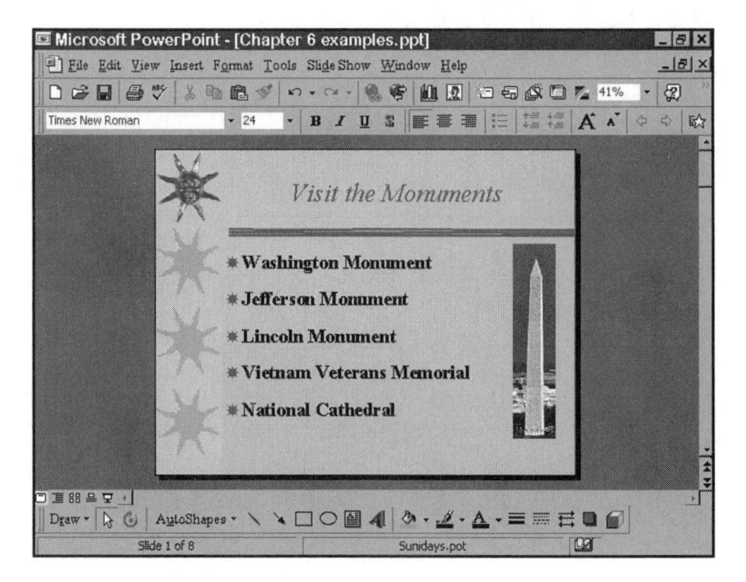

Figure 6.1.
A sample slide with a picture.

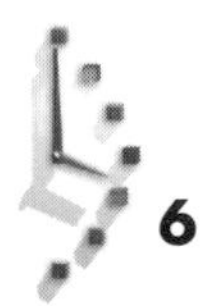

Using AutoClipArt

When you don't have time to browse through the clip art images and pictures that come with PowerPoint, use the nifty AutoClipArt command. AutoClipArt helps you find just the right clip art image for your presentation slides. Because PowerPoint is a smart application, it makes appropriate ClipArt suggestions from the gallery based on the keywords in your presentation. You need to supply only the concept word, and AutoClipArt does the rest. Figure 6.2 shows the AutoClipArt dialog box with keywords chosen and which slide they were chosen from.

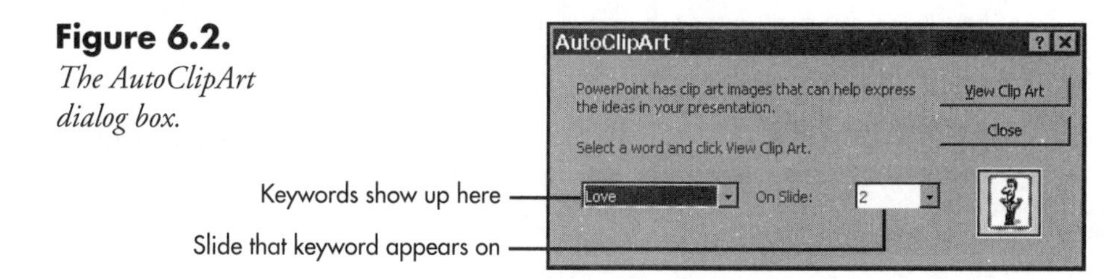

Figure 6.2.
The AutoClipArt dialog box.

Follow these steps to open AutoClipArt:

1. Switch to Slide View.
2. Display the slide where you want to add a clip art image.
3. Choose Tools | AutoClipArt from the menu.
4. Select the best word to describe your presentation from the drop-down list.
5. Click the View Clip Art button.

If you don't like the clip art that PowerPoint suggests, you can always browse through the Clip Gallery.

CAUTION

Your presentation must have a word or phrase that PowerPoint recognizes as a "concept." For example, the "Summer in DC" presentation used in this hour doesn't have a recognized word. In that case, PowerPoint displays the dialog box shown in Figure 6.3, saying that the application can't suggest a clip art image. You should browse the Clip Gallery to find the best image. Just because PowerPoint can't suggest an image, however, doesn't mean a good one isn't available. Remember, the computer isn't really smarter than you—it's just faster.

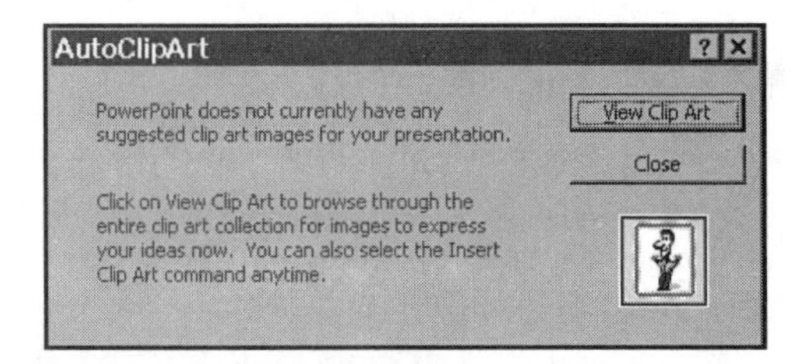

Figure 6.3.
The AutoClipArt dialog box when PowerPoint can't suggest an image.

Inserting Clip Art and Pictures

PowerPoint has several AutoLayouts with placeholders specifically designed to hold clip art images. You can also insert a clip art image or picture on any slide even if you don't have a placeholder. When you insert clip art images, PowerPoint displays the Clip Gallery, as shown in Figure 6.4, where you can browse through all the available clip art images and pictures. The nice folks at Microsoft have made bunches of clip art available for use in your presentations.

JUST A MINUTE

Although PowerPoint installs a lot of clip art on your hard drive, even more images are available on the Office 97 CD-ROM, so make sure that CD-ROM is handy. Those nice folks at Microsoft think of everything. The Clip Gallery even has a button you can click to quickly connect your machine to the Microsoft site, where you will find even more clip art you can download.

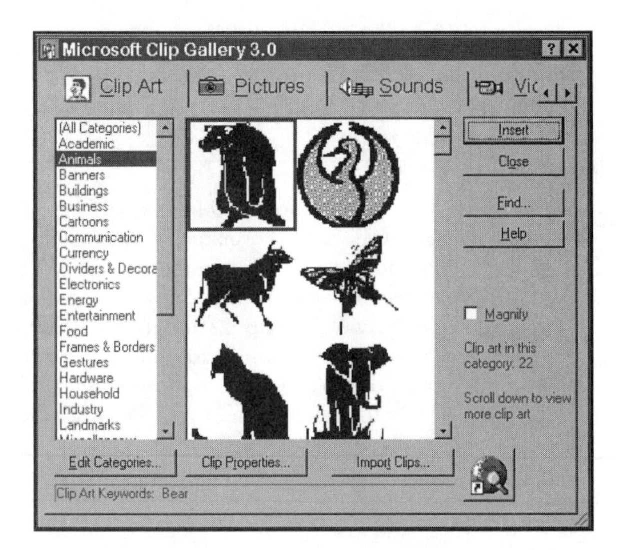

Figure 6.4.
The Clip Gallery.

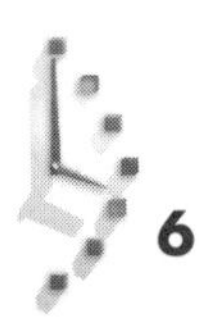

JUST A MINUTE

To delete an image, click once on it to select it, and then press the Delete key.

To insert a clip art image or picture into a presentation that already has a placeholder, follow these steps:

1. Open the slide where you want to add an image.
2. Double-click on the placeholder object where it says `Double click to add clip art.`
3. Select the ClipArt tab to display all available clip art images.

   or

3. Select the Pictures tab to display all available pictures.
4. From the Clip Gallery, select a category of images to display, or select the All Categories option to display all the images available.
5. Click an image.
6. Click the Insert button.

JUST A MINUTE

You can also use the Clip Gallery to select sounds and videos for your presentations. Multimedia options are covered in Hour 21, "Multimedia."

If your presentation does *not* have a placeholder, follow these steps to insert a clip art image or picture into a slide:

1. Display the slide where you want to add an image.
2. Choose Insert | Picture | ClipArt from the menu.
3. Click the ClipArt tab to display all available clip art images.

   or

3. Click the Pictures tab to display all available pictures.
4. From the Clip Gallery, select a category of images to display or select All Categories to display all the images available.
5. Click an image.
6. Click the Insert button.

PowerPoint inserts the clip art image in the center of the slide, as shown in Figure 6.5. You will probably want to resize or move the clip art image after it's been inserted on the slide.

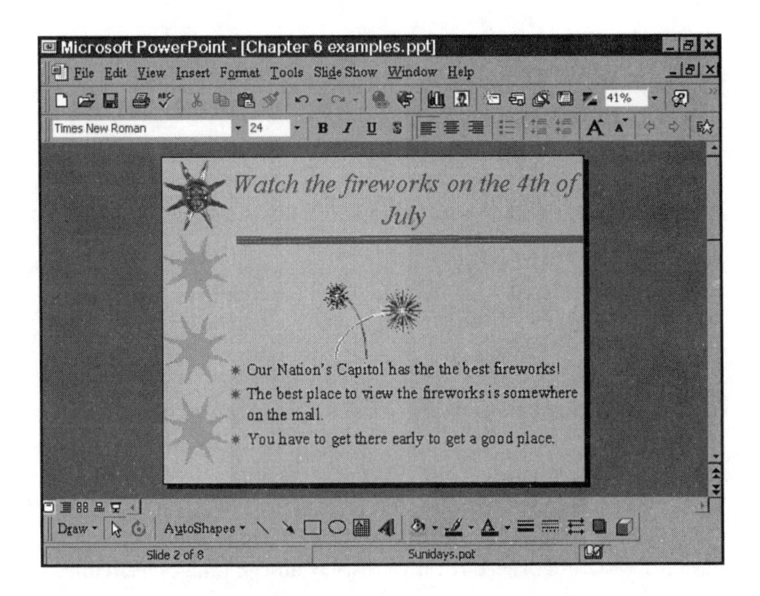

Figure 6.5.
Inserting clip art in the center of the slide.

Once an image has been inserted, PowerPoint automatically displays the picture toolbar. (See Figure 6.6.) The picture toolbar has several useful buttons with features such as Contrast, Brightness, Cropping, and Reset Picture that are helpful when you're working with images in PowerPoint.

Just a Minute

If you don't see the picture toolbar, choose View | Toolbars | Picture from the menu to display it.

Although the picture toolbar is initially a floating toolbar, you can dock it at any edge of the PowerPoint window. The picture toolbar is automatically displayed whenever you have a image selected. Refer to the section "Working with Image Objects" later in this hour to learn how to select an image.

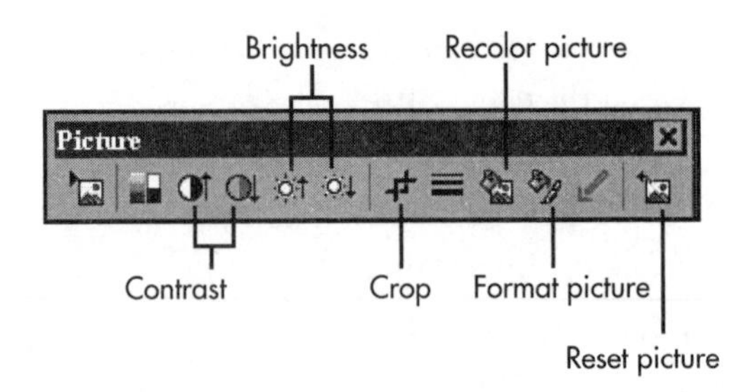

Figure 6.6.
The picture toolbar.

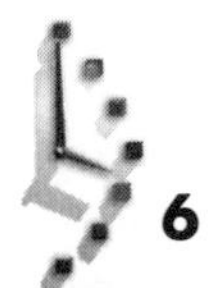

Adding Images to the Clip Gallery

The clip art images and pictures that come with PowerPoint are excellent, but what if you have several pieces of clip art you're constantly adding to your presentations? Having to find them every time you need them is time consuming, and you want to become a more efficient presentation designer so you can take Friday off. Well, here comes PowerPoint to the rescue again. You can add any clip art image or picture (or, for that matter, sound or video file) to the Clip Gallery, which stores frequently used resources that you want to get to quickly. To add an image to the Clip Gallery, follow these steps:

1. Open the Clip Gallery by choosing Insert | Picture | ClipArt from the menu.
2. Click the Import Clips button.
3. Select the drive and folder with the clip art or other file you want to add to the Clip Gallery.
4. Select the file.
5. Click the Open button to open the Clip Properties dialog box.
6. In the Clip Properties dialog box, type some keywords; you can separate keywords with a space and/or a comma.
7. Select the category or categories you want the file listed in, as shown in Figure 6.7.
8. If you don't see a category that applies, create a new one by clicking the New Category button.
9. Click the OK button.
10. Click the Close button in the Clip Gallery.

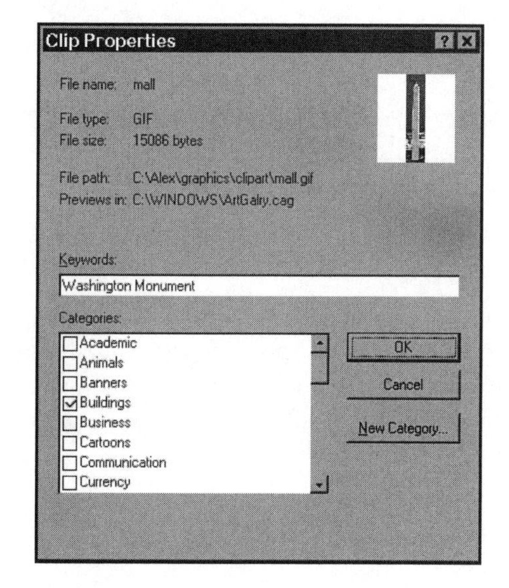

Figure 6.7.
The Clip Properties dialog box.

Working with Image Objects

Before you can move or resize any image, you need to know how to select the image object; it's not nearly as complicated as selecting a text object, however. Just a simple click, and the object is selected. To select multiple objects, hold the Shift key down while you click on each object you want to select.

Now you know the basics, so you can move, resize, and format at will. When an object is selected, you can see selection and resizing handles, as shown in Figure 6.8. Also, the picture toolbar is automatically displayed.

Figure 6.8.
Selecting the fireworks image object.

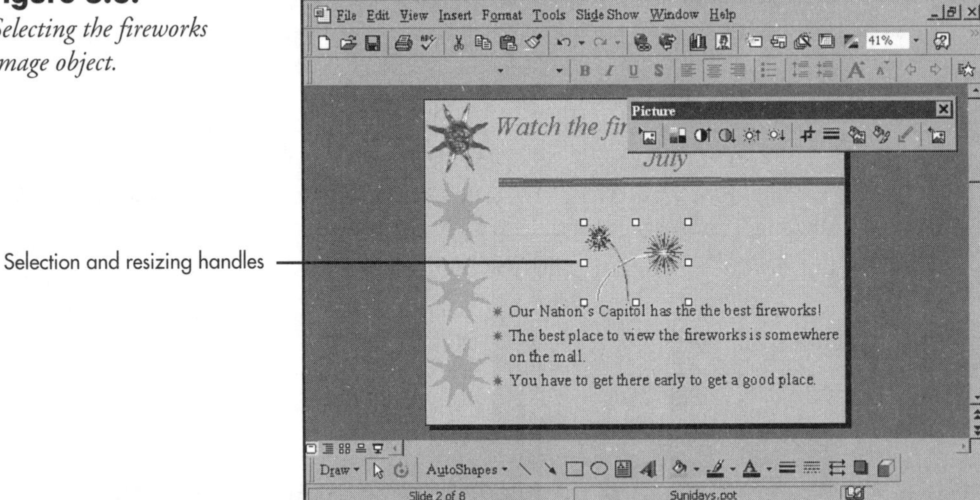

Moving or Copying Image Objects with the Mouse

When you insert a clip art image or picture into a slide that doesn't have a placeholder, you often need to move and/or resize the image. The slide you saw in Figure 6.8 has an image that needs to be moved, copied, and resized. Notice that it's currently in the middle of the slide and is very small. The slide would also look better with more fireworks.

To move or copy images, the simplest method is to use the mouse. You must be in Slide View to move or copy any graphical image. You can also use the menu to copy a clip art image or picture, but then you have to move it to the correct location. Why not copy *and* move the object at the same time? Follow these two simple steps to quickly move a clip art image or picture:

1. Click once on the object to select it; you should see selection and resizing handles surrounding it.

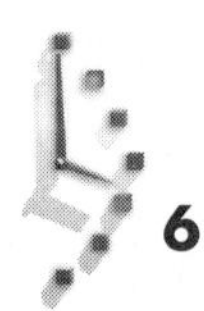

2. Place the mouse pointer anywhere on the clip art or picture so that it changes to a move pointer and drag the object to the location you want.

You can copy an object by using these same two steps; just hold down the Ctrl key while you're dragging the object. A small plus sign next to the mouse pointer appears when you do this, as shown in Figure 6.9.

Figure 6.9.
Copying the fireworks clip art image.

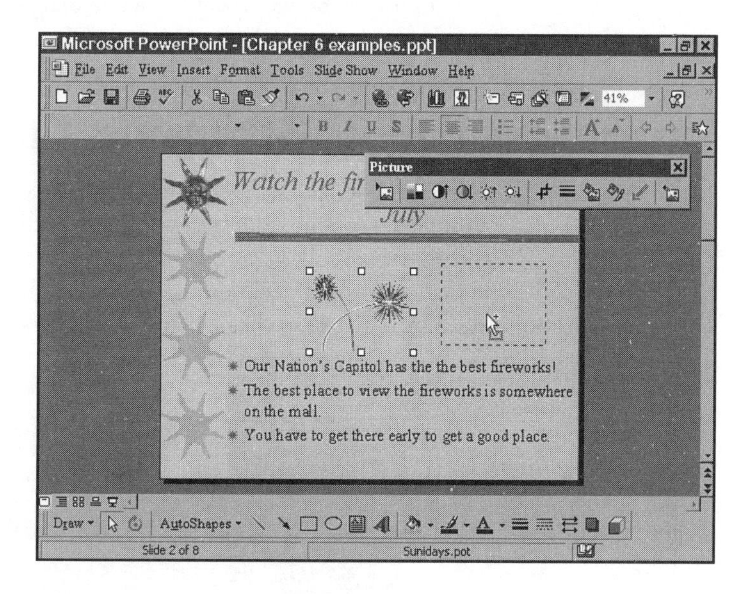

TIME SAVER

When you want a clip art image on two different slides, you have to use the copy-and-paste method described in Hour 5, "Working with PowerPoint Text Objects." After you paste an object, you usually have to move it to the location you want.

Resizing Image Objects with the Mouse

Unless you need an image to be an exact size, the easiest way to resize it is to use the mouse. As mentioned earlier, the fireworks image needs to be much larger. Who ever heard of the Fourth of July with puny fireworks? To resize an image, simply follow these steps:

1. Select the image.
2. Place the mouse pointer on any resizing handle, so that it looks like a resize (or four-headed) arrow, and drag the object until it's the size you want.

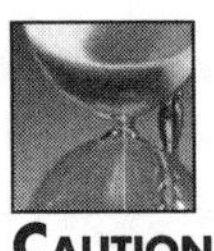

CAUTION

You can accidentally distort an image when you use a side, top, or bottom resize handle. Unless you want to distort the image on purpose, use the corner handles to resize. If you do accidentally distort an image, you don't have to fix it yourself. Just click the Reset Picture button on the picture toolbar. However, not every image can be reset. For those that can't, it's usually best to delete the image and reinsert it.

Ungrouping and Grouping Clip Art

The fireworks sample slide looks great, but the fireworks are all pretty much the same. However, PowerPoint gives you the ability to take a piece of clip art and ungroup it. You can then use just a portion of the image. Conversely, you can also group a bunch of images together. The bundled images interact as though they were one large image. In Figure 6.10, one of the fireworks clip art images has been ungrouped into two separate images; notice that each firework is surrounded by selection handles now.

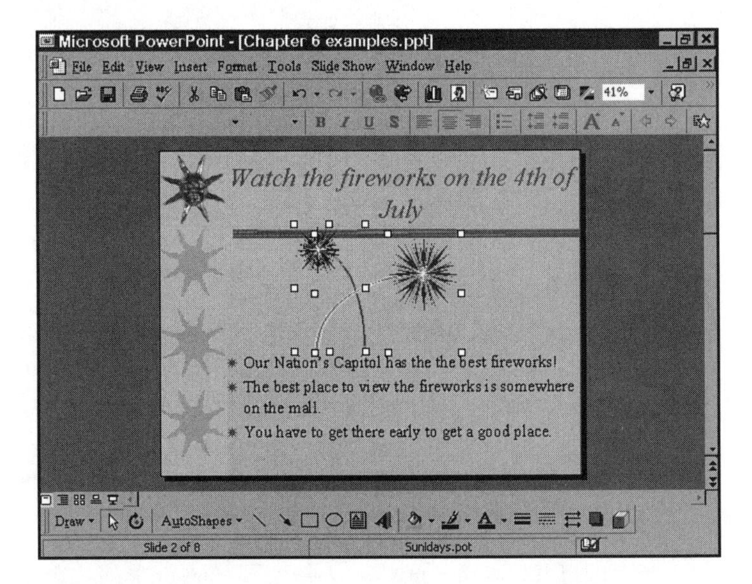

Figure 6.10.
Ungrouping the fireworks clip art image into two separate fireworks.

When you ungroup a clip art image, PowerPoint converts the image into a Microsoft Office drawing. Here are the steps for ungrouping a clip art image:

1. Select the clip art image.
2. On the drawing toolbar, choose Draw | Ungroup.
3. PowerPoint asks whether you really want to convert the object; click Yes.

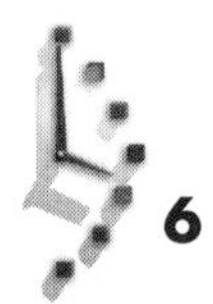

You will now have several separate image objects to work with.

TIME SAVER

> Some clip art images need to be ungrouped several times to get the portion you're looking for. Try ungrouping out on a simple piece of clip art first, and then on a more complicated one. You will work more with grouping and ungrouping in Hour 13, "Bringing Drawing Objects Together."

Grouping objects is the opposite of ungrouping them. In Figure 6.11, all the individual fireworks have been placed just so. You can now group all of them so that they act as one image, which makes it easier to copy, move, or resize the image object. (Maybe you can stay at home on Friday after all.) To group several objects together, follow these two simple steps:

1. Select all the objects you want to group together.
2. On the drawing toolbar, choose Draw | Group.

TIME SAVER

> You can quickly select multiple objects by dragging a lasso around the images. Place the mouse pointer above and to the left of all the images, hold down the mouse button, and drag to the lower right. As you drag the mouse, a lasso surrounding all the images appears. When you let go of the mouse button, all the images within the lasso will be selected.

Figure 6.11.

The fireworks grouped together as one image object.

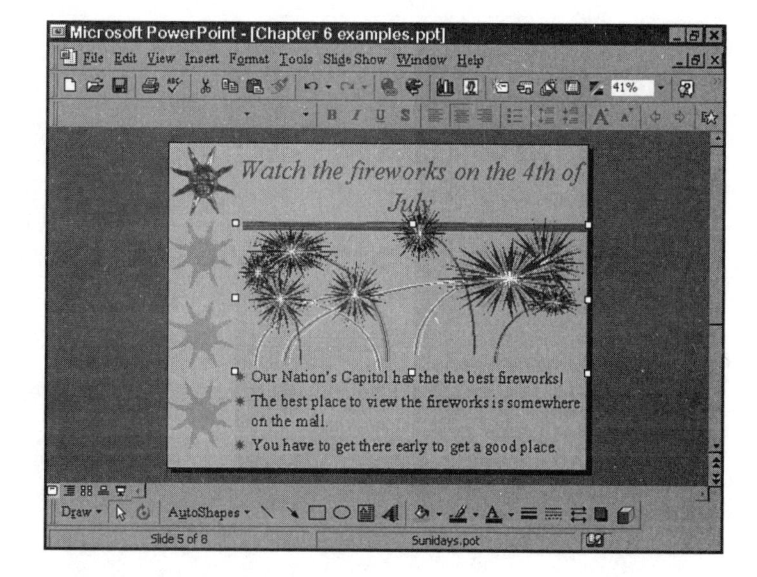

CAUTION

You will probably notice that grouped objects aren't properly formatted. When you group objects, sometimes they aren't formatted with the intended borders and shading. For this reason, I didn't leave the firework objects grouped for the next section, "Formatting Image Objects." If the objects had stayed grouped, there would have been a border or fill behind each set of fireworks when the formatting was applied. Even though they were grouped as one object, the formatting commands would have treated the images separately.

Formatting Image Objects

Now that you know how to resize and move the images, you're ready to learn different ways to control the image object. You have already covered most of the available options in Hour 5, and most of the options covered in this section work similarly. They are all found in the Format Picture dialog box. In the following sections, the fireworks clip art object is used as the example.

JUST A MINUTE

If you have ungrouped a clip art image, you won't see the Picture option in the Format menu. You see either an Object option or an Autoshape option. Whatever the case, when you want to change any image properties, selecting the last menu option in the Format menu gives you the Format dialog box.

Adding a Border or Fill

The first feature is how to add a border or fill to an image object. The border option really makes an image stand out; however, adding a fill to an image is an option that should be used sparingly, if at all. As mentioned previously, always consider the proper presentation for the image. Don't apply options just because you can. If you don't like the effect, you can always change the image back with the Undo command. Figure 6.12 shows a filled image object with a border.

JUST A MINUTE

A gradient fill effect called Early Sunset was used for the fireworks image. The image looks spectacular in color.

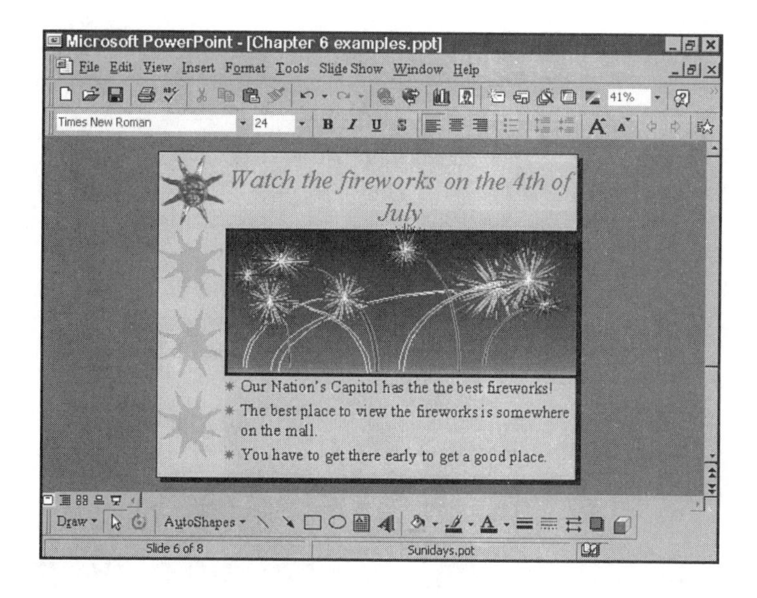

Figure 6.12.
The fireworks image with a border and fill.

To add a border to an image object, follow these steps:

1. Select the object you want to border or fill.
2. Choose Format | Picture from the menu.
3. Select the Colors and Lines tab. (See Figure 6.13.)

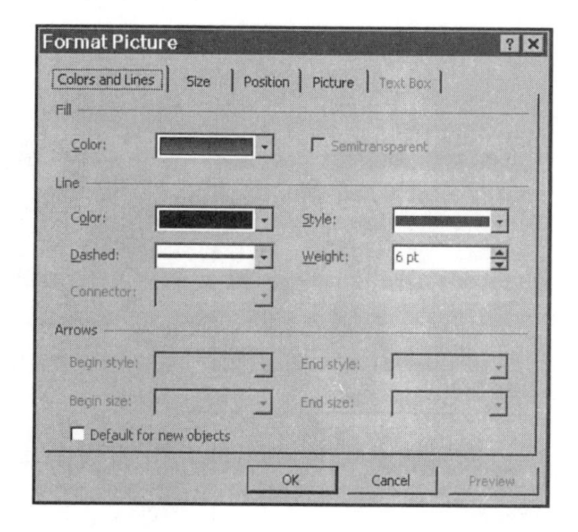

Figure 6.13.
The Colors and Lines tab of the Format Picture dialog box.

4. If you want to add a fill, select a fill option from the Color drop-down list in the Fill section of the dialog box.

Just a Minute

Use the Fill Effects options from the Color drop-down list when you want to apply a gradient or other effect to your text object. There are a lot of effects to choose from; just remember that your audience must be able to view the picture.

5. If you want a border, select a line color from the Color drop-down list in the Line section of the dialog box.
6. Change the Style, Dashed, and Weight options for the border, if you like.
7. Click the Preview button to preview your changes before accepting them.
8. Click the OK button when you're finished.

Sizing, Scaling, or Rotating a Picture

With PowerPoint, you have all kinds of control over an image object. You can scale an image or set it to an exact size. You can also rotate image objects in varying degrees, from 0 to 359. As with text objects, an image object is rotated in a clockwise direction.

To change the size, scale, or rotation of image objects, use these directions:

1. Click once on the image object to select it.
2. Choose Format | Picture from the menu to open the Format Picture dialog box.
3. Click the Size tab. (See Figure 6.14.)

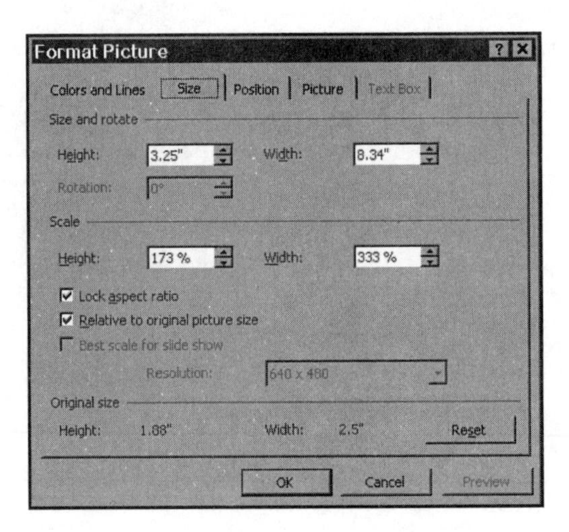

Figure 6.14.
The Size tab of the Format Picture dialog box.

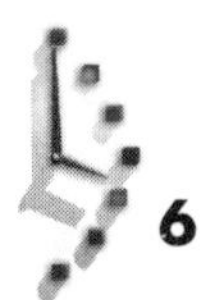

4. Enter an exact height and/or width for the image.

   or

4. Scale the image by entering a percentage for height and width in the Scale section of the dialog box.
5. Enter the amount in degrees by which you want to rotate the image object.
6. Click the Preview button to preview your changes before accepting them.
7. Click the OK button when you're finished.

TIME SAVER

Setting an exact size is the best method when you know the exact size you need for the image.

PowerPoint also allows you to free-rotate or flip any object. These options are covered in Hour 13.

Positioning an Image Exactly

Moving an image object with the mouse is probably the best method available. However, in certain situations you might need an image object placed in an exact location. In those instances, use the position option in the Format Picture dialog box. To position an image object in an exact location, follow these steps:

1. Select the image object you want to position.
2. Choose Format | Picture from the menu.
3. Click the Position tab.
4. Enter the horizontal position you want for the image object.
5. Enter the vertical position you want for the image object.
6. Click the Preview button to preview your changes before accepting them.
7. Click the OK button when you're finished.

CAUTION

PowerPoint positions objects by using their upper-left edges as origin points. If it doesn't seem as though PowerPoint is placing the object in the correct location, the image's corner offset is probably the reason.

Cropping, Color, Brightness, and Contrast

The Picture tab in the Format Picture dialog box has options for cropping an image and controlling an image's color, brightness, and contrast. Figure 6.15 shows the fireworks clip art image cropped (so you see just the top rightmost firework), and the color set to Watermark, which makes an image dimmer than normal.

Cropping an image is like taking a pair of scissors and cutting out just the portion of the image you need. In the fireworks example, the image was cropped so that just the top of it is displayed.

Figure 6.15.
The fireworks image cropped and set as a watermark.

When I crop an image, I usually use the cropping tool on the picture toolbar, as opposed to the measurement boxes in the Format Picture dialog box. It's much easier to crop an image when you can see what you're doing. To use the picture toolbar to crop an image, follow these steps:

1. Select the image you want to crop.
2. Click the Crop button on the picture toolbar.
3. Place the mouse pointer on any handle of the image; it should turn into a cropping pointer (which looks like the picture on the Crop button).
4. Drag the handle to crop the image.
5. Repeat as necessary.
6. Click the Crop button to turn cropping off.

Here are the steps for using the Format Picture dialog box to crop an image:

1. Select the image you want to crop.
2. Choose Format | Picture from the menu.

3. Click the Picture tab.
4. Enter the measurements to crop the image in the "Crop from" area. See Figure 6.16 for an example.

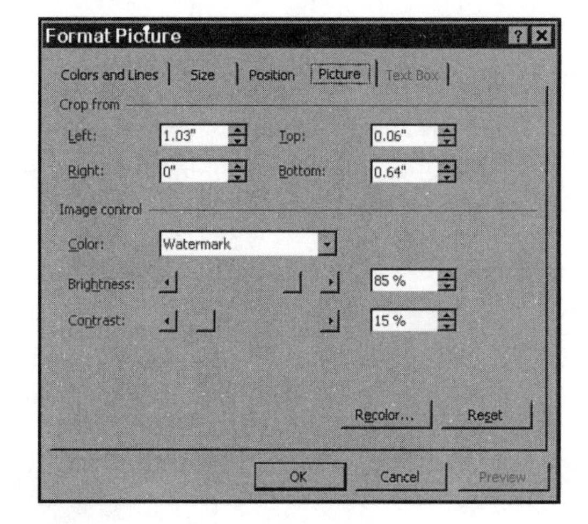

Figure 6.16.
Cropping an image in the Format Picture dialog box.

5. Click the Preview button to preview your changes before accepting them.
6. Click the OK button when you're finished.

You can choose to change an image into a watermark by setting the color option to Watermark. PowerPoint formats the picture with preset brightness and contrast settings. To set an image as a watermark, follow these steps:

1. Select the image you want to set as a watermark.
2. Choose Format | Picture from the menu.
3. Click the Picture tab.
4. Select Watermark from the Color drop-down list.
5. Click the Preview button to preview your changes before accepting them.
6. Click the OK button when you're finished.

Customizing the Color of Clip Art

The last option in the Format Picture dialog box is the one for changing the colors in a clip art image. This feature is new in PowerPoint 97. If you don't like the preset colors of an image, PowerPoint allows you to customize them.

CAUTION

Not all images allow color changes. All the clip art images that come with PowerPoint can be customized, but if you have images from another source, you might not be able to customize the colors.

Here's how to customize the color scheme of a clip art image:

1. Select the image you want to customize.
2. Click the Recolor Picture button on the picture toolbar, and then go to step 5.

   or

2. Choose Format | Picture from the menu.
3. Click the Picture tab.
4. Click the Recolor button.

   Either choice displays the Recolor Picture dialog box, as shown in Figure 6.17.

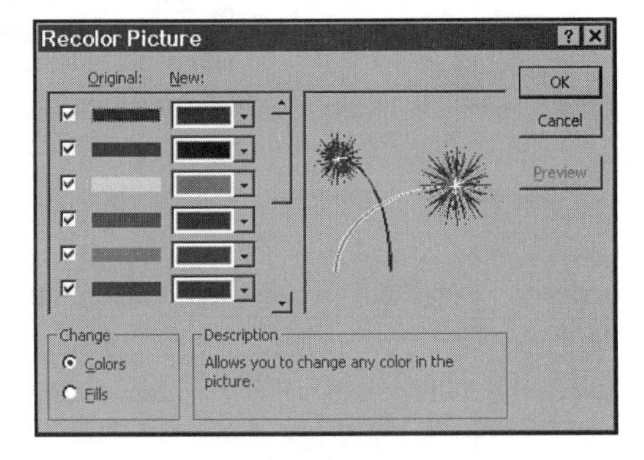

Figure 6.17.
The Recolor Picture dialog box.

5. Change the color options by clicking on any drop-down arrow and selecting another color.
6. Click the Preview button to preview your changes before accepting them.
7. Click the OK button to accept your changes.

Adding Shadows

Another interesting effect you can apply to an image is adding a shadow. PowerPoint 97 enhances the shadow effect by allowing the designer to fully customize the presentation. You can move a shadow up, down, left, or right. Figure 6.18 shows the fireworks image with a shadow that has been nudged up and to the left a bit.

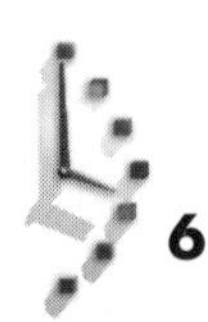

Figure 6.18.
A clip art image with a shadow.

To shadow a clip art image, follow these covert operations:

1. Select the image you want to place a shadow behind.
2. Click the Shadow button on the drawing toolbar to display all the shadow options.
3. Click the shadow option you want.

If you're extremely adventurous, you can add a custom shadow:

1. Select the image you want to place a shadow behind.
2. Click the Shadow button on the drawing toolbar.
3. Click the Shadow Settings option to display the shadow settings toolbar. (See Figure 6.19.)
4. Click the Shadow On/Off button to turn the shadow on.
5. Click any of the Nudge buttons to move the shadow.
6. Click the Shadow Color button to change the color of the shadow, if you want.
7. Click the Close button to close the shadow settings toolbar.

Figure 6.19.
The shadow settings toolbar.

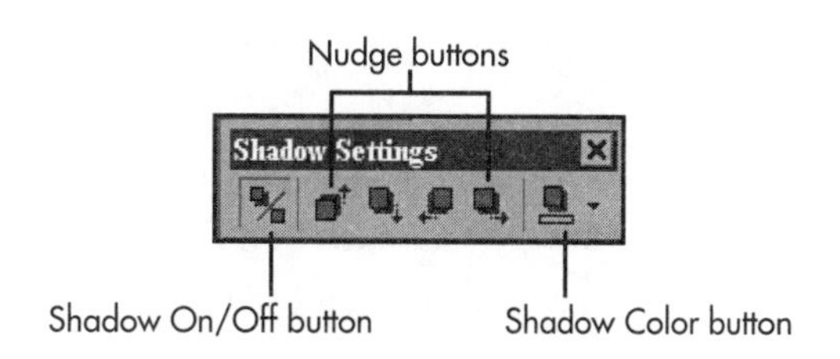

Summary

In this hour, you have learned about all the clip art and other graphical image options available in PowerPoint 97. If you can't decide which piece of clip art to use for your presentation, let the new AutoClipArt feature help you narrow the choices. You can insert a clip art image or other graphical image into any slide at any time, and you can add your favorite images to the Clip Gallery with a few simple clicks.

Moving or copying an image object is simple, whether you use the mouse or the menu. You can size any image to fit your needs. The Ungroup command lets you select a smaller portion of the image to display or change. Formatting a graphical image has never been simpler with the new Format | Object dialog box: Add a border or fill; scale or rotate an object; crop an image; change the color, brightness, and contrast; and even customize the color of clip art images. Don't forget—you can also add any one of numerous shadow options to an image to create the effect of depth.

Congratulations! You're now 1/4 of the way to becoming a PowerPoint 97 expert. Part III, "Putting Polish on a Presentation," covers how to customize your presentation with even more color options, use and customize the slide masters, and create that extra-special, exciting slide show. You've done a great job so far, and by now you're probably thinking of all kinds of really cool things you can do. What are you waiting for? Show Bob how a real presentation is done.

Workshop

Are you ready to shift to 5th gear and test what you've learned about clip art and all the fun and exciting places you can take your audience using clip art? Roll up those sleeves and give yourself some time. When I start working with graphics, I have a hard time stopping. And don't forget the last section with all those nifty questions and answers. You never know—someone might be asking about the one thing that has been driving you batty for the last half hour.

Test What You've Learned

1. Start PowerPoint and start a new presentation.
2. Use the Blank Slide Layout option.
3. Insert a simple clip art image (the symbols group has quite a few simple images to choose from).
4. Move the image to the upper-left corner of the slide.
5. Copy the image to the lower-right corner of the slide.
6. Resize the image on the left to be bigger.
7. Ungroup the left image, and move or copy one piece of the image.

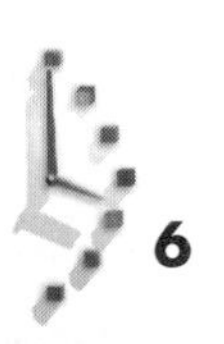

JUST A MINUTE

You might find that you need to use the Ungroup command more than once to be able to get to each little individual piece. For example, an image of a person might be several groups of groups of groups. When you're first starting to use the Ungroup feature, it's best to start with the simplest image and kind of work your way up.

8. Group all the images on the left into a single image.
9. Delete the image on the left.
10. Move the remaining image to the middle of the slide.

TIME SAVER

One of the Q&As answers how to do this, but to recap: Choose View | Guides from the menu, then move the image so that the top and side handles are positioned on the guides. Usually PowerPoint snaps the object to the guides. Choose View | Guides to turn the guides off, if you want.

11. Resize the image to be bigger.
12. Add a border to the image (and a fill, if you want).
13. Recolor the image.
14. Add a shadow to the image.
15. Save the presentation as `Hour 6 TWYL`.

Q&A

Q I have an image that someone gave me on a disk. Can I use it in my presentation?

A Certainly. First, insert the image on your slide by choosing Insert | Picture | From File from the menu. Once PowerPoint displays the Insert Picture dialog box, simply specify the drive and/or folder where the file is located, and click the Insert button.

TIME SAVER

Make sure the "Files of type" box shows the correct image file type. If you don't know the image type, select the All Files (*.*) option.

Q When I try to rotate a clip art image, the rotate option isn't available. How can I rotate the clip art?

A PowerPoint won't let you rotate a clip art image. However, you can trick PowerPoint into letting you rotate the clip art image in this manner:

1. Select the clip art image.
2. Choose Draw | Ungroup from the drawing toolbar.
3. Click the Yes button to convert the clip art to a Microsoft drawing object.
4. With all the objects still selected, choose Draw | Group from the drawing toolbar. You now have one Microsoft drawing object you can rotate.

CAUTION

Once you ungroup a clip art image you can't use the Recolor Picture option. You have to color each piece of the object separately. This topic is covered in more depth in Hour 12, "Drawing Shapes in PowerPoint." If you want to recolor and rotate a clip art image, recolor it first and then ungroup, group, and rotate the object.

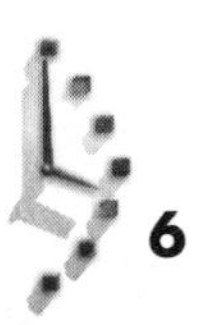

Part III

Putting Polish on a Presentation

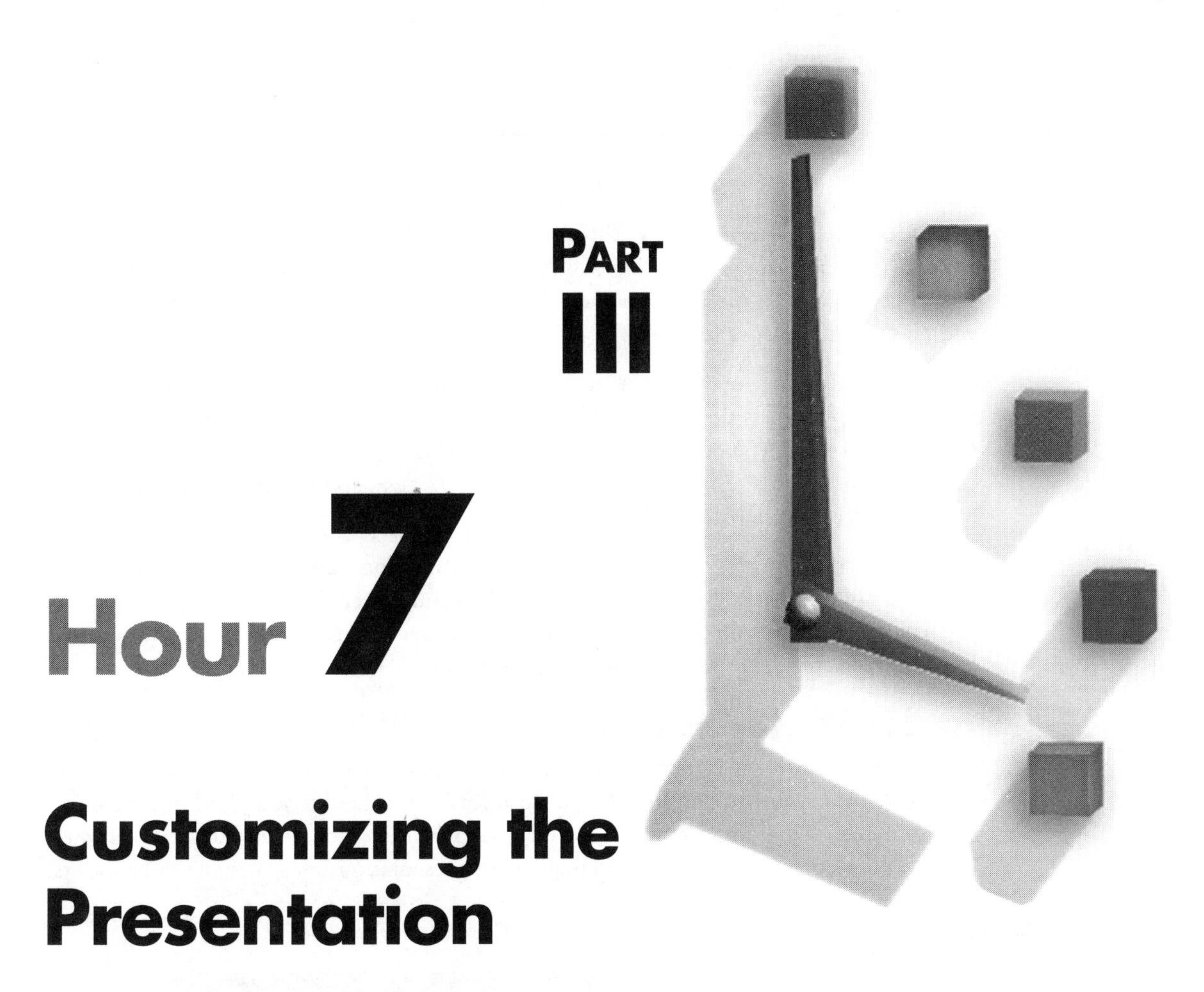

Part III

Hour 7

Customizing the Presentation

The next four hours cover all you need to know to customize, polish, and prepare your presentation for audience viewing. You will learn all the tricks for creating fabulous presentations. When you're done, the presentation will look as though it were created by a professional marketing firm. During this hour that covers applying all-important custom touches to your presentation, you will learn how to do the following:

- Create a custom color scheme
- Create a custom background
- Create and print speaker's notes
- Create handouts for your audience

Customizing the Color Scheme

When you choose one of PowerPoint's presentation designs or presentation templates, you aren't required to choose coordinating colors for the slide objects. Each design and template has eight coordinating colors for the background, regular text, title text, fills, and accents. The color scheme can affect every slide in your presentation or just one single slide—you make the choice. There's no need to go to each slide and change the color for every text item; let PowerPoint apply the color scheme and do the tedious work for you.

There might also be times when you don't need any color, such as for a company in Iowa that's trying to keep its costs down. You will be giving your presentation on a black-and-white overhead projector. You don't want to lose all the panache that the template gives you, but you do need to clearly sell your ideas. PowerPoint 97 gives you the option of showing the presentation clearly in black and white.

At other times, you might want to use your own custom colors, rather than the standard color scheme those nice folks at Microsoft have created for you. When situations such as these arise, you have two options: you can choose from one of the standard color schemes already created or you can create your very own custom color scheme.

Standard Color Schemes

Each presentation design or template has a standard color scheme that is first displayed when you create the presentation. You will also see at least one other black-and-white scheme, as shown in Figure 7.1. You should use the black-and-white option for those occasions when you can't use a color printer and need to generate presentation transparencies or handouts.

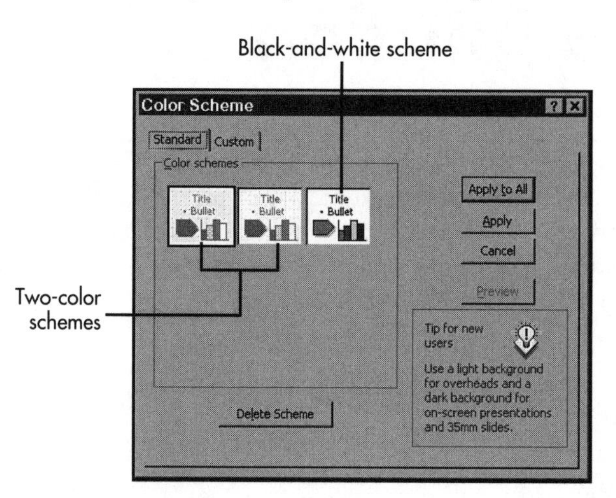

Figure 7.1.
Three color schemes in the Standard tab of the Color Scheme dialog box.

Some templates and presentation designs have several other predesigned standard color schemes for you to choose from. Figure 7.2 shows a template with nine color schemes.

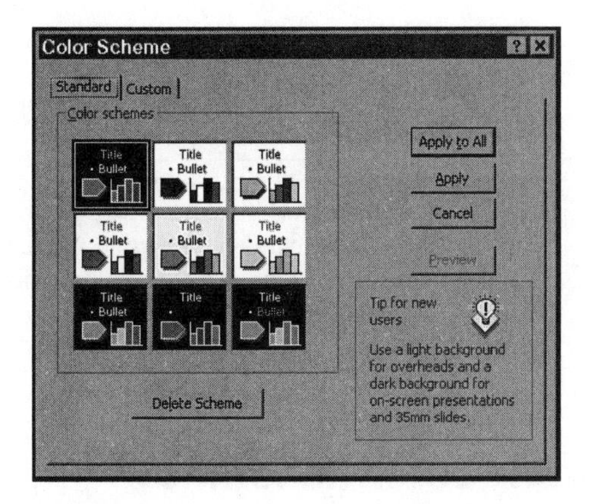

Figure 7.2.
Nine color schemes in the Color Scheme dialog box.

To select another predesigned standard color scheme for the entire presentation, follow these steps:

1. Choose Format | Slide Color Scheme from the menu.
2. Select the Standard tab.
3. Click any color scheme; the black-and-white color scheme is usually the top-right color scheme.
4. Click the Preview button to see a preview of the selected scheme.

JUST A MINUTE

Once again, you will probably need to move the dialog box out of the way to see the preview. To move a dialog box, place the mouse pointer in the title bar of the dialog box, click and hold down the mouse button, and drag the box to another location.

5. Click the Apply to All button to accept the change.

When selecting a color scheme, PowerPoint also allows you to change the color scheme for just one individual slide. This feature lets you add emphasis to a specific slide.

To change the color scheme for just one slide, follow these steps:

1. Choose Format | Slide Color Scheme from the menu.
2. Select the Standard tab.
3. Click any color scheme. The black-and-white color scheme is usually the top-right color scheme.

4. Click the Preview button to see a preview.
5. Click the Apply button to accept the change.

TIME SAVER

In many cases in PowerPoint, you can make a change to either the current slide (or selected slides) or to the entire presentation. If you want to change only the current selected slide(s), click the Apply button. If you want to change all the slides in the presentation, click the Apply to All button.

Custom Color Schemes

If you don't like any of the standard color schemes, you can always create your own custom color scheme. When you create a custom color scheme, you can select a custom color for the following eight options: background, text and lines, shadows, title text, fills, accent, accent and hyperlink, and accent and followed hyperlink. As you select a new color for each of these eight options, PowerPoint shows you a preview of what your choice will look like. Figure 7.3 shows the custom Color Scheme dialog box.

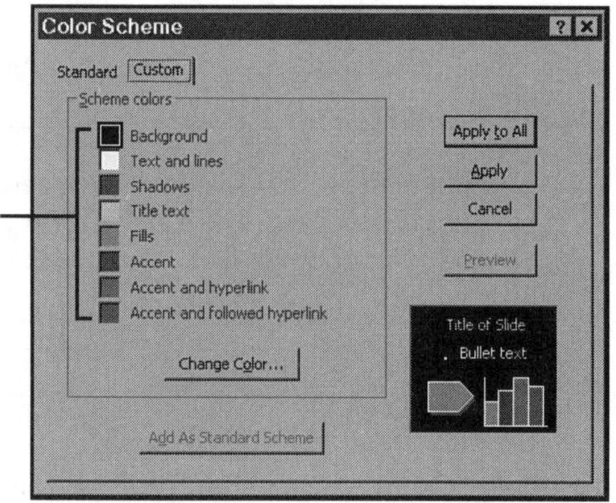

Figure 7.3.
The Custom tab of the Color Scheme dialog box.

To create a custom color scheme, follow these steps:

1. Choose Format | Slide Color Scheme from the menu.
2. Click the Custom tab.
3. Click the color box of the feature you want to change in the Scheme Colors section.
4. Click the Change Color button.
5. Select a standard color, as shown in Figure 7.4, from the Color dialog box or choose a color from the Custom window.

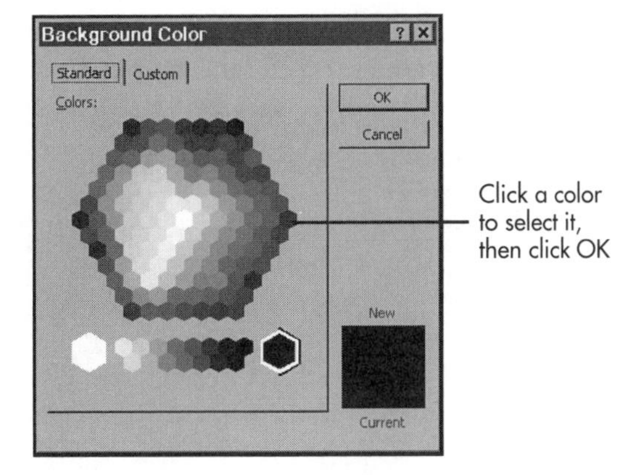

Figure 7.4.
The Color dialog box.

6. Click the OK button.
7. Repeat the preceding steps for each feature you want to customize.
8. Click the Preview button to see a preview.
9. Click the Apply or Apply to All button to accept the change.

Just a Minute

If you want to create a custom color, use the Custom tab in the Color dialog box, as shown in Figure 7.5. You can then either drag the cross hair and scroll arrow to select a color, or be more scientific and type in the number (0–255) for the Red/Green/Blue and Hue/Saturation/Luminance color component options.

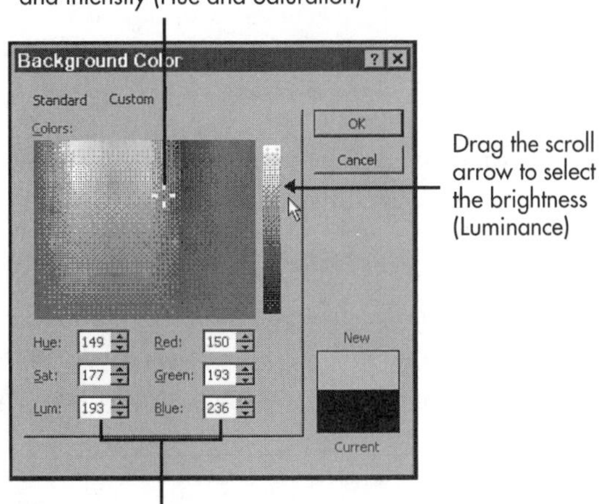

Figure 7.5.
The Color dialog box showing the Custom tab.

Once you have created a color scheme, you can add that color scheme to the standard list. That can save you time in the future if Bob wants to use the same colors over and over and over…

Follow these steps to save a custom color scheme:

1. Choose Format | Slide Color Scheme from the menu.
2. Click the Custom tab.
3. Create a custom color scheme by changing the Scheme Colors.
4. Click the Preview button to see a preview.
5. Click the Add as Standard Scheme button.

JUST A MINUTE

You can also delete a color scheme just as easily by selecting the scheme and clicking the Delete Scheme button.

Customizing the Background

PowerPoint allows you to not only change the color scheme of your slides, but also change the appearance of the presentation or slide background. If you want to change the background, you have many options available: color, shade, pattern, texture, or picture (watermark).

CAUTION

Although you can choose from all these background options, you can use only a single type of background for a specific slide. For example, you can have either a gradient shaded background or a picture as the background, but not both.

Just like changing the color scheme, you can change the background for only one slide or for the entire presentation.

Changing the Background Color

In addition to changing the background color through the Custom tab of the Color Scheme dialog box, PowerPoint has a quick way to change the background color with the Format | Background command. You can change the background color for just the current

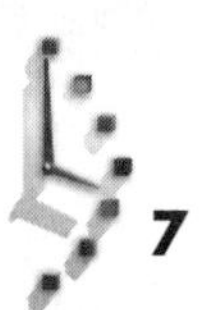

slide or for all the slides in your presentation. To change the background color, follow these steps:

1. Choose Format | Background from the menu.
2. Click the drop-down list in the Background Fill section of the dialog box, as shown in Figure 7.6.
3. Click one of the color boxes.

   or

3. Click More Colors and select another color from the Colors dialog box.
4. Click the OK button (from the Colors dialog box).
5. Click the Preview button to see a preview.
6. Click the Apply or Apply to All button to accept the change.

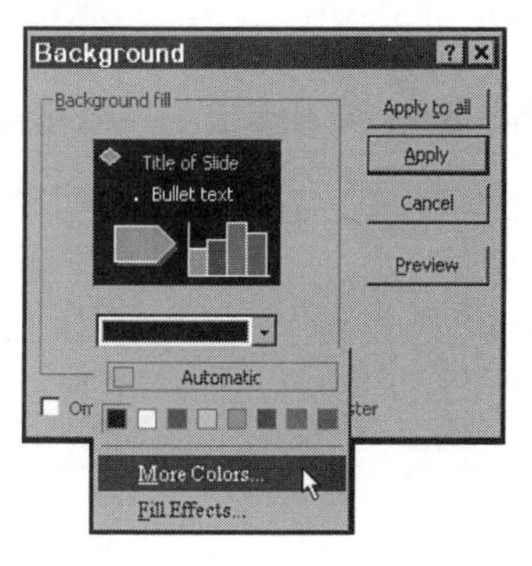

Figure 7.6.
The Background dialog box.

CAUTION

> If your slides have graphics, and you want to change only the background color (not add gradient shading or use a pattern), try changing the background color by using the Format | Color Scheme command. When you create the custom color scheme, change only the background color. Although you can change the background color using the Format | Background command, this option doesn't give you a good display when slides have certain graphical elements.

Changing the Fill Effects

One way to add special effects to a slide is to modify the fill effects for the background. You have four options for the background fill:

- Gradient
- Texture

- Pattern
- Picture

Each option, when used skillfully, can visually enhance a presentation or slide and add emphasis for a particular topic of discussion.

Gradient

Gradient shading is the most frequently used fill effect, not only for the slide background, but for drawing shapes as well. This effect can produce a dazzling visual display. For example, you could gradually transform one solid color into a lighter or darker color, fade two colors from one to the other, or use preset PowerPoint gradient choices with exotic names, such as Early Sunset or Rainbow. Gradient shading also includes six different shading styles, most of which have four different variants to choose from. Table 7.1 illustrates one sample variant for each of the available shading options. Explore every avenue—you might be surprised where you end up. Figure 7.7 is an example of a slide with a shaded background.

Table 7.1. Shading styles and variant options.

Shading style	Sample Variant
Horizontal	
Vertical	
Diagonal up	
Diagonal down	
From corner	
From title	

To select a gradient shading option for the background, use these steps:

1. Choose Format | Background from the menu.
2. Select Fill Effects from the Background Fill drop-down list.
3. In the Fill Effects dialog box, click the Gradient tab, as shown in Figure 7.8.

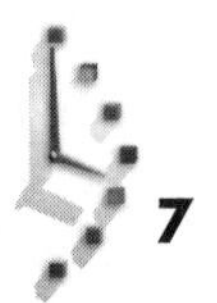

Figure 7.7.
A slide with a horizontal shaded background.

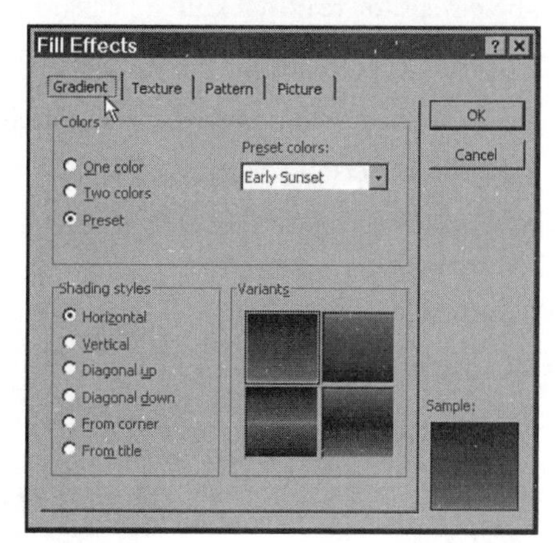

Figure 7.8.
The Gradient tab of the Fill Effects dialog box.

4. Select a color option, such as Preset, from the radio buttons in the Colors section.
5. Select one of the radio buttons, such as Horizontal or Vertical, in the Shading Styles section.
6. Select an option (most shading styles have four) in the Variants section; the one you pick is displayed in the Sample box.
7. Click the OK button.
8. Click the Preview button to see a preview.
9. Click the Apply or Apply to All button to accept the change.

Texture

You can add texture to your slide background to give it the appearance of marble, granite, walnut, sand, or one of several other options. Figure 7.9 shows a slide with a marble textured background.

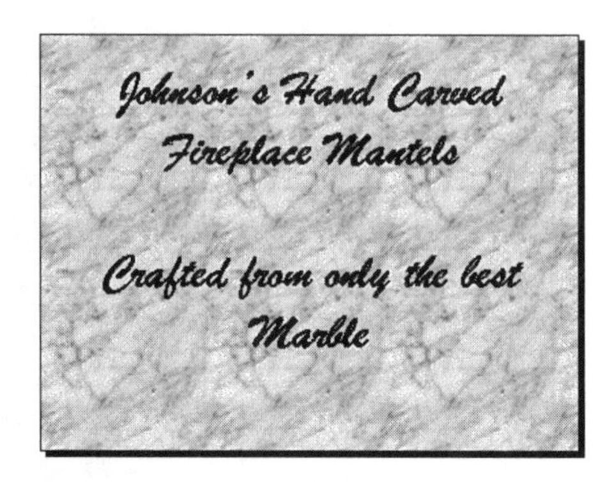

Figure 7.9.
A slide with a marble textured background.

Follow these steps to create a textured background:

1. Choose Format | Background from the menu.
2. Click Fill Effects from the Background Fill drop-down list.
3. In the Fill Effects dialog box, click the Texture tab, as shown in Figure 7.10.
4. Select an option in the Textures section; to see more choices, click the Other Texture button.
5. Click the OK button.
6. Click the Preview button to see a preview.
7. Click the Apply or Apply to All button to accept the change.

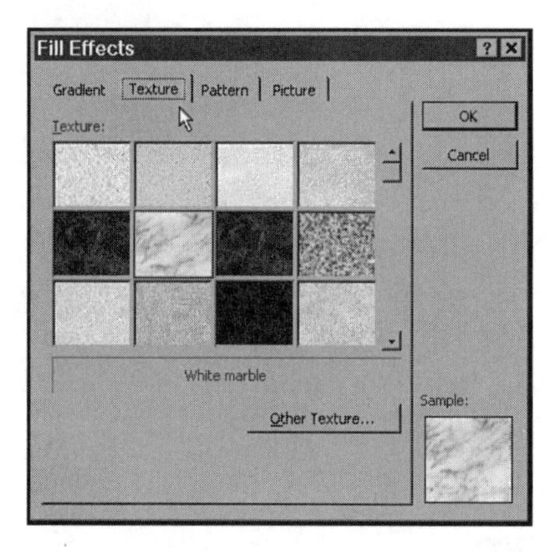

Figure 7.10.
The Texture tab of the Fill Effects dialog box.

Pattern

Patterns are repeated, two-color designs that can add an interesting visual effect to your slide. Figure 7.11 shows a slide with the brick pattern selected as the background.

Figure 7.11.
A slide with a brick-patterned background.

To select a pattern for the background, follow these steps:

1. Choose Format | Background from the menu.
2. Click Fill Effects from the Background Fill drop-down list.
3. In the Fill Effects dialog box, click the Pattern tab, as shown in Figure 7.12.
4. Select an option in the Pattern section.
5. Select a color in the Foreground drop-down list.
6. Select a color in the Background drop-down list.
7. Click the OK button.
8. Click the Preview button to see a preview.
9. Click the Apply or Apply to All button to accept the change.

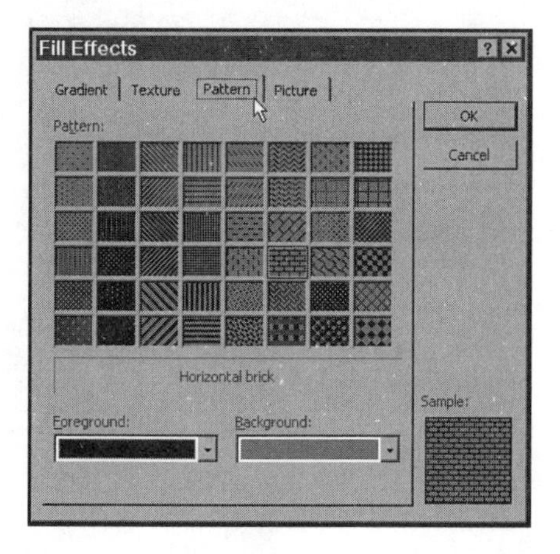

Figure 7.12.
The Pattern tab of the Fill Effects dialog box.

Picture

The picture option is a great feature to use if you have a company logo or graphic that you would like to appear in the background of your slide or presentation. Figure 7.13 shows a slide with a clip art picture as the slide background.

Figure 7.13.
A slide with a picture as the background.

To select a picture for the background, follow these steps:

1. Choose Format | Background from the menu.
2. Click Fill Effects from the Background Fill drop-down list.
3. In the Fill Effects dialog box, click the Picture tab, as shown in Figure 7.14.

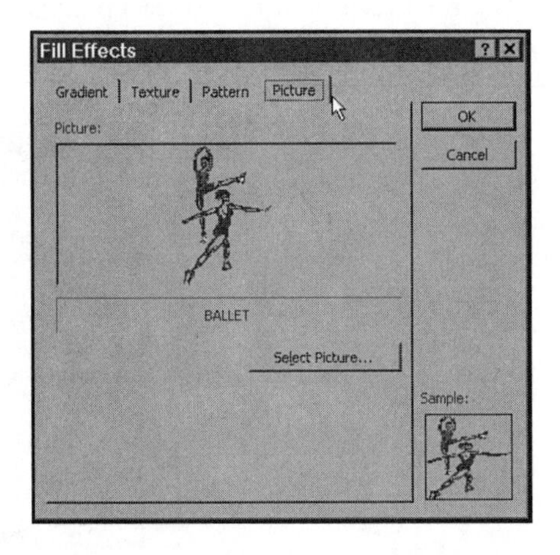

Figure 7.14.
The Picture tab of the Fill Effects dialog box.

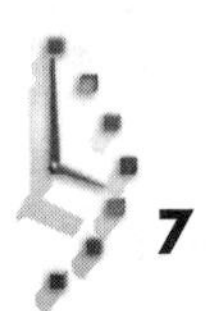

4. Click the Select Picture button.
5. Select the picture you want for the slide background from the Select Picture dialog box.
6. Click the OK button in the Select Picture dialog box to select the picture.
7. Click the OK button in the Picture tab of the Fill Effects dialog box.
8. Click the Preview button to see a preview.
9. Click the Apply or Apply to All button to accept the change.

Hiding Master Slide Items

Hour 8, "Working with the Masters," covers master slides. However, since you're learning about slide backgrounds, this is a good time to explain hiding master slide items. Basically, any object you see on a slide is probably represented on the master slide. These objects could be anything from a footer that displays the slide number to the slide's graphical components. Suppose you want an object to appear on every slide except one. That particular situation would be an opportunity to hide the master slide items, as explained in the following steps:

1. Select the slide you want to hide the master graphics on.
2. Choose Format | Background from the menu.
3. Select the "Omit background graphics from master" checkbox. (See Figure 7.15.)
4. Click the Preview button to see a preview.
5. Click the Apply or Apply to All button to accept the change.

Figure 7.15.
Hiding master slide items.

Preparing Speaker's Notes

When you create a presentation, you have done only half the job. Eventually, you have to go before an audience and speak! Showing the slides isn't enough; you need to extrapolate the information on each slide and present it to your audience. What will you say? You've created a stupendous presentation using PowerPoint, but now you need to create some notes pages for the verbal part of the presentation. Unlike other presentation programs, PowerPoint makes it very easy to create speaker's notes. You can do that by using either the Speaker Notes dialog box, as shown in Figure 7.16, or by typing directly on the slides while you're in the Notes Pages View.

To create speaker's notes using the Speaker Notes dialog box—a new feature in PowerPoint 97—follow these steps:

1. Display the slide you want to add notes to.
2. Choose View | Speaker Notes from the menu.
3. Type your speaker's notes.
4. Click the Close button when finished.

Figure 7.16.
The Speaker Notes dialog box.

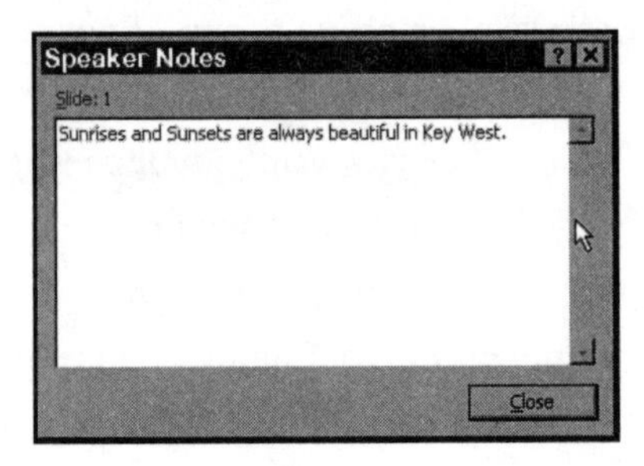

To create speaker's notes by using the Notes Pages View, follow these steps:

1. Display the slide you want to add notes to.
2. Switch to Notes Pages View by clicking the Notes Pages View button. (See Figure 7.17.)
3. Click inside the notes placeholder.
4. Type your notes.
5. Switch back to Slide View by clicking the Slide View button.

TIME SAVER

Usually the placeholder for your notes is so small that you can't see what you're typing. You might want to zoom in to 75 percent or 100 percent for a more legible display.

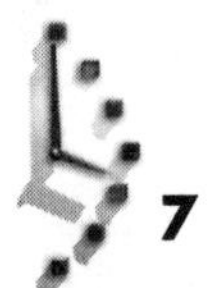

Figure 7.17.
A slide in Notes Pages View.

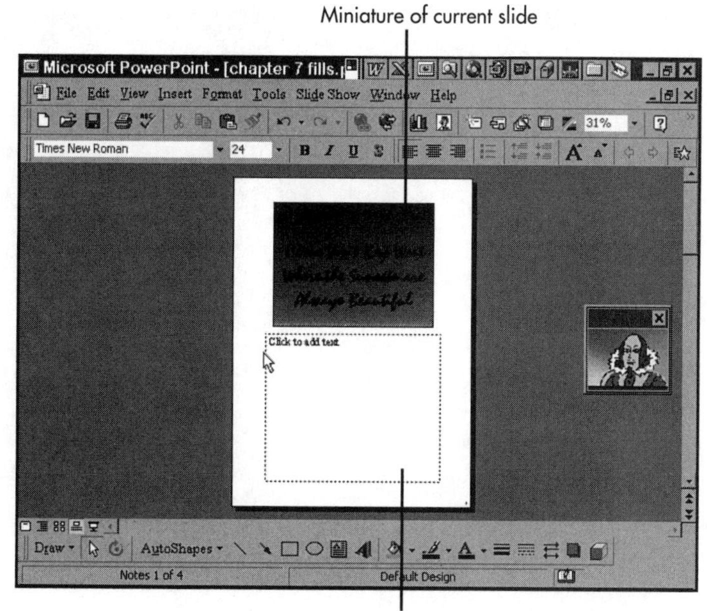

Printing Speaker's Notes

Typing your speaker's notes is only half the battle; now you need to print out those notes. Speaker's notes are shown only when you select the Notes Pages View, and you can print notes only when you select the print notes pages option from the Print dialog box. (See Figure 7.18.) To print speaker's notes, follow these steps:

1. Choose File | Print from the menu.

CAUTION

If you want to print speaker's notes, *do not* click the Print button because that prints your entire presentation, no questions asked. You need to specify that you want to print speaker's notes in the Print dialog box.

2. In the "Print what" drop-down list, select Notes Pages.
3. Change any other options needed.
4. Click the OK button.

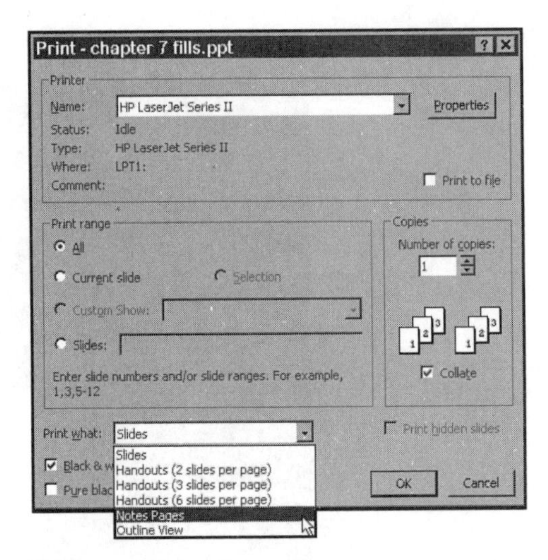

Figure 7.18.
The Print dialog box.

PowerPoint prints a miniature of each slide on the top half of the page, with the corresponding speaker's notes on the bottom half. Figure 7.19 shows a sample slide with speaker's notes.

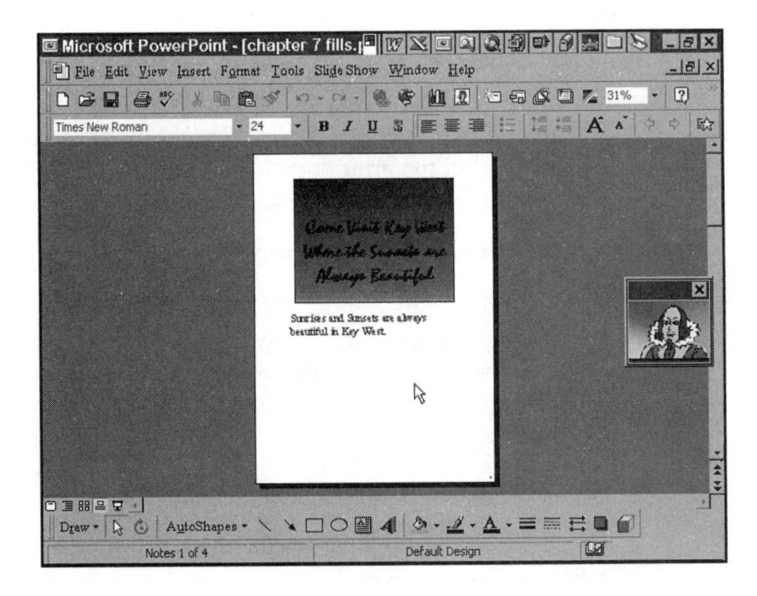

Figure 7.19.
A slide with speaker's notes.

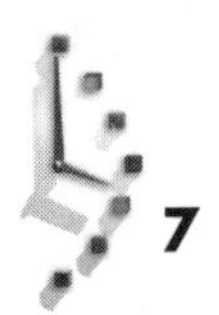

TIME SAVER

The font size has been enlarged a bit in Figure 7.19 to make the speaker's notes stand out more. You can add enhancements to the text in speaker's notes just as you would enhance text in a slide. Hour 5, "Working with PowerPoint Text Objects," covers text enhancements.

Preparing Audience Handouts

Now that you have finished your speaker's notes, wouldn't it be nice to have a printout of your presentation? You can give this printout to your audience so they can take home presentation handouts or add their own notes about the presentation's subject matter on the handouts. Well, here comes PowerPoint to the rescue. You can print audience handouts that have two, three, or six slides to a page by following these easy steps:

1. Choose File | Print from the menu.
2. In the "Print what" drop-down list, select Handouts (*x* slides per page).
3. Change any other options you want.
4. Click the OK button.

TIME SAVER

If you want your audience to have some room in which to write their own notes, use the Audience Handouts (3 slides per page) option. This option prints three slides on the left side of the page with lines on the right side for taking notes, as shown in Figure 7.20.

CAUTION

Unless you're printing color audience handouts, make sure the Black and White option in the Print dialog box is checked. Otherwise, you will have some very dark printouts. When you print audience handouts in black and white, PowerPoint prints only the basic information from each slide. All of the text, some of the graphics, and usually none of the background options are printed.

Figure 7.20.
Audience handouts with three slides per page.

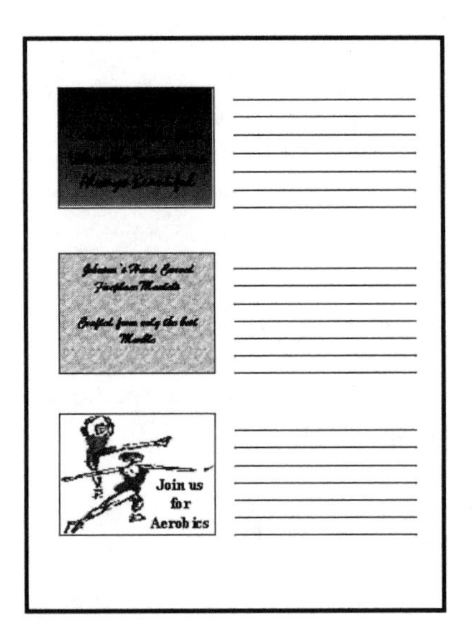

Summary

Even though PowerPoint 97 creates excellent initial presentation designs, the customization work you add will make the difference between a captivating presentation and just another canned speech. This hour has demonstrated some useful features to help you create a great presentation. Adding a custom color scheme or background can make your presentation stand out, and printing speaker's notes and handouts for your audience is an easy step that shows your preparation for the presentation. In the next hour, you learn how to use master slides to set reusable custom presentation features.

Workshop

Hi-ho, hi-ho, it's off to work we go...Well, not really when you're using PowerPoint 97. Once again, you have come to the ever-popular end-of-the-hour workshop. Be good kids and do your homework, and one day...well, you know the rest. Lots of great questions at the end, too. Have fun, be young, and play around a bit.

Test What You've Learned

1. Open the presentation file Hour 5 TWYL that you saved from Hour 5, "Working with PowerPoint Text Objects."

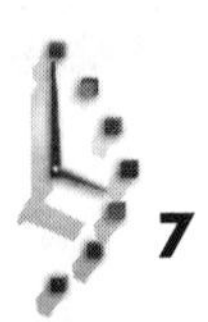

JUST A MINUTE

If you're "clicking around" this book and didn't do the "Test What You've Learned" section for Hour 5, just start a new presentation using the AutoContent Wizard. Answer the questions, and save the file as `Hour 5 TWYL`.

2. Change the color scheme of the presentation to the black-and-white standard scheme.
3. Create a custom color scheme with the options shown in Table 7.2.

Table 7.2. The TWYL custom color scheme.

Option	Color
Background	Green
Text and Lines	Aqua
Shadows	Blue
Title Text	Purple
Fills	Pink
Accent	Red
Accent and hyperlink	Orange
Accent and followed hyperlink	Yellow

4. Change the background color to a darker green.
5. Change the background to a shaded (gradient) background.
6. Hide the master items for one slide.
7. Create and print speaker's notes.
8. Print audience handouts with three slides per page.
9. Save the presentation as `Hour 7 TWYL`.
10. Close the presentation.

Q&A

Q I want to change the color scheme for several (but not all) of the slides in my presentation. Is there a quick way to do this without having to change the color scheme one slide at a time?

A Yes. You need to switch to Slide Sorter View and select all the slides you want to change. Hold the Shift key down while you click on each slide. Then simply choose Format | Color Scheme from the menu, make your changes, and click the Apply button to apply the changes to only those slides that have been selected.

Q I love the gradient shading that PowerPoint has, but I want to use a combination of the available options. How can I do this?

A You can't do this using the background option. PowerPoint allows you to choose only one shading option per object. You can "trick" PowerPoint, however, and get the effect you want by using drawing objects. If you use this trick, make sure your shapes have no lines. I usually group my shapes and send them to the back, also. Refer to Hours 12, "Drawing Shapes in PowerPoint," and 13, "Bringing Drawing Objects Together," for more information on working with drawing objects.

Q I have a graphic that would look great as a textured background. Can I use it?

A Sure. Just click the Other Texture button in the Fill Effects dialog box, and then select the graphics file. Any graphic that displays well as a repeated image can be used as a texture. You can either create your own by using any graphics program or use a graphic created by some other source.

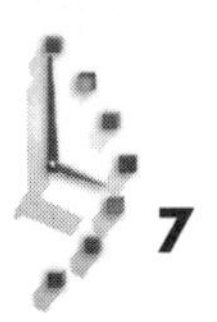

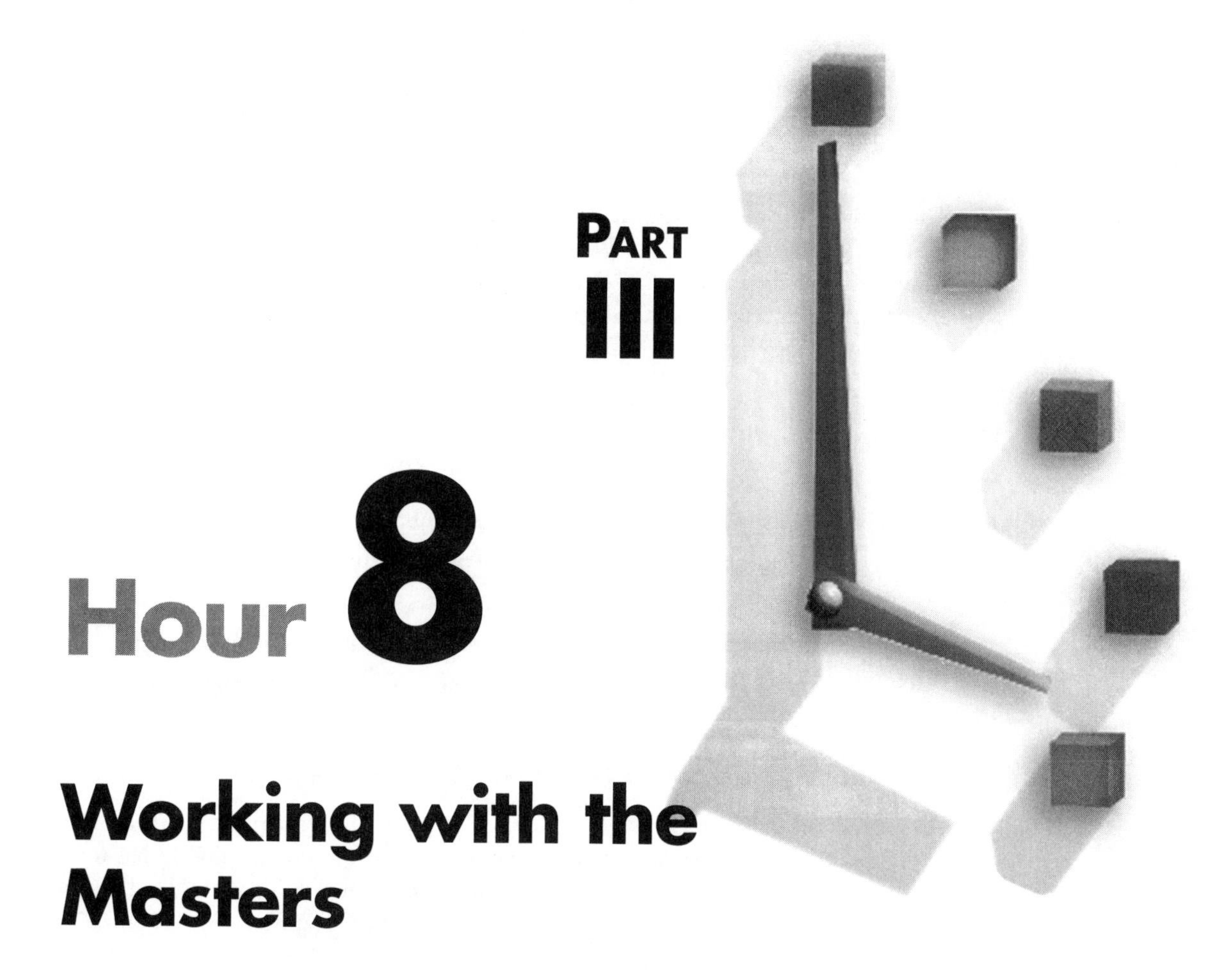

Part III

Hour 8

Working with the Masters

PowerPoint 97 has four "hidden" slides that control the overall look and feel of your presentation. These slides are called the *masters*—the Slide Master, Title Master, Notes Master, and Handout Master. You will probably find yourself working with the Slide Master and Title Master most often. These master slides control all the characteristics of your presentation and make it easier for you to place common elements for each slide. For example, if you want your company logo to appear on every slide in the same location, there's no need to insert the logo individually on the slides. You can simply place the logo on the Slide (and Title) Master, and it will automatically appear on every slide of your presentation.

If you want a customized, consistent look to your presentation, it's best to make any modifications you want in the Slide or Title Master, rather than slide by slide. Using the masters is a much more efficient way to create that special look. Also, when Bob tells you to make one little change, you have to change just the master, not 57 slides! (Yes, you *will* get Friday off.)

Any changes you make to the Slide Master affect every slide in your presentation, unless you make changes to individual slides. When you make changes to individual slides, those changes override the Slide Master defaults. Therefore, you're not stuck with the default Slide Master items. You can override the Slide Master at any time by either changing the slide objects or by selecting the "Omit background graphics from the master" checkbox in the Background dialog box, which was discussed in Hour 7, "Customizing the Presentation."

In this hour, you will learn how to do the following:

- View the four types of masters
- Set the default font for your presentation titles, subtitles, and body text
- Change the default bullet style for the entire presentation
- Add a header, footer, or page numbers to your presentation
- Add your company logo to your presentation so that it appears on every slide
- Save a presentation as a template so you can reuse the same formatting options

The Four Types of Masters

A *master* is a special slide that allows you to define all the formatting attributes and add any common graphical objects that will appear in your presentation. PowerPoint 97 has four masters, described in Table 8.1. Earlier versions of PowerPoint didn't have a Handout or Notes Master. These masters are a new (and much appreciated) feature of PowerPoint 97.

Table 8.1. The masters.

Title	Description
Slide Master	Controls most of the slide attributes.
Title Master	Controls attributes for the title slide.
Handout Master	Formats audience handouts.
Notes Master	Formats the speaker notes.

If you want to apply a particular slide format, or have pictures and text that should appear on every slide, add the attributes to the Slide Master. You can also make the same modifications for the title slide, notes pages, or audience handouts by editing the corresponding master.

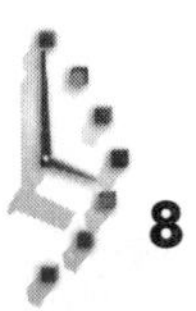

JUST A MINUTE

If you have made changes on individual slides, any changes made in the master won't seem to have taken effect. When customizing a presentation, you should first make changes to the Slide Master. If more specific changes are necessary, change the individual slides. If you have previously made changes to a particular slide and want to switch back to the Slide Master defaults, follow these steps:

1. Click the Slide Layout button on the standard toolbar.
2. Click the Reapply button.

JUST A MINUTE

Refer to Hour 4, "Working with Slides," for more information on reapplying the Slide Layout.

CAUTION

Reapplying the layout doesn't bring back background graphical items that have been omitted. To redisplay the background graphics, choose Format | Background from the menu, and uncheck the "Omit background graphics from the master" checkbox.

Slide Master

Think of the Slide Master as Elvis, the King of all the masters. The Slide Master controls every slide of your presentation except for the title slide. The Slide Master controls how the text is formatted, where it's positioned, what bullet characters are used, the color scheme, and what graphical items appear on every slide in your presentation. Figure 8.1 shows the Slide Master screen. To display the Slide Master, you have two choices:

- Choose View | Master | Slide Master from the menu.

  or

- Hold down the Shift key and click the Slide View button at the lower-left area of the screen.

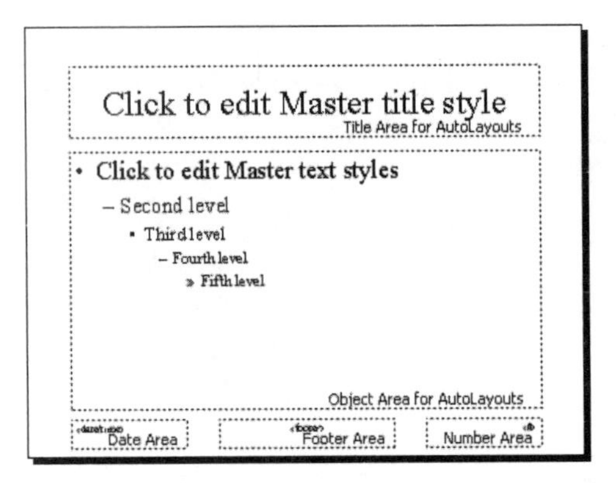

Figure 8.1.
The Slide Master for a blank presentation.

When you make changes to the Slide Master, you shouldn't be concerned with the specific text information. You're more concerned with formatting the text. The Slide Master looks almost identical to a regular bullet slide, but it *is* different. First, notice that the Slide Master has five placeholders, listed in Table 8.2.

Table 8.2. Slide Master placeholders.

Placeholder	Description
Title area	Used to format, position, and size the title text for all slides. You can change the font type, size, color, and any other effects you want.
Object area	Used to format, position, and size the body text for all slides. You can change the font attributes, just as with the title, and change the bullet style.
Date area	Used to add, position, resize, and format a date on every slide in the presentation.
Number area	Used to add, position, resize, and format automatic slide numbering.
Footer area	Used to add, position, resize, and format footer text for every slide in your presentation.

Title Master

The Title Master allows you to control pretty much the same attributes as the Slide Master, but only for a title slide (usually there's only one title slide in a presentation). The Title Master controls how the title and subtitle text on a slide are formatted and positioned. If you want a graphical item to appear on the title slide, you should place it on the Title Master in addition to the Slide Master. Figure 8.2 shows the Title Master, which you open by choosing View | Master | Title Master from the menu.

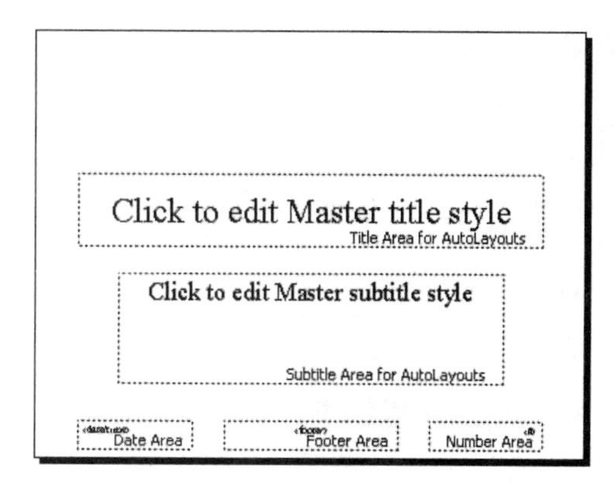

Figure 8.2.
The Title Master for a blank presentation.

If the Title Master option isn't available from the menu, you must first view the Slide Master, and then create the Title Master. Choose Insert | New Title Master from the menu or click the Insert New Title Master button on the standard toolbar to create the Title Master.

JUST A MINUTE

When you're in normal Slide View, the Insert New Title Master button is usually the New Slide button.

You might want to portray the presentation of the Title Master differently than the Slide Master so that you add some emphasis to your presentation's title slide.

TIME SAVER

Start a few new presentations with the presentation design templates. You will notice that the title slide has a slightly different look than the other slides do, but the presentation is still consistent with the overall theme of the presentation design.

The Title Master, just like the Slide Master, has five placeholders, described in Table 8.3.

Table 8.3. Title Master placeholders.

Placeholder	Description
Title area	Used to format, position, and size the title text of the title slide. You can change the font type, size, color, and any other effects you want.
Subtitle area	Used to format, position, and size the subtitle text of the title slide. You can change the font attributes, just as with the title.

continues

Table 8.3. continued

Placeholder	Description
Date area	Used to add, position, resize, and format a date for the title slide.
Number area	Used to add, position, resize, and format automatic slide numbering for the title slide.
Footer area	Used to add, position, resize, and format footer text for the title slide.

Handout Master

The Handout Master is used to format your audience handouts. Similar to the Slide and Title Masters, you can add graphical and text objects to the Handout Master, shown in Figure 8.3. The Handout Master is associated with a corresponding handout master toolbar that allows you to choose from one of four views: outline, or two, three, or six slides per page. To display the Handout Master, you have two choices:

- Choose View | Master | Handout Master from the menu.

  or

- Hold down the Shift key and click either the Outline View button or the Slide Sorter View button at the lower-left area of the screen.

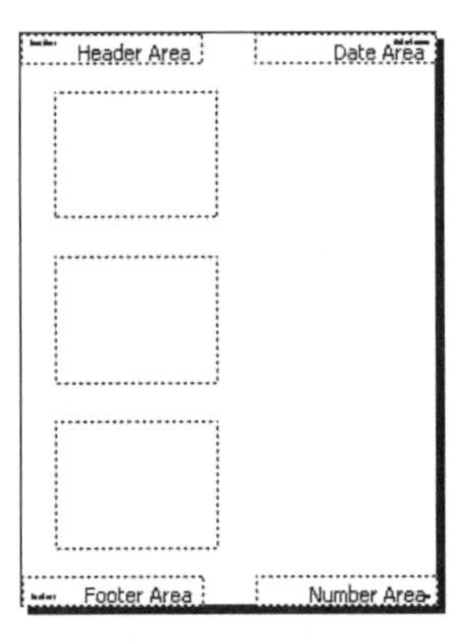

Figure 8.3.
The Handout Master for a blank presentation.

Just a Minute

If the handout master toolbar isn't automatically displayed, choose View | Toolbars | Handout Master from the menu.

The Handout Master has four small placeholders, two at the top and two at the bottom of the page. Additionally, you can have one, two, three, or six placeholders displayed in the middle of the page, depending on the view selected. Table 8.4 covers these placeholders.

Table 8.4. Handout Master placeholders.

Placeholder	Description
Header area	Used to add, position, resize, and format text that should appear on the top of every page of the handouts.
Date area	Used to add, position, resize, and format a date on every page of the handouts.
Footer area	Used to add, position, resize, and format text that should appear at the bottom of every page of the handouts.
Number area	Used to add, position, resize, and format automatic page numbering.
Slide or Outline placeholders	Used to show the positioning of the slides or outline in the handouts. These placeholders can't be moved or resized.

Notes Master

The Notes Master is used to format the presentation of the speaker's note pages. As always, you can add graphical items and text to the Notes Master. The Notes Master also allows you to resize the slide area. To display the Notes Master, you have two choices:

- Choose View | Master | Notes Master from the menu.

  or

- Hold down the Shift key and click the Notes Pages View button.

Figure 8.4. displays the Notes Master.

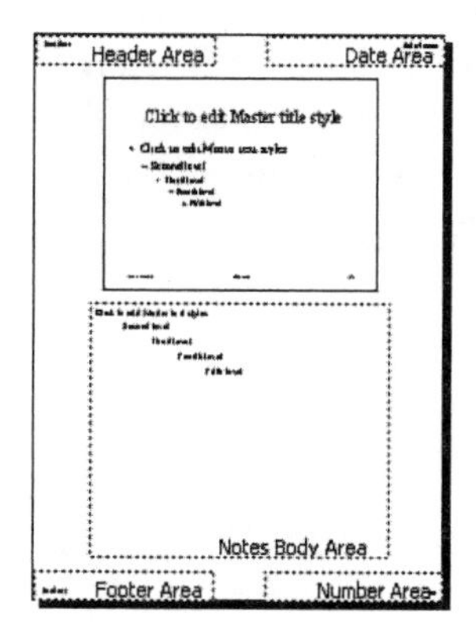

Figure 8.4.
The Notes Master for a blank presentation.

The Notes Master should have six placeholders; they are described in Table 8.5. Two placeholders are located at the top, two at the bottom of the page, and two larger placeholders are in the middle of the page.

Table 8.5. Notes Master placeholders.

Placeholder	Description
Header area	Used to add, position, resize, and format text that should appear on the top of every page in the speaker notes.
Date area	Used to add, position, resize, and format a date on every page of speaker notes.
Footer area	Used to add, position, resize, and format text that should appear at the bottom of every page in speaker notes.
Number area	Used to add, position, resize, and format automatic page numbering for speaker notes.
Slide placeholder	Used to show the positioning of the corresponding slide. This image can be resized or moved.
Notes Body area	Used to format, position, and resize the body text in the speaker's notes. You can change the font type, size, color, and other attributes.

Setting a Default Font

You can change the mood of your entire presentation by simply changing the font face. The font can be changed for the title, subtitle, or body text of your entire presentation by using the Slide and Title Master. Select a font and font attributes that are appropriate for your presentation, making sure to keep your audience in mind. For example, a financial presentation to the board of directors of Mary Kay Cosmetics could use a pretty script font in pink on the title slide. The other slides in the presentation could use a more conservative font in the same color. Figures 8.5 and 8.6 show the title slide and first slide for this fictitious board meeting.

Figure 8.5.
The title slide for the Mary Kay Cosmetics financial presentation.

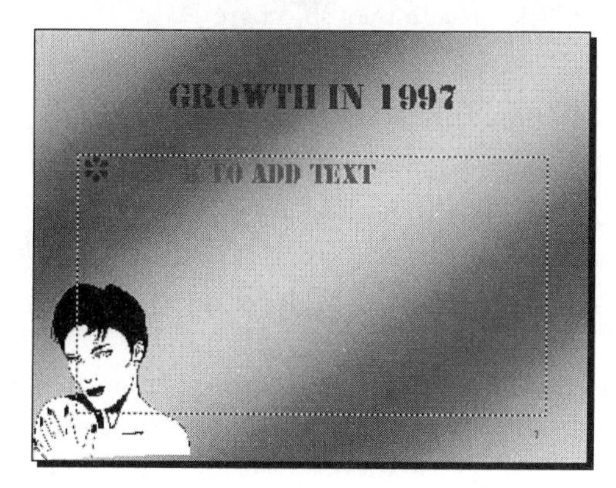

Figure 8.6.
The first slide for the Mary Kay Cosmetics financial presentation.

To set a default font for the title or subtitle, follow these steps:

1. View the Slide Master by choosing View | Master | Slide Master or Title Master from the menu.
2. Click once on the Title or Subtitle area.
3. Choose Format | Font from the menu.
4. Make any font changes you want.
5. Click the OK button.

Follow these steps to set a default font for all the body text:

1. View the Slide Master by choosing View | Master | Slide Master from the menu.
2. Click once on the Object area.
3. Click a second time on the placeholder border to select the entire object.
4. Choose Format | Font from the menu.
5. Make any font changes you want.

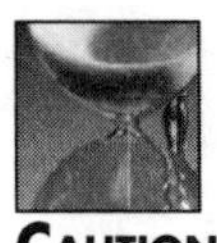

CAUTION

If the font size contains a plus sign, don't set the size setting to an exact number. Setting an exact number indicates that all the bullet-level text will be displayed in the same size. Instead, use the Increase Font Size or Decrease Font Size buttons on the standard toolbar to change the font size.

6. Click the OK button.

Follow these steps to set a default font for individual bullet levels:

1. View the Slide Master by choosing View | Master | Slide Master from the menu.
2. Click once on the Object area.
3. Click a second time on the level you want to change.
4. Choose Format | Font from the menu.
5. Make any font changes.
6. Click the OK button.

Changing Bullet Styles

You can add some life to your presentation by selecting bullets that fit the theme of the presentation. This feature is one of the easiest ways to customize and coordinate the entire look of the presentation, especially when you're using one of the presentation design templates. Changing the bullet style to reflect the overall theme of the presentation can add that special touch. Your audience will think that you have put hours into designing the presentation. Figure 8.7 shows the fictitious Mary Kay Cosmetics financial presentation with custom bullets.

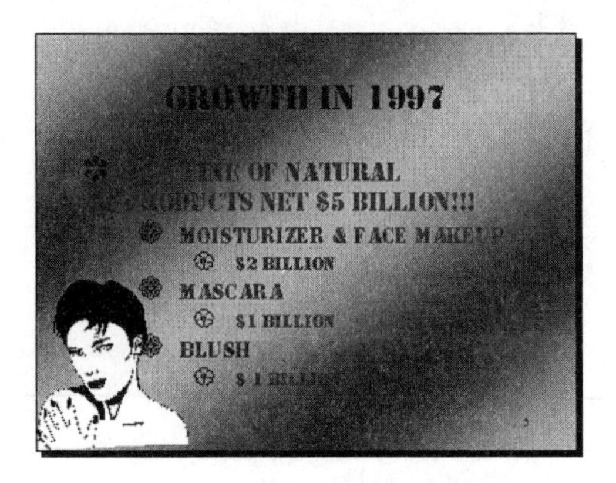

Figure 8.7.
The Mary Kay Cosmetics presentation with custom bullets.

To change the default bullet style for the entire presentation, follow these instructions:

1. View the Slide Master by choosing View | Master | Slide Master from the menu.
2. Click once on the Object area.
3. Click a second time on the bullet level you want to change.
4. Choose Format | Bullet from the menu.
5. Select a font from the "Bullets from" drop-down list.
6. Select a color for the bullet from the Color drop-down list.
7. Set the size of the bullet in the Size box.
8. Click a symbol from the symbol grid.

TIME SAVER

The two most popular fonts are Monotype Sorts and Wingdings. Click on the first symbol in the grid (the symbol "pops up" so you can see it better) and use the arrow keys on the keyboard to see each symbol. If you can't find just the right symbol, try a different font.

9. Click the OK button.

Headers and Footers

If you have ever used a word processing program, you know that the header and footer is any piece of information you want to appear at the top or bottom of every page in your document. Examples of header or footer information are page numbers, dates, or company addresses. In PowerPoint, headers and footers work pretty much the same way. However, PowerPoint has predesigned areas for the date and slide number, with a separate area designed for extra header or footer information. To add the date, the slide number, or a footer to the slides in your presentation, follow these steps:

1. Choose View | Header and Footer from the menu.
2. Select the Slide tab, shown in Figure 8.8.
3. Select the items you want displayed on your slides.
4. Type in text for the footer, if you like.
5. Click the OK button.

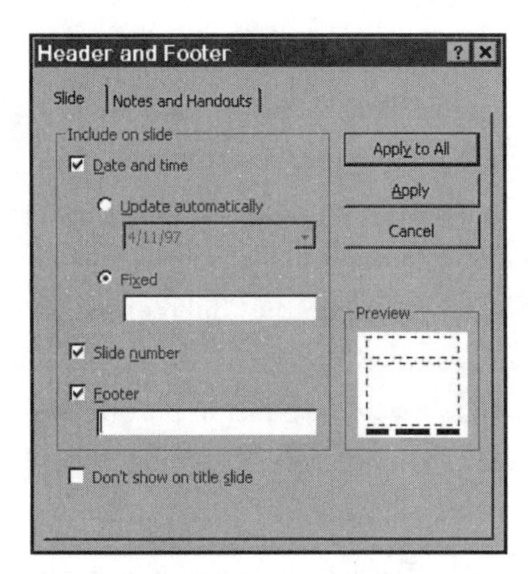

Figure 8.8.
The Slide tab of the Header and Footer dialog box.

You can also choose to add the same information in your speaker's notes or audience handouts. To add the date, the slide number, a header, or a footer to your audience handouts or notes pages, follow these steps:

1. Choose View | Header and Footer from the menu.
2. Select the Notes and Handouts tab, shown in Figure 8.9.
3. Select the items you want displayed on your notes and handouts.
4. Type in text for the header and/or footer, if you want.
5. Click the OK button.

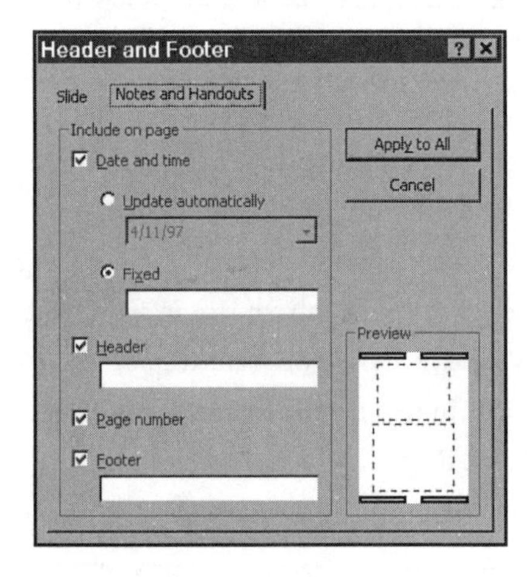

Figure 8.9.
The Notes and Handouts tab of the Header and Footer dialog box.

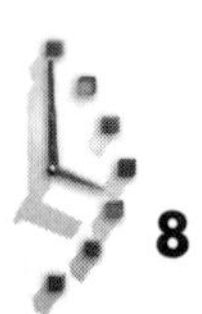

8

Adding a Company Logo to the Master

You can very easily add your company logo to every slide in the presentation, the handouts, or your speaker's notes. Before you can add your company logo, you do need to have the logo already created and saved as a graphic on your system. In Figure 8.10, you can see the company logo added to the master for the fictitious Mary Kay Cosmetics financial report.

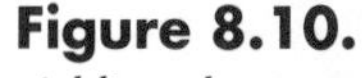

Figure 8.10.
Adding the company logo to the Mary Kay Cosmetics financial report.

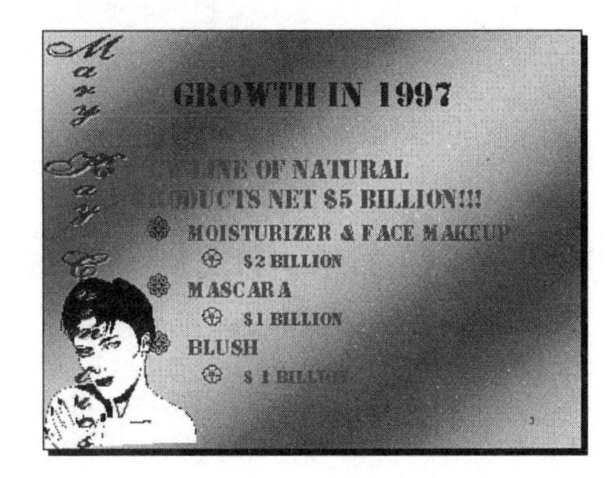

To add your company logo (or any other graphic) to the master, follow these steps:

1. Choose View | Master | Slide Master or Title Master from the menu.
2. Choose Insert | Picture | From File from the menu.
3. Select the drive and folder that contains your company logo.
4. Select the graphics file that has the company logo.
5. Click the Insert button.
6. Position and resize the graphic as necessary.
7. Switch to Slide View.

Time Saver

You need to place the logo on both the Title and Slide Master. Place the logo in a different place on the Title Master to give your presentation a more professional look. (See Figure 8.11.)

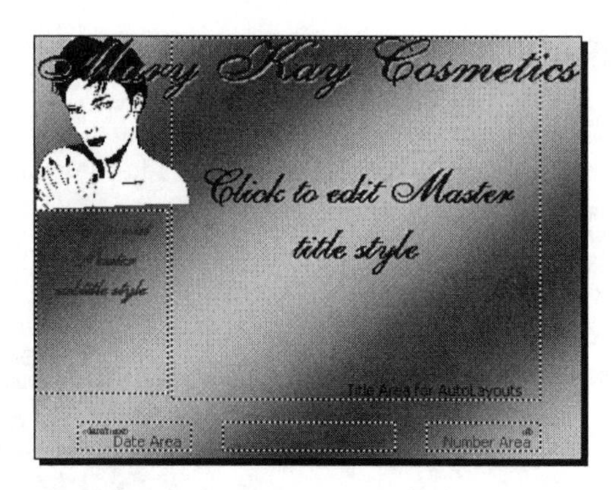

Figure 8.11.
A title slide with the logo placed at the top.

Saving a Presentation as a Template

In this hour, you have seen how to fine-tune the format of the Mary Kay financial presentation by choosing the best font and bullet styles, moving the text objects to the perfect position, and adding the company logo. Doing all this was fairly painless using the Slide and Title Masters, but why do all that work again for the next presentation if you don't have to? Guess what? With PowerPoint 97, you don't have to duplicate all your hard work. So not only will you get to take this Friday off, but maybe next Friday as well! What you need to do is save your presentation as a template.

A *template* is a presentation that has been saved in a special format so that you won't accidentally delete the original file.

A PowerPoint template usually has preformatted text, background graphics, and color schemes. You can also include macros, menu and key assignments, and custom toolbars to a template, if you like. Although you can create a template from scratch, the easiest way by far to create a custom template is to use an existing presentation that you have modified to suit your needs. To save an existing presentation as a template, follow these steps:

1. Open the existing presentation, or create a new presentation based on a presentation design.
2. Make any other changes you want.
3. Delete any extra text or slides you don't need in every presentation.

Time Saver

Since a template is usually just the overall design of the presentation, not the actual slides themselves, you probably won't need any slides in your presentation except for the first one. To have a complete template, you should make all your changes in the Slide or Title Master.

4. Choose File | Save As from the menu.
5. Type a name for your template.
6. In the "Save as type" drop-down list, select Presentation templates.
7. Click the Save button.

Summary

If you're modifying a global presentation attribute, use one of the four master slides, which lets you control all the characteristics of the presentation and offers an easy way to give a consistent look to the presentation slides. Modifications to the masters can change the default font, bullet styles, headers, footers, and background graphics for your slides. Changes to the Slide Master, for example, affect every slide in your presentation. After you have taken the time to develop a great presentation template, you can even save the template and reuse the settings later. In the next hour, you learn how to wrap up the presentation and polish your delivery.

Workshop

Here we go—the end-of-the-hour workshop again. You get a chance to test what you've learned this hour and change the Slide Master. Once again, don't forget to read the questions and answers at the end of the section.

Test What You've Learned

1. Start a new presentation by using the AutoContent Wizard. Take note of the font and bullet styles used throughout the presentation.
2. View the Slide, Title, Handout, and Notes Master for the presentation.
3. Change the font style in the Slide and Title Master (make the change dramatic so you notice the difference).
4. Move the Title placeholder on the Title Master to a different location.

TIME SAVER

You move a placeholder in a master the same way you move any other text object in Slide View.

5. Take a look at the presentation and notice the change.
6. Change the bullet style of the first and second levels on the Slide Master.
7. Add your company logo or other graphic to the Slide, Title, Handout, and Notes Masters.
8. Add the date and slide number to the Slide, Handout, and Notes Masters.
9. Save the presentation as `Hour 8 TWYL`.
10. Save the presentation again as a template.
11. Close the presentation.

Q&A

Q I have several slides that I made changes to, and now I want them to follow the master slide. Can I reapply the master to all of them at the same time?

A You can always switch to Slide Sorter View, select all the slides, and reapply the master layout. This technique works perfectly if all the slides follow the same layout (for example, if all the slides in your presentation use the bullet slide layout). If they follow different layouts, you should select only the slides that follow the same layout and reapply the master layout. The process should be repeated for each set of slides. If your presentation slides follow different layouts, and you globally reapply a layout to all the slides in a presentation, you could end up with a big mess.

Q I accidentally deleted the Title placeholder in the Slide Master. How do I get it back?

A Since you can't reapply the master layout to the master, the Slide Master has a special option for adding missing placeholders to any master. To add a placeholder, just follow these steps:

1. Choose Format | Master Layout from the menu or click the Master Layout button on the standard toolbar.
2. In the Master Layout dialog box, click the checkbox for the placeholder you're missing.
3. Click the OK button.

Q How can I get the word *Slide* to appear in front of the automatic slide numbering in my slides?

A First, add slide numbering as explained in this chapter. Then, follow these steps in the Slide Master:

1. Click once on the Number placeholder.
2. Zoom to 75 percent or 100 percent.

3. Click once in front of the <#> symbol.
4. Type the word `Slide`, followed by a space.
5. Zoom back to Fit.
6. Switch to Slide View.

You should now have the word *Slide* in front of the slide number.

PART

III

Hour 9

Basics of Slide Shows

Now that you have created and edited several presentations, you're finally ready to show off all your hard work. This hour and the next covers everything you need to know about running a slide show. In this hour, you will learn how to do the following:

- View the presentation
- Make temporary annotations on the presentation
- Set slide timings, either custom or rehearsed
- Hide a slide
- Create a summary slide

After learning these skills, you'll be ready to give that important speech.

Viewing the Presentation

Viewing your presentation is the easy part, but deciding which option to use can be a bit more difficult. Although there are several ways to view a presentation, you'll learn just two options in this hour:

- Starting the slide show in PowerPoint
- Saving a presentation so that it always starts as a slide show

Hour 10, "Adding Pizzazz to a Slide Show," explains setting up the slide show to run as a self-running presentation at a kiosk.

Starting the Slide Show in PowerPoint

During the initial presentation design, you need to start and view your presentation in PowerPoint. Doing so gives you the opportunity to fine-tune your presentation and add timings, transitions, and any other finishing touches to your show. To start a slide show in PowerPoint, you have four main options:

- Choosing View | Slide Show from the menu
- Choosing Slide Show | View Show from the menu
- Choosing Slide Show | Rehearse Timings from the menu
- Clicking the Slide Show View button

Each option gives you basically the same result. You can view the entire presentation from start to finish, clicking the mouse to advance to the next slide. The Rehearse Timings option has the only difference from the other options. When you choose Slide Show | Rehearse Timings from the menu, PowerPoint displays the presentation starting from the first slide, recording the time you spend on each slide before you advance the display to the next slide. Figure 9.1 demonstrates PowerPoint during a rehearsal.

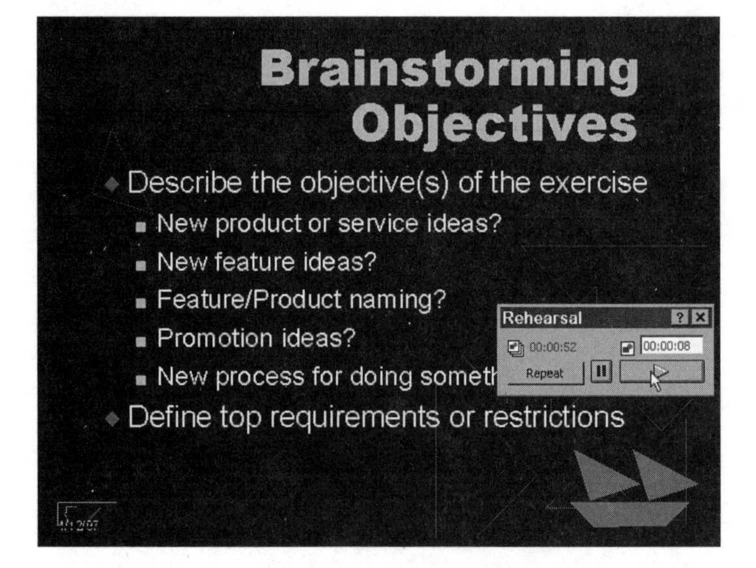

Figure 9.1.
Viewing the slide show while rehearsing timings.

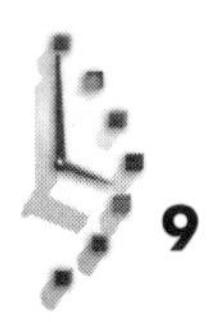

CAUTION

When you click the Slide Show View button, you usually start the slide show from the currently active slide. If you want to start the presentation from the beginning, select the first slide before going into Slide Show View.

CAUTION

If you find that you're not viewing the presentation in a linear fashion from slide one to the end, check out the Slide Show | Set Up Show options. When you view a slide show, PowerPoint follows the slide order that has been set in this dialog box.

JUST A MINUTE

With older versions of PowerPoint, you could view a presentation by either choosing View | Slide Show from the menu or clicking the Slide Show View button. When you chose the menu option, you were prompted to rehearse new timings, if you wanted. In PowerPoint 97, you choose Slide Show | Rehearse Timings from the menu to perform the same action.

TIME SAVER

If you're viewing a presentation and want to stop before you reach the end, press the Esc key on your keyboard. The slide show is then terminated.

Saving a Presentation to Start as a Slide Show

After you have finished adding all the custom touches to your presentation, you might want to save it as a self-running presentation. Every time you open the presentation file, the show will run. This action saves you some time and effort, and your audience won't have to see the PowerPoint 97 screen before the actual show. To save a presentation as a slide show, follow these steps:

1. Make sure the presentation is open and onscreen.
2. Choose File | Save As from the menu.
3. In the "File name" box, type a name for your presentation, if necessary.
4. In the "Save as type" drop-down list, select PowerPoint Show. (See Figure 9.2.)
5. Click the Save button.

Now every time you open the file, it will start the show.

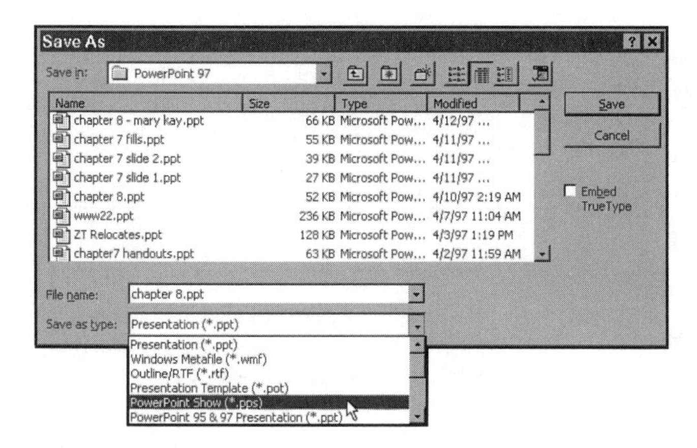

Figure 9.2.
The Save As dialog box for a PowerPoint Show.

JUST A MINUTE

When you save a presentation as a show, PowerPoint saves the file with a .PPS extension. You might notice in the Open dialog box that the icons for a show (.PPS) and a regular presentation (.PPT) are a little different.

TIME SAVER

You can save a presentation as a show, and then put a shortcut to the show on your Windows 95 desktop, which makes the show only a click away. To create a shortcut on your desktop, follow these steps:

1. Find the file by using My Computer.
2. Right-click on the file and drag it to your desktop.
3. Release the mouse button and select Create Shortcut(s) Here, as shown in Figure 9.3.
4. To run the show, simply right-click the icon and choose Show from the pop-up menu.

Setting and Using the Slide Show Settings

When you view a slide show, you have several options for its display, most of which are available in the Set Up Show dialog box. (See Figure 9.4.) From this dialog box, you can choose whether the show is going to be presented by a speaker, browsed by an individual, or run at a kiosk. You can also determine which slides or custom shows to display, how the slides

should advance, and the default pen color (explained in the following section, "Using the Pen"). To change any show settings, follow these steps:

1. Choose Slide Show | Set Up Show from the menu.
2. Change any options needed.
3. Click the OK button.

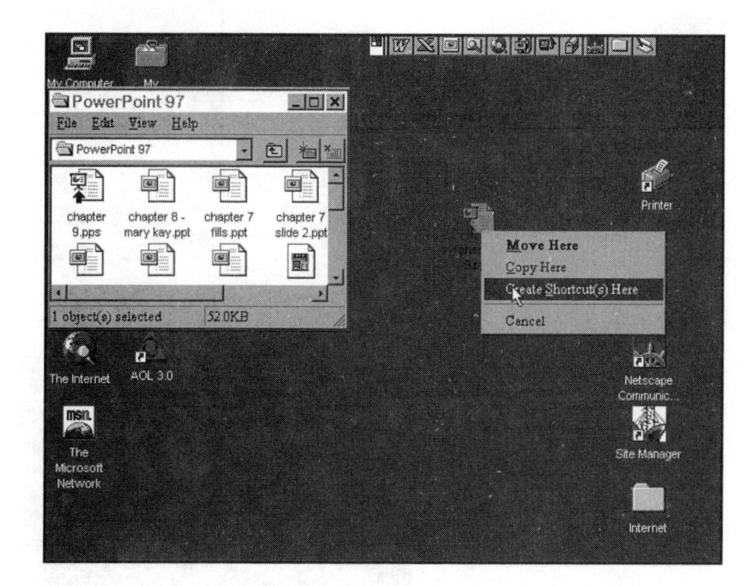

Figure 9.3.
Creating a shortcut on the desktop.

Time Saver

If you plan on annotating a slide show, it's usually best to manually advance each slide.

Using the Pen

When you're viewing a presentation, you have the ability to temporarily annotate each slide by turning your mouse pointer into a pen, as shown in Figure 9.5. This is a great feature when you have audience participation. To display the pen during a slide show, select one of the following options:

- Press Ctrl+P.

  or

- Right-click and select Pen from the menu.

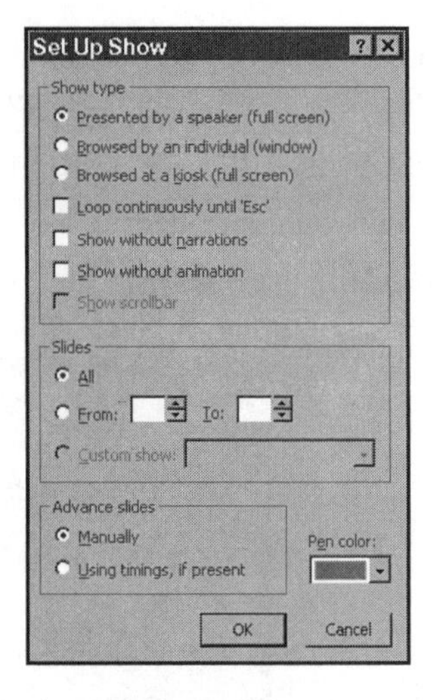

Figure 9.4.
The Set Up Show dialog box.

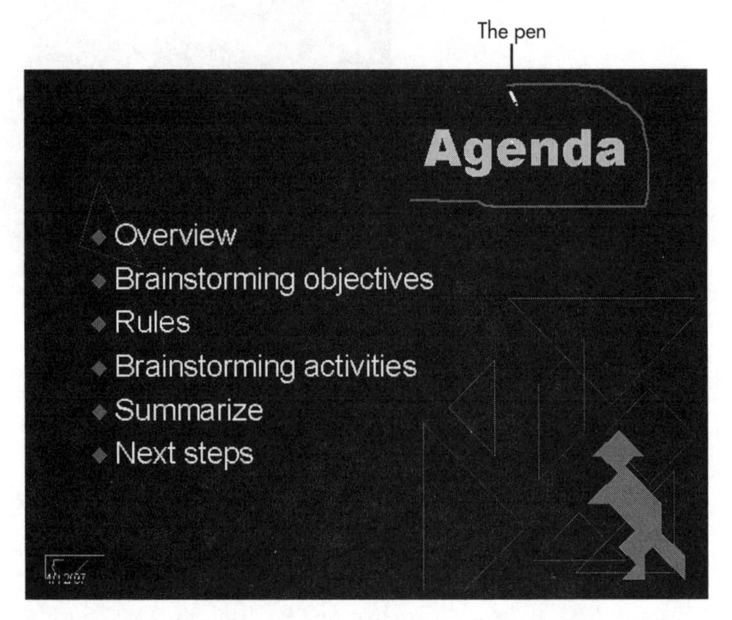

Figure 9.5.
The pen has been turned on for easy annotation of the slide.

To use the pen, simply hold down the left mouse button and handwrite or draw annotations by moving the mouse. The annotations you make during the slide show aren't permanent, so they disappear for the next show.

It's a good idea to get some practice using the pen before the actual slide show. Sometimes your annotations can end up as illegible handwriting. Typically, the pen is used to underline or emphasize a specific point during our presentation. Another neat trick is to hold down the Shift key while you're drawing lines. This keeps your lines straight, as shown in Figure 9.6.

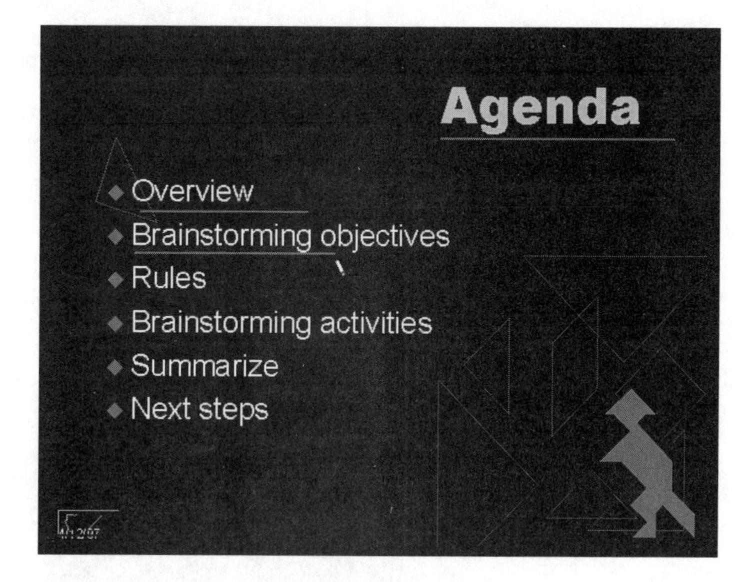

Figure 9.6.
Drawing straight lines.

To change the pen back to the pointer arrow, use one of these methods:

- Press Ctrl+A.

  or

- Right-click and select Pen from the menu.

Change the Pen Color

You can change the color of the pen before you actually run the slide show or during a slide show. To change the pen color before running the show, use the Set Up Show dialog box, as shown in Figure 9.7. To change the pen color, follow these steps:

1. Choose Slide Show|Set Up Show from the menu.
2. Select a new color for the pen from the "Pen color" drop-down list.
3. Click the OK button.

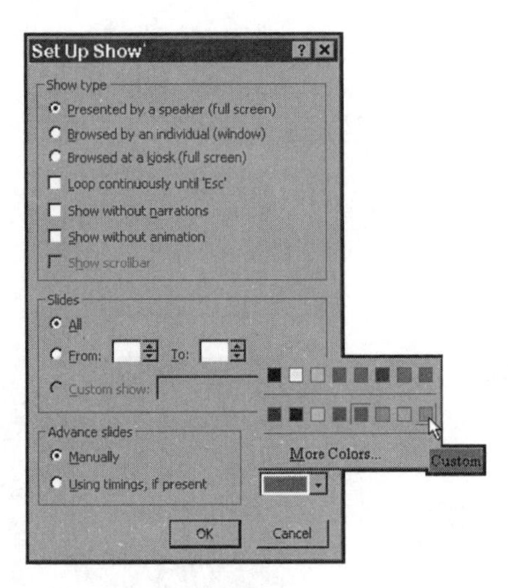

Figure 9.7.
Changing the pen color.

During the slide show, you might want to change the pen color to differentiate commands. To change the pen color during a show, use the following steps:

1. Right-click and choose Pointer Options | Pen Color.
2. Select a new color, as shown in Figure 9.8.

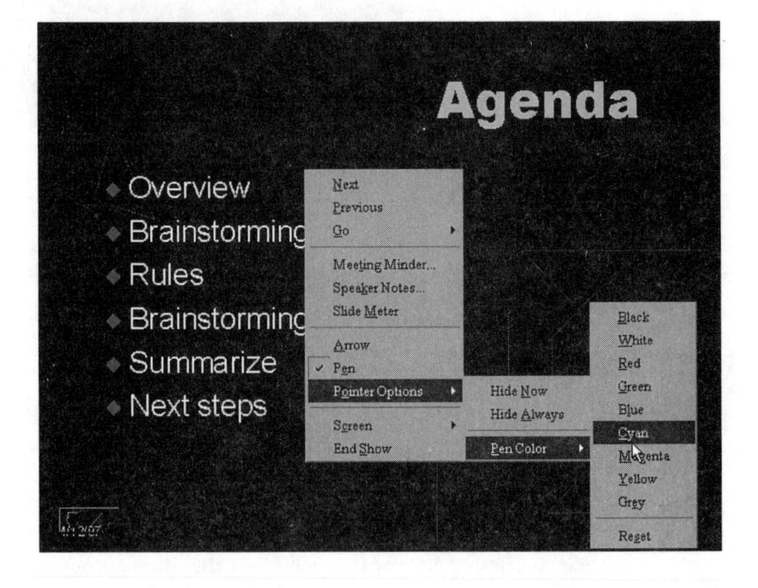

Figure 9.8.
Changing the pen color during a presentation.

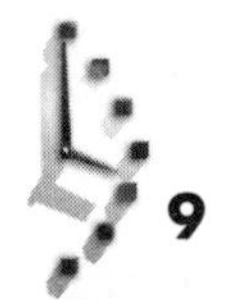

You can always set the pen color back to the original color, if you want. To reset the pen color during a slide show, use these two steps:

1. Right-click on the slide.
2. Choose Pointer Options | Pen Color | Reset.

Erase Annotations

Any annotations made on a slide usually automatically disappear once you have advanced to the next slide. However, it might be necessary to delete the annotations before advancing to the next slide. Follow these steps to erase the annotations on a slide during a slide show:

- Press the E key.

  or

- Right-click and choose Screen | Erase Pen.

Slide Sorter View

When you're adding all the finishing touches to your slide show, you'll find that the Slide Sorter View is the most useful. Slide Sorter View allows you to view several slides simultaneously, as shown in Figures 9.9 and 9.10. You can move slides around, add and view the timings for individual slides, hide slides, add transitions, and include animation (which is covered in Hour 10). Slide Sorter View has its own unique toolbar with buttons that make most tasks just a click away.

Just a Minute

The number of slides you see depends on your screen resolution. My screen resolution is set for 640×480. However, at 800×600, for example, you might see six complete slides at 100 percent zoom.

Time Saver

You can view more slides or fewer slides onscreen by changing the zoom option for the Slide Sorter View.

While in Slide Sorter View, you can see little icons underneath the individual slides. The icons represent transitions, animation, hidden slides, and timings that have been added.

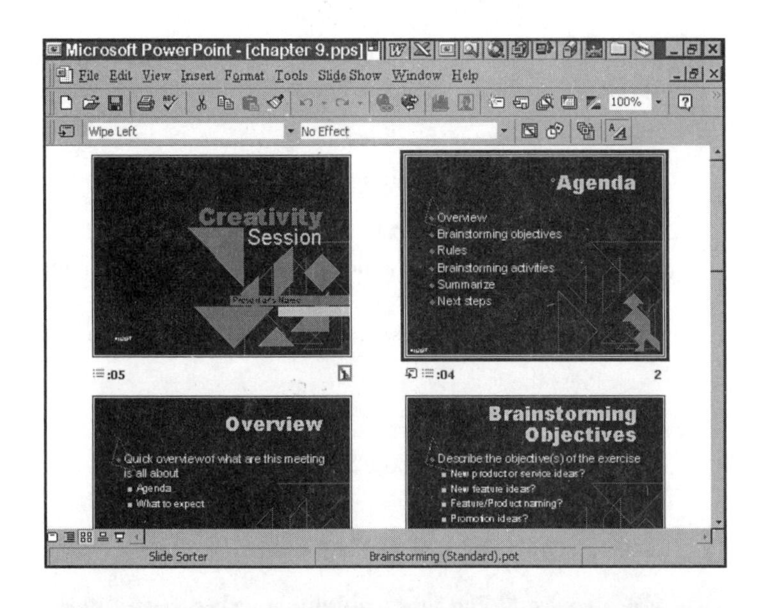

Figure 9.9.
Slide Sorter View at 100 percent zoom, showing two complete slides.

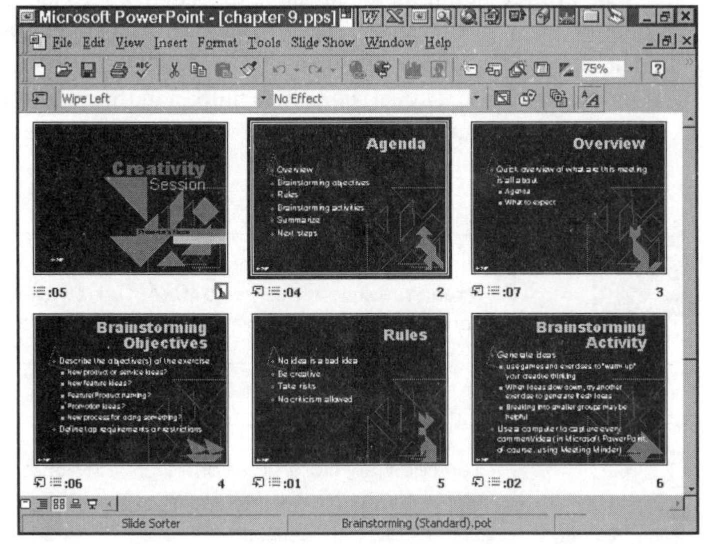

Figure 9.10.
Slide Sorter View at 75 percent zoom, showing six slides.

Moving Slides

When you need to rearrange your slides, Slide Sorter View is the easiest place to do that. If possible, set the zoom control so that you can see all of the slide you want to move and the destination position, as shown in Figure 9.11. To move a slide, follow these steps:

1. Place your mouse pointer on the slide you want to move.
2. Hold down the left mouse button.

3. Drag the mouse pointer to the new position; you should see a vertical line indicating the placement of the slide.
4. Release the mouse button.

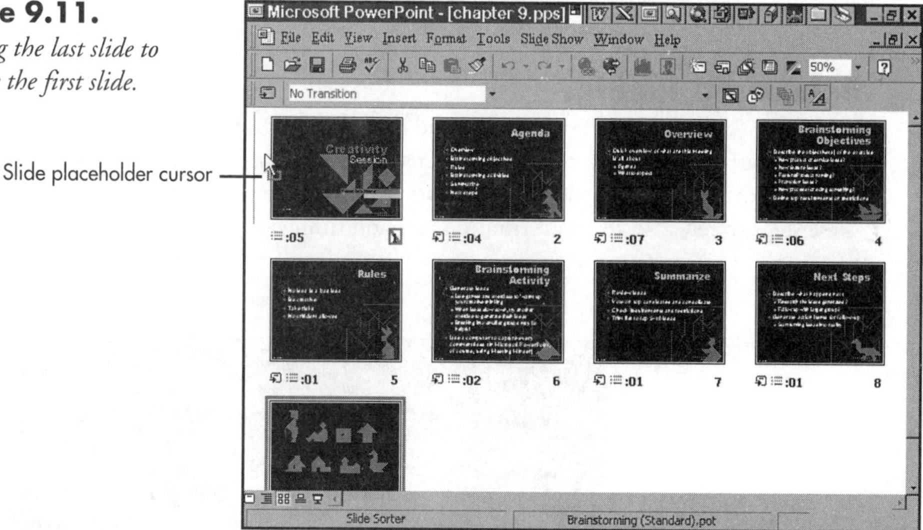

Figure 9.11.
Moving the last slide to become the first slide.

Timing

When you run an automatic slide show, or a slide show that advances from slide to slide without any help from yours truly, you need to set timings for each slide. You can either make an educated guess as to how long the slide should be displayed (custom timings) or rehearse your presentation and have PowerPoint record the duration (rehearsed timings) before you advance to the next slide.

Custom Timings

It's easiest to set custom timings while you're in Slide Sorter View. To set custom timings for your presentation, follow these steps:

1. Select the slide or slides you want to set timings for.
2. Choose Slide Show | Slide Transition from the menu.
3. Under Advance, click the Automatically After checkbox.
4. Type the number of seconds you want the slide to be displayed onscreen.
5. Click the Apply button.

Time Saver

To select a slide, just click on the slide. To select multiple slides, hold down the Shift key and click on each slide you want to select.

If you want to set the same show timings for all the slides in your presentation, click the Apply to All button in the Slide Transition dialog box.

Rehearsed Timings

You can also rehearse your presentation and have PowerPoint automatically add timings for each of your slides. While you're rehearsing your show timings, PowerPoint displays the Rehearsal dialog box in the lower-right corner of the slide show. (See Figure 9.12.) Follow these steps to rehearse your presentation and add timings:

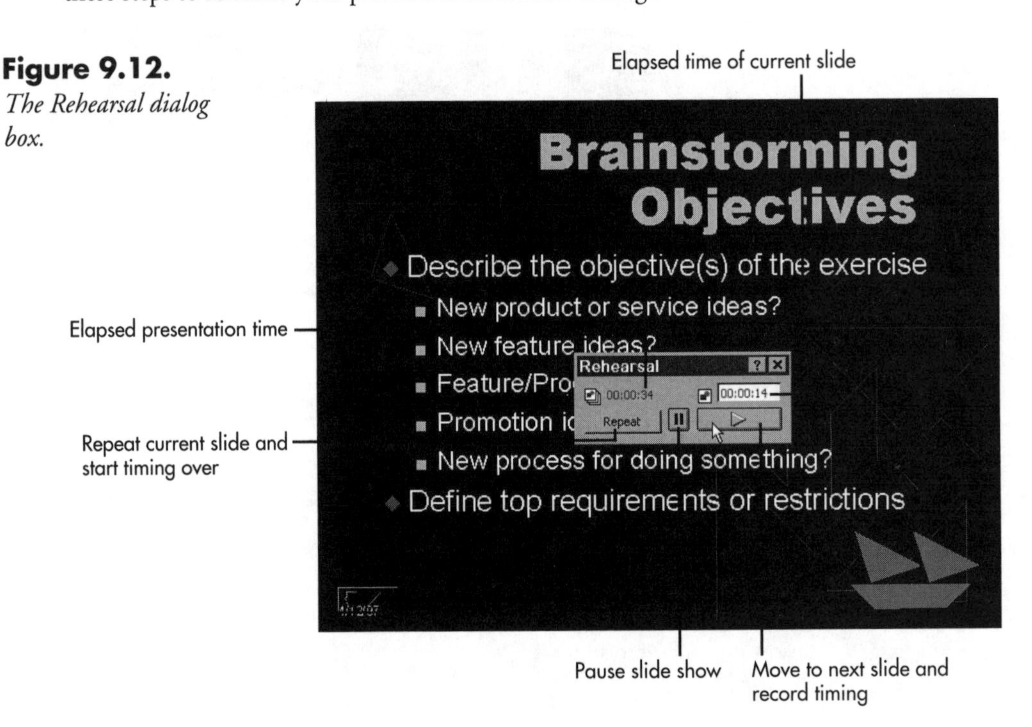

Figure 9.12.
The Rehearsal dialog box.

1. Choose Slide Show | Rehearse Timings from the menu.
2. Practice your entire presentation as though you were in front of your audience. Click the right-arrow button to advance to the next slide and record the time for the current slide.
3. At the end of the show, click the Yes button to record your timings.
4. Click the Yes button to review your timings in Slide Sorter View.

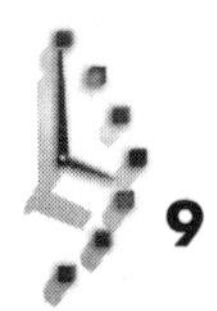

You can now edit your timings if you want, or rehearse your show again to get new timing values.

Keeping Your Time

Sometimes even the best plans get sidetracked, but PowerPoint 97 gives you a nifty tool to keep you on track. The tool is especially useful if you have a preset amount of time for a presentation but are giving your presentation to an unfamiliar group. If you have planned a question-and-answer period after the presentation, timing is very critical. The Slide Meter, shown in Figure 9.13, keeps track of the time allotted for the current slide and the entire presentation and lets you know if you're moving along too fast and should slow down, or if you need to put a little more coal on the fire.

Figure 9.13.
The Slide Meter.

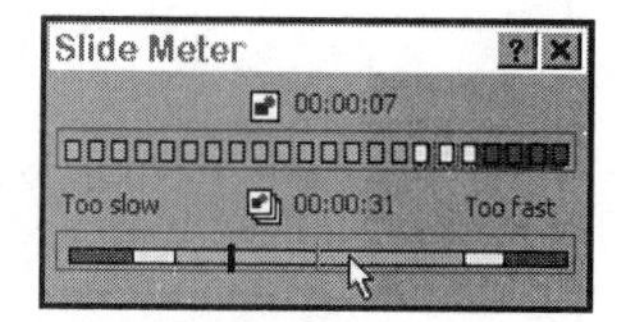

The top number on the meter indicates the elapsed time for the current slide, and the bottom number shows the elapsed time for the entire presentation. The black line in the colored bar at the bottom of the Slide Meter indicates whether you're too slow, too fast, or just right. To view the Slide Meter, simply follow these steps:

1. Start your slide show.
2. Right-click and choose Slide Meter from the menu.

Hiding a Slide

Sometimes when you're creating a presentation, you might not be sure whether a piece of information is relevant. Of course, you always want to be prepared (even if you're not a Boy Scout), no matter what might come up. If you have a slide that doesn't need to be shown, you can always leave it in the presentation file, but hide it from the show by following these steps:

1. Select the slide you want to hide.
2. Choose Slide Show | Hide Slide from the menu.

   or

2. Click the Hide Slide button from the Slide Sorter toolbar.

Time Saver

> If you're hiding slides, you might not want to have them numbered. Although PowerPoint doesn't display a slide that has been hidden, it doesn't renumber the slides automatically.

Creating a Summary Slide

Creating a summary slide quickly is a new feature in PowerPoint 97. PowerPoint creates the summary (or agenda) slide from the titles of the slides you select, which is almost the reverse of the Expand Slide option discussed in Hour 4, "Working with Slides." To create a summary slide, follow these steps:

1. Switch to Slide Sorter View.
2. Select the slide(s) that you want to be included in the summary.
3. Click the Summary Slide button on the Slide Sorter toolbar. (See Figure 9.14.)

PowerPoint creates the summary slide in front of the first slide selected. Move the summary slide to the end to close your presentation powerfully.

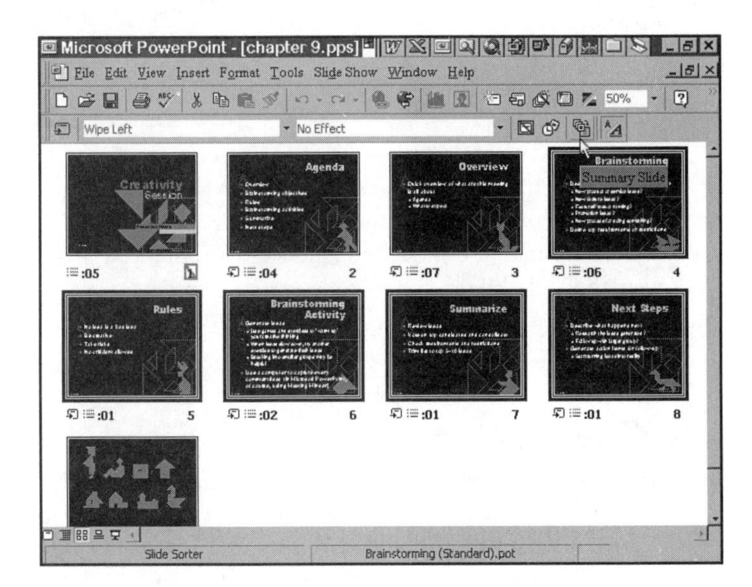

Figure 9.14.
Creating a summary slide.

Summary

You have now completed your PowerPoint presentation from design to delivery. Creating a slide show is the finishing touch to your hard work. It's important to apply creativity and thought to the slide show and remember that you're judged on the pacing, as well as the cool color scheme. You can now easily view the presentation, make temporary annotations, set slide timings, hide a slide, or create a summary slide. The presentation includes many features that make you look like a presentation expert. This hour caps the basics. Future chapters add more advanced features to your knowledge base. This hour and the next cover everything you need to know about running a slide show.

Workshop

This hour's "Test What You've Learned" section starts you off with a basic slide show. Get ready, Francis—the fun is really going to start now. You'll have a chance to show off all the new skills you have learned. This hour's "Q&A" has some great tips, so don't forget to stop in on your way home.

Test What You've Learned

1. Create a presentation by using the AutoContent Wizard or open an existing presentation.
2. Save the presentation as `Hour 9 TWYL`.
3. View the presentation as a slide show.
4. Save the presentation as a slide show so that whenever you open it, the show starts.
5. Run the slide show again and use the pen to make annotations for the show.
6. Change the color of the pen.
7. Erase the annotations from the current slide.
8. Switch to Slide Sorter View.
9. Set the timing for all the slides to five seconds.
10. Rehearse the timings for the slide show and record the new times.
11. Hide a slide.
12. Create a summary slide for your slide show and move it to the end of the presentation.
13. Save your show again.
14. View your show.
15. Close the show.

Q&A

Q When viewing a slide show, can I go back to the previous slide?

A Yes. You can either display the Slide Show menu or press the P key. (By the way, the N key takes you to the next slide.) If you find you're running a lot of slide shows, it's a good idea to learn the "hot keys" for working with slide shows. Appendix A, "Hot Keys and Menus," has a pretty complete list of the available ones, as well as the PowerPoint 97 help files.

Q Now that I've saved my presentation as a slide show, how do I make changes to it?

A You need to open the show in PowerPoint and either let it run or press the Esc key to stop it. Once the show is stopped, you can make any changes needed. Don't forget to save the show before you close it.

Q How do I redisplay a slide I have hidden?

A The Hide Slide command works like an on/off button; the option is either on or off. To redisplay a slide that has been hidden, simply select the slide and then choose Slide Show|Hide Slide from the menu.

Part III

Hour 10

Adding Pizzazz to a Slide Show

Now that you have learned the basics necessary to set up a slide show, it's time to get into the special features that add extra sparkle to your show. In this hour, you will learn about the following:

- Adding special effects, such as slide transitions and animation
- Setting up a show to be browsed by an individual or at a kiosk
- Setting up your show on two screens, one for the presenter and one for the audience
- Customizing the same show for two different audiences

Adding Transitions

When you first view your slide show, moving (or transitioning) from slide to slide can be a little boring. But never fear—PowerPoint 97 is here. You can add a special effect called a *transition* that changes the way individual slides appear onscreen. There are over three dozen types of transitions to choose from. For example, you can indicate that one slide should dissolve into the next or specify a checkerboard transition. Not only do you have a choice of transition effects, but you can also set the speed of each transition.

But enough talk; the best way to understand the transition effect is to get in there and try it. To do that, follow these steps:

1. Switch to Slide Sorter View.
2. Select the slide(s) you want to add a transition to.
3. Choose Slide Show | Slide Transition from the menu or click the Slide Transition button on the Slide Sorter toolbar.
4. In the Slide Transition dialog box, select a transition in the drop-down list in the Effect section. (See Figure 10.1.)
5. Select a speed: Slow, Medium, or Fast.
6. Click the Apply button.

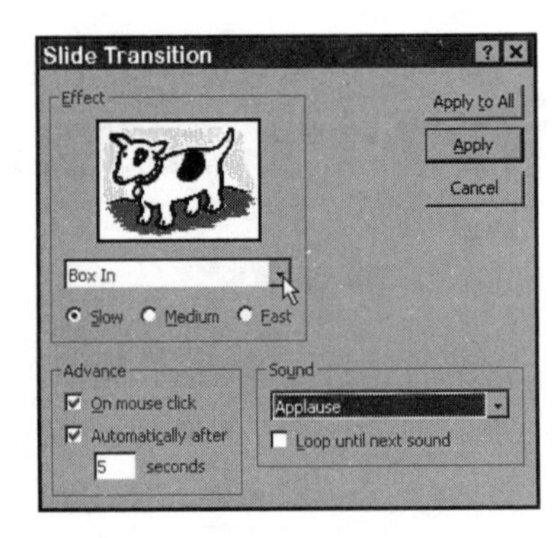

Figure 10.1.
In the Slide Transition dialog box, the dog changes to a key to display the transition effect you have chosen.

TIME SAVER

To quickly apply the same transition to every slide in your presentation, click the Apply to All button.

After adding a transition effect to a slide, you will notice that a small slide transition icon appears under the slide's left corner, as shown in Figure 10.2. This icon lets you know that you have been successful in adding the transition effect.

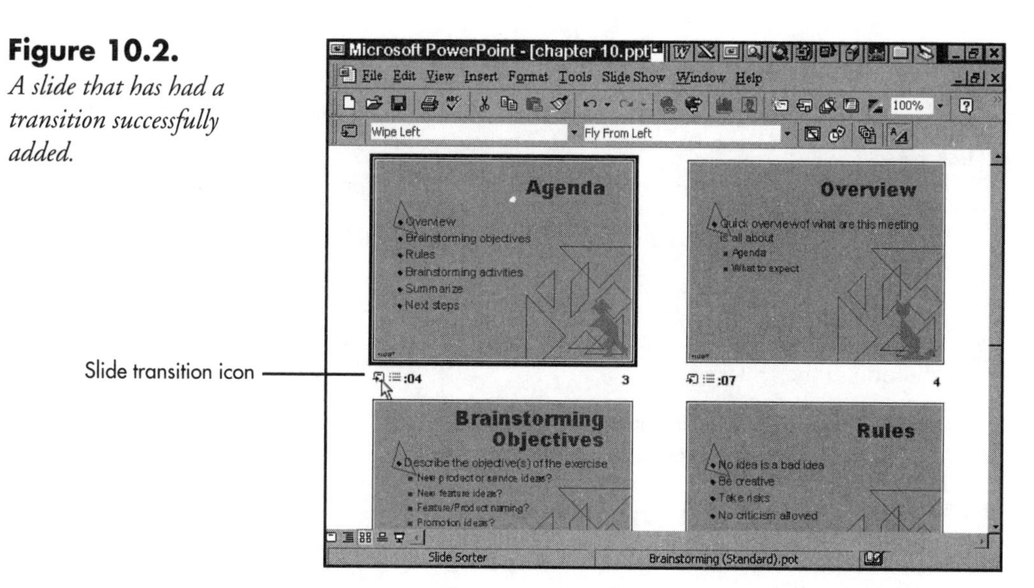

Figure 10.2.
A slide that has had a transition successfully added.

TIME SAVER

In addition to the standard display that indicates what the transition effect will look like, you can also click the transition icon to see what the effect will look like on the actual slide.

Including Animation

PowerPoint 97 comes with state-of-the-art animation options for your slide shows. You can animate almost anything. Animation is commonly added to text items, drawing items, charts, and clip art.

The ability to animate charts is a new feature in PowerPoint 97. For more information on charts, refer to Hours 17, "Creating Charts and Graphs with Microsoft Graph," and 18, "Editing Charts and Graphs," later in this book.

NEW TERM *Animation* is the ability to add cool visual or sound effects to any object. Some of these effects can be quite complex. For example, your presentation could have the sound of a drum roll or have the individual letters of a text item fly onto the screen (like a typewriter typing them). When an object is animated, you can see the full effect during the slide show.

TIME SAVER

The best view available when you're setting animation effects is the Slide Sorter View. This view allows you to set animation for any PowerPoint object and use the custom animation settings.

You have two options available when setting animation. You can use one of PowerPoint's preset animation settings, or you can create your own custom animation. Preset animation is the way to go when you're in a time crunch, yet want to add a little extra pizzazz to your presentation. Custom animation is an excellent choice when you want to add sound in addition to the visual effects.

Once you have added animation to the objects on your slide(s), you can preview the animation settings from either Slide or Slide Sorter View.

Using Preset Animation

PowerPoint 97 has eight preset animation settings available. Use them to quickly add motion to any PowerPoint object. To set animation using one of the available preset options, follow these steps:

1. Select the object you want to animate.
2. Choose Slide Show | Preset Animation from the menu.
3. Click the animation setting you want.

JUST A MINUTE

The Drive-In, Flying, and Camera preset options include sound effects with the visual animation.

Using Custom Animation

The preset animation settings are nice, but when you want to control all facets of the animation effects, you need to roll up those shirt sleeves and get into the custom animation settings. Custom animation is where PowerPoint lets you choose from over 40 visual effects, multiple sounds, and timings. You can also set the order in which the objects are animated. Follow these steps to set custom animation:

1. While you're in Slide View, display the slide you want to animate.
2. Choose Slide Show | Custom Animation from the menu.
3. Select the Timing tab. (See Figure 10.3.)

Just a Minute

You must be in Slide View to add custom animation.

Figure 10.3.
The Timing tab of the Custom Animation dialog box.

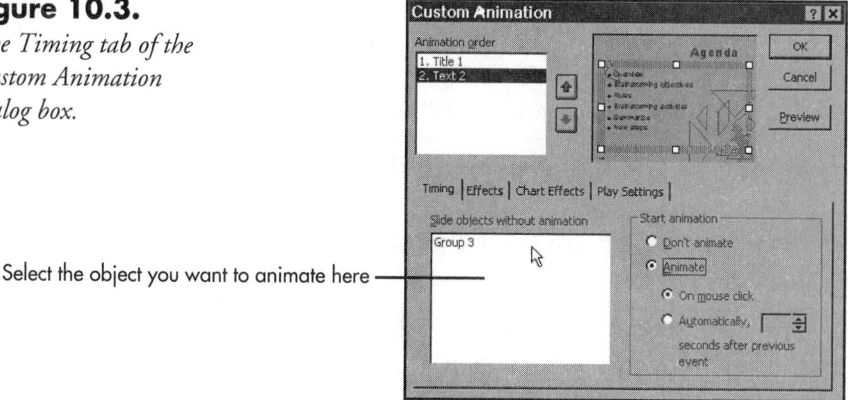

4. In the "Slide objects without animation" box, select the text or object to animate.
5. In the "Start animation" section, select the Animate radio button.
6. Select how the animation is to start by setting either "On mouse click" or "Automatically, *x* seconds after previous event."
7. Click the Effects tab. (See Figure 10.4.)

Figure 10.4.
The Effects tab of the Custom Animation dialog box.

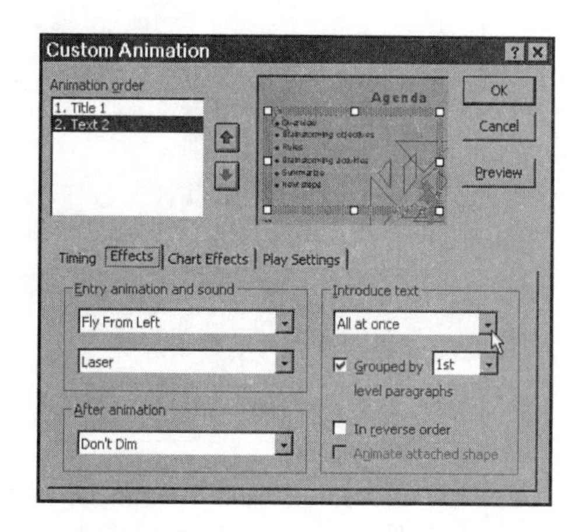

8. In the "Entry animation and sound" section, select the animation and sound settings you want.

9. If you're animating a text object, in the "Introduce text" section select how you want PowerPoint to introduce the text: All at once, By word, or By letter.
10. Select the paragraph level to introduce the text.
11. Change any other settings you want.
12. Repeat steps 3 through 11 for each object to animate.
13. Click the Preview button to see a preview of the animation settings.
14. Click the OK button when you're done adding animation to the slide.

Previewing Your Animation Effects

You can preview your animation settings at any time by viewing the slide show. PowerPoint 97 also has a new option that lets you preview animation settings for the current slide without starting the entire slide show.

To preview the animation for just one slide, display the slide and choose Slide Show | Animation Preview from the menu. PowerPoint then shows a slide miniature, shown in Figure 10.5, that displays all the currently set animation options for the slide.

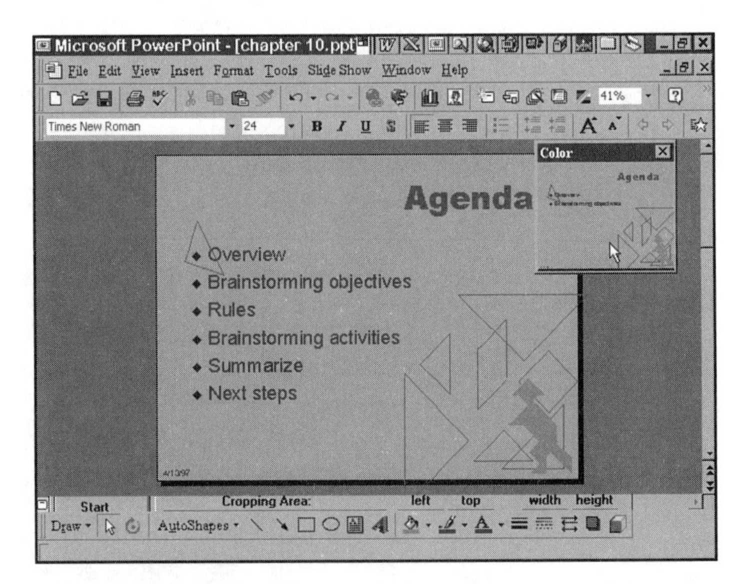

Figure 10.5.
A preview of the animation settings.

TIME SAVER

If you already have the slide miniature displayed, you can preview animation settings at any time by simply clicking on the slide miniature.

Running a Slide Show

PowerPoint 97 gives you three options in the Set Up Show dialog box for running your slide show, so you can pick the option that best fits your needs. You can run the slide show by using the standard presentation method—the presentation is viewed full screen with a speaker controlling the show. This presentation method is the most common and the one that's been used so far in this book.

The second option is to create a slide show that people can browse at their convenience. An orientation presentation for new employees is a good example of this kind of presentation method.

The third and final option, a self-running presentation, is useful when the show will be displayed on a kiosk, such as you often see at a trade show.

Presented by a Speaker

Up to this point, you have been viewing the slide shows with the Presented by a Speaker method, the most common of the three methods because there's usually a speaker who controls the show. Use this method, too, if you're running a presentation conference.

To set a slide show to be presented by a speaker in full-screen mode, follow these steps:

1. Choose Slide Show | Set Up Show from the menu.
2. Select the "Presented by a Speaker (full screen)" option.
3. Click the OK button.

Browsed by an Individual

The Browsed by an Individual option is very useful when you have a standalone presentation, such as those used at employee orientations or a training seminar that you would like people to watch at their convenience. You can create a slide show and save it to the local area network so that employees can open and view the show whenever they want.

In this option, the show runs in a small window with menu options for printing, copying, and editing the show. The Browse menu item, as shown in Figure 10.6, has commands for the different methods of advancing through the presentation.

To save a presentation to be viewed by individuals in a window, follow these steps:

1. Choose Slide Show | Set Up Show from the menu.
2. Select the "Browsed by an Individual (window)" option.
3. Click the OK button.

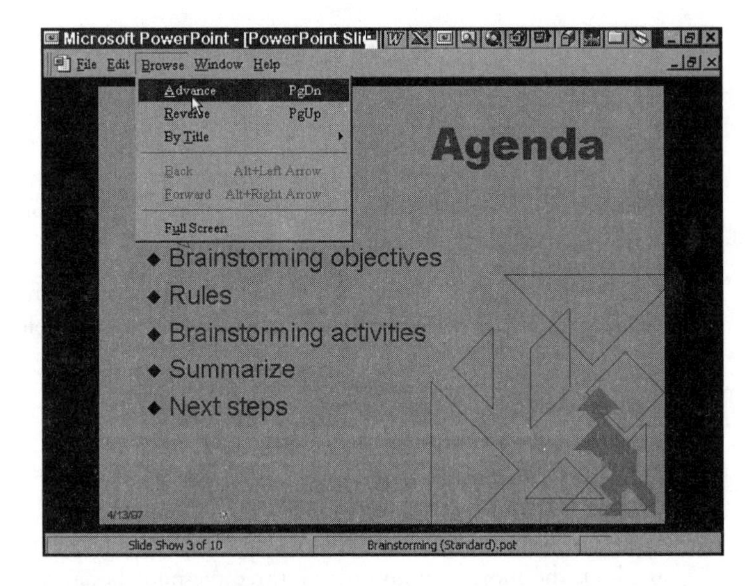

Figure 10.6.
Browsing the show with the Browse menu selections.

When you view the show, use the Page Up and Page Down keys to move from slide to slide. To print the presentation while viewing, choose File | Print from the menu. You can also quickly advance to a particular slide by choosing Browse | By Title from the menu.

TIME SAVER

When you want people to browse a presentation on a network, it's useful to save the presentation as a PowerPoint Show. This task is discussed in Hour 9, "Basics of Slide Shows." You might also want to ask your network administrator to place a shortcut to the presentation file somewhere that's convenient for all personnel to easily open and view the show.

TIME SAVER

When you use the browse option, keep in mind that not everyone viewing the show is familiar with PowerPoint. You might want the first slide to explain how to navigate the presentation. Figure 10.7 illustrates common page-navigation instructions. Another option is to include a summary of the most important instructions at the bottom of each slide, such as Next=PgDn and Previous=PgUp. If you do that, someone coming in at the middle of the presentation can still figure out how to navigate.

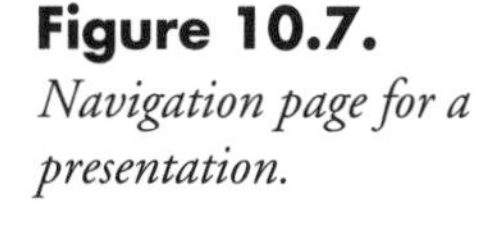

Figure 10.7.
Navigation page for a presentation.

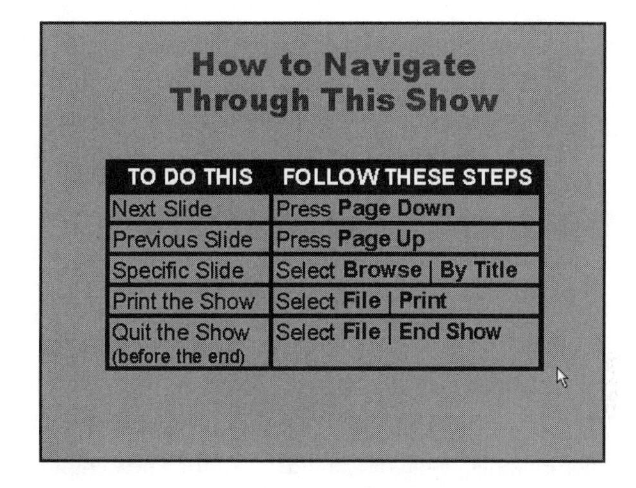

Browsed at a Kiosk

The Browsed at a Kiosk option in the Set Up Show dialog box saves the presentation as a self-executing show. Use this option when a person won't be available to advance the show from slide to slide, as is the case when the show runs automatically from a kiosk at a trade show or convention. To set up a show so it can be browsed at a kiosk, follow these steps:

1. Choose Slide Show | Set Up Show from the menu.
2. Select the "Browsed at a Kiosk (full screen)" option.
3. Click the OK button.

When you select this option, PowerPoint automatically sets the show to run in a continuous loop until the Esc key is pressed.

Just a Minute

See Hour 21, "Multimedia," for information about adding voice narration to your show. Also, refer to Hour 22, "Creating Web Pages," for information about adding hyperlinks to a presentation.

Deciding Which Slides to Show

As discussed in Hour 9, you can hide slides that shouldn't appear in your slide show. This feature is useful if you want to hide one or two slides. However, if you want to display only a certain range of slides, it's easier to use the Set Up Show dialog box to specify which slides should be included in your show. To specify a range of slides to display in a show, follow these steps:

1. Choose Slide Show | Set Up Show from the menu.
2. In the Slides section, select the From/To option.
3. Type the beginning slide number in the From box and the ending slide number in the To box.

Creating Custom Shows

If you need to create several similar slide shows for different audiences, you will appreciate PowerPoint 97's new Custom Shows feature. This feature allows you to create a show within a show that specifies which slides to display for each audience, so you don't need to create several shows that are almost the same. To use this feature, you group together the slides that will be different, and then switch to those slides during your custom show.

For example, if you have a slide show for a new employee orientation, you might want one show for new managers and one show for new staff personnel. Both of these shows would have similar slides for all new employees, but the custom shows would have slides specifically for managers or staff, depending on the custom show selected. After showing the first few general slides, you would then branch to the slides directed to the specific audience.

To create a custom show, first create a slide show that has all the slides that will be used for all the shows. After the slides are created, use these following steps:

1. Choose Slide Show | Custom Shows from the menu.
2. Click the New button to open the Define Custom Show dialog box.
3. Type a name for your custom show, such as Staff or Manager.
4. In the "Slides in presentation" box, select the slides you want displayed in the custom show.

TIME SAVER

You can select multiple slides by holding down the Ctrl key on the keyboard while you click on each slide.

5. Click the Add >> button to add slides to the "Slides in custom show" listbox, as shown in Figure 10.8.

TIME SAVER

If the slides aren't listed in the order in which they should appear, use the up-arrow or down-arrow buttons to move individual slides to the correct location.

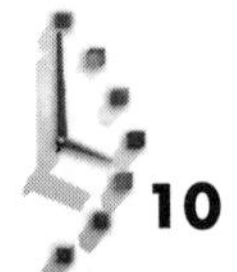

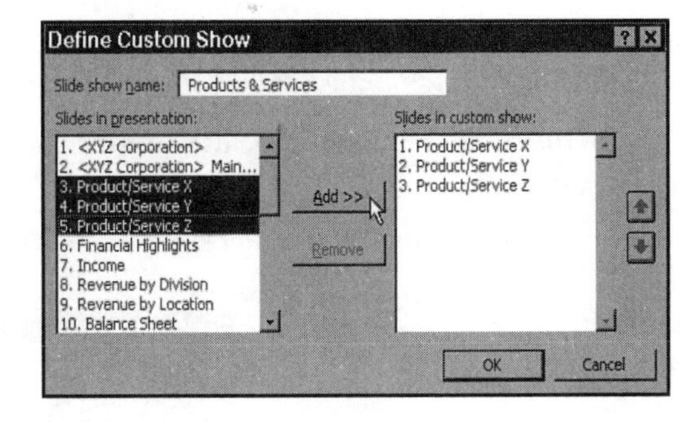

Figure 10.8.
Selecting slides for the Products & Services custom show.

6. Click the OK button when you're done to go back to the Custom Show dialog box.
7. Repeat steps 2 through 6 to create another show.
8. Click the Close button to close the Custom Show dialog box when you're finished.

Follow these steps to add or remove slides from a custom show:

1. Choose Slide Show | Custom Shows from the menu.
2. Select the name of the custom show you want to edit.
3. Click the Edit button.
4. Add or remove slides from the "Slides in custom show" listbox.
5. If the slides aren't in the order you want, use the up-arrow or down-arrow buttons to move individual slides to the correct location.
6. Click the OK button when you're done.
7. Click the Close button to close the Custom Show dialog box when you're finished.

TIME SAVER

You can add hyperlinks from any PowerPoint object to a custom show. The link quickly takes you to another custom show. See Hour 22 for more information about hyperlinks.

Viewing on Two Screens

The last option covered in this hour explains the steps for viewing a slide show on two screens. This feature is new in PowerPoint 97 and allows the audience to view a slide show on one computer while the presenter controls the show from another computer. To view a presentation on two screens, you need two computers with an available COM port and a single null-modem cable. Both PCs must have PowerPoint installed. To set up the slide show for viewing on two computers, follow these steps:

1. On the computer that will be used for the control, open the presentation you want to show.
2. Choose Slide Show | View on Two Screens from the menu. (See Figure 10.9.)

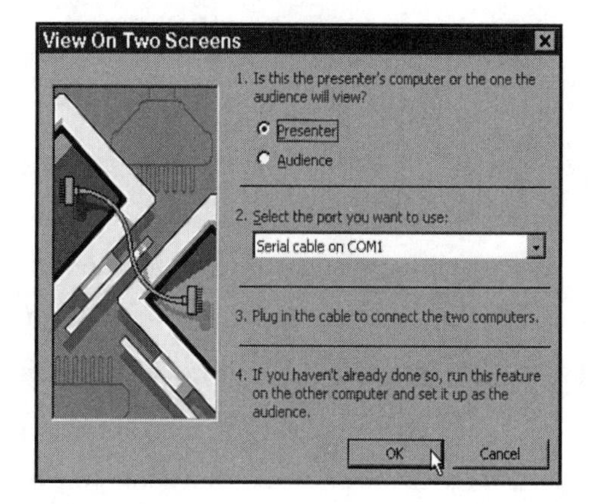

Figure 10.9.
Setting up a slide show on two computers in the View on Two Screens dialog box.

3. Select the Presenter option.
4. Select the COM port the cable will be connected to (COM1 or COM2).
5. Run PowerPoint on the second computer and choose Slide Show | View on Two Screens from the menu.
6. Select the Audience option.
7. Select the COM port the cable will be connected to (COM1 or COM2).
8. Click the OK button.

This option should be used when you don't want the audience to see the control menu used during a presentation.

Summary

This hour is over, but you should have an excellent understanding of slide show special effects. Experiment with preset and custom slide transitions and animation; the effort will keep your audience from being hypnotized by boring slide flips.

Other features explained during this hour give you the ability to run the show in a standalone mode or to hide the control menu. The individual and kiosk displays are useful formats when

a presenter isn't available to run the show, and the dual-screen option adds extra magic to the presentation. For full wizardry, create custom shows so that a single presentation can target multiple audiences. PowerPoint 97 makes using all these special features an easy task.

Workshop

Don't stop the clock—it's still time to rock. This workshop will put the fun in your work. Complete the "Test What You've Learned" and "Q&A" sections, and you'll be well on your way to becoming the next PowerPoint 97 wizard.

Test What You've Learned

1. Open an existing presentation or start a new presentation by using the AutoContent Wizard.
2. Switch to Slide Sorter View.
3. Add transition effects to each slide. Use a different transition effect for each slide, just to see what they all look like.
4. Switch to Slide View and add some custom animation effects to your slides. Again, play around with all the different animation options available.
5. Save the presentation as `Hour 10 TWYL`.
6. In the Set Up Show dialog box, set the show type to the Browsed by an Individual option.
7. View the slide show.
8. Use the Set Up Show dialog box to set the show type to the Browsed at a Kiosk option.
9. View the slide show.
10. Use the Set Up Show dialog box to set the show type to the Presented by a Speaker option.
11. View the slide show.
12. Save the presentation again.
13. Close the presentation.

Q&A

Q My slide transition is too fast. I can hardly tell that a transition effect was added. How can I fix this?

A Try selecting either Slow or Medium as your transition speed. I always set the speed to Slow because it results in a much nicer show.

Q Can't I just click on the Slide Transitions Effects drop-down list on the Slide Sorter toolbar to select a transition?

A You certainly could do that, but then you don't get to see a preview of the effect you have chosen, and you can't change the timing of the transition. To change the timing of the transition, you need to go into the Slide Transition dialog box.

Q Can you animate items that are on the master slide?

A Yes! This is a new feature with PowerPoint 97. In older versions of PowerPoint, you couldn't animate items on the Slide Master. To quickly set animation for Slide or Title Master items, follow these steps:

1. Choose View | Master | Slide (or Title) Master from the menu.
2. Click the object you want to animate.
3. Choose Slide Show | Preset Animation from the menu.
4. Click the Animation option you prefer.

You can also set up a custom animation for any object. Custom animation gives you more animation options.

PART IV

Drawing with PowerPoint 97

Hour

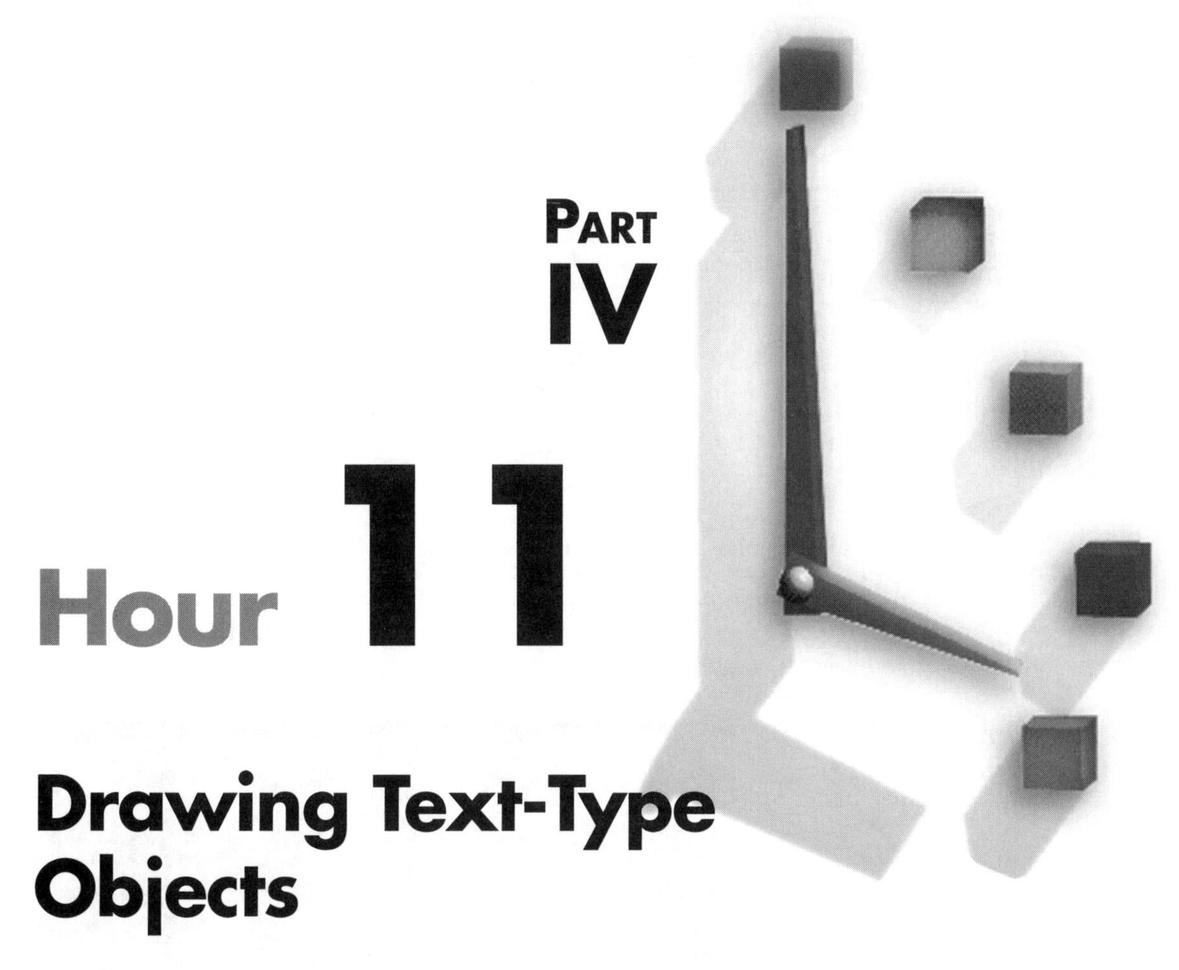

Drawing Text-Type Objects

In the next four hours, you will be learning about the different drawing options available in PowerPoint 97. This hour covers drawing text objects and using the guides to position objects. You will learn how to work with the following:

- Text boxes
- WordArt
- PowerPoint guides

Text box and WordArt objects are considered drawing objects, even though they also use text. These objects serve as the introduction to the drawing section of this book.

Text Boxes

You have already been adding text to your slides. The preplaced text object placeholders have been the primary vehicle for the text additions. When you need text added to your slide outside the placeholders, however, you can use the Text Box tool on the drawing toolbar. (See Figure 11.1.)

JUST A MINUTE

Text that's in a text box is included in spellchecks of your presentation, but isn't included in the Outline View or printout of your presentation.

Figure 11.1.
Use the Text Box tool to add additional text to a slide.

When you add a text box to a slide, it behaves in one of two ways:

- As a label, as shown in Figure 11.2, in which the text within it doesn't word wrap. This option is useful when you need a short caption, such as under a graph or a clip art image.

Figure 11.2.
A text label for a clip art image.

- As a word processing box, as shown in Figure 11.3, in which the text within the text box does word wrap, and the text box can expand, if necessary.

Figure 11.3.
Supplying information in a word processing box.

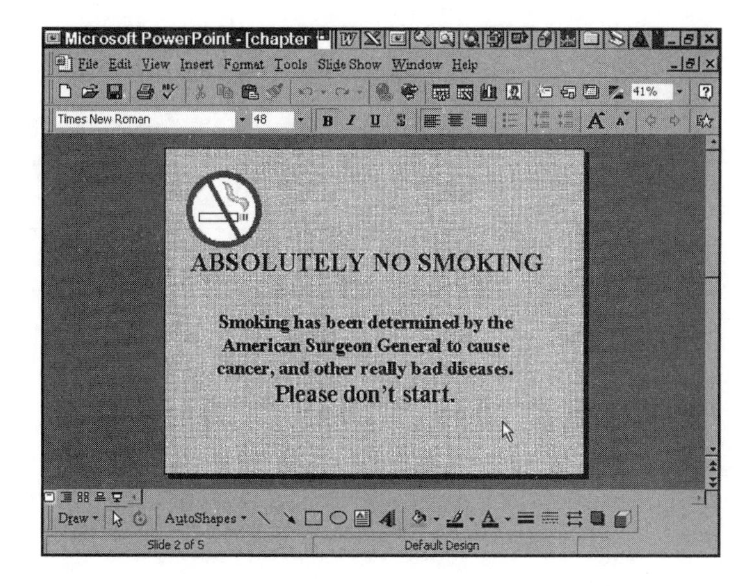

Text Labels

To create a text label, follow these steps:

1. Click the Text Box tool on the drawing toolbar.
2. Click on the slide where you want to position the text label.
3. Start typing. (See Figure 11.4.)

Figure 11.4.
Creating a text box label.

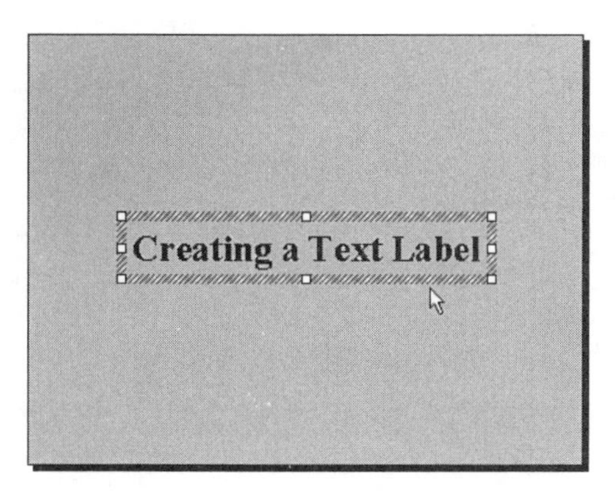

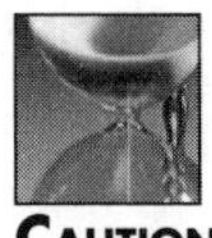

CAUTION

Be careful when typing text labels. Don't type too much text, or the text box will run off the slide. When there's a chance you might have too much information, create a word processing box instead. If the text does overrun the edge, you can either add hard returns manually or resize the text box object.

Word Processing Boxes

A *word processing box* is a fancy name for a text box that has the size defined before you start typing (as opposed to just clicking on the slide and typing). Follow these steps to create a word processing box:

1. Click the Text Box tool on the drawing toolbar.
2. Drag a box on the slide where you want the text box to appear.
3. Start typing.

JUST A MINUTE

The easiest method for dragging a box is to imagine the text on the slide with a box around it. Place the mouse pointer on the upper-left corner of the imaginary box, click and hold the left mouse button, and then drag the pointer to the lower-right corner of the box, as shown in Figure 11.5. Release the mouse button. You now have a word processing box.

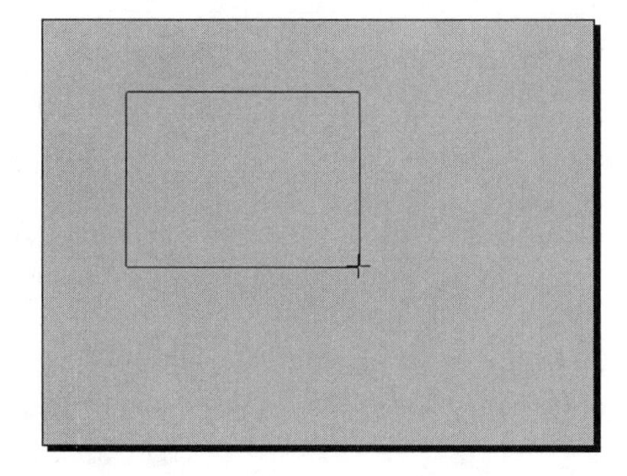

Figure 11.5.
Dragging from the upper-left corner to the lower-right corner to create a word processing box.

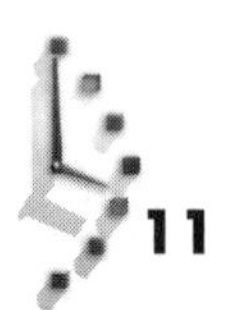

Formatting a Text Box

You can add many special effects to a text box for emphasis and impact, such as including a fill or border. PowerPoint also allows you to control the size and position of the text box and change the text anchor point and internal margins of the text. All these options are available in the Format Text Box dialog box.

Adding a Fill or Border

By adding a border or fill to your text box, you can really make the text stand out. Figure 11.6 illustrates how a text box can be formatted by using the fill and border options.

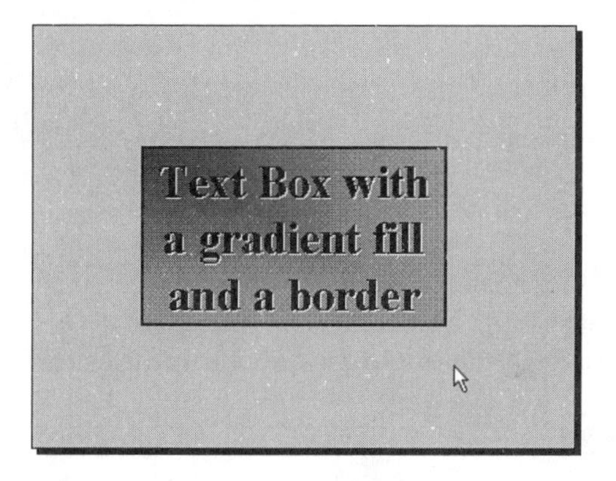

Figure 11.6.
A text box with a gradient fill and a border.

To add a fill or border to a text box, follow these steps:

1. Select the text box you want to format.
2. Choose Format | Text Box from the menu.
3. Click the Colors and Lines tab. (See Figure 11.7.)
4. Select a color or fill option from the Color drop-down list in the Fill section.

Just a Minute

Use the Fill Effects option from the Color drop-down list to apply a gradient or other fill effect to your text object. Although it's easy to get carried away with all the special effects, just remember that the text is what you want the audience to focus on, not the fancy formatting.

5. If you want a border, click the Color drop-down list under the Line section.
6. Change the Style, Dashed, and Weight options for the line, if you want.

7. Click the Preview button to preview your changes before accepting them.
8. Click the OK button when you're finished.

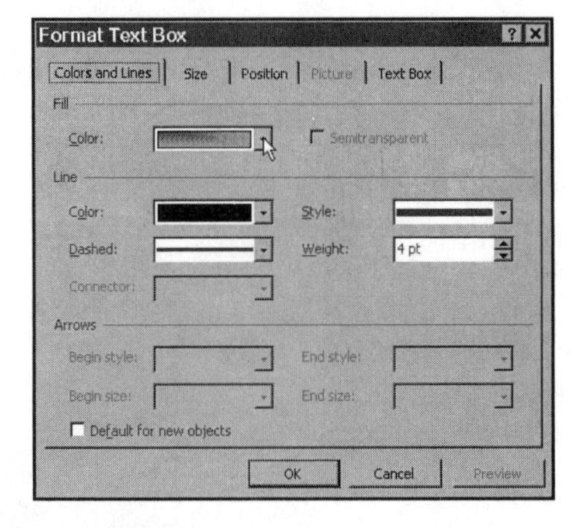

Figure 11.7.
The Colors and Lines tab of the Format Text Box dialog box.

Changing the Size of a Text Box

Usually, a text box fits the size of the text that it holds. You can resize the text box by dragging the sizing handles, but the text box usually automatically resizes to fit the text.

JUST A MINUTE

Remember that when you change the size of a text box, you're *not* changing the text's font size.

If you want a text box to be a bit bigger than the text it holds, the only way you can do this is to set the size in the Format Text Box dialog box. To do that, follow these steps:

1. Click once on the text object to select it.
2. Choose Format | Text Box from the menu.
3. Click the Size tab, shown in Figure 11.8.
4. Enter an exact height and/or width for the bounding box.
5. Click the Preview button to preview your changes before accepting them.
6. Click the OK button when finished.

JUST A MINUTE

PowerPoint also allows you to free-rotate or flip any object. These options are covered in Hour 13, "Bringing Drawing Objects Together."

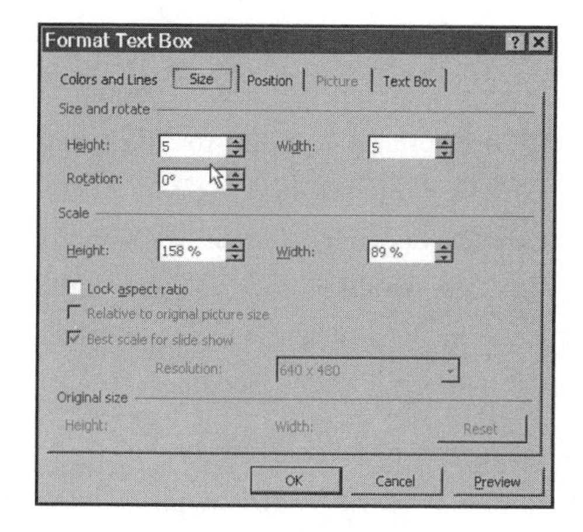

Figure 11.8.
The Size tab of the Format Text Box dialog box.

Moving a Text Box

After you create your text box, you might decide later that it needs to be moved to another location on the slide. PowerPoint has two options for moving the text box. You can either drag the text box to the new location or set the position in the Format Text Box dialog box.

To drag a text box to a new location, follow these steps:

1. Click once on the text box to select it.
2. Place the mouse pointer on the box's border so you can see the move pointer, as shown in Figure 11.9.
3. Click and hold down the left mouse button.
4. Drag the box to the new location.
5. Release the mouse button.

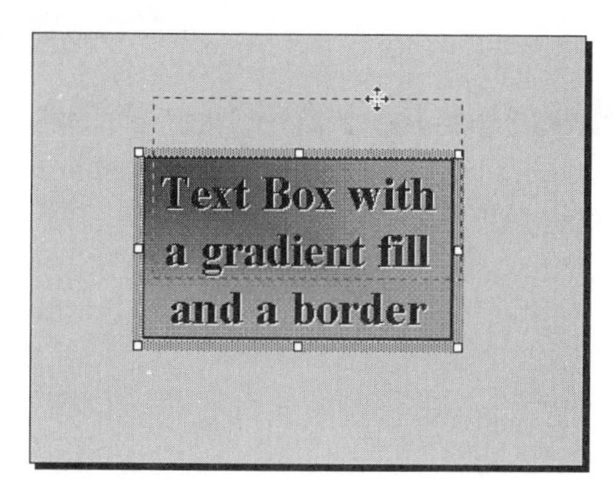

Figure 11.9.
Moving a text box.

Here's how to position a text object in an exact location:

1. Select the text box you want to position.
2. Choose Format | Text Box from the menu.
3. Click the Position tab.
4. Enter the horizontal position you want for the text box.
5. Enter the vertical position you want for the text box.
6. Click the Preview button to preview your changes before accepting them.
7. Click the OK button when finished.

CAUTION

PowerPoint positions objects by using their upper-left edges. If you want to center a text object, it's much easier to turn on the guides, by choosing View | Guides from the menu, and drag the object to the center, as shown in Figure 11.10. The object should snap to the guides automatically.

Figure 11.10.
A text object centered by using the guides.

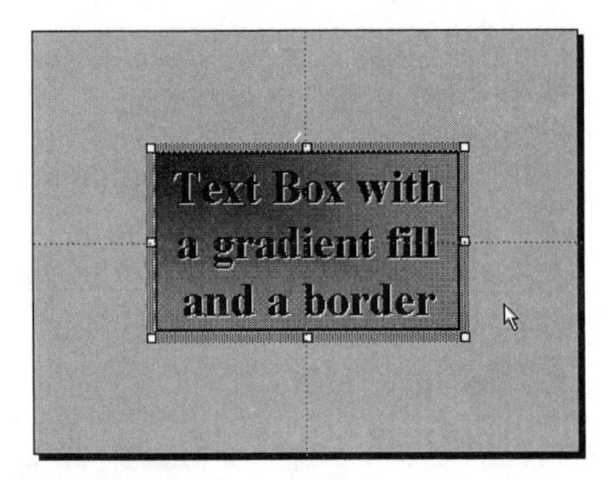

Setting the Text Anchor Point

Text can be anchored to the top, middle, bottom, top center, middle center, or bottom center of the text box. Figure 11.11 shows two text objects, each with a different anchor point.

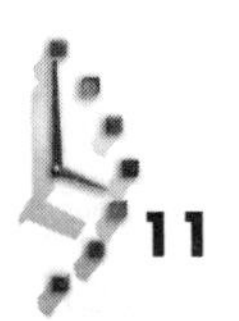

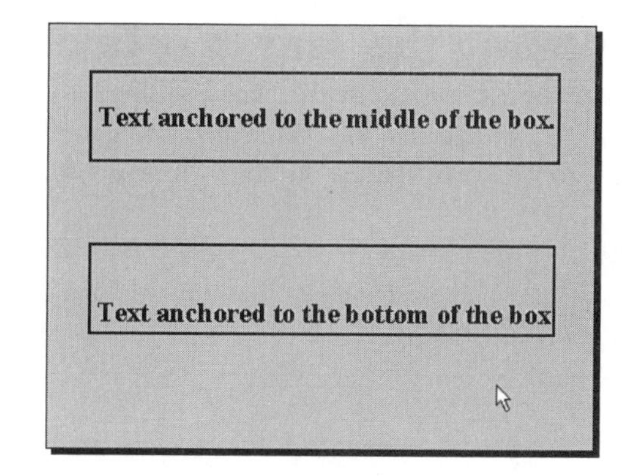

Figure 11.11.
Text anchored to the middle and bottom of text boxes.

To change the anchor point of the text in a text box, follow these steps:

1. Select the text object.
2. Choose Format | Text Box from the menu.
3. Click the Text Box tab. (See Figure 11.12.)
4. Select a new anchor point from the "Text anchor point" drop-down list.
5. Click the Preview button to see a preview of your change.
6. Click the OK button.

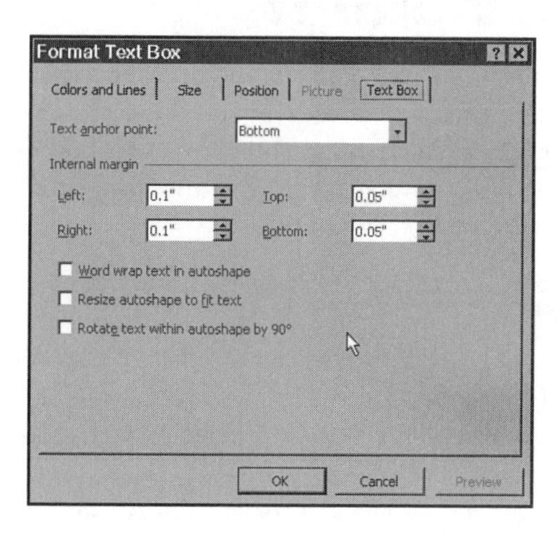

Figure 11.12.
The Text Box tab of the Format Text Box dialog box.

Formatting the Text in a Text Box

You can format the text in a text box by using the Format Font dialog box or by selecting any of the text formatting tools on the formatting toolbar. Make the text bigger or smaller, select a new font face, or change the color. So many font choices, so little time.

Just a Minute

The drawing toolbar has only one button for formatting text: the Text Color button.

To format text in a text box, follow these steps:

1. Select the text you want to format. If you want to format all the text in the text box, click once on the text box to select it and a second time on the text box border to select the entire text box.
2. Choose Format | Font from the menu.
3. Change any options you want.
4. Click the Preview button to see a preview of your changes before accepting them.
5. Click the OK Button.

Using WordArt

In earlier versions of PowerPoint, drawing required a separate program—WordArt—which was used to create text with special effects. However, PowerPoint 97 has the WordArt feature built in. Special effects and other tricks are now only a click away. The WordArt button has all the same features as the WordArt program, plus many exciting new features, such as 3-D effects and textured fills.

New Term *WordArt* is a feature that takes plain old ordinary text and embellishes it with shadowing, stretching, and fitting the text to several predefined shapes, as shown in Figure 11.13. You can also change the look of the object by adding many color enhancements.

Just a Minute

When you create WordArt, the text is changed to a drawing object, so it's not included in spellchecks or the Outline View.

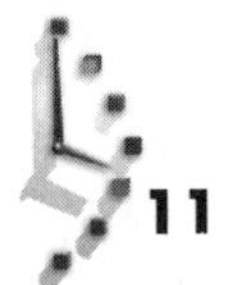

Figure 11.13.
A slide with WordArt.

Follow these steps to create WordArt:

1. Click the WordArt button in the middle of the drawing toolbar (the blue A at an angle).
2. Select a WordArt style from the WordArt Gallery. (See Figure 11.14.)
3. Type your text.
4. Change the font or font size, if you want.
5. Add bold or italics, if you like.
6. Click the OK button.

Figure 11.14.
The WordArt Gallery.

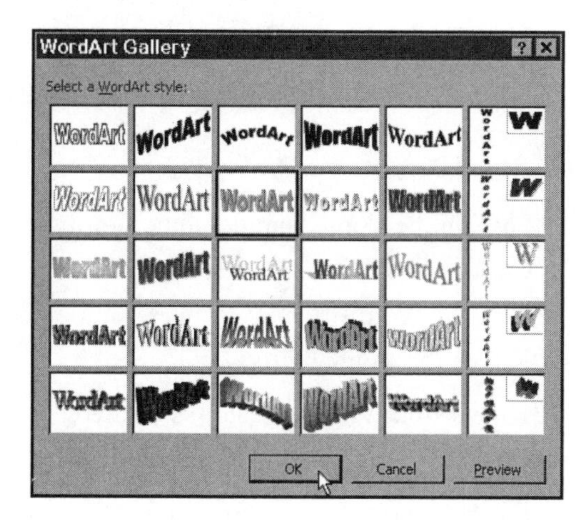

The WordArt object will be added to the middle of your slide, and is ready to be resized and repositioned as necessary. To resize WordArt, follow the steps:

1. Click once on the WordArt to select it.
2. Position the mouse over any white sizing handle.
3. Hold down the left mouse button and drag the sizing handle to a new location, as shown in Figure 11.15.
4. Release the mouse button.

Figure 11.15.
Resizing a WordArt object.

Here's how to move a WordArt object:

1. Position the mouse pointer on the WordArt object.
2. Click and hold down the left mouse button; you should see a move pointer.
3. Drag the WordArt object to a new location on the slide.
4. Release the mouse button.

To edit the text in WordArt, follow these steps:

1. Double-click the WordArt object.
2. Edit the text.
3. Click the OK button.

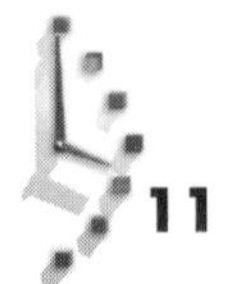

Using the WordArt Toolbar

When you click on a WordArt object, the WordArt toolbar usually appears. (See Figure 11.16.) Use this toolbar to add or change any of the special effects of a WordArt object. Some of the features you can change are the WordArt object's shape and format. You can also rotate the WordArt object, and switch the text to a vertical or horizontal orientation.

Figure 11.16.
The WordArt toolbar.

Changing the WordArt Shape

There are 40 custom shapes you can use for your WordArt object, as shown in Figure 11.17. To change the shape of a WordArt object, follow these steps:

1. Select the WordArt object by clicking on it.
2. On the WordArt toolbar, click the WordArt Shape button.
3. Click a new shape.

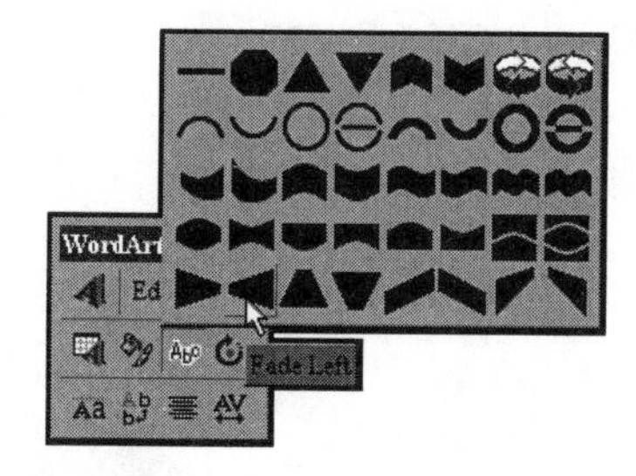

Figure 11.17.
WordArt shape options.

Formatting WordArt

You can format WordArt in the same manner as any other object. You can change the color and line options for the WordArt. The fill option is an excellent method for coloring the WordArt object and making it stand out.

To add color and fill to a WordArt object, follow these steps:

1. Select the WordArt object you want to format.
2. Click the Format WordArt button on the WordArt toolbar.
3. Click the Colors and Lines tab. (See Figure 11.18.)
4. Select a fill option from the Color drop-down list.

5. If you want, select color, style, dashed, and weight options for a border.
6. Click the Preview button to preview your changes before accepting them.
7. Click the OK button when you're done.

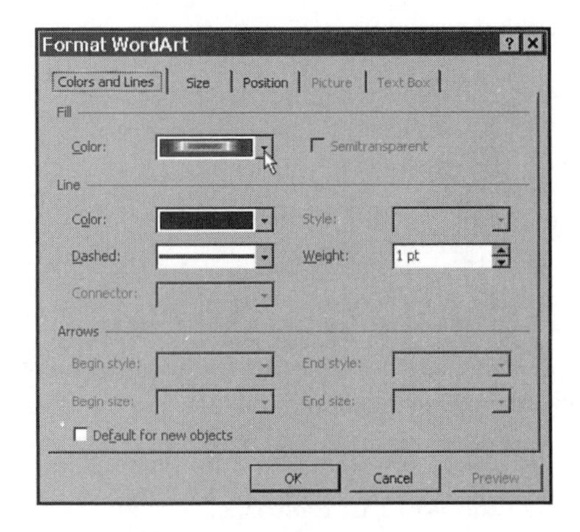

Figure 11.18.
The Colors and Lines tab of the Format WordArt dialog box.

Creating Vertical Text

Figure 11.19 illustrates vertical WordArt. To make the WordArt text vertical instead of horizontal, follow these steps:

1. Select the WordArt object you want to change.
2. Click the WordArt Vertical Text button on the WordArt toolbar.

Figure 11.19.
WordArt with vertical text.

Time Saver

To change the WordArt text back to a horizontal orientation, click the WordArt Vertical Text button again.

Rotating WordArt

You can easily rotate WordArt by using the Free Rotate button on the WordArt toolbar; just follow these steps:

1. Select the WordArt object you want to rotate.
2. Click the Free Rotate button on the WordArt toolbar. You should see four green rotate handles in each corner of the WordArt object, as shown in Figure 11.20.
3. Place the mouse pointer on any rotate handle, and hold the left mouse button down.
4. Rotate the WordArt object.
5. Release the mouse button when the WordArt object is in the position you want.

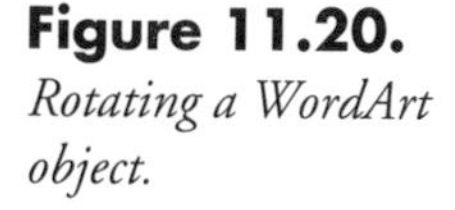

Figure 11.20.
Rotating a WordArt object.

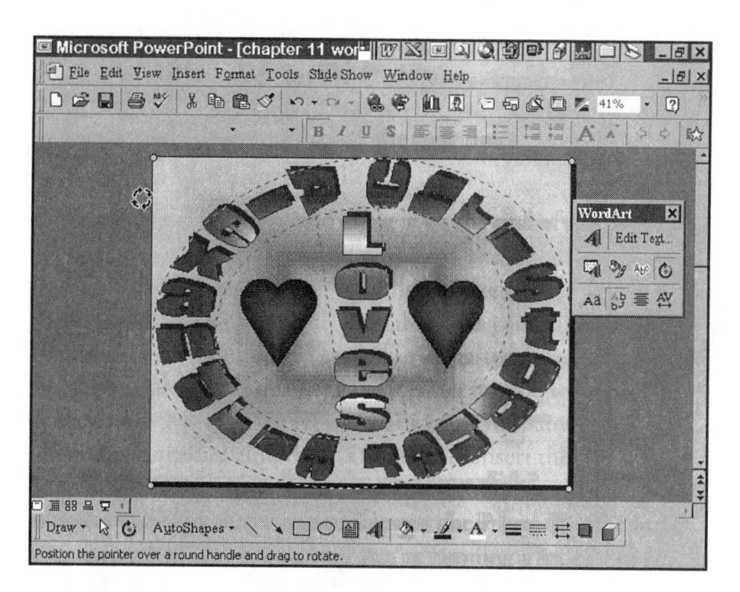

Summary

Drawing objects allow you to add depth to your presentation and more clearly define your message. In this hour, you have learned how to create text objects, use the WordArt program, and the steps for using the guides to position objects.

Workshop

This hour started your introduction into drawing objects. If you thought WordArt was fun to read about, get ready for some hands-on experience. After a brief "Test What You've Learned" section, you will soon be venturing into the land of drawing in the next hour, where all things are possible.

P.S. Once again, don't forget to read those all-important questions and answers.

Test What You've Learned

1. Start a new blank presentation, using the blank slide as the layout.
2. Create a text box label.
3. Create a word processing box.
4. Select one of the text boxes you created and change the color and line style.
5. Create a WordArt object.
6. Change the shape of the WordArt object.
7. Change the fill color of the WordArt object.
8. Make the WordArt object text vertical.
9. Change the WordArt object text back to horizontal.
10. Rotate the WordArt object.
11. Save the presentation as `Hour 11 TWYL`.
12. Close the presentation.

Q&A

Q I created a text box, but now I think I would rather have a shape with the text inside it. Is there an easy way to do this?

A To quickly change a text box to an AutoShape (AutoShapes are covered in the next hour), follow these steps:

1. Click on the text box to select it.
2. Choose Draw | Change AutoShape from the drawing toolbar.
3. Select an AutoShape category.
4. Click the AutoShape you want.

At first glance, it might not seem that the text box has indeed changed shape. This is usually because text boxes have no lines or fill effects. After you change the shape, you might need to turn on the fill and line options in the Format AutoShapes dialog box. You might also find that the AutoShape needs to be resized. Hour 12, "Drawing Shapes in PowerPoint," covers formatting AutoShapes.

Q What is the little yellow diamond I see when I select a WordArt object?

A This is an adjustment handle. You can use it to change the appearance of the WordArt shape. Simply click and drag the adjustment handle. An adjustment handle's function depends on where it appears on the WordArt; the best thing to do is just experiment with them (they all work a little differently). Don't forget, if you make a change that you really don't like, you can always use the Undo command.

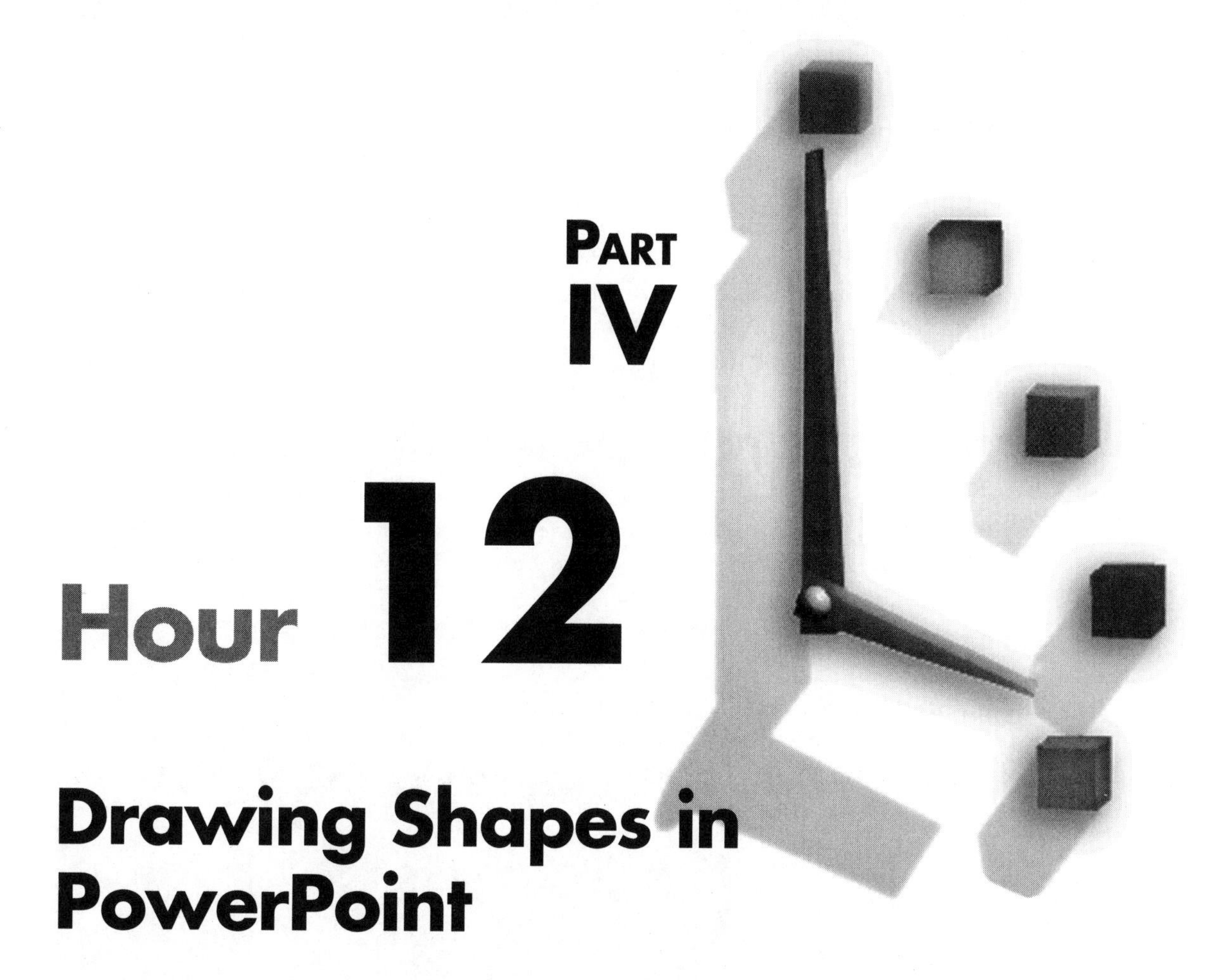

PART IV

Hour 12

Drawing Shapes in PowerPoint

PowerPoint supplies drawing tools that inspire unlimited creativity, and in this hour, you learn the fundamentals for drawing eye-catching graphics. This hour should be very enjoyable because you'll be drawing interesting objects in PowerPoint. Better than oils and canvas, PowerPoint and a high-resolution monitor allow you to experiment with unique digital effects. If you have the time, creating custom drawing objects in PowerPoint is an energizing, artistic experience. Exciting drawing features have been added to PowerPoint 97, so people who have used previous versions of PowerPoint will discover new AutoShapes: connectors, callouts, and action buttons. This hour introduces you to the basics of successfully working with PowerPoint drawing objects; during it, you will learn the following:

- ☐ What an AutoShape is and how to draw it
- ☐ How to draw lines and connectors
- ☐ How to add text to an AutoShape
- ☐ How to apply formatting to AutoShapes and lines

The material covered in Hours 13, "Bringing Drawing Objects Together," and 14, "Drawing Special Effects," teaches more basic knowledge needed to join drawing objects so you can create standalone graphic images. An interesting side effect of this knowledge is that you start to look at everyday graphical objects and envision them reproduced as a result of combining different PowerPoint drawing objects. The possibilities are endless, so without further ado....

Drawing AutoShape Objects

When you look at Figure 12.1, you probably see a Manhattan cocktail with a cherry (dry, shaken, not stirred). I see two trapezoids, a rectangle, an oval, a circle, and a curved line. Each of these objects has also been formatted to create a particular effect.

Figure 12.1.
Using PowerPoint 97's drawing objects to make a simple picture.

Just a Minute

Even though you can't tell at a glance, the shapes in this picture have also been grouped to interact as a single vector graphic. The Group and Ungroup features are explained in more detail in Hour 13.

New Term

Vector graphics are a type of graphic image composed of shapes grouped together. The shapes are stacked on top of each in an order that creates a picture in the mind's eye. Think back to when you were in kindergarten. Remember cutting out a bunch of circles, squares, and triangles? After gluing the shapes together, you had formed a picture of a house underneath clouds. Vector graphics work by the same principles.

Are you ready to start drawing? I am. Get ready to learn about the basic PowerPoint object types.

Lines

PowerPoint 97 has six different line styles to choose from: three straight and three curved line styles. Each line style can also be formatted with many different options. PowerPoint always has the type of line you need for a project. This hour covers how to work with straight lines, and Hour 14 covers curved lines. The line, arrow, and double-arrow options all draw straight lines; here are the steps for drawing them:

1. Select AutoShapes from the drawing toolbar or choose View | Picture | AutoShapes.
2. Select Lines.
3. Click on either Line, Arrow, or Double Arrow.
4. Move the mouse to the area on the slide where you want the line to start. The mouse pointer should look like Figure 12.2, a thin cross (also called a *cross hair*).
5. Click and hold down the left mouse button.
6. Drag the mouse to the location where the line should end, and release the mouse button.

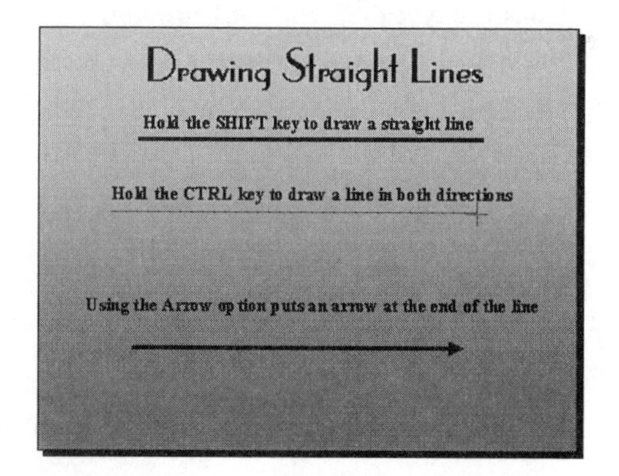

Figure 12.2.
The mouse pointer is ready to draw a line.

Just a Minute

If you selected Arrow, the arrow appears on the end of the line (the position where you released the mouse button). Therefore, if you're drawing a line from left to right, the arrow appears on the right end of the line. Depending on the settings, the arrow might be so small that you can't see it, so refer to the upcoming section "Using Arrowheads" for more information on formatting arrowheads.

Time Saver

If you want to draw a straight, or constrained, line, hold down the Shift key while dragging. This method keeps the line constrained to 15-degree angles and makes drawing less tedious.

Holding down the Ctrl key while dragging causes the line to draw in both directions from the starting point.

Use Ctrl+Shift while dragging the mouse to get a straight line drawn in both directions.

Connectors

A *connector* is a valuable, time-saving drawing object used to visually connect two points. Using connector lines instead of normal lines is helpful when you move an object because the lines stay connected (hence the name *connectors*). To connect any object, use one of PowerPoint 97's three types of connector lines—straight, angled, or curved—and follow these steps:

1. Select AutoShapes from the drawing toolbar.
2. Select Connectors.
3. Click the type of connector you want.
4. Position the mouse on the first object to connect.
5. Click on a blue connection site. (See Figure 12.3.)
6. Move the mouse to the second object and click on a connection site. Wow, you're really connected now!

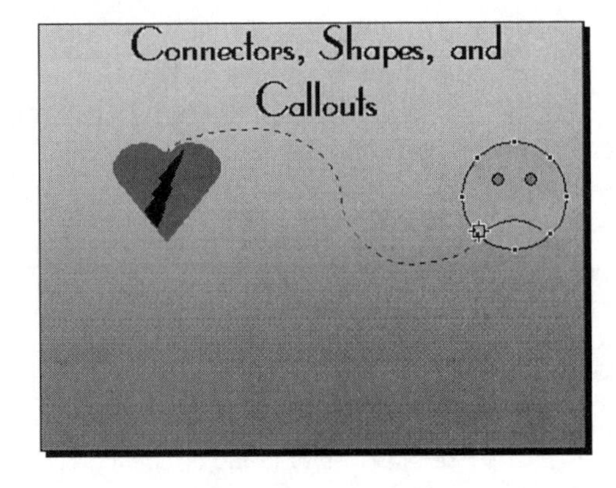

Figure 12.3.
Click on a connection site to use a connector.

Once you have connected two objects, the connection lines show locked connectors as red squares. If a connector isn't locked to an object (unlocked), the connector is shown as a green square. You can also use the yellow adjustment controls to "snake" the connector the way you want. This feature is one you need to actually experiment with to really get the hang of it.

Basic Shapes, Block Arrows, Flow Chart Symbols, and Stars and Banners

The next four AutoShape options—Basic Shapes, Block Arrows, Flow Chart Symbols, and Stars and Banners—all interact in basically the same way. The main difference between the objects is the specific shape. There are many closed shapes that can be easily drawn and grouped to create almost any kind of picture. Remember the sample cocktail shown at the beginning of this chapter? Your drawing can be very simple or extremely complex, enough to create an intricate work of art.

Follow these steps to draw an AutoShape:

1. Select AutoShapes from the drawing toolbar.
2. Select Basic Shapes, Block Arrows, Flow Chart Symbols, or Stars and Banners.
3. Click the AutoShape you want to draw.
4. When drawing any kind of AutoShape, imagine a box that will contain the AutoShape image. Click and hold the left mouse button on the upper-left corner of the imaginary box.
5. Drag to the lower-right corner of the imaginary box.
6. Release the mouse.

Callouts

A *callout* is a text description for part of a graphical image. Callout objects are useful AutoShapes when you need to use text with a connecting line back to an object. For example, you might need to describe a particular object, or you might want your happy face drawing to say something, as shown in Figure 12.4.

Whatever your need, PowerPoint 97 is up to speed. To draw a callout, follow these familiar steps:

1. Select AutoShapes from the drawing toolbar.
2. Select Callouts.
3. Click the callout you want.
4. As with drawing an AutoShape, imagine a box that will contain the callout on your slide. Click and hold down the left mouse button on the upper-left corner of the imaginary box.

5. Drag to the lower-right corner of the imaginary box.
6. Release the mouse.

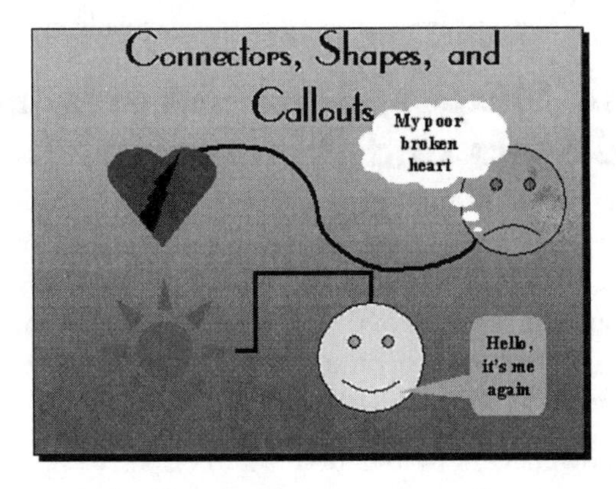

Figure 12.4.
Sad and happy faces with something to say.

Action Buttons

Action buttons, the last available option on the AutoShapes menu, allow you to create navigation buttons like the ones you see displayed on World Wide Web pages. You draw these buttons just as you do any other AutoShape. Once you release the mouse button, PowerPoint 97 displays the Actions Settings dialog box where you can set the specific action you want the button to perform. Action buttons are covered in more detail in Hour 22, "Creating Web Pages."

Adding Text in Drawing Objects

You can add text quickly and easily to any AutoShape. The one exception is lines, which can't have text added to them. Many people draw the shape, and then draw a text box on top of the shape. However, resist the urge to add text to your shapes in this manner because this method actually creates two objects: the AutoShape and the text box. If you were to move the AutoShape, the text wouldn't move with it (unless you took the extra step of grouping them together). What a time-consuming mess! To avoid that potential problem, follow this simple sequence to add text to any AutoShape:

1. Select the shape.
2. Start typing.

Wow—that was almost *too* easy! The text is automatically centered in the AutoShape and can be formatted in the same manner as other text objects, as shown in Figure 12.5.

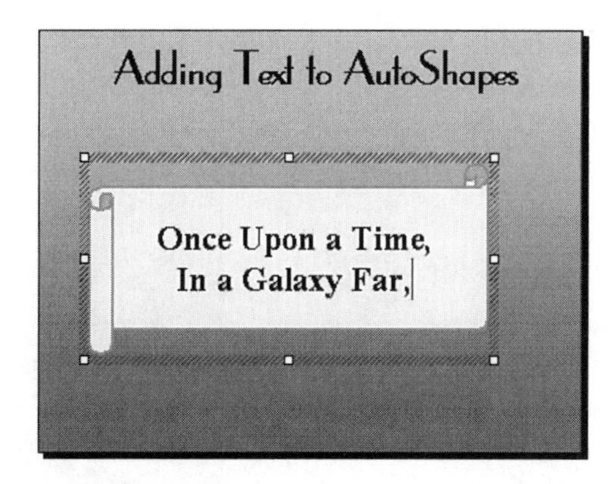

Figure 12.5.
An AutoShape with text.

Formatting Drawing Objects

Do you want color? Lines? What type of arrows do you want on your lines? Do you need the arrow to be placed at the other end of the line? The drawing objects you have learned to draw in this hour can be formatted in so many different ways. PowerPoint 97 is like that famous fast-food chain—yes, you *can* have it your way!

Working with Shapes

The shape of AutoShape objects can easily be formatted with color and lines, and you can adjust the size or position, if needed. The Manhattan cocktail pictured at the beginning of this chapter had different color and line options set for each object. The three shapes that made up the glass were colored white, with no lines. The liquid was colored light brown (a whiskey color) and enhanced with gradient shading and no lines. The cherry, colored red, had gradient shading and no lines, and its stem was a single curved line that was three points thick.

12

Using Colors and Lines

You can add or change the color and lines of any AutoShape. How you combine these options depends on the effect you want. At first, it might seem as though it takes a while to figure out how to get a certain special effect, but eventually you will find yourself seeing every object in your home as a combination of PowerPoint AutoShapes with color and lines. To change or add color or lines to any AutoShape, follow these steps:

1. Select the AutoShape you want to format.
2. Choose Format | AutoShape from the menu.
3. Click the Colors and Lines tab. (See Figure 12.6.)
4. Select a color or fill option from the Color drop-down list.

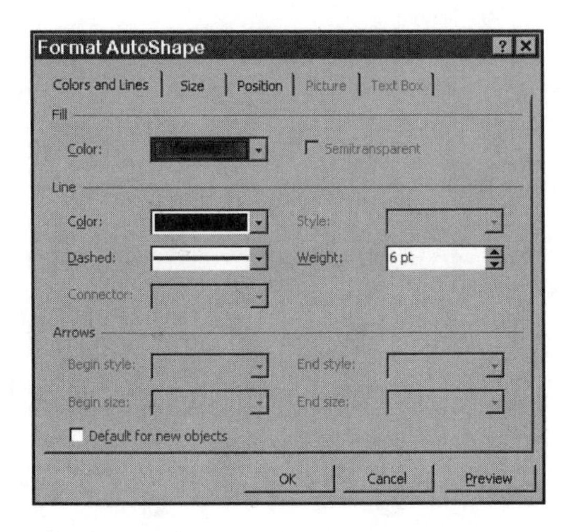

Figure 12.6.
The Colors and Lines tab of the Format AutoShape dialog box.

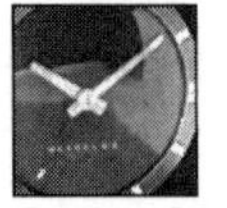

Just a Minute

> Use the Fill Effects option from the Color drop-down list to apply a gradient or other fill effect to your text object. Unlike working with text boxes, it's fun to just let your imagination run wild. Remember, however, that you're drawing a picture, and don't include unnecessary effects that detract from the image.

5. If you want a border, click the Color drop-down list under the Line section.
6. Change the Style, Dashed, and Weight options for the line for different effects.
7. Click the Preview button to preview your changes before accepting them.
8. Click the OK button when finished.

Resizing AutoShapes

The easiest way to resize an AutoShape is to drag a sizing handle, as shown in Figure 12.7.

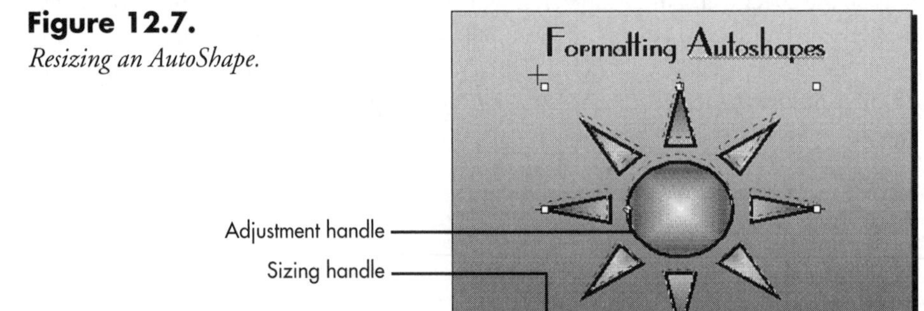

Figure 12.7.
Resizing an AutoShape.

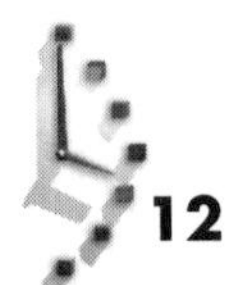

However, if you want an AutoShape to be a specific size, you can set it in the Format AutoShape dialog box:

1. Click once on the AutoShape to select it.
2. Choose Format | AutoShape from the menu.
3. Click the Size tab. (See Figure 12.8.)
4. Enter an exact height and/or width for the bounding box.
5. Click the Preview button to preview your changes before accepting them.
6. Click the OK button when finished.

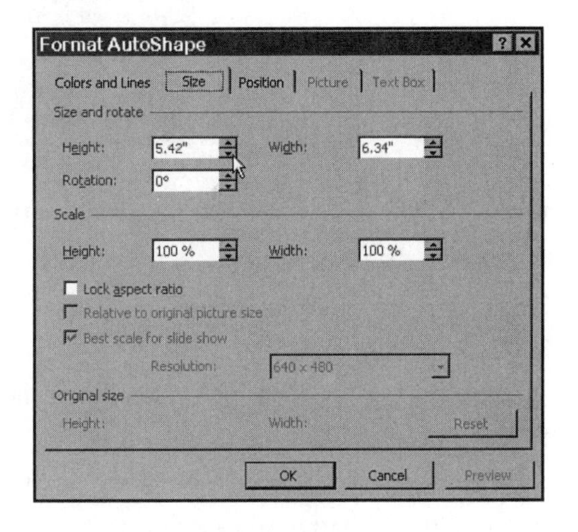

Figure 12.8.
The Size tab of the Format AutoShape dialog box.

JUST A MINUTE

PowerPoint also allows you to free-rotate or flip any object. These options are covered in Hour 13.

Moving or Positioning an AutoShape

Even when you try to draw everything in just the right place, you often need to move AutoShapes around. You have two options for repositioning AutoShapes: the fast-draw mouse method of dragging the AutoShape to the appropriate location or the position option in the Format AutoShape dialog box.

To drag an AutoShape to a new location, follow these easy steps:

1. Position the mouse pointer on the AutoShape.
2. Click and hold down the left mouse button.

3. Drag the AutoShape to the new location. (See Figure 12.9.)
4. Release the mouse button.

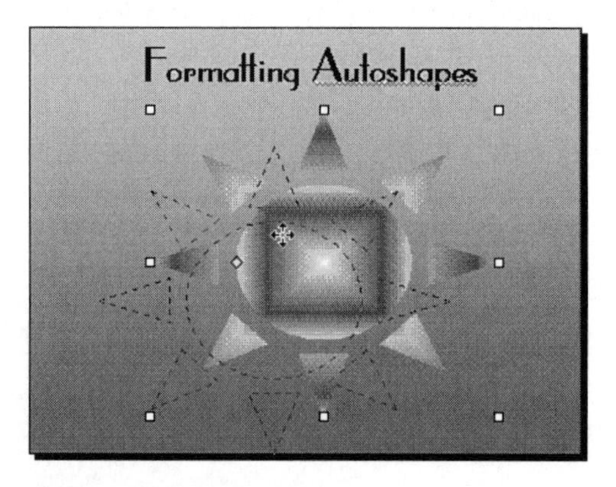

Figure 12.9.
Moving an AutoShape.

If accuracy is important, follow these steps to position an AutoShape in an exact location:

1. Select the AutoShape you want to position.
2. Choose Format | AutoShape from the menu.
3. Click the Position tab.
4. Enter the horizontal position you want for the AutoShape.
5. Enter the vertical position you want for the AutoShape.
6. Click the Preview button to preview your changes before accepting them.
7. Click the OK button when finished.

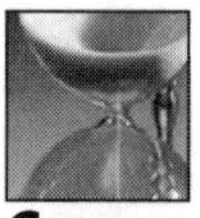

CAUTION

PowerPoint positions objects by using their upper-left edge. If you want to center an AutoShape, it's much easier to turn on the guides by choosing View | Guides from the menu and dragging the object to the center, as shown in Figure 12.10. The object should snap to the guides automatically.

JUST A MINUTE

You can align several AutoShapes by using the Draw | Align or Distribute command from the drawing toolbar. Aligning objects is covered in Hour 13.

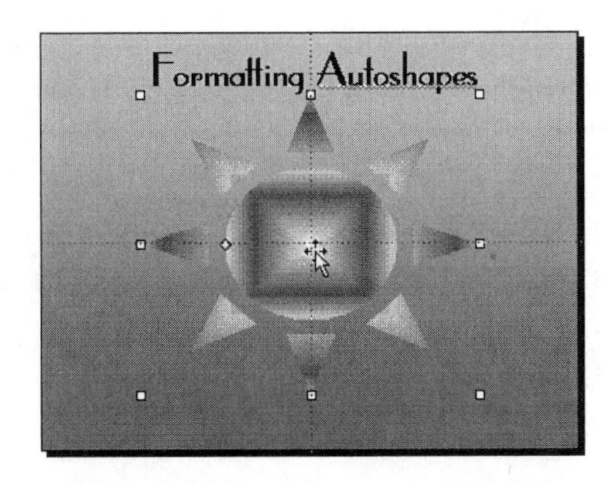

Figure 12.10.
An AutoShape centered by using the guides.

Formatting Text

If you have entered text into an AutoShape, you can format its appearance just as you would any other text object. You can use the Format Font dialog box or any of the text formatting tools on the formatting toolbar.

JUST A MINUTE

The drawing toolbar has one button for formatting text, the Text Color button.

To format AutoShape text, follow this sequence:

1. Select the text you want to format.

TIME SAVER

If you want to format all the text in the AutoShape, click once on the AutoShape to select it and a second time on the AutoShape border to select the entire AutoShape.

2. Choose Format | Font from the menu.
3. Change any options you want.
4. Click the Preview button to see a preview of your changes before accepting them.
5. Click the OK button.

Refer to Hour 5, "Working with PowerPoint Text Objects," for all the nitty-gritty details of formatting text.

In the Format AutoShape dialog box's Text Box tab, there are a few additional options to help you get certain tasks done quickly. As discussed previously, you can change how the text is anchored in the text object. There are also options for changing the internal margins, word wrapping the text, fitting the AutoShape to the text, and rotating text. To change any of these options, follow these steps:

1. Select the AutoShape.
2. Choose Format | AutoShape from the menu.
3. Click the Text Box tab. (See Figure 12.11.)
4. Change any options you want.
5. Click the Preview button to see a preview of your changes.
6. Click the OK button.

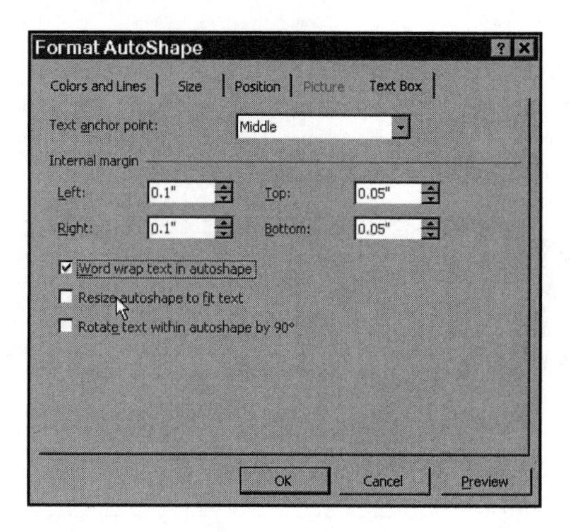

Figure 12.11.
The Text Box tab of the Format AutoShape dialog box.

Working with Lines

There are hundreds of different ways to format a line. PowerPoint 97 offers you choices for changing the look for any type of line you might have drawn. The following sections cover the available options for these attributes:

- Line styles
- Color
- Thickness
- Arrowheads
- Connectors

Formatting Line Styles

All the lines you draw can be formatted with many options for just the right look. You can change the line color, select one of PowerPoint's dashed line styles, or choose a custom line

pattern. You can also change the line's thickness simply by changing the line weight to a larger point size. Figure 12.12 shows a line drawn in a two-color, 15-point thick (or heavy), diamond pattern.

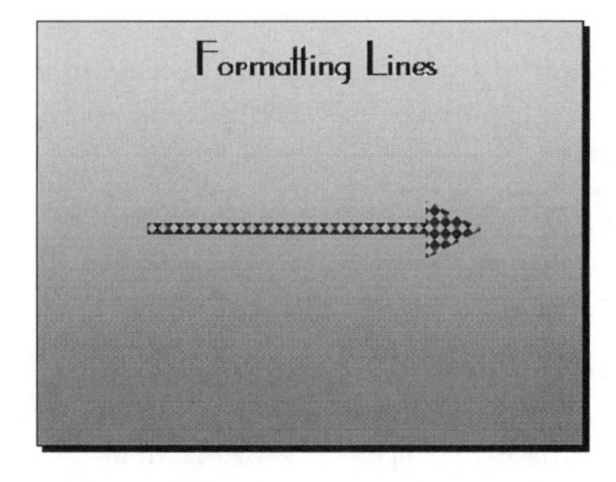

Figure 12.12.
Changing the look of the line.

TIME SAVER

If you use a pattern option for a line, set the line's thickness at 10 or more points so that the pattern is properly displayed.

To change the line style, follow these steps:

1. Select the line you want to format.
2. Choose Format | AutoShape from the menu.
3. Click the Colors and Lines tab. (See Figure 12.13.)

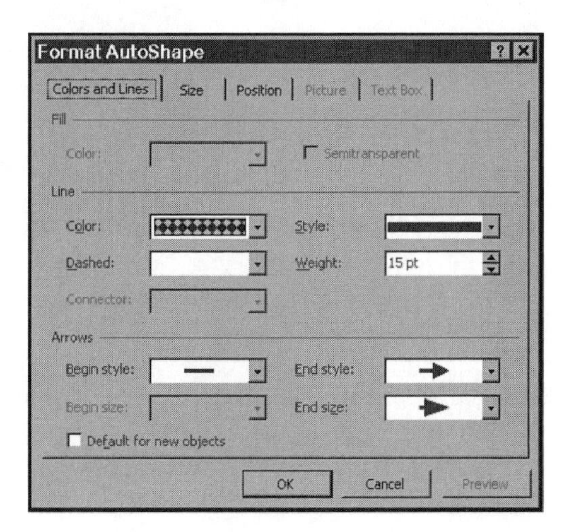

Figure 12.13.
The Colors and Lines tab of the Format AutoShape dialog box.

4. Under the Line section, select a color or pattern option from the Color drop-down list.
5. Change the Style, Dashed, and Weight options for the line for different effects.

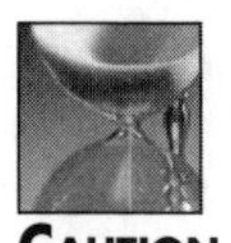

CAUTION

If you use a pattern, you can't select a style, too. You must choose one option or the other.

6. Click the Preview button to preview your changes before accepting the modifications.
7. Click the OK button when finished.

Using Arrowheads

You can easily add or edit arrowheads on a line. You might realize that you need arrowheads or that an arrowhead ended up on the wrong side of the line after you drew it. You also have several different arrowhead styles to choose from.

The option of adjusting the arrowhead size without changing the line's thickness is a new feature in PowerPoint 97. Not only can you adjust the size, but for double-arrowhead lines, you can also have a different style and size for each end of the line! Figure 12.14 illustrates a line with different arrowhead styles and varying sizes for each end of the line.

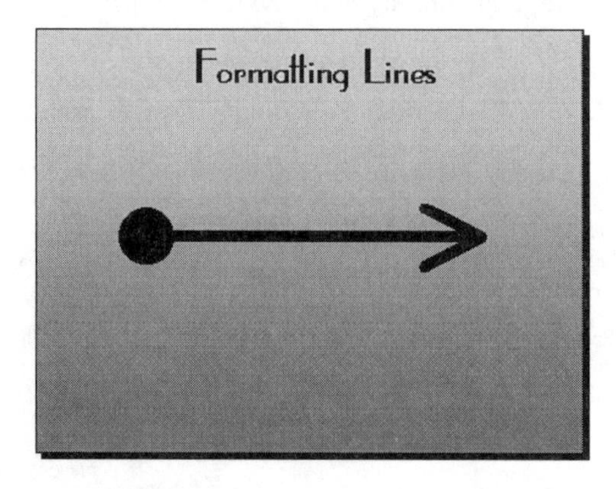

Figure 12.14.
A line formatted with different arrowheads.

Follow these steps to add, move, or change the arrowhead style:

1. Select the line you want to format.
2. Choose Format | AutoShape from the menu.
3. Click the Colors and Lines tab.

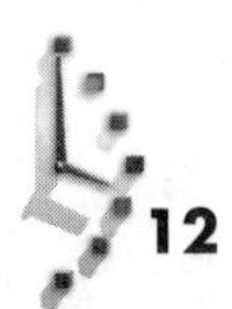

4. Under the Arrows section, select a begin style and/or end style of arrow for the line.
5. Select a begin size and/or end size for each arrow style.
6. Click the Preview button to preview your changes before accepting them.
7. Click the OK button when finished.

Using Connector Lines

Connector lines can also be formatted with all the options previously discussed. In addition to the standard formatting options, you can also change the connector line style, if you want. The connector can have the following styles:

- Straight
- Elbow
- Curved

To change the style of a connector line, follow these steps:

1. Select the line you want to format.
2. Choose Format | AutoShape from the menu.
3. Click the Colors and Lines tab.
4. Under the Line section, select the connector style you want from the Connector drop-down list.
5. Select a begin size and/or end size for each arrow style.
6. Click the Preview button to preview your changes before accepting them.
7. Click the OK button when finished.

Summary

In this hour, you have learned about options for drawing and formatting AutoShapes in PowerPoint, and you have been introduced to the concept of using the AutoShape features available with PowerPoint 97 to create a picture. You have seen a picture with simple formatting created with AutoShape lines and shapes.

You have also learned how to draw straight, curved, and connector lines, seen the quick, easy methods available for drawing any other AutoShape, and learned how to make an AutoShape take on new and exciting dimensions by simply changing the color, fill, line, and other options found in the Format AutoShape dialog box.

Stay tuned, because in the next two hours this book covers more features that will transform you into a novice graphical artist. You'll find that once you start drawing, you won't want to stop.

Workshop

For this hour's workshop, I thought it would be fun to create a picture during the TWYL section. The following steps explain how to create the picture of the Manhattan cocktail you saw at the beginning of this hour. If you don't want to be the bartender, you could make a picture of the Cheshire Cat, if you like. Get some practice, and have fun, Alice.

Test What You've Learned

JUST A MINUTE

Don't forget to save your art frequently while you work. This is so important when you start to draw because drawing takes a lot more memory than normal and could cause your system to stop responding. I have had my machine lock up on me on several occasions, usually when I was drawing something really fun and fancy. I was so glad I had used the Save button frequently.

1. Start a new blank presentation.
2. Choose Blank Slide as the layout for the first slide.
3. Change the background color to a light gray so you can see the glass.
4. The first object you'll create is the glass. It's three AutoShapes, all from the Basic Shapes menu:
    - The top is a trapezoid.

TIME SAVER

Use the yellow adjustment handle to squeeze the bottom of the trapezoid almost closed.

    - The stem is a rectangle.
    - The base is an oval.
5. Select all three AutoShapes and format the fill color to white with no line.
6. For the drink, draw another trapezoid inside the first one.
7. Format the drink trapezoid with a horizontal gradient fill, selecting a brown color with no line.
8. Use the oval AutoShape again to draw a cherry (hold the Shift key down while drawing to make the oval a perfect circle).
9. Format the cherry with a horizontal gradient fill, selecting a dark red color with no line.

10. Use a curved line for the stem.
11. Format the line to have a weight of 4 points.
12. Save the file as `Hour 12 TWYL`.

Q&A

Q I noticed that your AutoShapes menu is floating on the left of the screen like a toolbar. How did you do that?

A Any toolbar menu has a thin title bar at the top (like the AutoShape menu). You can drag the menu to a new location and create a floating toolbar. To perform this incredible feat (I've used the AutoShape menu as the example), just follow these steps:

1. Select AutoShape from the drawing toolbar.
2. Move the mouse pointer to the top of the menu into the title bar.
3. Click and hold down the left mouse button.
4. Drag to the location you want.
5. Release the mouse button.

TIME SAVER

Any floating toolbar can also be resized.

Q How do I add text to a line so that the text moves with the line?

A Unfortunately, there's not really a quick way to add text to a line. You need to create a text box (use the label method discussed in Hour 11). If you want the text to move with the line, you need to select both objects and group them together. Grouping is covered in Hour 13.

Q What's the little yellow diamond that appears on the AutoShapes when selected?

A This is an adjustment handle. You can use it to change the appearance of the AutoShape object, just as you can with WordArt shapes.

Q When I type text in my AutoShape, it doesn't word wrap; in fact, it appears outside the shape. Help?

A Unfortunately, this usually happens if you type a lot of text on an AutoShape. I guess those nice folks at Microsoft assumed that you wouldn't be typing anything lengthy on a shape. Here's how you can fix the problem:

1. Select the AutoShape.
2. Choose Format | AutoShape from the menu.

3. Click the Text Box tab.
4. Select the "Word wrap text in autoshape" checkbox.
5. Click the OK button.

You can also use the "Resize autoshape to fit text" option. I sometimes use the two options together; it just depends on the situation. Experiment with both options to see which one you prefer.

PART
IV

Hour 13

Bringing Drawing Objects Together

Now that you know how to draw and format any of PowerPoint 97's AutoShapes to create a simple picture, you're ready to learn how to create a more complicated picture. This hour covers four important tasks that are often used when creating an image:

- Pulling several objects into a group or ungrouping a single object
- Stacking and using the order of the stack to create the effect you need
- Using the different methods for aligning objects
- Rotating objects

Ungrouping and Grouping Objects

Some of the best lessons I've learned have been from inserting a clip art image and ungrouping it to see how the image was created. After ungrouping an image, you can see the components used to create the picture. When you're first learning, start with a simple image and then progress to more complicated pictures.

NEW TERM *Object ungrouping* means taking an image, such as a piece of clipart, and *decomposing* the object (taking it apart) to see all the smaller pieces that make up the larger image. *Grouping* is the exact opposite. You take several objects and then bind (or group) them together to make one larger image. Most clip art images are just a bunch of small shapes that have been grouped together to create a coherent image.

To ungroup an image, follow these steps:

1. Select the image.
2. Choose Draw | Ungroup from the drawing toolbar.
3. Click Yes to convert the object to a drawing object.

Figure 13.1 shows a simple clip art image that has been ungrouped. Notice that there are selection handles surrounding each separate object in the group.

CAUTION

Some objects have image groups that have been grouped together. For example, to completely ungroup the dice clip art, I had to choose the Draw | Ungroup command three times.

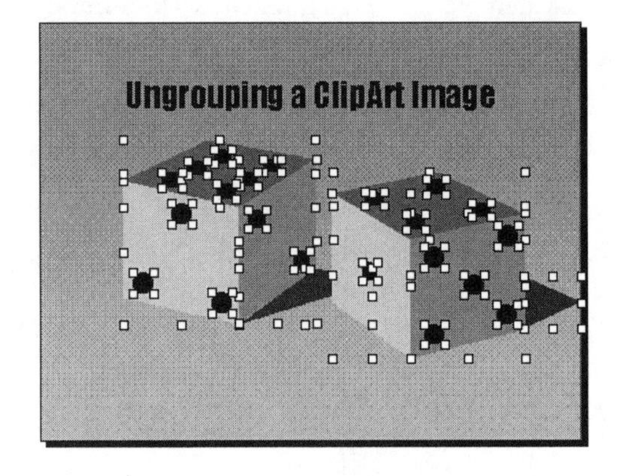

Figure 13.1.
A clip art image that has been ungrouped.

Figure 13.2 shows the Manhattan cocktail image, from the previous hour, with all the AutoShapes grouped together to make a single object.

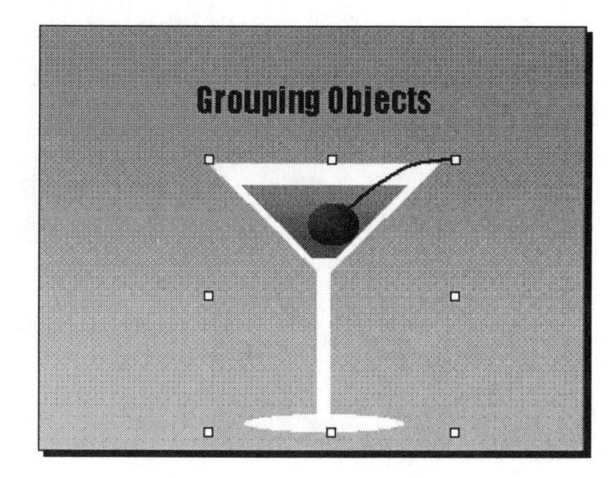

Figure 13.2.
The Manhattan cocktail image, grouped together as one object.

When you have grouped all the objects that make up an image, there are several advantages. Because the collection of objects becomes a single image construct, the image is much easier to move, resize, or copy. To group several objects into a single image, follow these steps:

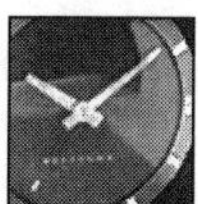

Just a Minute

You must have at least two objects selected to use the Group command.

1. Select all the objects you want to group together.
2. Choose Draw | Group from the drawing toolbar.

Time Saver

You can easily select several objects by using the mouse to drag a lasso around all the ones you want to select. Figure 13.3 shows a lasso selecting several objects. Or, you can hold down the Shift key and click on each object you want to select.

Time Saver

If you have ungrouped a clip art image—to see how it was created, for example—select one of the objects and then choose Draw | Regroup from the drawing toolbar to regroup the entire image.

Figure 13.3.
Lassoing several objects to select them.

Stacking Objects

You can change the entire presentation of a drawing by changing the order in which the objects are stacked on top of one another. Objects toward the front of the stack hide and overlap background objects. When you're drawing AutoShapes or inserting other objects, PowerPoint stacks each object in the order that they're drawn or inserted. To see how this feature works, draw any AutoShape and choose Edit | Duplicate from the menu. Choose Edit | Duplicate a few more times, and you can see how the AutoShapes are stacking on top of each other in a sweep, as shown in Figure 13.4.

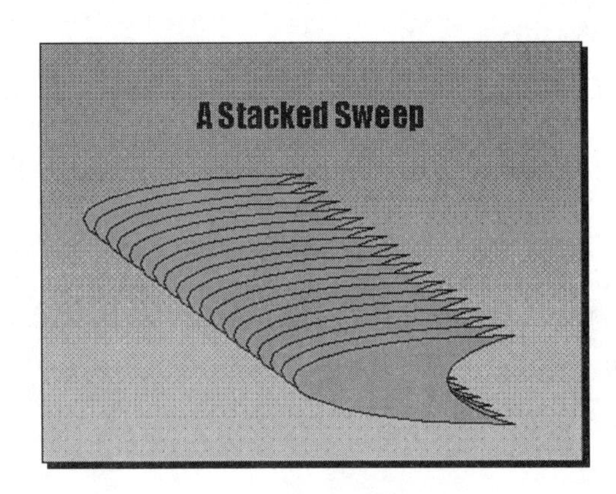

Figure 13.4.
AutoShapes stacked on top of each other in a sweep.

NEW TERM A *sweep* is a repeating series of identical objects that are displayed as evenly spaced and overlapped.

When you want to change the stacking order of objects, you can move an object to the front or back of the stack quickly. If you want the object somewhere in the middle of the stack, you need to move the object up or down through each layer.

Figure 13.4 is a sample picture with several AutoShape objects. The sun is behind the cloud, the lightning is on top of the cloud, and the clip art of Seattle is the central focus. Using this picture, you'll see how to work with the Order options.

Figure 13.5.
A nasty day in Seattle.

To brighten up the day, move the sun object to the top of the stack with these steps:

1. Select the object you want to move.
2. Choose Draw | Order | Bring to Front from the drawing toolbar. (See Figure 13.6.)

Figure 13.6.
The sun has come out.

TIME SAVER

Sometimes you can't see or select the object you want to move because it's hidden by other screen objects. If you select an object and then press the Tab key (or the Shift+Tab key combination), you can scroll through all the objects available in the picture. PowerPoint selects each object sequentially.

In the Seattle example, you now want to move the deadly lightning bolt to the back of the picture (bottom of the stack). To move an object to the bottom of the stack, follow these steps:

1. Select the object you want to move.
2. Choose Draw | Order | Send to Back from the drawing toolbar. (See Figure 13.7.)

Figure 13.7.
The lightning is gone (hidden).

The clouds also had to be stacked properly to get the correct effect. When you need a little more precision in the stacking order, you might want to move the object up and/or down one layer at a time. To move an object up one layer in the stack, follow these steps:

1. Select the object you want to move.
2. Choose Draw | Order | Bring Forward from the drawing toolbar.

Here's how to move an object down one layer in the stack:

1. Select the object you want to move.
2. Choose Draw | Order | Send Backward from the drawing toolbar.

Aligning and Distributing Objects

PowerPoint 97 has some great features for precisely lining up or distributing any object, drawing, clip art, or text. When aligning and distributing is combined with the grouping, order, and formatting features, you can start to really create some serious artwork. Who knows—you might be the next Pablo Picasso.

Aligning Objects

In previous hours, you have seen how to center objects by using the Guides option in the View menu. Okay, great—but what if you have several objects, as you might for a custom border,

that you want placed in a straight line? What to do, what to do? Well, here comes PowerPoint to the rescue. The Draw | Align or Distribute command lets you line up several objects. You can align the selected objects vertically by the left, center, or right sides, or you can align them horizontally by the top, middle, or bottom.

To align objects vertically, as shown in Figure 13.8, follow these steps:

1. Select all the objects you want to align.
2. Choose Draw | Align or Distribute from the drawing toolbar.
3. Choose either Align Left, Align Center, or Align Right from the submenu.

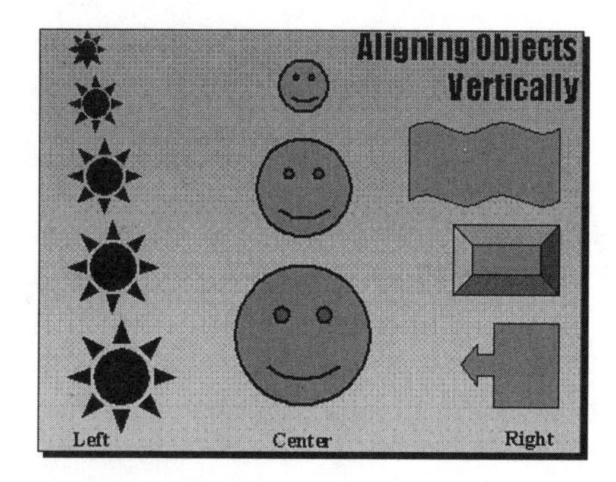

Figure 13.8.
Aligning objects vertically.

Follow these steps to align objects horizontally, as shown in Figure 13.9:

1. Select all the objects you want to align.
2. Choose Draw | Align or Distribute from the drawing toolbar.
3. Choose either Align Top, Align Middle, or Align Bottom from the submenu.

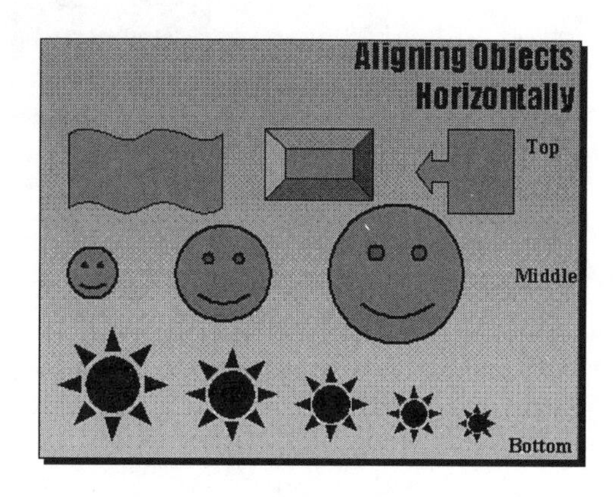

Figure 13.9.
Aligning objects horizontally.

You can also use a combination of the vertical and horizontal alignment options to stack objects precisely. Figure 13.10 shows two different combinations.

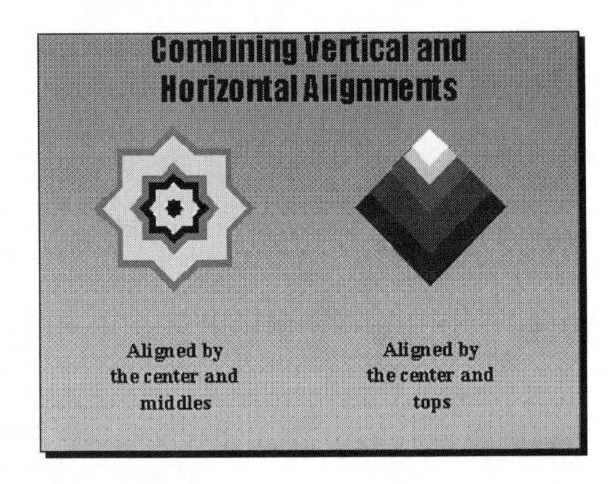

Figure 13.10.
Combining the vertical and horizontal alignment options to stack objects.

Distributing Objects

If you have several objects that would look good spaced equal distances from one another, use one of PowerPoint 97's Distribute options. Distribute takes all the objects selected and spaces them an equal distance apart between the first and last object. You can distribute either horizontally or vertically, as shown in Figure 13.11.

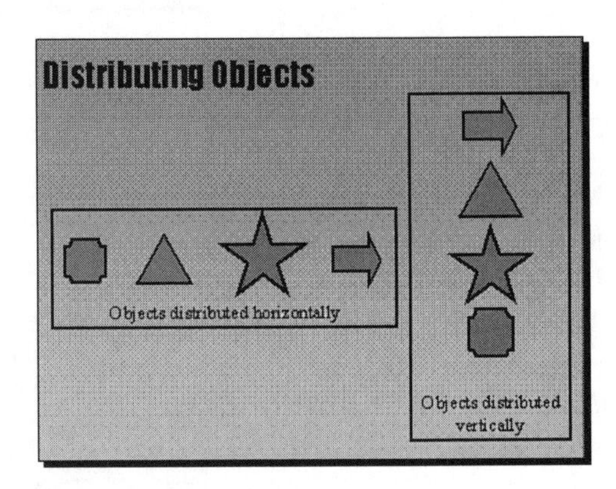

Figure 13.11.
Evenly distributing selected objects horizontally or vertically.

To distribute objects, follow these steps:

1. Select all the objects you want to align.
2. Choose Draw | Align or Distribute from the drawing toolbar.
3. Choose either Distribute Horizontally or Distribute Vertically from the submenu.

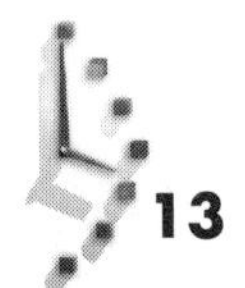

TIME SAVER

When you need the same object repeated evenly, as shown in Figure 13.12 for the posts on the picket fence, use the Edit | Duplicate command. As mentioned earlier, Duplicate is a great way to make sweeps and arrays with drawing objects. To create an array, follow these steps:

1. Draw the first object.
2. Select the object.
3. Choose Edit | Duplicate from the menu.
4. Drag the new object the distance you want all objects to be spaced.
5. Choose Edit | Duplicate from the menu for each duplicate object you need.

You might want to align the objects after you're finished.

NEW TERM An *array* is a series of identical objects that are evenly spaced but *not* overlapped, as they are in a sweep.

Figure 13.12.
Using the Duplicate command to create a picket fence with flowers.

Rotating and Flipping Objects

PowerPoint has many shapes you can use while drawing. However, by using PowerPoint 97's rotating and flipping options, you have even more possibilities. Figure 13.13 shows a picture that was created with the heart AutoShape. The four hearts are individually rotated and grouped to form a four-leaf clover. Once again, you're limited only by your imagination.

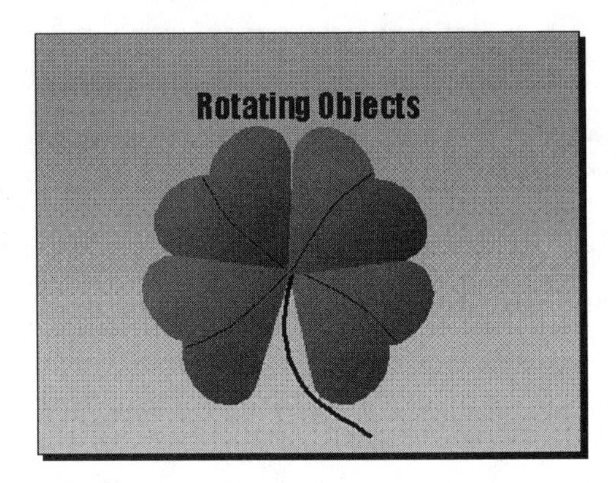

Figure 13.13.
A four-leaf clover created with PowerPoint 97's Free Rotate tool.

To apply the rotate effect to an object, follow these steps:

1. Select the object you want to rotate.
2. Click the Free Rotate tool on the drawing toolbar.
3. Position the mouse over a green rotate handle and drag to rotate, as shown in Figure 13.14.
4. Click anywhere off the object to deselect it.

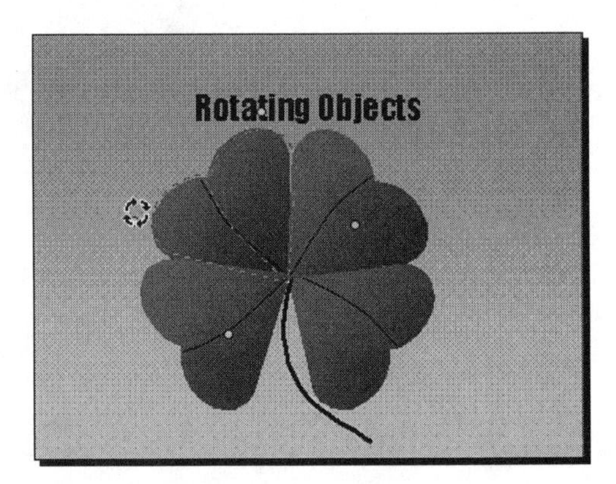

Figure 13.14.
Rotating an object using the Free Rotate tool.

TIME SAVER

Hold down the Shift key to rotate in 15-degree increments.

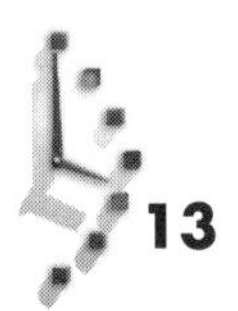

TIME SAVER

From the Draw | Rotate or Flip menu, you can also choose either Rotate Left or Rotate Right to rotate an object in 90-degree increments.

Use the Flip options when you want to rotate an object 180 degrees. Flipping is much easier than free rotating when you want to produce upside-down or mirror images. Figure 13.15 shows a clip art image that has been flipped vertically.

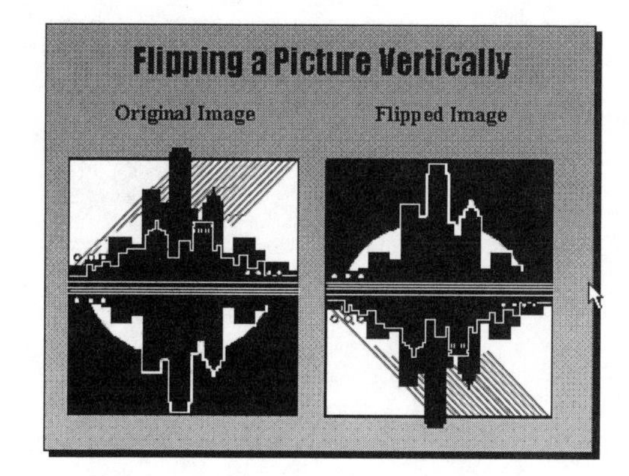

Figure 13.15.
Flipping the clip art image vertically gives you a completely different look.

Follow these steps to flip an object:

1. Select the object you want to flip.
2. Choose Draw | Rotate or Flip from the drawing toolbar.
3. Depending on the effect you want, select either Flip Horizontal or Flip Vertical.

Summary

This hour has covered many different PowerPoint 97 drawing methods that can be applied to almost any object in your PowerPoint presentations. You have learned how to group several drawing objects to create a single object and how to ungroup objects, such as clip art. Ungrouping an image can be used to get just a portion of the picture.

PowerPoint's stack, align, and distribute methods can be powerful tools when you need precision object placement. And, last but not least, you have learned how to rotate and flip objects to give you more flexibility when you're creating your own drawings. Stay tuned, because the last drawing hour gives you some great tips, tricks, and hints to create phenomenal drawings.

Workshop

In this hour's workshop, you create a simple border using the skills you have learned. Although the border you're creating is only on the left side of the slide, you could create a border for an entire slide. If you want the border to appear on each slide in your presentation, just place the entire drawing on the Slide (and Title Slide) Master. Voilà! Look out, Dali.

Figure 13.16 shows what the end result should look like.

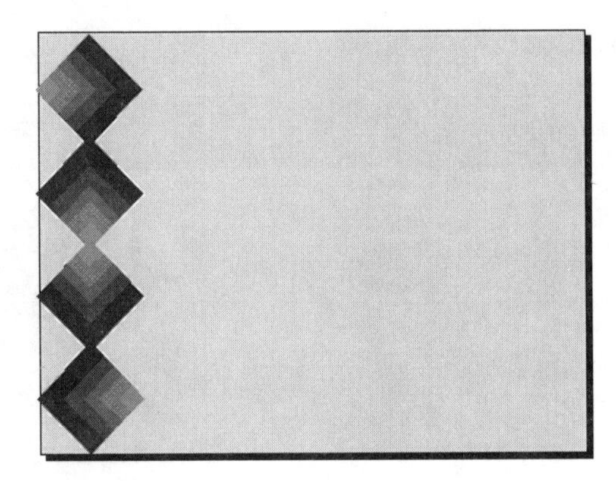

Figure 13.16.
A border created with PowerPoint's drawing tools.

Test What You've Learned

1. Start a new blank presentation, using the Blank layout as the first slide.
2. Draw a diamond.
3. Format the diamond's size to 2 inches for both the height and width.
4. Duplicate the diamond, and scale it to 80 percent for the height and width. Repeat this step so that there are six diamonds. Each diamond should be drawn a little smaller than the one before.
5. Select all six diamonds and align them on the center and top.
6. Select each diamond and using your favorite color—green, maybe—make the diamonds progressively lighter in color (the largest is the darkest and the smallest is the lightest).
7. Select the diamonds and select No Line for them all.
8. Select all the diamonds and group them into one object.
9. Duplicate the object three times (you will have four diamonds).
10. Move the diamonds to the left of the slide (don't worry about them being lined up).

11. Align the four diamonds on their centers.
12. Distribute the diamonds vertically in relation to the slide.
13. Change the stacking order so that the bottom dark corner is on top of the top light corner for each diamond.
14. Rotate the first diamond to the left.
15. Flip the second diamond vertically.
16. Rotate the fourth diamond to the right.
17. Select all four diamonds and group them together.
18. Save the file as `Hour 13 TWYL`.

Q&A

Q I tried to ungroup a graphic that my friend created in Photoshop, but the command was dimmed out. Am I doing something wrong?

A Probably not. The only types of graphics that can be ungrouped are vector graphics. Graphics that have been created with a drawing program like Photoshop or Paintbrush can't be ungrouped. This is also true for photographs that you might have scanned.

Q The Duplicate command you mentioned is great. However, I need to duplicate an object, in a sweep, with the object getting progressively smaller. Will Duplicate do that for me?

A Duplicate just creates an exact copy of the object at the same size. You have to do a little extra work for this task. The following instructions should get you started on the right track:

1. Draw the object.
2. Select the object.
3. Choose Edit | Duplicate from the menu.
4. Choose Format | AutoShape from the menu.
5. Click the Size tab.
6. Under the Scale section, type the same percentage for height and width, such as `90%`.
7. Click the OK button.
8. Repeat steps 3 through 7 for each object you need.

You might want to align the objects after you have finished. Use the Draw | Align or Distribute command from the drawing toolbar. You can use this feature to create cool images.

Q I want to align several objects by their bottom sides, as well as on the bottom of the slide, to create a border. Can PowerPoint 97 do that for me?

A Sure. Here are the instructions for doing that:

1. Choose Draw | Align or Distribute | Relative to Slide from the drawing toolbar.
2. Select the objects.
3. Choose Draw | Align or Distribute | Align Bottom from the drawing toolbar.

This procedure aligns the objects not only with each other, but also on the bottom of the slide.

Q I tried to rotate a clip art image, but the command is not available—what's wrong?

A Before you can rotate a clip art image, you have to ungroup it (this converts the image to a PowerPoint drawing). I usually ungroup the clip art (sometimes you have to select Ungroup several times), then group the sub-objects back together again so that I have a single PowerPoint image. Once a clip art image has been ungrouped, you can use the Free Rotate or Flip options.

Part IV

Hour 14

Drawing Special Effects

This last PowerPoint drawing hour concentrates on special effects for drawing lines and AutoShapes. PowerPoint 97 still has the Freeform line-drawing feature you might be familiar with from previous versions. In addition, Microsoft has added two new line-drawing options: Curves and Scribble.

This hour also covers adding a shadow effect to a drawing object and using the new 3-D feature. Finally, you will learn how to add motion to drawing objects by using animation. You will learn the about the following:

- Drawing curved lines and freeform objects and scribbling
- Adding and customizing shadows to your objects
- Adding and customizing 3-D effects to your objects
- Animating drawing objects

Drawing Curved Lines

With the Curve tool, you can draw lines with curves. Although you can draw curved lines with the Freeform and Scribble tools, the Curve tool gives you more control when you need to draw precise curved lines. PowerPoint 97 lets you decide how much of a curve should be applied to the line and where the curve will be placed. You also have full editing power to change or add more curves, if needed. To draw a line with curves, follow this sequence:

1. Select AutoShapes from the drawing toolbar.
2. Select Lines.
3. Click Curve.
4. Move the mouse to the area on the slide where you want the line to start and click.
5. Move the mouse to the point where you want the curve to turn, and then click. See Figure 14.1 for an example.
6. Repeat for each curve you need.
7. Double-click to end.

Figure 14.1 shows a curved line and where to click.

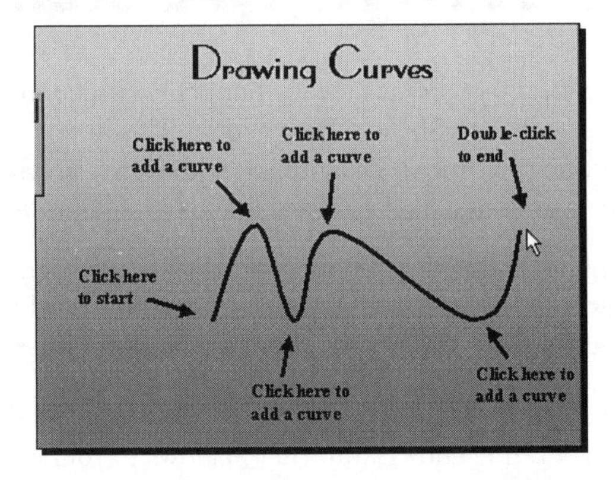

Figure 14.1.
Drawing a line with many curves is easy with the Curve tool.

TIME SAVER

To create a closed curve, end the line as close to the beginning as possible and then double-click. Figure 14.2 shows a closed curve.

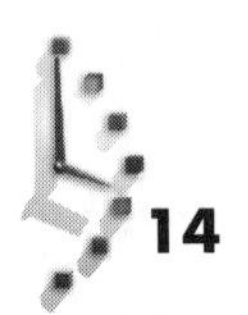

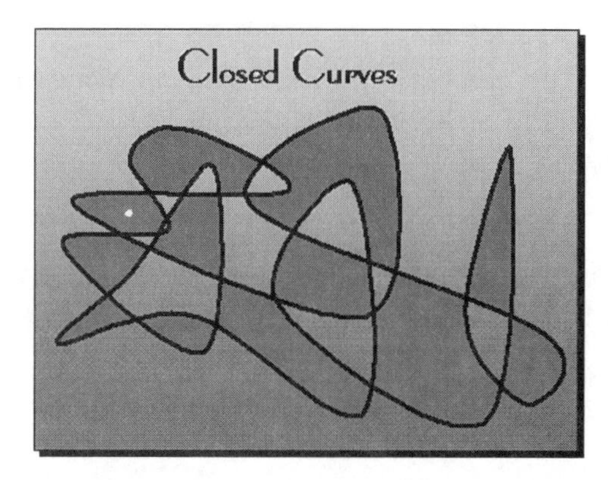

Figure 14.2.
A closed curve.

Drawing Freeform Lines

Use the Freeform tool when you need a bit more freedom for your lines or when you want to create a shape that's not a stock AutoShape. Drawing freeform is very similar to drawing curves. To draw a freeform object, use this method:

1. Select AutoShapes from the drawing toolbar.
2. Select Lines.
3. Click Freeform.
4. Move the mouse to the area on the slide where you want to start the freeform and click.
5. Move the mouse to the first point and click.
6. Repeat for each point you want.
7. Double-click to end the line. (See Figure 14.3.)

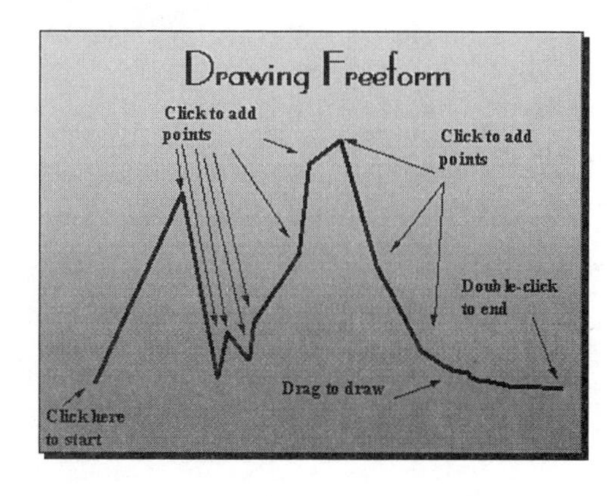

Figure 14.3.
A freeform AutoShape that looks like mountains.

Time Saver

While drawing in Freeform Mode, you can add uncontrolled curved lines (scribble) by dragging the mouse.

Time Saver

To close the freeform and create a shape, release the mouse button near the starting point. PowerPoint automatically snaps the endpoints together to signal that the shape is closed.

Scribbling

Use the Scribble feature when what you want total freedom. Scribble allows totally unconstrained drawing at all times in your creative adventures. You could even write your name, as shown in Figure 14.4.

Figure 14.4.
Using the Scribble feature to write my name.

To scribble (as if you needed instructions), follow these steps:

1. Select AutoShapes from the drawing toolbar.
2. Select Lines.
3. Click Scribble.
4. Move the mouse to the area on the slide where you want to start and drag.

The Scribble option is a new feature for PowerPoint 97. It can be fun, but at first it can make you feel like you're back in the first grade, learning to write all over again.

Editing Lines

You can easily edit the shape of a curved, freeform, or scribble line by using the Edit Points option in the Draw menu. When you edit the points of a line object, you're moving a vertex. Figure 14.5 shows a closed curve with the Edit Points option turned on.

NEW TERM A *vertex* is the point where two line segments meet or the highest point of a curve.

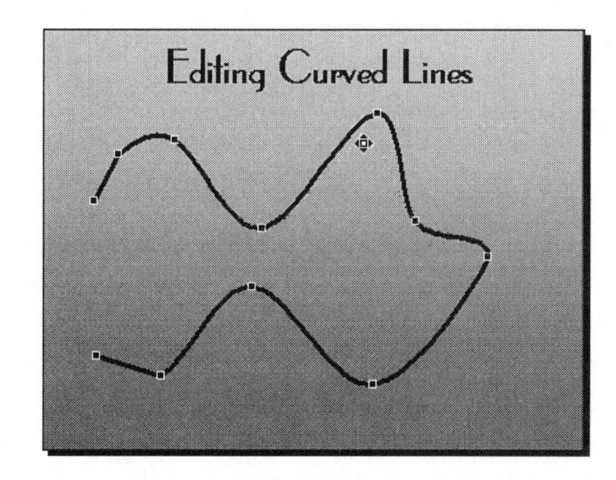

Figure 14.5.
Click and drag a vertex to edit the curve.

To edit a curved, freeform, or scribble line, follow these steps:

1. Select a curved, freeform, or scribble line.
2. Choose Draw | Edit Points from the drawing toolbar.
3. Click and drag any vertex point on the object.
4. Click off the object to deselect it when you're finished.

In addition to letting you edit the existing vertex points on a curved, freeform, or scribble line, PowerPoint 97 also allows you to add or delete a vertex. To add a vertex, follow these steps:

1. Select a curved, freeform, or scribble line.
2. Choose Draw | Edit Points from the drawing toolbar.
3. Click and drag the line where you want to add a vertex.
4. Edit the line.
5. Click off the object to deselect it when you're finished.

Here's how to delete a vertex:

1. Select a curved, freeform, or scribble line.
2. Choose Draw | Edit Points from the drawing toolbar.
3. Hold the Ctrl key and click the vertex point you want to delete.

4. Edit the line.
5. Click off the object to deselect it when you're finished.

Time Saver

For greater control over the shape of a curve, use this method. After you choose Draw | Edit Points, right-click a vertex. A shortcut menu appears with curve point options you can use to refine the shape of the curve.

Using Shadows and 3-D Effects

You can add a shadow or 3-D effect to almost any PowerPoint object to add depth. Each effect can be fully customized to create the exact image you want.

Shadows

Shadows add the illusion of depth to PowerPoint objects. You can add a shadow to any PowerPoint object, including text objects, clip art, AutoShapes, lines, freeforms, WordArt, charts, and more. Although PowerPoint has 20 predefined shadow styles to choose from, you can also create your own custom shadow by modifying the shadow position or color. Follow these steps to add a shadow to an object:

1. Select the object you want to add a shadow to.
2. Click the Shadow button on the drawing toolbar.
3. Select the shadow style you want.

Figure 14.6 shows several different PowerPoint objects with a shadow effect.

Figure 14.6.
Adding shadows to give the illusion of depth.

Time Saver

If you don't like any of the shadow styles available, pick the one closest to the effect you want and then edit the shadow.

Caution

Not all shadow styles are available for all objects. For example, PowerPoint objects such as clip art, lines, and charts have only eight of the shadow styles available.

To change the shadow's color, follow these steps:

1. Select the object you want to edit.
2. Click the Shadow button on the drawing toolbar.
3. Click Shadow Settings to display the Shadow Settings toolbar.
4. Click the Shadow Color drop-down arrow. (See Figure 14.7.)
5. Select a color, or click More Shadow Colors to pick a color from the Color dialog box.

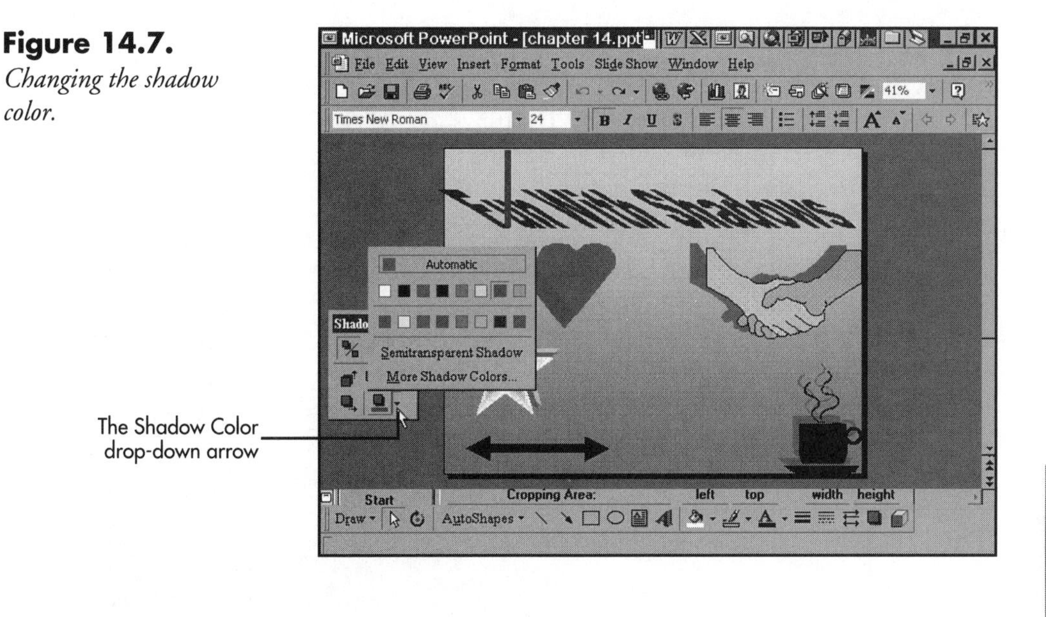

Figure 14.7.
Changing the shadow color.

Here's how to move (or *nudge*) a shadow:

1. Select the object you want to edit.
2. Click the Shadow button on the drawing toolbar.
3. Click Shadow Settings to display the Shadow Settings toolbar.
4. Depending on the direction you want to move the shadow, click the Nudge Shadow Up, Down, Left, or Right drop-down arrow.

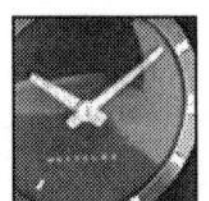

JUST A MINUTE

Each time you click the Nudge Shadow buttons, the shadow moves one pixel. When you hold down the Shift key and click a Nudge Shadow button, the shadow moves six pixels.

If you decide that the shadow doesn't add the effect you want, you can remove it by using this method:

1. Select the object you want to edit.
2. Click the Shadow button on the drawing toolbar.
3. Click the No Shadow button.

3-D Effects

With PowerPoint 97's new 3-D feature, you can add a 3-D effect to AutoShapes, lines, and freeform objects and customize the 3-D settings after they have been applied. You can change the rotation (or *tilt*), depth, direction, lighting, and surface texture. Figure 14.8 shows several PowerPoint objects with 3-D effects.

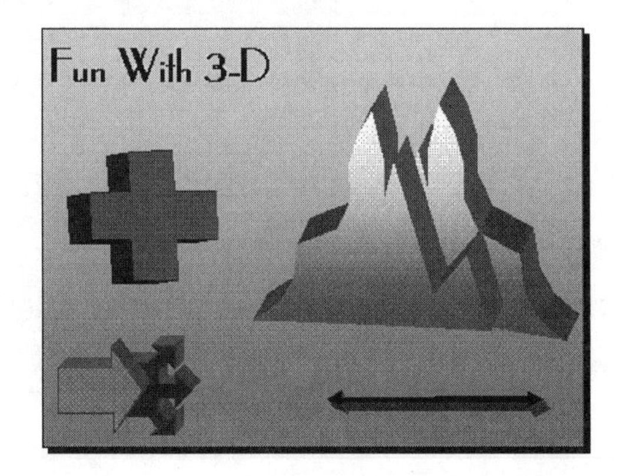

Figure 14.8.
Using 3-D effects with PowerPoint objects.

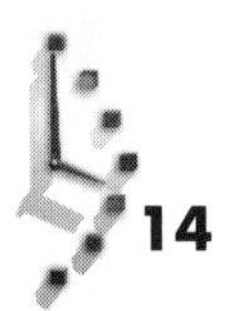

Follow these easy steps to add a 3-D effect to an object:

1. Select the object you want to add 3-D to.
2. Click the 3-D button on the drawing toolbar.
3. Select the 3-D style you want.

TIME SAVER

> If you really don't like any of the 3-D styles available, pick the one closest to the effect you want and then edit the effect.

To change the color of the 3-D effect, follow these steps:

1. Select the object you want to edit.
2. Click the 3-D button on the drawing toolbar.
3. Click 3-D Settings to display the 3-D Settings toolbar.
4. Click the 3-D Color drop-down arrow. (See Figure 14.9.)
5. Select a color, or click More 3-D Colors to pick a color from the Color dialog box.

Figure 14.9.
Changing the 3-D color.

The 3-D Color drop-down arrow

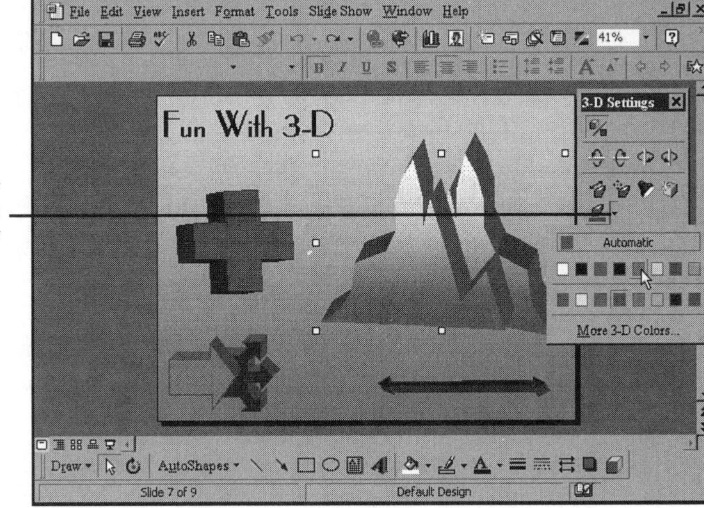

The Tilt option rotates the object around a horizontal or vertical axis. The object appears to turn onscreen and present different sides. To tilt a 3-D object, follow these steps:

1. Select the object you want to edit.
2. Click the 3-D button on the drawing toolbar.
3. Click 3-D Settings to display the 3-D Settings toolbar.
4. Depending on the direction you want to tilt the object, click the Tilt Down, Up, Left, or Right button.

JUST A MINUTE

When you click the Tilt buttons, the object moves in 6-degree increments. If you hold down the Shift key while you click a Tilt button, however, the object moves in 45-degree increments.

TIME SAVER

Use the Direction button before using the Tilt buttons. You might find that a simple change in direction gives you the effect you're looking for without having to use several Tilt commands.

If all these 3-D effects were just too much dazzle for the monthly budget, you might want to remove them. Here's how you can do that quickly:

1. Select the object you want to edit.
2. Click the 3-D button on the drawing toolbar.
3. Click the No 3-D button.

Animating Drawing Objects

PowerPoint 97 has state-of-the-art animation options that you can apply to drawing objects. As discussed in Hour 10, "Adding Pizzazz to a Slide Show," you can animate almost anything, including drawing objects.

You have two options for setting animation. You can use one of PowerPoint's preset animation settings, or you can create your own custom animation. Preset animation saves time because you don't have to make a lot of choices. You simply set the animation with one mouse click. Custom animation is an excellent choice when you want to add not only visual animation effects, but sounds, too.

Once you have included animated objects on your slide(s), you can preview the animation settings from Slide View.

Preset Animation

Selecting one of PowerPoint 97's eight preset animation settings is the quick way to add animation to any PowerPoint drawing object. To set animation using one of the available preset options, follow these steps:

1. Select the object you want to animate.
2. Choose Slide Show | Preset Animation from the menu.
3. Click the animation setting you want.

JUST A MINUTE

> The Drive-In, Flying, and Camera preset options include sound effects, too.

Custom Animation

Use custom animation settings when you want total control over every aspect of the object's animation. The Custom Animation dialog box gives you access to every animation option available in PowerPoint 97. You can choose from over 40 visual effects and many sound options. You can also set the animation order for the objects and the timings for the animation.

To set custom animation, use this method:

1. While in Slide View, display the slide you want to animate.
2. Choose Slide Show | Custom Animation from the menu.
3. Click the Timing tab. (See Figure 14.10.)

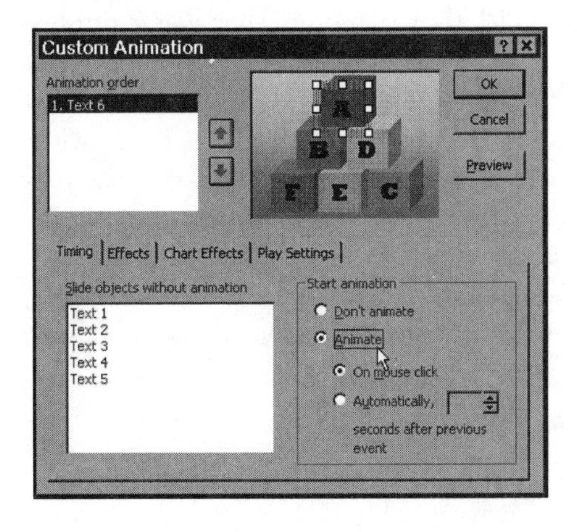

Figure 14.10.
The Timing tab of the Custom Animation dialog box.

4. In the "Slide objects without animation" box, select the object to animate.
5. In the "Start animation" section, select the Animate radio button.
6. Select how the animation is to start by selecting one of these checkboxes: "On mouse click" or "Automatically, after *x* number of seconds" (*x* is the number of seconds you choose).
7. Click the Effects tab. (See Figure 14.11.)

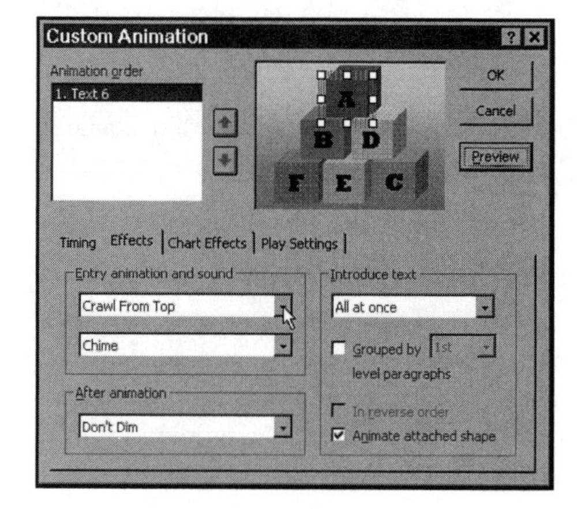

Figure 14.11.
The Effects tab of the Custom Animation dialog box.

8. In the "Entry animation and sound" section, select the animation and sound settings you want.
9. Repeat steps 3 through 8 for each object to animate.
10. Click the Preview button to see a preview of the animation settings.
11. Click the OK button when you're finished adding animation to the slide.

Preview Your Animation

After you have applied animation to the drawing objects, you can preview the animation in one of two ways. The most obvious choice is viewing the slide show. However, PowerPoint 97 also has a new option that lets you preview animation for the current slide without viewing the entire slide show. Just choose Slide Show | Animation Preview from the menu. This option displays a slide miniature, as shown in Figure 14.12, that shows all the current animation settings for the slide in full motion.

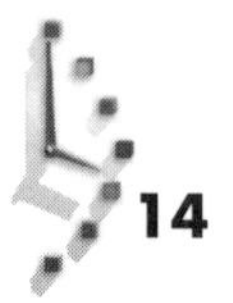

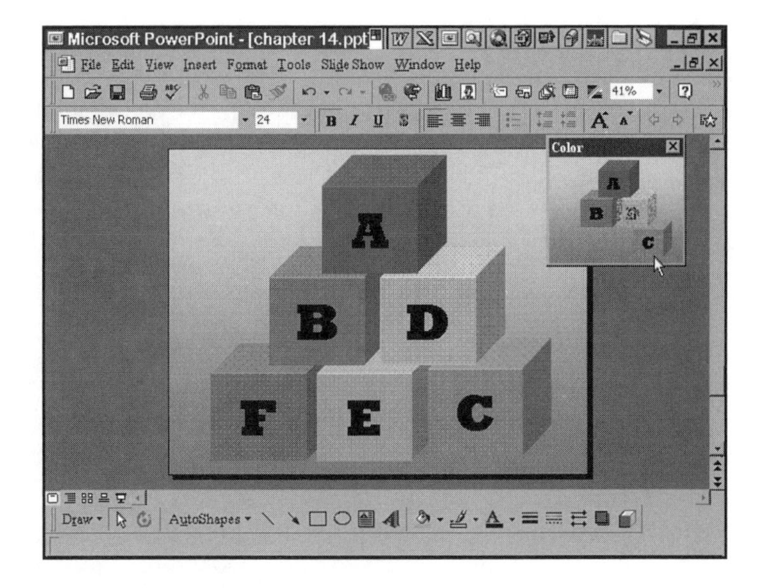

Figure 14.12.
The slide miniature shows a preview of the animation settings.

TIME SAVER

If you already have the slide miniature displayed, you can preview the current animation settings at any time by simply clicking on the slide miniature.

Summary

In this hour, you have quickly covered the PowerPoint 97 basics for including professional drawing effects in your presentations. Curves, freeform objects, and scribbling give you extra flexibility when you're drawing lines. In addition, you can add depth to almost any two-dimensional object by adding either a shadow or a 3-D effect; both can be fully customized. For example, you can change the color or create a custom theme. You have also seen the dazzling animation features available with PowerPoint 97.

You've spent the last four hours learning how PowerPoint's drawing features can help you create simple graphics. If you really want to do some serious drawing with PowerPoint's tools, the best way is learning from other people. When I first started drawing, I would insert a clip art image and ungroup it to see what shapes were beneath the final creation. I learned how they were colored and discovered how the image was composed. Experimentation and reverse engineering is the best method of learning about expert tricks that can be used to draw PowerPoint pictures.

Workshop

This workshop's exercise steps you through the process of drawing a mountain range with clouds and hills, as shown in Figure 14.13. You might find that after you have finished the exercise, you want to do more. That's perfectly normal, so don't resist the urge—give into it. The more you practice drawing, the better you get. You will also discover that the ideas just keep flowing. To me, PowerPoint is like potato chips—betcha can't have just one!

There are some great questions and answers at the end of this section, so be sure to check them out before you move on the next hour.

Figure 14.13.
In this hour's TWYL exercise, you draw this mountain range with hills and clouds.

Test What You've Learned

1. Start a new, blank presentation, using the Blank layout.
2. Change the slide background to the preset gradient "Daybreak," using the horizontal shading option with the light end on the bottom.
3. Use the Freeform tool to draw mountains. I drew two sets of mountains for the sample image.
4. Format the freeform object with a brown or green gradient shading, very light. Use the horizontal effect with the white end at the top (for snow).

TIME SAVER

> You might want to edit the points of the freeform object to make sure the starting and ending points are positioned below any of the other points. Otherwise, you might get a very strange-looking mountain range.

5. Format the freeform object so that it has no lines.

TIME SAVER

> If you drew more than one freeform object, as I did, you might need to reorder the stacking of the objects. I had to send my second mountain range to the back.

6. Using the Curve tool, draw some hills.
7. Format the hills in a green color and use the gradient shading (just not as light as for the mountains).
8. Format the curve so that it has no lines.
9. Using the Curve tool, draw some clouds. The clouds are a closed curve.
10. Format the clouds as white, semitransparent, and with no lines.

JUST A MINUTE

> Just for fun, I drew the sun rising behind the mountains.

11. Give your mountains a 3-D effect.
12. Change any settings you want (go ahead—it's okay to play).
13. Save the presentation as `Hour 14 TWYL`.
14. Close the presentation.

Q&A

Q I've been drawing with the Scribble tool, trying to write my name, but it still looks awful. How can I fix it?

A You can try editing the points of the scribble line, as previously explained in this hour. If you're still having a tough time getting a legible image, try zooming in to get a better view of what you're working on. Setting the zoom to 150 percent or higher can make a big difference. Also, you might want to go into the Windows Control Panel and set the mouse pointer speed as slow as possible. A slow pointer speed helps when you're creating freeforms and scribbles.

Q Whenever I add a shadow to an object that has a 3-D effect, the 3-D disappears. What's going on?

A PowerPoint 97 doesn't allow you to have both a shadow and a 3-D effect. You must choose one or the other.

Q I used the Text Shadow tool to add a shadow to my text. How can I change the color and edit the shadow?

A When you use the Text Shadow tool on the formatting toolbar, you can't edit the shadow. The shadow is preset. If you want full shadow-editing capabilities with text, your best bet is to add a shadow to the text object. As long as the object has no fill, the text takes the shadow of the object.

Q How do you add a 3-D effect to a clip art image?

A You can't add a 3-D effect to a clip art image unless you ungroup the image first. Be careful when choosing clip art for this effect. Usually the simple clip art looks just fine with 3-D, but the more complicated clip art doesn't.

PART V

Inserting Tables, Worksheets, Graphs, and Organizational Charts

Part V

Hour 15

Word Tables

The next six hours cover different types of objects that can be created in other programs. PowerPoint 97 allows you to embed the externally created documents in a slide show. The documents enhance the presentation by offering tables, charts, graphs, and organization charts. This hour covers Word tables, and Hour 16, "Excel Worksheets," discusses Excel worksheets. When deciding whether to use a table or a worksheet, ask yourself if you need to work with numbers. If the answer is no, use a table. If, however, you will be working with numbers and calculations, you will probably want to use an Excel worksheet. For example, if you're adding, subtracting, multiplying, or dividing, a worksheet is better.

You can embed a Word table in a slide in two distinct ways. You can either copy a table that has been previously created, or you can create a new table from scratch. In the next hour, you will learn how to do the following:

- Copy or link a preexisting Word table into a PowerPoint slide
- Insert (or embed) a new Word table into a PowerPoint slide
- Add information to an embedded Word table
- Edit and format an embedded Word table

Just a Minute

If you're already familiar with Microsoft Word and have used the table feature before, you might find that you don't need to read this entire chapter. I suggest that even proficient Word experts at least skim through this chapter. You might find that this chapter includes some tips or tricks that could prove extremely useful.

New Term Almost all Windows programs, like the programs in Microsoft Office, allow you to use *OLE* (*object linking and embedding*). In practice, OLE is the underlying structure that links objects and applications. It's simply a mechanism for taking any object, such as a Word table, and doing one of two things:

- Copy the object to another program document, such as a PowerPoint presentation, and *link* the object to the original. When an object is linked, whenever the original changes, so does the linked copy. This method lets you keep track of one base document that's reused in others.
- *Embed* another program object, such as a Word table, in your PowerPoint document. When you embed an object in PowerPoint, the object can be activated and edited in place. You can edit the object using all the tools available in the application that created the object. In this hour's example, you could edit the embedded Word object just as though you were using Word.

Copying a Word Table

Now try running through an example of table copying. You're given a Microsoft Word document with a table that should be included in your presentation. Figure 15.1 illustrates a Microsoft Word document with a table that should be included in the presentation. You can easily copy the table into a PowerPoint slide.

15

Figure 15.1.
A Microsoft Word document with a table.

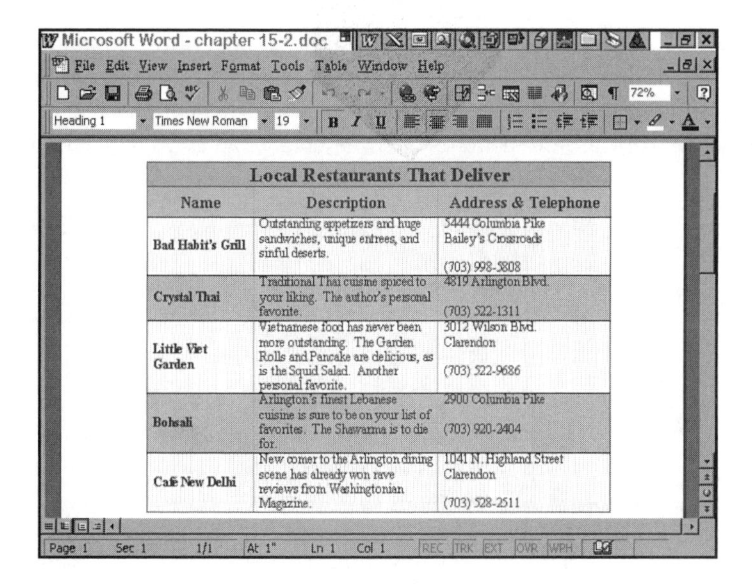

Local Restaurants That Deliver		
Name	**Description**	**Address & Telephone**
Bad Habit's Grill	Outstanding appetizers and huge sandwiches, unique entrees, and sinful deserts.	5444 Columbia Pike Bailey's Crossroads (703) 998-5808
Crystal Thai	Traditional Thai cuisine spiced to your liking. The author's personal favorite.	4819 Arlington Blvd. (703) 522-1311
Little Viet Garden	Vietnamese food has never been more outstanding. The Garden Rolls and Pancake are delicious, as is the Squid Salad. Another personal favorite.	3012 Wilson Blvd. Clarendon (703) 522-9686
Bohsali	Arlington's finest Lebanese cuisine is sure to be on your list of favorites. The Shawarma is to die for.	2900 Columbia Pike (703) 920-2404
Café New Delhi	New comer to the Arlington dining scene has already won rave reviews from Washingtonian Magazine.	1041 N. Highland Street Clarendon (703) 528-2511

When I want to copy information from one application (such as Microsoft Word) into another application (such as Microsoft PowerPoint), I always start both programs. When you have two (or more) programs running, you see buttons on the Windows 95 taskbar representing each program, as shown in Figure 15.2.

Figure 15.2.
The Windows 95 taskbar with Microsoft Word and PowerPoint running.

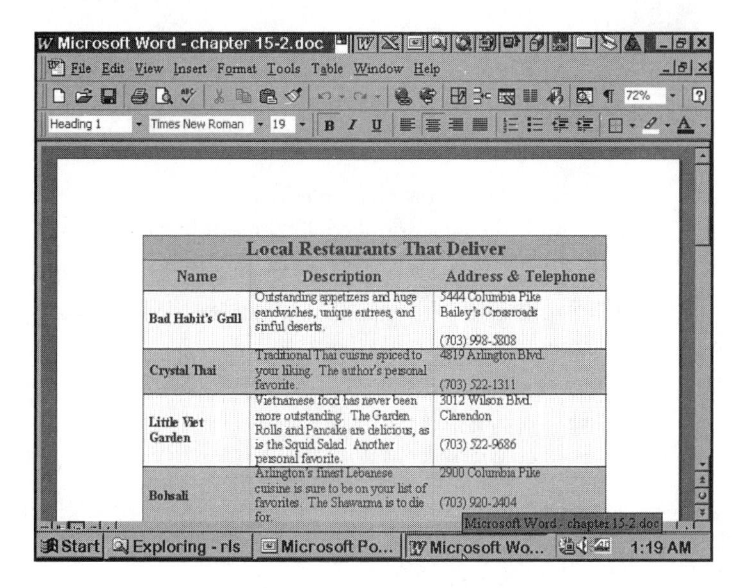

Local Restaurants That Deliver		
Name	**Description**	**Address & Telephone**
Bad Habit's Grill	Outstanding appetizers and huge sandwiches, unique entrees, and sinful deserts.	5444 Columbia Pike Bailey's Crossroads (703) 998-5808
Crystal Thai	Traditional Thai cuisine spiced to your liking. The author's personal favorite.	4819 Arlington Blvd. (703) 522-1311
Little Viet Garden	Vietnamese food has never been more outstanding. The Garden Rolls and Pancake are delicious, as is the Squid Salad. Another personal favorite.	3012 Wilson Blvd. Clarendon (703) 522-9686
Bohsali	Arlington's finest Lebanese cuisine is sure to be on your list of favorites. The Shawarma is to die for.	2900 Columbia Pike (703) 920-2404

There are several ways to copy information from one application into another—you can use Edit | Copy with the Edit | Paste command, toolbar buttons, drag and drop, or hot keys. Although all the methods work, in my experience it's best to use the menu command when copying information between different programs. To copy a table from Word into PowerPoint, follow these steps:

1. Make sure both programs are running, and that the documents you want to copy between are open.
2. Switch to Word.
3. Select the table.

TIME SAVER

The easiest way to select a table is to click once on the table, then choose Table | Select Table from the menu.

4. Choose Edit | Copy from the menu.
5. Switch to PowerPoint by clicking the PowerPoint button on the Windows taskbar.
6. View the slide you want to place the table on.
7. Choose Edit | Paste from the menu.

JUST A MINUTE

Over time, you might find that you prefer to use another method, and that's okay. Windows accepts and embraces diversity. Experiment with different methods and use the method you prefer.

You might want to link the table in your presentation to the original table in the Word document. If the table is linked, later modifications to the Word table are displayed in the presentation. Use the following steps to link the table:

1. Make sure both programs are running, and that the documents you want to copy from and to are open.
2. Switch to Word.
3. Select the table.
4. Choose Edit | Copy from the menu.
5. Switch to PowerPoint by clicking the PowerPoint button on the Windows taskbar.
6. View the slide you want to place the table on.
7. Choose Edit | Paste Special from the menu.
8. From the Paste Special dialog box, select Paste Link. (See Figure 15.3.)

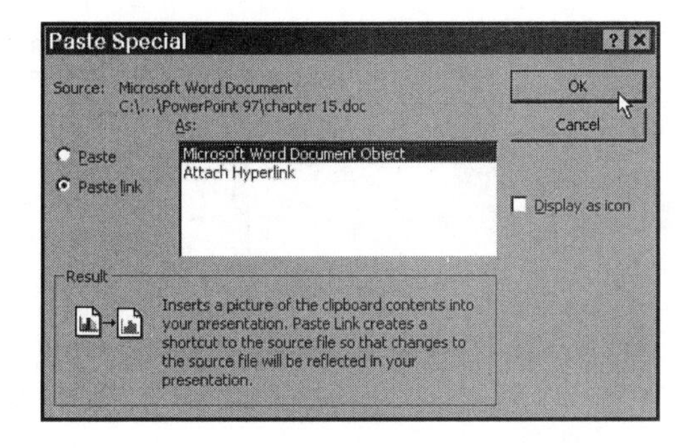

Figure 15.3.
The Paste Special dialog box.

9. Select Microsoft Word Document Object.
10. Click the OK button.

Now you can make changes to your original Microsoft Word document and the changes will show up in your presentation. When you open your presentation file, PowerPoint displays the window shown in Figure 15.4, asking whether you want to update your links. Simply click the OK button to update your presentation.

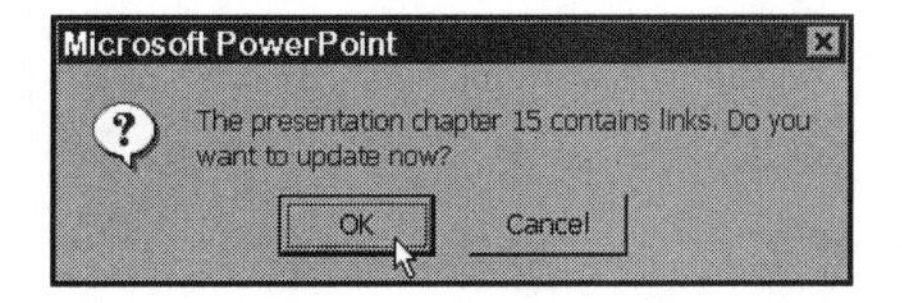

Figure 15.4.
PowerPoint asks whether you want to update your links.

JUST A MINUTE

You should save your Microsoft Word document before you perform the steps needed to link the object to PowerPoint. When you create a link, PowerPoint uses the name of the original document to make any necessary updates. If you haven't saved the original document, PowerPoint gets confused and doesn't know where to find the linked table when you view the presentation later. Another fact to keep in mind is that moving or renaming the document can also break the link.

Inserting (or Embedding) a Word Table

When you want to create a table from scratch that will be used only in your PowerPoint presentation, you can easily insert one into a slide. In fact, PowerPoint has a layout just for this purpose, as shown in Figure 15.5, or you can use the Insert Microsoft Word Table button on the standard toolbar.

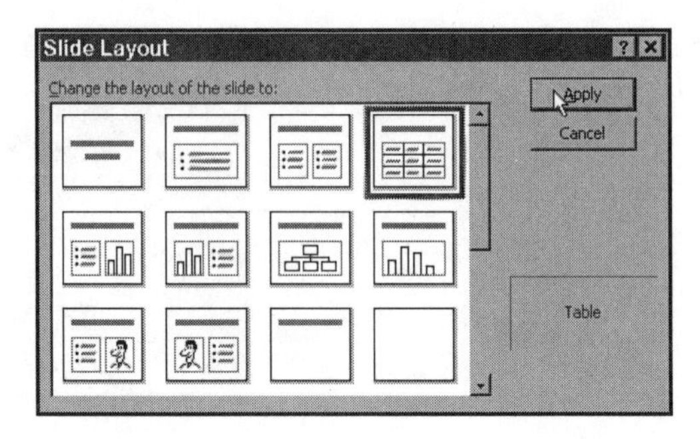

Figure 15.5.
Selecting the Table Slide Layout.

Follow these steps to insert a table by using the Table Slide Layout:

1. Start a new slide with the Table Slide Layout.
2. Double-click the table placeholder.
3. Select the number of columns and rows needed. (See Figure 15.6.)
4. Click the OK button.

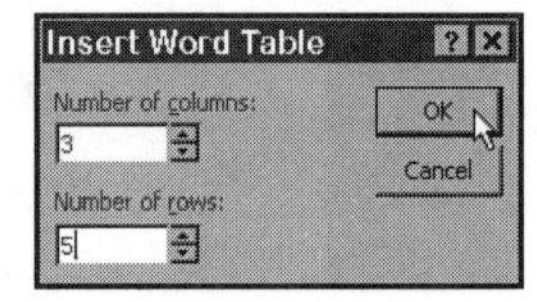

Figure 15.6.
Select the number of columns and rows for your table.

There's another method you can use to insert a table into any slide; just follow these steps:

1. Display the slide where you want to insert a table.
2. Click the Insert Microsoft Word Table button on the standard toolbar.
3. Select the number of columns and rows you want and click. (See Figure 15.7.)

CAUTION

Although you can add rows and columns to the table later, it's best to specify the exact number of columns and rows when you first create the table. When you add rows or columns later, you might have to do some serious reformatting and resizing. There have been times when I have just started all over again and re-created the entire table rather than fuss with all the reformatting for a proper table display.

Regardless of the method used to insert a table, PowerPoint should now be active in Table Edit Mode. Figure 15.8 shows a PowerPoint window in Table Edit Mode. Notice that although the toolbars and menu bar are similar to PowerPoint, they actually belong to Microsoft Word. While you're in Table Edit Mode, you're actually using Microsoft Word to change, update, and create the table.

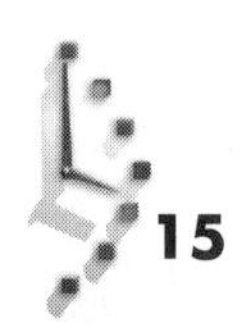

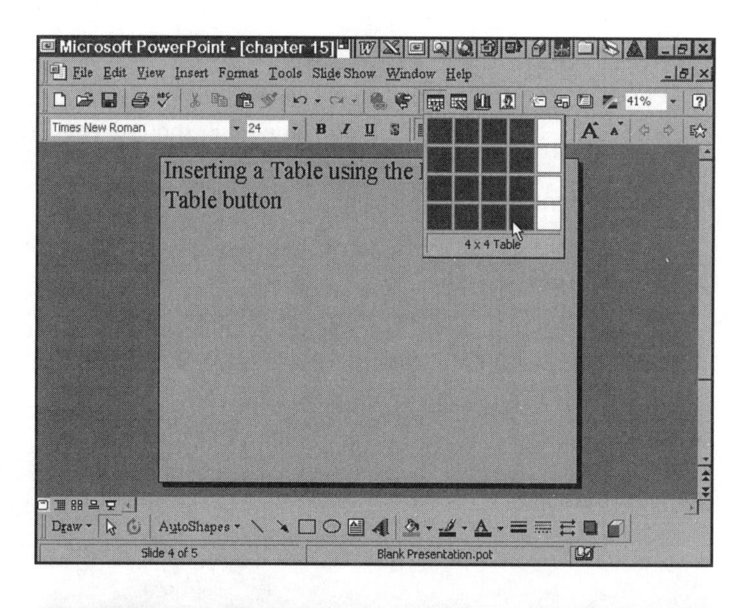

Figure 15.7.
Select the number of columns and rows for your table.

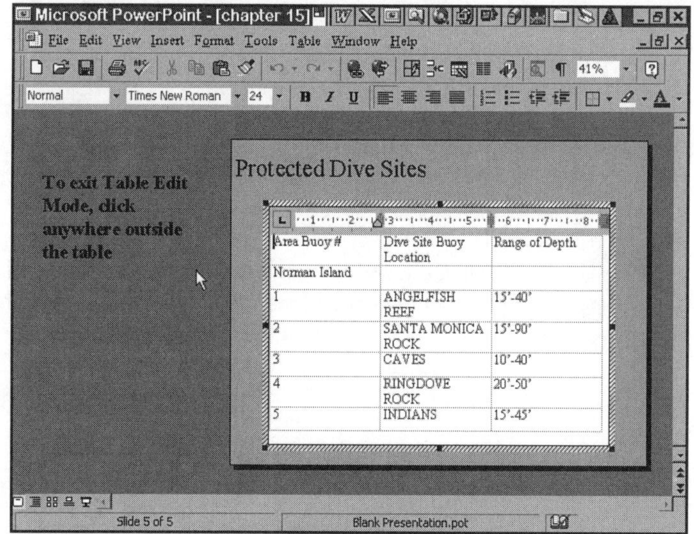

Figure 15.8.
Working on a table in Table Edit Mode.

To quickly exit from Table Edit Mode, click anywhere outside the table.

Once you have inserted a table into a presentation, the table becomes an embedded object. The object can have information inserted or be reformatted. If you want to directly edit the table, simply double-click the table to switch to Table Edit Mode.

Inserting Information

Once you have inserted a table, you need to type in the information that should appear in the table. Remember that a presentation slide shouldn't have too much information jammed into the display area. The table information should be short, sweet, and to the point. To insert information, follow this step:

- ☐ Make sure the cursor is in the cell to which you want to add information, and type the information.

You can quickly move from cell to cell while typing information by pressing the Tab key. Pressing the Shift+Tab key combination moves the cursor backward one cell at a time. Figure 15.9 illustrates adding information to a table.

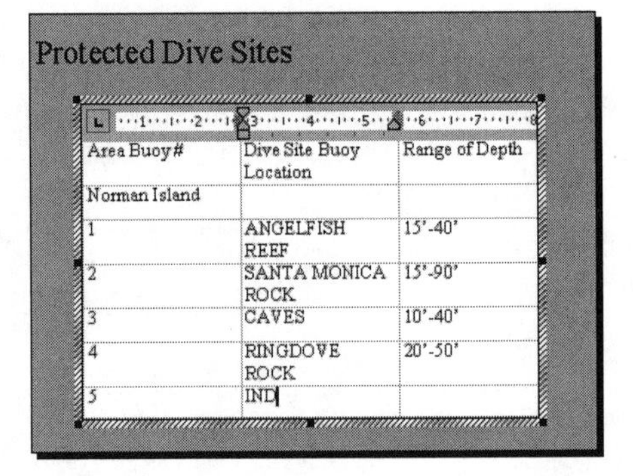

Protected Dive Sites

Area Buoy#	Dive Site Buoy Location	Range of Depth
Norman Island		
1	ANGELFISH REEF	15'-40'
2	SANTA MONICA ROCK	15'-90'
3	CAVES	10'-40'
4	RINGDOVE ROCK	20'-50'
5	IND	

Figure 15.9.
Adding information to a new table.

CAUTION

If you press the Tab key while in the last cell of the table, you will add a row to the end of the table. If you don't want the additional row, just click the Undo button on the standard toolbar.

Formatting a Word Table

Once all the information has been inserted into the table, you will probably want to add lines to the table and format the text. You might also need to edit the size of the columns or rows. Figure 15.10 shows a finished table that has been formatted with lines, shading, and text formatting.

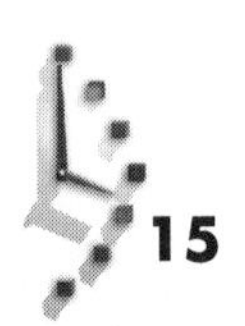

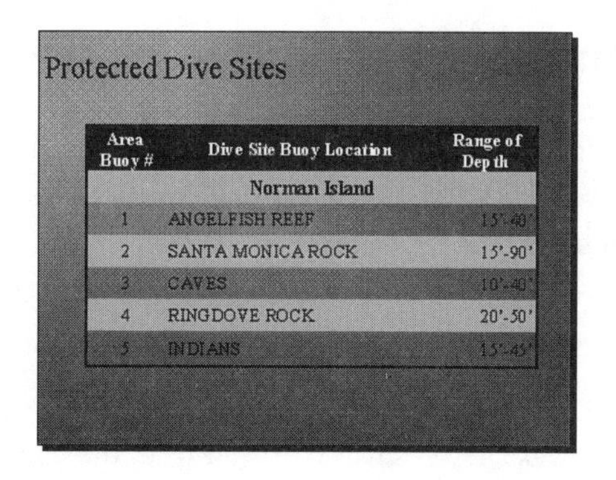

Protected Dive Sites

Area Buoy #	Dive Site Buoy Location	Range of Depth
	Norman Island	
1	ANGELFISH REEF	15'-40'
2	SANTA MONICA ROCK	15'-90'
3	CAVES	10'-40'
4	RINGDOVE ROCK	20'-50'
5	INDIANS	15'-45'

Figure 15.10.
A table that has been formatted with lines, shading, and text formatting.

Adding Lines to a Table

Although Word doesn't automatically add lines to a table, adding lines is very simple. You also get to choose the line style and width. To add lines to the entire table, follow these steps:

1. Double-click the table to go into Table Edit Mode.
2. Choose Table | Select Table from the menu.
3. Click the Tables and Borders button on the standard toolbar to turn on the Tables and Borders toolbar. (See Figure 15.11.)
4. Select a line style from the Line Style drop-down list.
5. Select the line thickness from the Line Weight drop-down list.
6. Click the Borders button drop-down arrow and select All Borders to add a border to all the cells in your table.

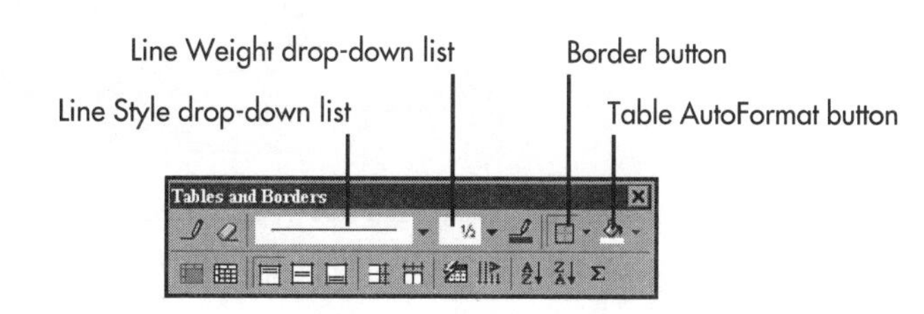

Figure 15.11.
The Tables and Borders toolbar.

Caution

Unless the line weight is 3 points or more, the lines sometimes don't appear onscreen.

Time Saver

Use the Table AutoFormat button, shown in Figure 15.11, to select from many preformatted table styles.

Formatting the Text in a Table

To format the text in a table, you use Word's toolbars and menus. This shouldn't be a problem. The nice folks at Microsoft have made the toolbar buttons and menu commands almost identical to the tools you have been using in PowerPoint. To format text in a table, simply do the following:

1. Double-click the table to go into Table Edit Mode.
2. Select the text you want to edit.
3. Choose Format | Font from the menu. (See Figure 15.12.)
4. Make any changes you want from the Font dialog box.
5. Click the OK button.

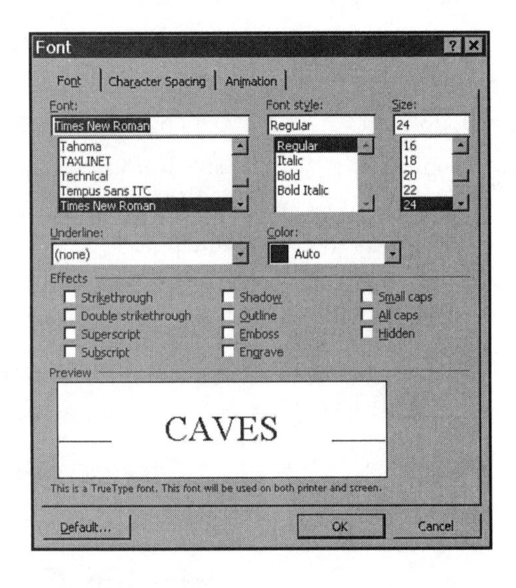

Figure 15.12.
The Font dialog box offers many choices for changing the look of your text.

Time Saver

You also can use the buttons on the formatting toolbar to quickly format text.

You might want to change the alignment of the text in the cells of your table. For example, currency amounts should be right-aligned. To change the alignment, follow these steps:

1. Double-click the table to go into Table Edit Mode.
2. Select the cells you want to change the alignment of.

   Depending on the type of alignment you want, click the Align Left, Center, Align Right, or Justify button on the formatting toolbar. (See Figure 15.13.)

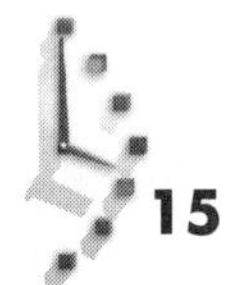

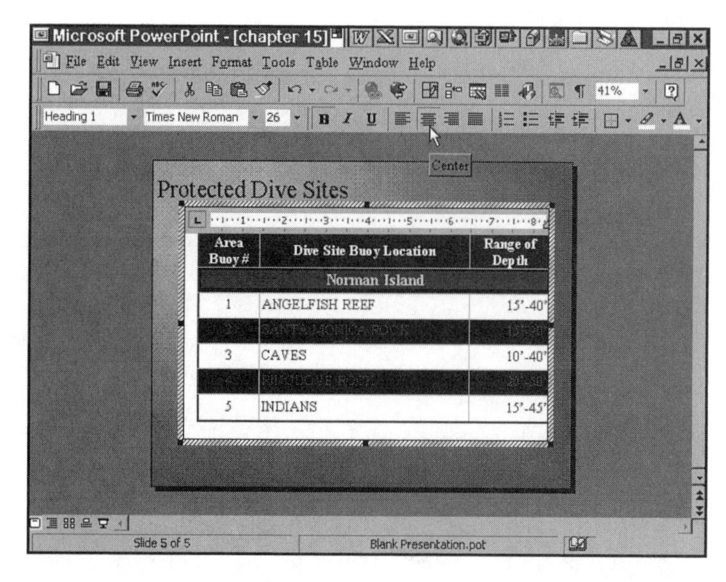

Figure 15.13.
Click one of the alignment buttons to change the text's alignment.

A new feature in Word 97 allows you to vertically align text in a cell. To do this, simply select the cell you want to align, and click either the Align Top, Center Vertically, or Align Bottom button on the Tables and Borders toolbar.

Adding and Resizing Rows or Columns

You can easily add extra columns or rows to a table at any time. When you add extra columns or rows to a table, you might need to make the font size a little smaller to fit the new table on your slide. The easiest task to perform is adding a row to the end of the table; just follow these steps:

1. Double-click the table to go into Table Edit Mode.
2. Position the cursor in the last cell.
3. Press the Tab key.

When adding a row in the middle of a table, Word adds the new row above the row (or rows) you have selected. To add an extra row to a table, follow these steps:

1. Double-click the table to go into Table Edit Mode.
2. Click in the row under where you want the new row and choose Table | Select Row from the menu.
3. Choose Table | Insert Rows from the menu.

Just a Minute

To insert more than one row, select the number of rows you want to insert. For example, to insert three rows, you should select three rows.

When you add an extra column, Word adds the new column to the left (or in front of) the column (or columns) you have selected. To add an extra column to a table, follow these steps:

1. Double-click the table to go into Table Edit Mode.
2. Click in the column to the left of where you want the new column, and choose Table | Select Column from the menu.
3. Choose Table | Insert Columns from the menu.

Just a Minute

To insert more than one column, select the number of columns you want to insert. For example, to insert three columns, you should first select three columns.

After you have formatted the text in a table, you might find that the width of the columns should be smaller or wider. Or, you might want the height of the rows to be thinner or taller. You can either manually adjust the size of columns or rows, or you can let Word quickly change the row height or column width based on the information that's in your table. To manually adjust the row height or column width, perform the following steps:

1. Double-click the table to go into Table Edit Mode.
2. Make sure nothing is selected.
3. Place the mouse pointer over the border of the row or column you want to adjust so that it looks like a double-headed arrow, as shown in Figure 15.14.
4. Click and hold the mouse button.
5. Drag the border to the new size.
6. Release the mouse button.

Time Saver

To quickly resize a column to get the best fit, double-click a column border.

Caution

If there's anything selected when you're resizing rows or columns, chances are you might end up resizing only certain cells, instead of the entire row or column. This is great if that effect is your intention, but usually it isn't. If this does happen, just click the Undo button on the standard toolbar.

Figure 15.14.
Resizing a column with the mouse.

Area Buoy #	Dive Site Buoy Location	Range of Depth
	Norman Island	
1	ANGELFISH REEF	15'-40'
2	SANTA MONICA ROCK	15'-90'
3	CAVES	10'-40'
4	RINGDOVE ROCK	20'-50'
5	INDIANS	15'-45'

TIME SAVER

If you have added extra columns or rows, let Word adjust the row height and column width for you. Then you can go back and make manual adjustments where you think it's necessary.

To quickly change the row height to the best fit, do the following:

1. Double-click the table to go into Table Edit Mode.
2. Choose Table | Select Table from the menu.
3. Choose Table | Cell Height and Width from the menu.
4. Click the Row tab.
5. Under Height of Rows, click the drop-down arrow and select Auto. (See Figure 15.15.)
6. Click the OK button.

To quickly change the width of the columns to the best fit, perform the following steps:

1. Double-click the table to go into Table Edit Mode.
2. Choose Table | Select Table from the menu.
3. Choose Table | Cell Height and Width from the menu.
4. Click the Column tab.
5. Click the AutoFit button. (See Figure 15.16.)

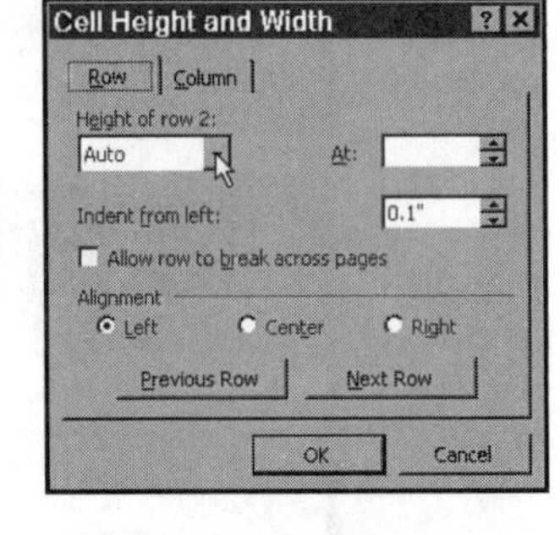

Figure 15.15.
Select Auto for the row height.

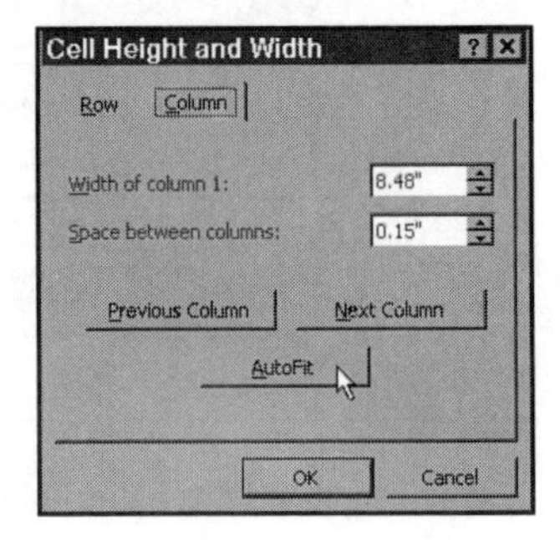

Figure 15.16.
Click the AutoFit button to resize the columns based on the text in the cells.

TIME SAVER

If you want the columns in your table to be an exact size, simply enter an amount in the Width box. If you want all the columns in your table to be the same size, select the table and then enter an amount in the Width box.

Summary

In this hour, you have learned about the different methods for inserting a Microsoft Word table into a presentation. You can either copy an existing table from Microsoft Word, or you can embed a brand-new Microsoft Word table into your presentation. When you copy an existing table, you can link the PowerPoint copy to the original Microsoft Word table if modifications or updates are likely.

When editing an embedded table, you might use all the tools and commands that would normally be available in Microsoft Word. You can format the table by adding lines, changing the text font, or modifying the alignment. Microsoft Word allows you to quickly add extra rows or columns, just in case you need them.

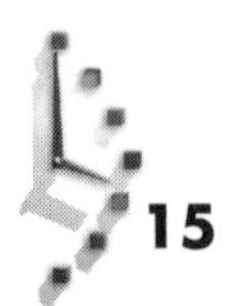

Workshop

In this workshop, you will be working with—yes, you guessed it—a Word table. Sometimes working with embedded (or inserted) objects can be tricky; it's a skill that takes lots of practice to master. If you run into a snag, try to fix it first, but if it seems your table is getting worse and worse, just start again. Often, it's not worth the time to fix something; it's just faster and easier to begin again.

Be sure to read the questions and answers at the end of the section. The first question is a good one.

Test What You've Learned

1. Start a new blank presentation. Use the Table layout.
2. Insert a title, such as `TWYL - Using Tables`.
3. Double-click to add a table.
4. Make the table three columns by five rows.
5. Type three headings for each column, and four of your favorite music selections, as shown in Table 15.1.

Table 15.1. Sample data.

Artist	Title	Type
Candy Dulfer	Saxuality	New Age
Johann Strauss	Waltzes & Polkas	Classical
Mixed	Pulp Fiction	Movie Soundtrack
Nirvana	Unplugged in New York	Alternative

6. Add lines to the entire table.
7. Format the heading row to have a bigger font.
8. Change the row height for the entire table to Auto.
9. Change the column width for the entire table to AutoFit.
10. Exit from Table Edit Mode to view your table.
11. Double-click the table to do some more editing.
12. Use the Table AutoFormat option and select a preformatted table style.
13. Exit from Table Edit Mode.
14. Save the file as `Hour 15 TWYL`.
15. Close the file.

Q&A

Q I resized a table, and now the text is all distorted. How can I resize a table without having that happen?

A Be very careful when resizing tables. Always use a corner handle when resizing, which should keep everything in proportion. If you want to be extra sure, hold the Shift key down while you're dragging a corner handle.

Q My linked objects aren't updating—what's wrong?

A Usually, the links have somehow been turned to manual update. You can fix this attribute in two ways. You can manually update your links or change them to automatically update. To manually update links, follow these steps:

1. Choose Edit | Links from the menu.
2. Select the links you want to update from the Links listbox.
3. Click the Update Now button.
4. Click the Close button.

To change the links to automatically update, follow these steps:

1. Choose Edit | Links from the menu.
2. Select the links you want to change to automatic updates from the Links listbox.
3. Select Automatic as the Update option.
4. Click the Close button.
5. If the object isn't available in the Links listbox, or the Edit | Links command isn't available, the link(s) have somehow been broken. There's no way to fix this short of deleting the object and recopying it into your slide show.

Q I want a title row on the top of my table. Can I combine all the cells into one cell?

A Yes. To merge cells, select the cells you want to combine, then choose Table | Merge Cells from the menu. The cells that have been merged will now act as one cell.

PART V

Hour 16

Excel Worksheets

You can easily copy or embed a Microsoft Excel worksheet into your presentation, just as you can with a Microsoft Word table. PowerPoint 97 allows you to copy an externally created worksheet in a slide show or embed a new worksheet. This hour covers Microsoft Excel worksheets. Once again, when you're trying to decide whether to use an Excel worksheet or a Word table, ask yourself if you need to work with numbers or text. If the answer is more num-bers and calculations than text, use an Excel worksheet. If the answer is more text than numbers you should look at Hour 15, "Word Tables." For example, if you're adding, subtracting, multiplying, or dividing, a worksheet is preferred.

Inserting an Excel worksheet in a slide can be done in two different ways. You can either copy a worksheet that has been previously created by Bob, or you can create a new worksheet from scratch right in PowerPoint! In the next hour, you learn how to do the following:

- Copy or link a preexisting Excel worksheet into a PowerPoint slide
- Insert (or embed) a new Excel worksheet into a PowerPoint slide
- Add information to an embedded Excel worksheet
- Edit and format an embedded Excel worksheet

JUST A MINUTE

If you're already familiar with Microsoft Excel, you probably don't need to study this entire chapter in depth. However, even proficient Excel experts might want to at least skim through this chapter. You could find a useful trick or two.

Copying an Excel Worksheet

Similar to the process for copying a Word table, you can copy a preexisting Excel worksheet, or part of it, into your PowerPoint presentation. Try walking through the steps for copying a sample worksheet. Figure 16.1 shows a Microsoft Excel worksheet with information that should be included in the presentation. You can easily copy part of the worksheet (or the entire worksheet, depending on the size) into a PowerPoint slide.

Figure 16.1.
A Microsoft Excel worksheet.

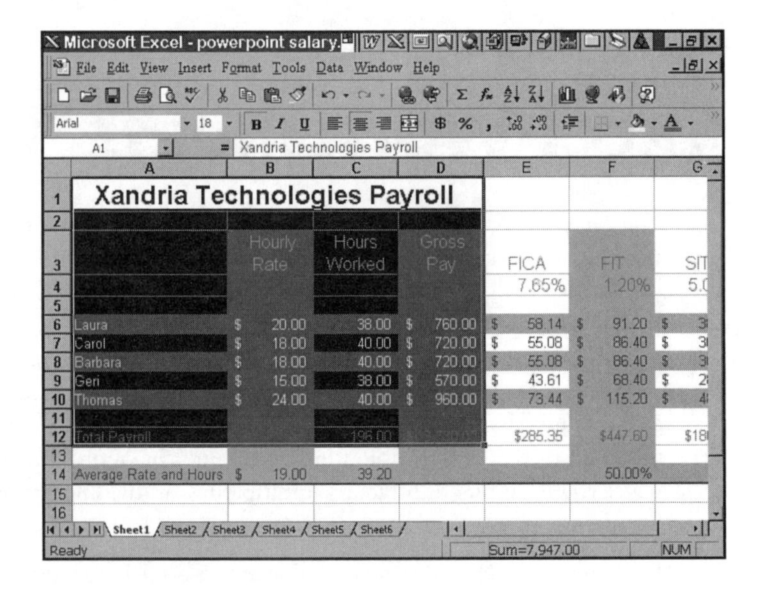

JUST A MINUTE

Most worksheets can be quite large, so I suggest copying only the information that's needed to make your point for the particular presentation. Remember that the fundamental design concept for a presentation is not to overwhelm your audience with onscreen gymnastics. You can always expand on any information when you're giving the presentation.

Whenever I copy information from one application (such as Microsoft Excel) into another application (such as Microsoft PowerPoint), I always start both programs. When you have two or more programs running, you can see buttons on the Windows 95 taskbar representing each program.

There are several ways to copy information from one application into another; you can use Edit | Copy with the Edit | Paste command, toolbar buttons, the drag-and-drop procedure, or hot keys. Although all the methods work, in my experience it's best to use the menu commands when copying information between different programs. To copy worksheet information from Excel to PowerPoint, follow these steps:

1. Make sure both programs are running, and that the documents you want to copy between are open.
2. Switch to Excel.
3. Select the cells you want to copy.

TIME SAVER

> The easiest way to select cells is to simply drag through the cells you want to select.

4. Choose Edit | Copy from the menu.
5. Switch to PowerPoint by clicking the PowerPoint button on the Windows taskbar.
6. View the slide you want to place the information on.
7. Choose Edit | Paste from the menu.

You might want to link the worksheet information in your presentation to the original worksheet in the Excel workbook. If the information is linked, later modifications to the Excel worksheet are displayed in the presentation. Use the following steps to link the worksheet information:

1. Make sure both programs are running, and that the documents you want to copy from and to are open.
2. Switch to Excel.
3. Select the cells you want to copy.
4. Choose Edit | Copy from the menu.
5. Switch to PowerPoint by clicking the PowerPoint button on the Windows taskbar.
6. View the slide you want to place the worksheet information on.
7. Choose Edit | Paste Special from the menu.
8. From the Paste Special dialog box, select Paste link. (See Figure 16.2.)

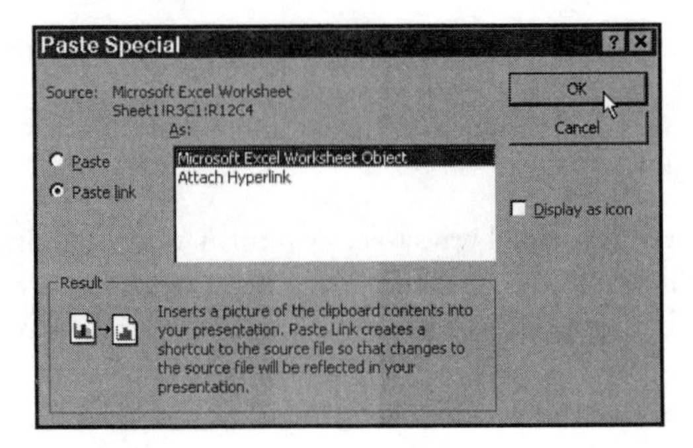

Figure 16.2.
The Paste Special dialog box.

9. Select Microsoft Excel Worksheet Object.
10. Click the OK button.

JUST A MINUTE

Over time, you might find that you prefer to use another method, such as toolbar buttons or the drag-and-drop technique. There's usually no problem with doing that. Experiment with different methods and use the method you prefer. The only caveat is when you want to link information from the original document to the destination document. In that case, you need to use the menu to paste the information.

Now you know how to make changes to your original Microsoft Excel worksheet and have the changes displayed in your presentation. When you open your presentation file, PowerPoint displays a window asking if you want to update your links. Simply click the Yes button to update your presentation.

JUST A MINUTE

You should save your Microsoft Excel worksheet before you perform the steps for linking the object to PowerPoint. When you create a link, PowerPoint uses the name of the original document to make any necessary updates. If you haven't saved the original document, PowerPoint will be confused and won't know where to find the linked information when you view the presentation at a later date. If you rename or move the document, the link will also be broken.

Inserting (or Embedding) an Excel Worksheet

In some instances, the worksheet for the PowerPoint presentation will already be created. You simply need to insert the worksheet into a slide. Unlike inserting a Microsoft Word table, PowerPoint doesn't have a specific layout for this purpose. You can use the Title Only layout, as shown in Figure 16.3, with the Insert Microsoft Excel Worksheet button on the standard toolbar, or you can use the Object layout.

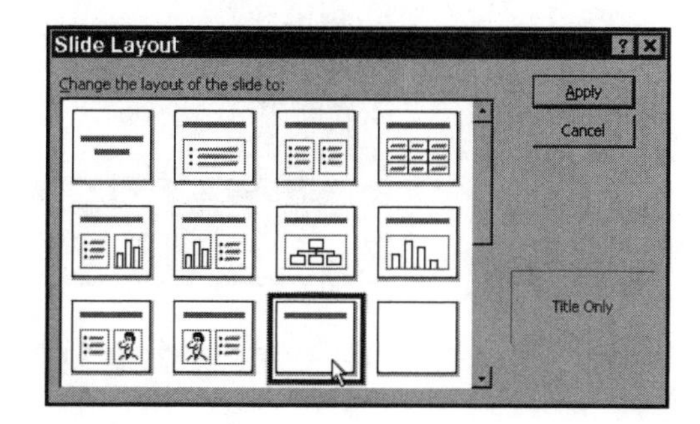

Figure 16.3.
Selecting the Title Only layout.

The best method, I find, is to insert an Excel worksheet by using the Title Only layout with the Insert Microsoft Excel Worksheet button on the standard toolbar. When you insert a worksheet as an object, much more formatting is required to display only the informational cells. To insert a worksheet using the Insert Microsoft Excel Worksheet button on the standard toolbar, perform the following steps:

1. Start a new slide with the Title Only layout.
2. Click the Insert Microsoft Excel Worksheet button on the standard toolbar.
3. Select the number of columns and rows you want, and then click. (See Figure 16.4.)

Follow these steps to insert a worksheet into your presentation using the Object layout:

1. Start a new slide using the Object Slide layout.
2. Double-click the object placeholder.
3. Select "Create new" from the Insert Object dialog box. (See Figure 16.5.)

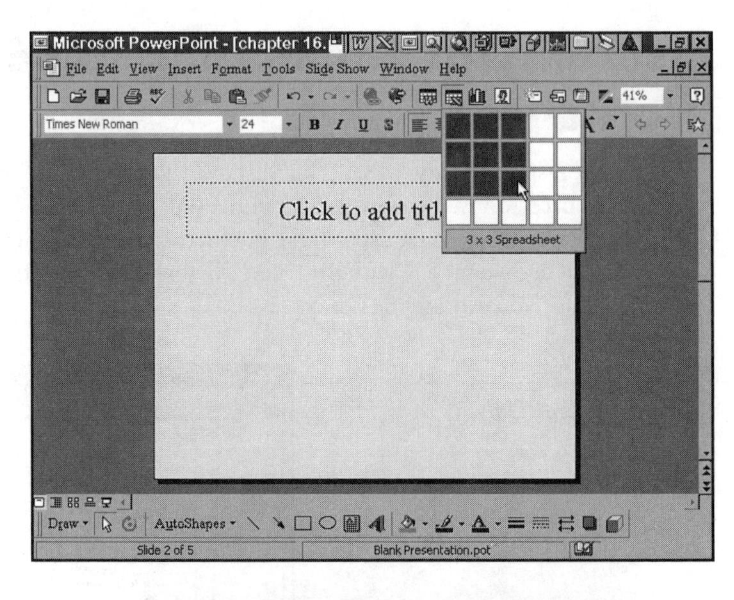

Figure 16.4.
Selecting the number of columns and rows for your worksheet.

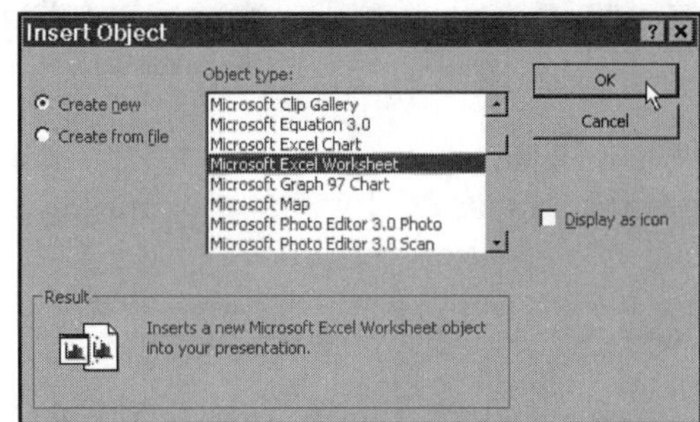

Figure 16.5.
Use the Insert Object dialog box to insert a Microsoft Excel worksheet into your presentation.

4. Select Microsoft Excel Worksheet from the "Object type" list.
5. Click the OK button.

CAUTION

After inserting a worksheet, you will have to do some resizing and moving to properly align the worksheet on the slide.

Regardless of the method used to insert a worksheet, Excel should now be active in PowerPoint. Figure 16.6 shows PowerPoint with the Excel tools. Notice that although the toolbars and menu bar are similar to PowerPoint, they actually belong to Microsoft Excel. While you are creating and editing the worksheet, you're actually using Microsoft Excel, not PowerPoint, to change, update, and create the worksheet.

Figure 16.6.
Working on a worksheet with Microsoft Excel's tools and menu.

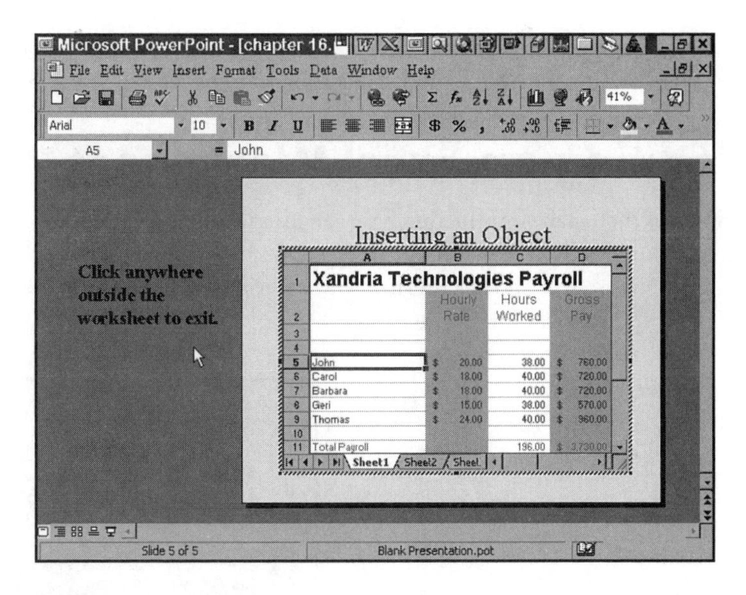

To exit from editing the worksheet, click anywhere outside the worksheet.

Once you have inserted a worksheet into a presentation, it becomes an embedded object. The object might need information inserted or require the cells to be reformatted. If you want to directly edit the worksheet, simply double-click the worksheet object and you will find yourself back in the land of Excel.

Inserting Information

When you first insert an Excel worksheet into a slide, the worksheet is often too small to see. You could just change the zoom control to 100 percent or 150 percent. Before you enter any information, you should resize the worksheet object so that it's big enough to work with and big enough to see later. To resize the worksheet object, follow these steps:

1. Click outside the object to exit from Excel editing.
2. With the worksheet selected, drag a corner-sizing handle to resize the worksheet.

CAUTION

Don't drag a top, bottom, left, or right sizing handle. This resizes the worksheet, but doesn't maintain the proportions for the information it will eventually contain.

To insert information in your worksheet, make sure the cursor is in the cell where you want to add information, and type the information.

You can quickly move from cell to cell while typing information by pressing the Tab key. Pressing the Shift+Tab key combination moves the cursor backward one cell at a time.

Editing an Excel Worksheet

Once all the information has been inserted into the table, you will probably want to add lines to the worksheet, format the text and numbers, and change the size of the columns or rows. Figure 16.7 shows a finished worksheet that has been formatted with lines, shading, and text and number formatting.

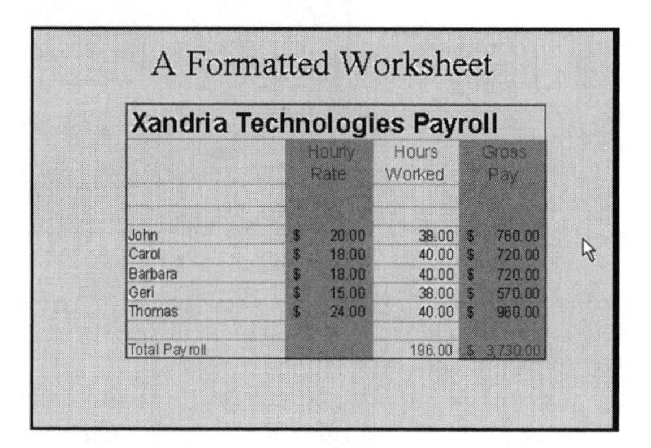
A Formatted Worksheet

Xandria Technologies Payroll

	Hourly Rate	Hours Worked	Gross Pay
John	$ 20.00	38.00	$ 760.00
Carol	$ 18.00	40.00	$ 720.00
Barbara	$ 18.00	40.00	$ 720.00
Geri	$ 15.00	38.00	$ 570.00
Thomas	$ 24.00	40.00	$ 960.00
Total Payroll		196.00	$ 3,730.00

Figure 16.7.
A worksheet that has been formatted.

Adding Lines and a Fill to a Worksheet

Although Excel automatically adds gridlines to the worksheet, you might want to enhance the lines or add shading. To add a border to a worksheet, follow these steps:

1. Double-click the worksheet to go into Excel editing.
2. Select the cells, columns, or rows you want to enhance.
3. Click the Borders button drop-down arrow on the formatting toolbar. (See Figure 16.8.)
4. Select a border style.

To add shading to a worksheet, follow these steps:

1. Double-click the worksheet to go into Excel editing.
2. Select the cells, columns, or rows you want to enhance.
3. Click the Shading button drop-down arrow on the formatting toolbar. (See Figure 16.9.)
4. Select a shading color.

Figure 16.8.
Selecting a border from the formatting toolbar.

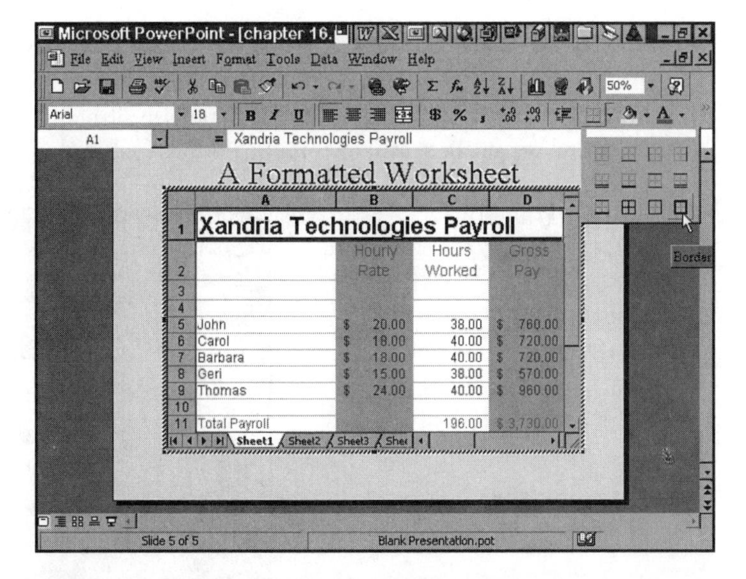

Figure 16.9.
Selecting shading from the formatting toolbar.

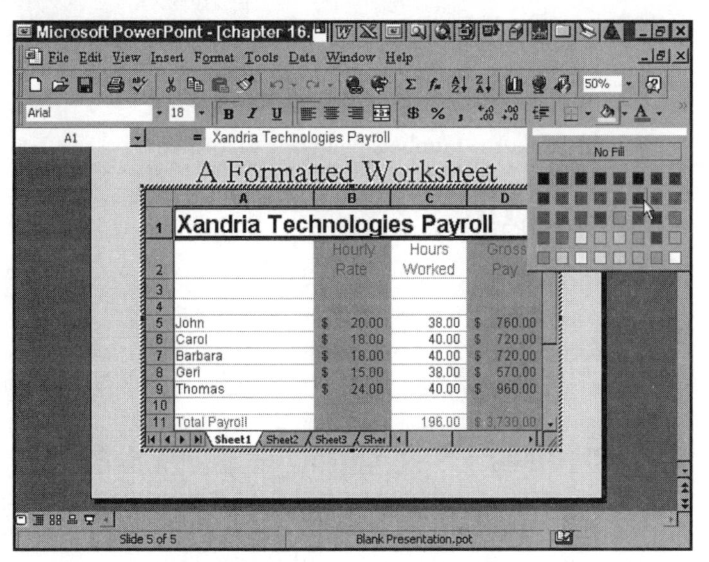

TIME SAVER

Choose Format | AutoFormat from the menu to select from many preformatted worksheet styles.

Formatting Numbers in a Worksheet

Excel offers easy access to many number formatting styles. Depending on the type of numbers you're working with, you have several options available, including currency, accounting, dates, and percentages, as shown in the Format Cells dialog box in Figure 16.10.

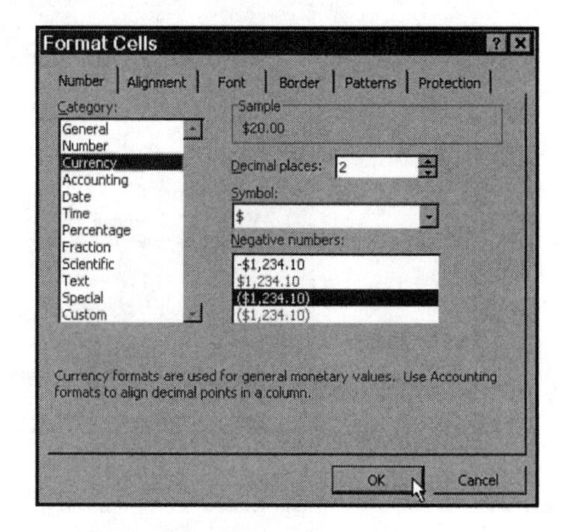

Figure 16.10.
The available number of formatting options.

To format numbers in a worksheet, follow these steps:

1. Select the numbers you want to format.
2. Choose Format | Cells from the menu.
3. Click the Number tab.
4. Select the category that matches the type of numbers you're using.
5. Select the number of decimal places to show.
6. Change any other options available, if you want.
7. Click the OK button.

Summing Numbers

When working with numbers, one of the most common tasks is to total a column or row of numbers. Excel gives you a quick way to total a column or row of numbers. To quickly sum a column or row of numbers, follow these steps:

1. Click the cell where you want the total to appear.
2. Click the AutoSum button on the standard toolbar.
3. Press Enter.

Resizing Columns

After you have formatted the text or numbers in a worksheet, you might find that the width of the columns should be smaller or wider. You can either manually adjust the size of columns, or you can let Excel quickly change the column width based on the information in the column. To manually adjust the column width, follow these steps:

1. Place the mouse pointer over the border of the column you want to adjust so that it looks like a double-headed arrow, as shown in Figure 16.11.

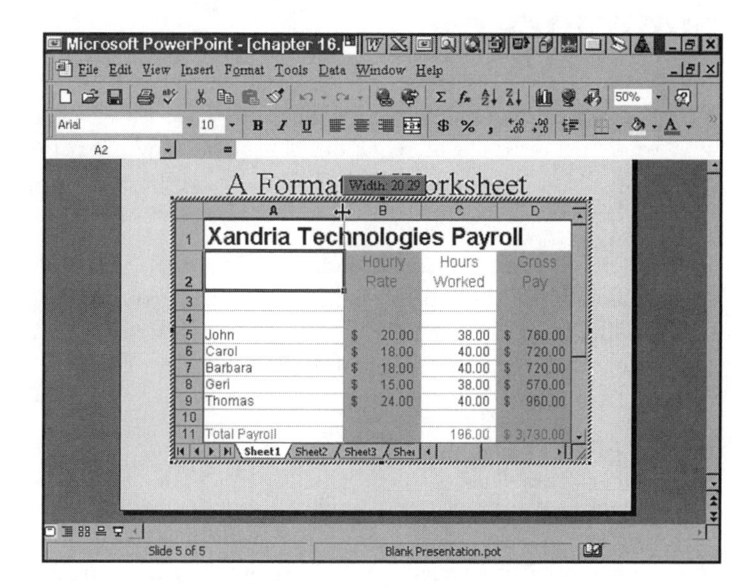

Figure 16.11.
Resizing a column with the mouse.

2. Click and hold the mouse button.
3. Drag the border to the new size.
4. Release the mouse button.

TIME SAVER

> You can quickly resize a column to get the best fit. Just double-click a column border.

If you want the columns in your worksheet to be an exact size, perform the following steps:

1. Select the column you want to resize.
2. Choose Format | Column | Width from the menu.

3. Enter an amount in the Column Width dialog box, as shown in Figure 16.12.
4. Click the OK button.

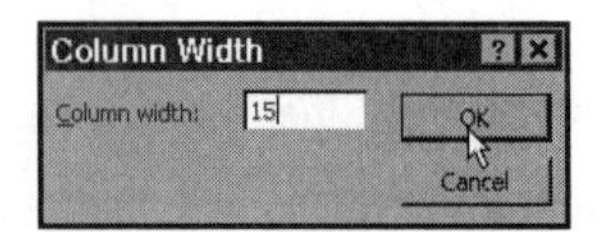

Figure 16.12.
Setting an exact column width.

Summary

In this hour, I have covered the different methods for inserting a Microsoft Excel worksheet into a presentation. You can either copy an existing worksheet or embed a brand-new worksheet into your presentation. When you copy an existing worksheet, you can link the PowerPoint copy to the original Microsoft Excel worksheet if modifications or updates are likely.

When editing an embedded worksheet, you have access to all the tools and commands that would normally be available in Microsoft Excel. You can format the table by adding lines or shading or by changing the number format. Microsoft Excel allows you to quickly resize columns and to sum a group of numbers.

Workshop

This hour's workshop is very similar to the previous hour's. You will be inserting and working with an Excel worksheet. Follow the step-by-step instructions, and you won't be lead astray. Remember, if things really get knocked out of whack, you might want to start over. And don't forget the question-and-answer session at the very end.

Test What You've Learned

1. Start a new blank presentation with the Title Only layout.
2. Type the title `What I Had for Lunch`.
3. Click the Insert Microsoft Excel Worksheet button on the standard toolbar.
4. Select 4×2 as the worksheet size.
5. Click outside the worksheet to exit from Excel edit.
6. Resize the worksheet object so that it's bigger.
7. Double-click the worksheet to edit it.

8. Type `Hamburger`.
9. Press Tab.
10. Type `5`.
11. Press the down-arrow key and then the left-arrow key.
12. Type `Fries`.
13. Press Tab.
14. Type `2.75`.
15. Press the down-arrow, then left-arrow keys.
16. Type `Large Coke`.
17. Press Tab.
18. Type `1.5`.
19. Press the down-arrow, then left-arrow keys.
20. Type `Total`.
21. Press Tab.
22. Click the AutoSum button and press Enter.
23. Select the cells with the words `Large Coke` and `1.5` (cells A3 and B3).
24. Click the Borders button on the standard toolbar and click the double-line border.
25. Resize column A to better fit the text (either by double-clicking or manual adjustment).
26. Format column B to have dollar signs and two decimal places.
27. Click outside the worksheet.
28. Save the file as `Hour 16 TWYL`.
29. Close the file.

Q&A

Q I just tried to copy some information from my Excel worksheet, but the Paste command is dimmed. Why can't I paste?

A Excel has a little quirk. When you select information and then choose Copy, you should see little dashes running around your selection. If you press the Esc key (or any other key that makes the running dashes disappear), the Paste command won't be available in any program. All you need to do is make sure you don't press Esc.

Q I would like an average of the numbers in my worksheet. Is there an easy way to do this?

A Yes, Excel has a function that gives you the average of a range of numbers. Here's how you do that:

1. Click in the cell where you want the average to display.
2. Click the Paste Function button on the standard toolbar (the button right next to the AutoSum button that has an *f* and *x* on it).
3. From the Function Category list, select Statistical.
4. From the Function Name list, select AVERAGE.
5. Click the OK button.
6. In the Number 1 box, Excel makes a guess as to the correct range of numbers to average for you. (If this range isn't correct, click the button that looks like a worksheet with a red arrow, select the correct range, then click the button next to the new, selected range with the little red arrow pointing down.)
7. Click the OK button to accept the range.

You should see an average of the numbers you have selected. The Office Assistant is a great help with this feature, especially from step 5 on. If you don't see him hanging around asking if you want help, press the F1 key on your keyboard.

Excel has tons of other functions to make your number life easier. If you want more information on using Excel, you might want to buy the *Teach Yourself Excel 97 in 24 Hours* (Sams Publishing) companion book.

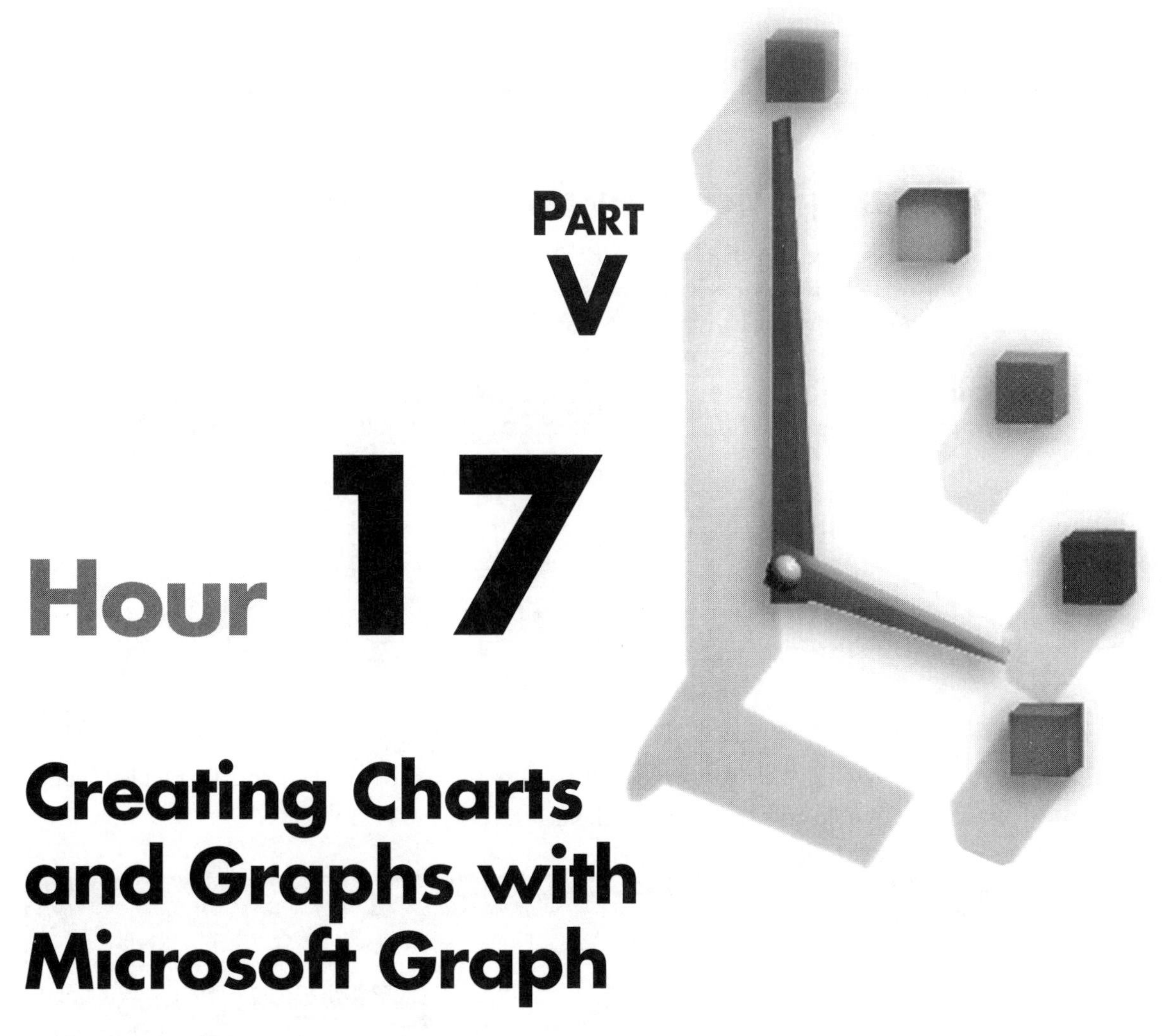

PART V

Hour 17

Creating Charts and Graphs with Microsoft Graph

In addition to tables and worksheets, you can also embed a graph or chart into your presentation. Charts and graphs are an excellent medium for visually presenting numeric data. PowerPoint 97 relies on the Microsoft Graph 97 program for creating the charts and graphs that will be embedded in your presentation. Several chart types are available, and each chart type has several subtypes as well, ensuring that there's a chart for any need. Most charts can be displayed in either two or three dimensions, and almost every aspect of a chart can be formatted to suit your requirements. The next two hours should give you a solid foundation for creating and inserting fantastic charts. This hour covers the basic chart tasks:

- Inserting and viewing a chart
- Entering the data that will be displayed on the chart
- Choosing the correct chart type for the job

So get started and create that chart for Bob!

Inserting and Viewing a Chart

It's easy to create a chart in PowerPoint when you use one of the available AutoLayouts. Figure 17.1 displays the chart layout selections. If you want to insert a chart on any other slide, just use the Insert Chart button on the standard toolbar.

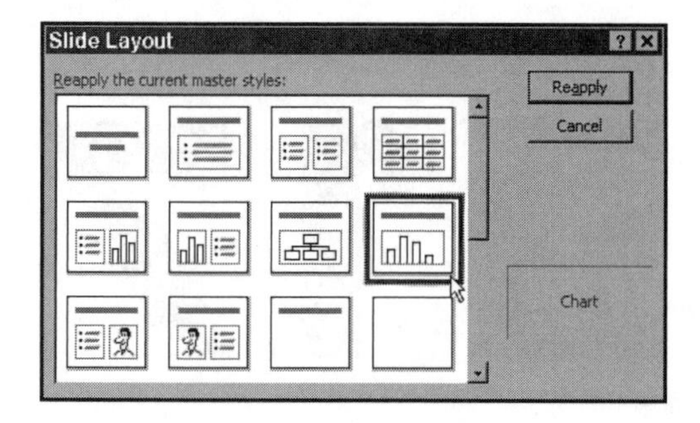

Figure 17.1.
Selecting a chart layout.

Follow these steps to insert a chart by using the Chart Slide Layout:

1. Start a new slide using the Chart, Text and Chart, or Chart and Text Slide Layout.
2. Double-click the chart placeholder. (See Figure 17.2.)

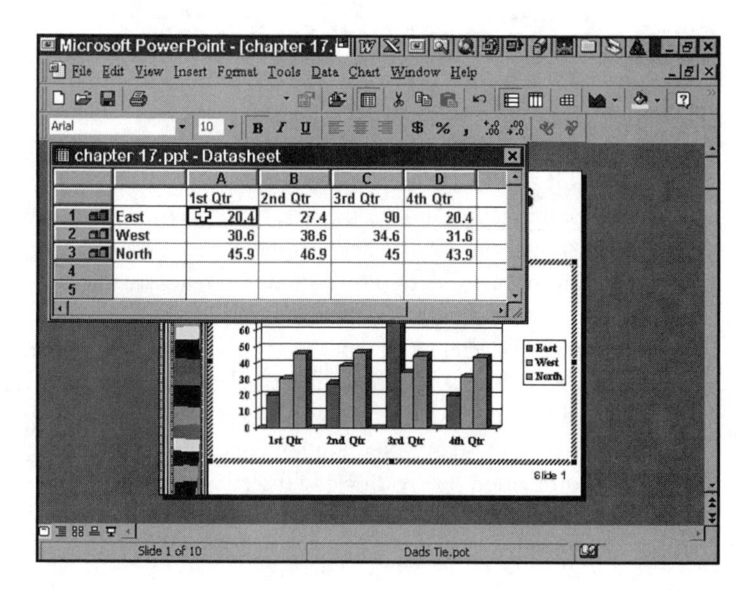

Figure 17.2.
The foundation for a chart.

There's another method for inserting a chart into any slide; just follow these steps:

1. Display the slide where you want to insert a chart.
2. Click the Insert Chart button on the standard toolbar.

JUST A MINUTE

> If you use the Insert Chart button, the chart is inserted in the middle of the current slide. If you have other objects on the slide, you might need to resize or move the chart. Use the corner handles to resize the chart so that all the chart components stay in proportion.

Entering Information in the Datasheet

After you have inserted the chart, you will be in what I call Chart Edit Mode, and while in Chart Edit Mode, you're actually working in Microsoft Graph 97. Microsoft Graph 97 is an extra program installed with PowerPoint 97. Just as you noticed when you were inserting a Microsoft Word table or Microsoft Excel worksheet, you will notice that the toolbars and menu commands have changed to reflect that you're now in Microsoft Graph 97. Any formatting or chart changes must be done while in Microsoft Graph's Chart Edit Mode.

The first item to take note of when you're in Chart Edit Mode is the chart *datasheet*, which is simply a small worksheet you can use to fill in the appropriate information that serves as the basis for your chart. The nice folks at Microsoft have given you a sample datasheet and chart (it's hiding behind the datasheet) to get you started. The first row and column are reserved for text (labels) that identify the actual numbers you will eventually enter. Figure 17.3 shows the sample datasheet and underlying chart.

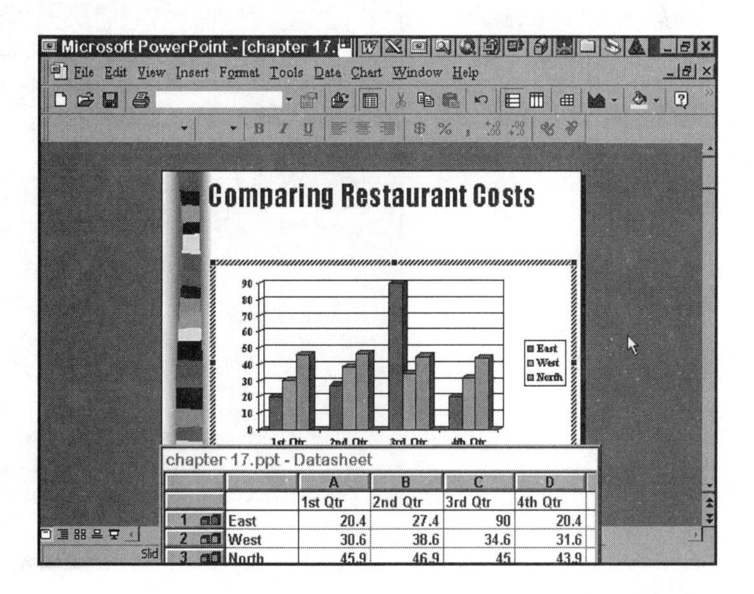

Figure 17.3.
A sample datasheet and corresponding chart to help get you started.

After you have inserted the information for your chart, you can turn the datasheet off, which gives you more room to format the chart. If you need to edit the chart data later, you can turn the datasheet back on with a simple mouse click. To turn the datasheet off or on, follow these steps:

- Choose View | Datasheet from the menu.

  or

- Click the View Datasheet button on the standard toolbar.

Just a Minute

> You can quickly close the datasheet by clicking the Close button in the upper-right corner of the datasheet window.

Time Saver

> Sometimes I just leave the datasheet on, but move it out of the way. To move the datasheet, place the mouse pointer in the datasheet title bar and drag the datasheet window to a new location. Figure 17.4 shows the datasheet moved to a new location.

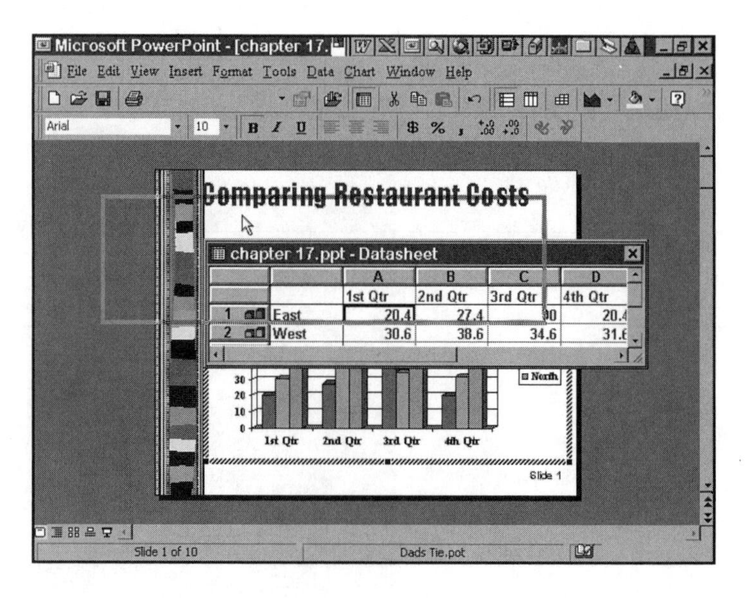

Figure 17.4.
Moving the datasheet to work on the chart.

To create a chart, all you need to do is replace the sample information in the datasheet with your real information.

Entering Information

Entering information in a Microsoft Graph datasheet is really no different from entering information in a table or worksheet. Although you can change the column width in a datasheet (new with Microsoft Graph 97), you don't really need to worry about this option unless you want to see the information as you work. The information you enter in the datasheet (whether you can see it or not) is displayed on the chart, and the chart is what your audience sees. To enter information in the datasheet, perform the following steps:

1. Click in the cell where you want to enter or change information.
2. Type.

Here are some helpful datasheet tips:

- Use the first row and column to label the information.
- Use the Tab key to move forward one cell.
- Use the Shift+Tab key combination to move backward one cell.
- The cell with the dark border is the current selected cell.
- To edit cell information, select the cell and press F2.

When entering information on a datasheet, keep in mind the type of chart you will eventually be using. For example, if you're using a pie chart like the one shown in Figure 17.5, you should enter only one row of information. On the other hand, if you're using a bar chart, you can enter as many columns and rows of information as needed.

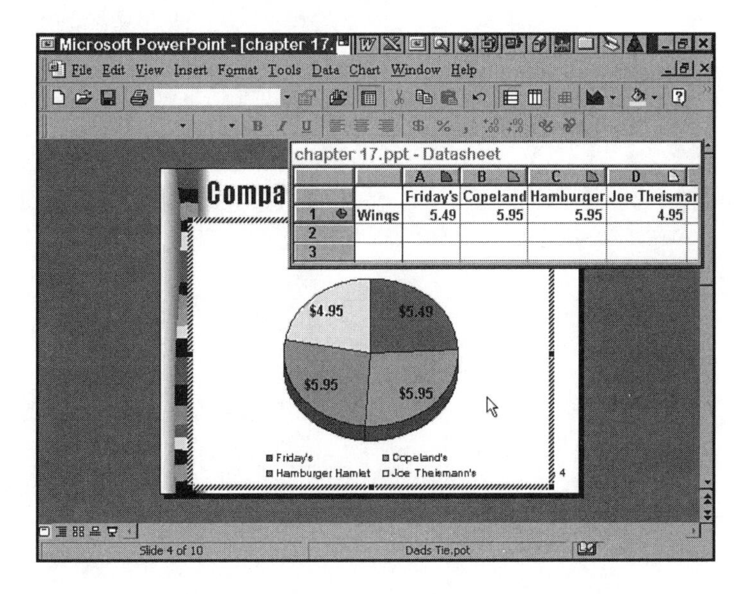

Figure 17.5.
A pie chart uses only one row and many columns.

Time Saver

If you have a lot of information you need to chart, you might want to create several slides. Each slide would display a pie chart.

Just a Minute

As always, remember that you don't want to get too detailed when entering information. Your audience has to be able to read and quickly understand the information onscreen. You can always expound on the information when you give the presentation.

Selecting Cells

When editing chart information, it's important to know how to select information cells. You can select multiple cells by simply using the mouse and dragging, as shown in Figure 17.6.

Figure 17.6.

Selecting several cells by dragging the mouse.

chapter 17.ppt - Datasheet

		A	B	C	D	E
		Friday's	Copeland'	Hamburger	Joe Theismann's	
1	Wings	5.49	5.95	5.95	4.95	
2	Caesar Sa	8.19	7.95	7.95	7.5	
3	Hamburge	6.09	6.95	5.95	5.75	
4						
5						
6						
7						
8						

To select an entire column, simply click the column heading at the top of the column, as shown in Figure 17.7.

Figure 17.7.

Selecting an entire column.

chapter 17.ppt - Datasheet

		A	B	C	D	E
		Friday's	Copeland'	Hamburger	Joe Theismann's	
1	Wings	5.49	5.95	5.95	4.95	
2	Caesar Sa	8.19	7.95	7.95	7.5	
3	Hamburge	6.09	6.95	5.95	5.75	
4						
5						
6						
7						
8						

To select an entire row, click the row heading at the left of the row, as shown in Figure 17.8.

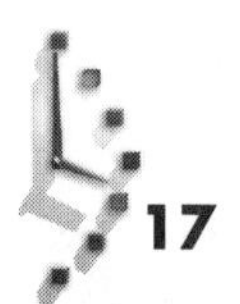

Figure 17.8.
Selecting an entire row.

chapter 17.ppt - Datasheet

		A	B	C	D	E
		Friday's	Copeland's	Hamburger	Joe Theismann's	
1	Wings	5.49	5.95	5.95	4.95	
2	Caesar Sa	8.19	7.95	7.95	7.5	
3	Hamburge	6.09	6.95	5.95	5.75	
4						
5						
6						
7						
8						

NEW TERM The column or row *headings* are the lettered or numbered gray areas at the top of each column or to the left of each row.

And last, to select the entire datasheet, click the Select All button, as shown in Figure 17.9.

Figure 17.9.
Selecting the entire datasheet.

chapter 17.ppt - Datasheet

		A	B	C	D	E
		Friday's	Copeland's	Hamburger	Joe Theismann's	
1	Wings	5.49	5.95	5.95	4.95	
2	Caesar Sa	8.19	7.95	7.95	7.5	
3	Hamburge	6.09	6.95	5.95	5.75	
4						
5						
6						
7						
8						

TIME SAVER

The Select All button is the gray rectangle in the upper-left corner of the datasheet.

Copying and Importing Information

If you already have the information available in a spreadsheet format, there's no need to retype the information into a datasheet. For example, an Excel or Lotus 1-2-3 worksheet might serve as the basis for the chart. You can either copy the information from the existing worksheet or import the information. The option you use depends on how much information you need.

Copying Information

If the worksheet you're using is large and has additional information that won't be used for the chart, use the Copy command. You should select and copy only the portion needed to populate the chart. Figure 17.10 shows a large Excel worksheet that's the basis for the copy. After the selection is made, use the Edit | Copy command to get the cells you want for the chart.

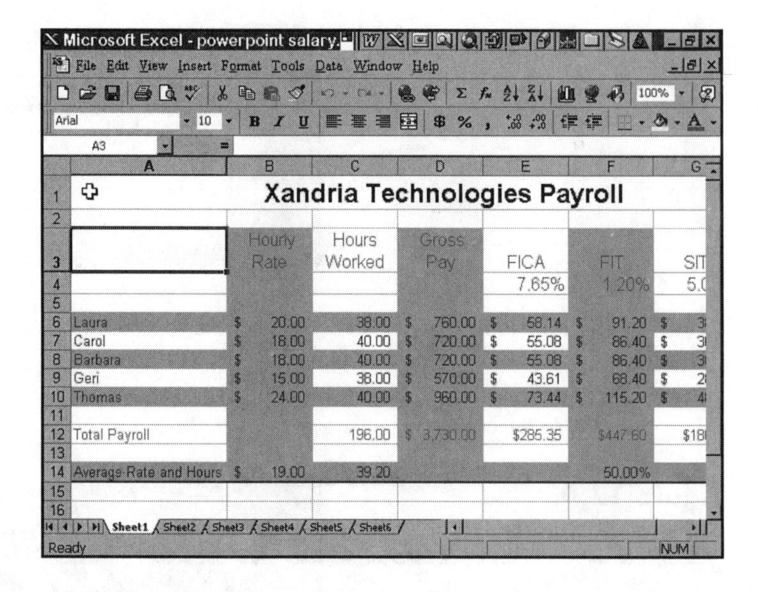

Figure 17.10.
A large Excel worksheet.

As previously mentioned, it's quite easy to copy information from one application into another and there are several different methods available for the task. Use the following method to copy information from an existing worksheet into the Microsoft Graph datasheet:

1. Make sure both programs are running, and that the documents you want to copy between are open.
2. Switch to Excel (or Lotus 1-2-3).
3. Select the cells that contain the information you need for the chart, as shown in Figure 17.11.
4. Choose Edit | Copy from the menu.
5. Switch to PowerPoint by clicking the PowerPoint button on the Windows taskbar.
6. View the slide where you want to place the chart.
7. Double-click the chart placeholder or insert a chart by using the Insert Chart button on the standard toolbar (if you haven't done this already).
8. Select the entire datasheet by clicking the Select All button.
9. Choose Edit | Paste from the menu.

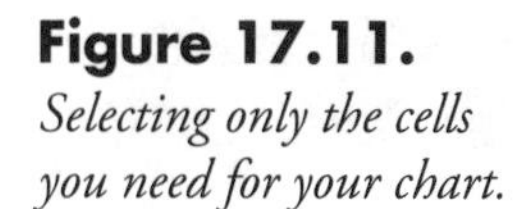

Figure 17.11.
Selecting only the cells you need for your chart.

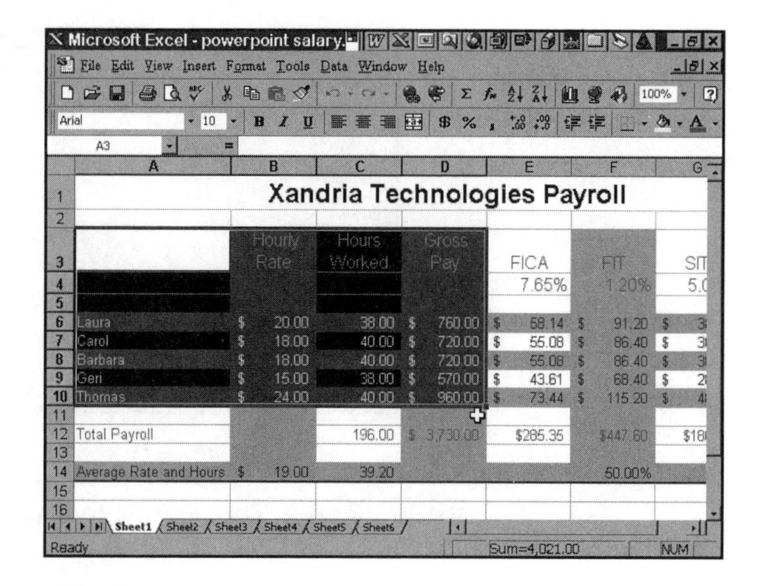

Importing Information

If the worksheet you're using contains just the information you need to create the chart, you might want to use the Import File option. Remember that you might need to clean the datasheet up a little bit by deleting extra rows and columns, but importing a file is much easier than re-entering all the information directly into the datasheet. To import a file into a Microsoft Graph datasheet, follow these steps:

1. View the slide where you want to place the chart.
2. Double-click the chart placeholder or insert a chart by using the Insert Chart button on the standard toolbar (if you haven't done this already).
3. Choose Edit | Import File from the menu.
4. Select the drive and folder from the "Look in" drop-down box.
5. Select the filename from the list of files, as shown in Figure 17.12.

JUST A MINUTE

If you're importing a Lotus 1-2-3 file, you might need to change the "Files of type" drop-down list to display All Files (*.*).

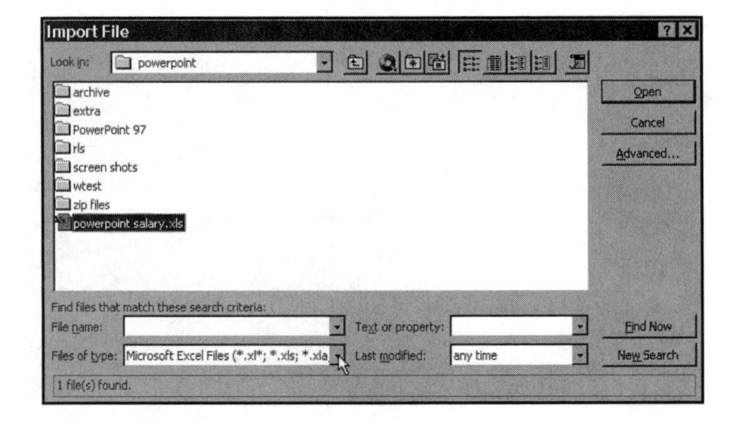

Figure 17.12.
Selecting a file to import.

6. Click the Open button.
7. Select the worksheet you want to import from the Import Data Options dialog box, as shown in Figure 17.13.

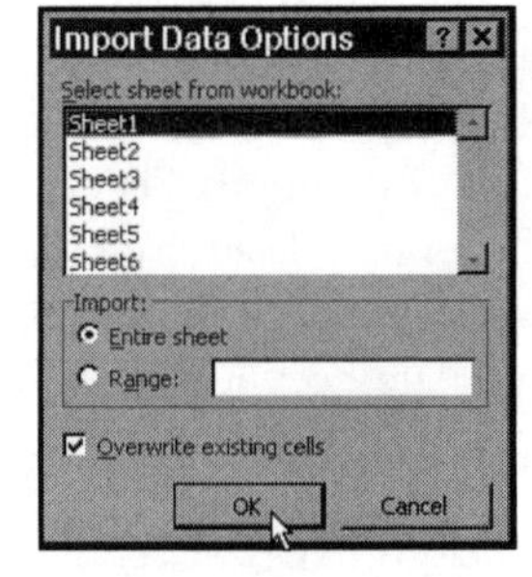

Figure 17.13.
Selecting the Sheet1 worksheet to import.

8. Make sure the "Overwrite existing cells" checkbox is checked.

Time Saver

> If you know the range of cells you want to import, such as A1–G10, you can enter the range in the Import Data Options dialog box.

9. Click the OK button.

Sometimes extraneous rows of information are transferred to the datasheet. To delete the extra rows of information, follow these steps:

1. Select the rows or columns you want to delete from the datasheet.
2. Choose Edit | Delete from the menu.

CAUTION

> Pressing the Delete key deletes only the contents of the cells, not the rows or columns.

A Word About Undo

You're probably used to having unlimited access to undoing your mistakes. Although Microsoft Graph 97 does have an Undo command, you get only one chance. In other words, if you make a mistake, don't do anything else—click the Undo button right away. If you even type one extra letter, you will have to fix your mistake all by yourself. To undo a mistake, you have these two choices:

- Choose Edit | Undo from the menu.

  or

- Click the Undo button on the standard toolbar.

17

Choosing a Chart Type

Now that you have fully entered all your charting information into the datasheet, you have the option of changing the type of chart. Chart types designate the display characteristics of the graph. The default chart is the standard 3-D Column chart, as shown in Figure 17.14.

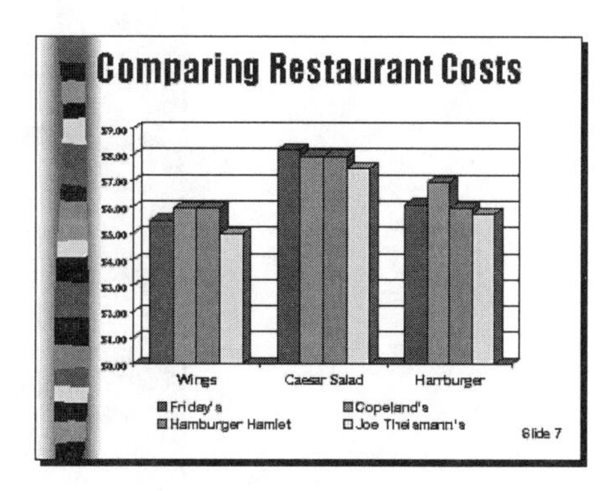

Figure 17.14.
The default chart type, a 3-D Column.

Microsoft Graph has over a dozen standard charts, many of them with several subtypes. In total, there are over 70 different charts from which to choose. In addition to all the different standard charts that come with Microsoft Graph, there are 20 predesigned custom chart types to choose from. For even more flexibility, you can create your own custom chart types to use in the future.

If you find that you're always changing the chart type to your favorite variation, such as a 3-D pie chart, you can change the default chart type.

Just a Minute

All the instructions that follow assume that you're already in Chart Edit Mode. The instructions don't apply if you're in PowerPoint Slide Edit Mode. To edit a chart, double-click the chart object.

Standard Types

You can change the type of chart at any time. When you do, you're usually affecting the entire chart. To change the type of the entire chart, perform the following steps:

1. Choose Chart | Chart Type from the menu.
2. Click the Standard tab.
3. Select a chart type from the list.
4. Select a chart subtype from the samples at the right side of the window.
5. Click the "Press and hold to view sample" button to see a sample of your chart before accepting any changes, as shown in Figure 17.15.
6. Click the OK button to accept the new Chart type.

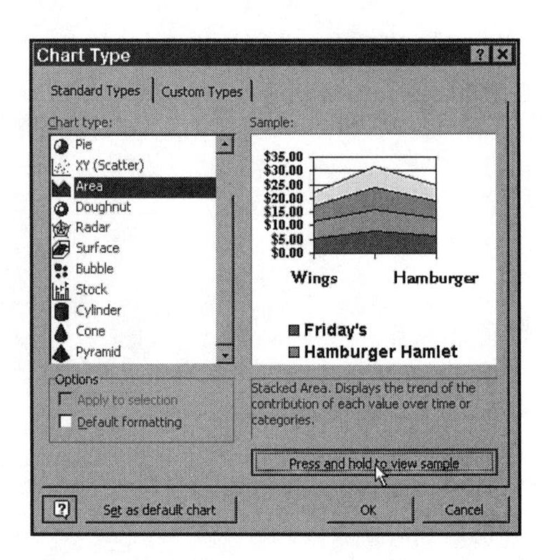

Figure 17.15.
Previewing a chart type selection before accepting the change.

The ability to preview the chart type you select, populated with your custom information, is new with Microsoft Graph 97, as is being able to combine different chart types into a single chart. Figure 17.16 shows two separate data series combined onto one chart.

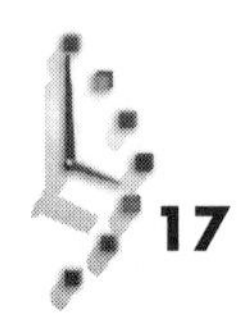

Figure 17.16.
Combining chart types.

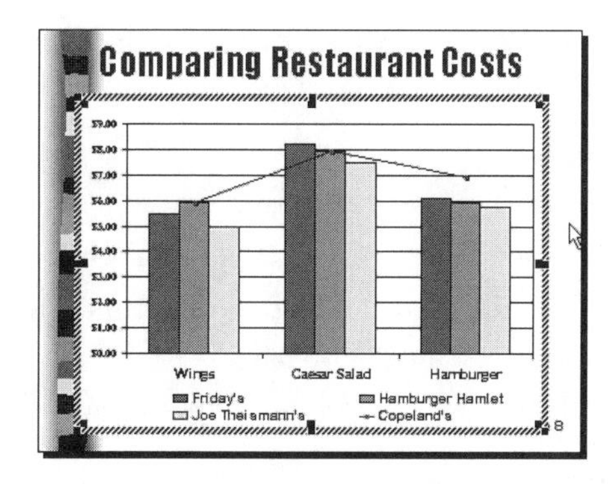

The combination feature is available when using 2-D charts, with the exception of the XY (Scatter) and Bubble types. The 3-D Column and Bar types also allow you to use a Cylinder, Cone, or Pyramid type. To change the chart type for a single data series, perform the following steps:

1. Select the data series you want to change.

JUST A MINUTE

> You can select any item on a chart by single-clicking it. You also can select a chart item by choosing the item from the Chart Objects drop-down box on the standard toolbar, as shown in Figure 17.17.

Figure 17.17.
Selecting a chart item from the Chart Objects drop-down box on the standard toolbar.

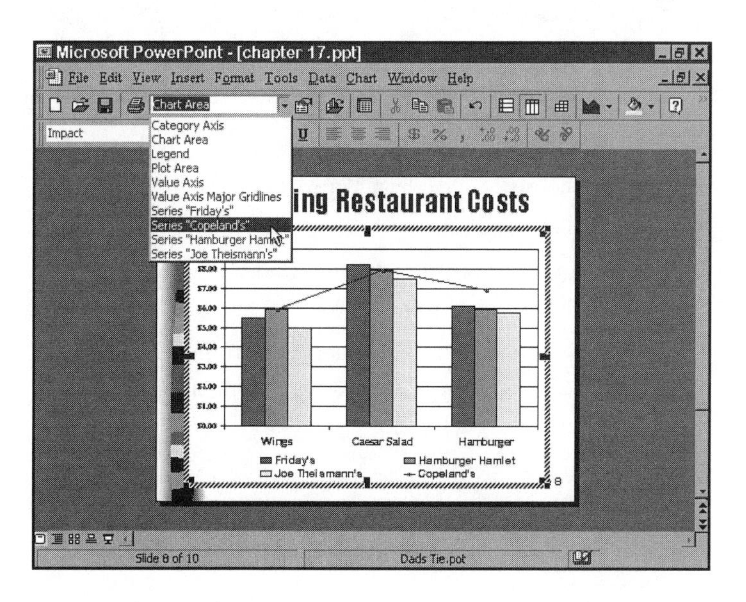

2. Choose Chart | Chart Type from the menu.
3. Click the Standard tab.
4. Select a chart type from list.
5. Select a chart subtype from the samples at the right side of the window.
6. Make sure the "Apply to selection" checkbox is checked.
7. Click the Press and hold to view sample button to view a sample of your chart before accepting any changes.
8. Click the OK button to accept the new Chart type.

Custom Types

A custom chart type is similar to a template that stores all the custom formatting information. Usually the coherent, custom formatting scheme takes considerable time to create. If you think there's even a remote chance you will want to create a similar chart, it's worthwhile to save the chart as a custom chart type.

JUST A MINUTE

I haven't covered formatting a chart yet—that material is covered in Hour 18, "Editing Charts and Graphs."

The custom chart type is a new feature in Microsoft Graph 97. Once again, a big round of applause for the Microsoft folks.

Take a peek at all the predefined custom chart types available to help give you ideas for your own custom chart types. To save a chart as a custom chart type, perform the following steps:

1. Format the chart as desired.
2. Choose Chart | Chart Type from the menu.
3. Click the Custom tab. (See Figure 17.18.)
4. Select User-defined for the chart type.
5. Click the Add button.
6. Type a name for your chart type in the Name box.
7. Type a description, if you like, in the Description box. (See Figure 17.19.)
8. Click the OK button.

Q When I change the chart type, I lose all the formatting that took me hours to do. Help!

A Whenever you change the chart type, Microsoft Graph will, by default, apply the formatting of the chart type to your chart. If you have made formatting changes to your chart, such as changing the font face, font size, color, background, or anything else, you might want to uncheck the "Default formatting" box under Options in the Chart Type dialog box.

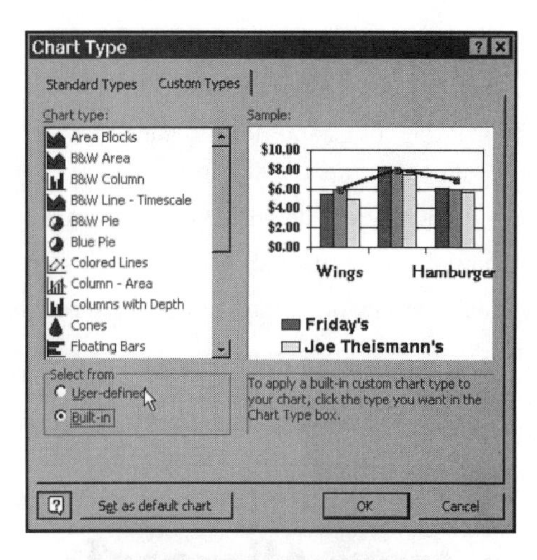

Figure 17.18.
The Custom tab for adding or selecting a custom chart type.

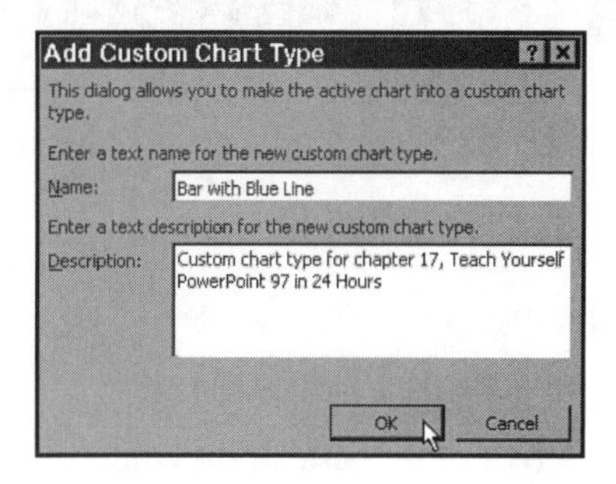

Figure 17.19.
Type a name and description for your custom chart type.

Whenever you want to apply your custom chart type (or one of Microsoft's), all you need to do is follow these steps:

1. Choose Chart | Chart Type from the menu.
2. Click the Custom tab.
3. Select either User-defined or Built-in.
4. Select a chart type from the list on the left.
5. Click the OK button to accept the new chart type.

Changing the Default Chart Type

To save time in the future, you might want to modify the default chart type. Microsoft Graph makes it easy to change the default chart type; simply follow these steps:

1. Choose Chart | Chart Type from the menu.
2. Click the Standard tab.

3. Select a chart type from the list.
4. Select a chart subtype from the samples at the right side of the window.
5. Click the "Press and hold to view sample" button to see a sample of your chart before accepting any changes.
6. Click the "Set as default chart" button.
7. Click the Yes button to accept the change to the default chart.
8. Click the OK button to accept the new chart type.

JUST A MINUTE

You also can set a custom chart type as the default chart.

Exiting from Microsoft Graph

As with all embedded objects, you can exit from Microsoft Graph by clicking outside the chart area. To get back into Chart Edit Mode and edit the chart, simply double-click the chart.

Summary

This hour has introduced you to the power available with Microsoft Graph 97. You can display any type of numeric information imaginable with a visual chart. There are several methods available for inserting a chart into your presentation, but the easiest is to use the Chart AutoLayout.

Every chart is derived from a base dataset. Entering data on the chart datasheet is easy. If you already have the information in an Excel or Lotus 1-2-3 worksheet, you can quickly copy or import the information into your chart datasheet. If you make a mistake, use the Undo feature right away, as Microsoft Graph remembers only the last thing you have done.

Microsoft Graph 97 has dozens of chart types available and also has many built-in custom chart types. If you still can't find just the right chart type, you have the option of creating your own custom chart type.

Stay tuned, because the next hour covers all the different formatting options to really make those charts stand out.

Workshop

In this hour's workshop, you create a chart to compare some of the dive depths the British Virgin Islands. This helps prepare you for your upcoming paid vacatic will give you since you will soon be a true PowerPoint 97 wizard. Oh, yes—the couple of questions after the short exercise.

Test What You've Learned

1. Start a new blank presentation with the Chart AutoLayout.
2. Type the Title `Dive Site Minimum & Maximum Depths.`
3. Double-click the chart placeholder.
4. Enter the data in Figure 17.20 in the datasheet.

Figure 17.20.
The data for your practice chart.

Chapter 17 TWYL.ppt - Datasheet

		A	B	C	D	E
		Caves	Indians	Angelfish	Spyglass Wall	
1	Minimum	10	15	15	20	
2	Maximum	40	45	40	55	
3						
4						
5						
6						
7						

5. Change the chart type to the Standard 2-D Bar Chart.
6. Change the chart type to the Custom Built-in Tubes.
7. Save the file as `Hour 17 TWYL` (you will use this file for Hour 18's "Test Wh You've Learned" section.)
8. Close the file.

Q&A

Q I have all my chart information in an Excel worksheet as well as an Exc chart. Can't I just use the chart I have already created in Excel?

A By all means, please do. The charting features in Excel are actually better th those available with Microsoft Graph. If you know how to use the chart fea Excel or have charts already created, the best thing to do is to select the char your Excel worksheet and copy it into your PowerPoint presentation slide. N to do extra work if the job is already done (remember, you want to take Fric

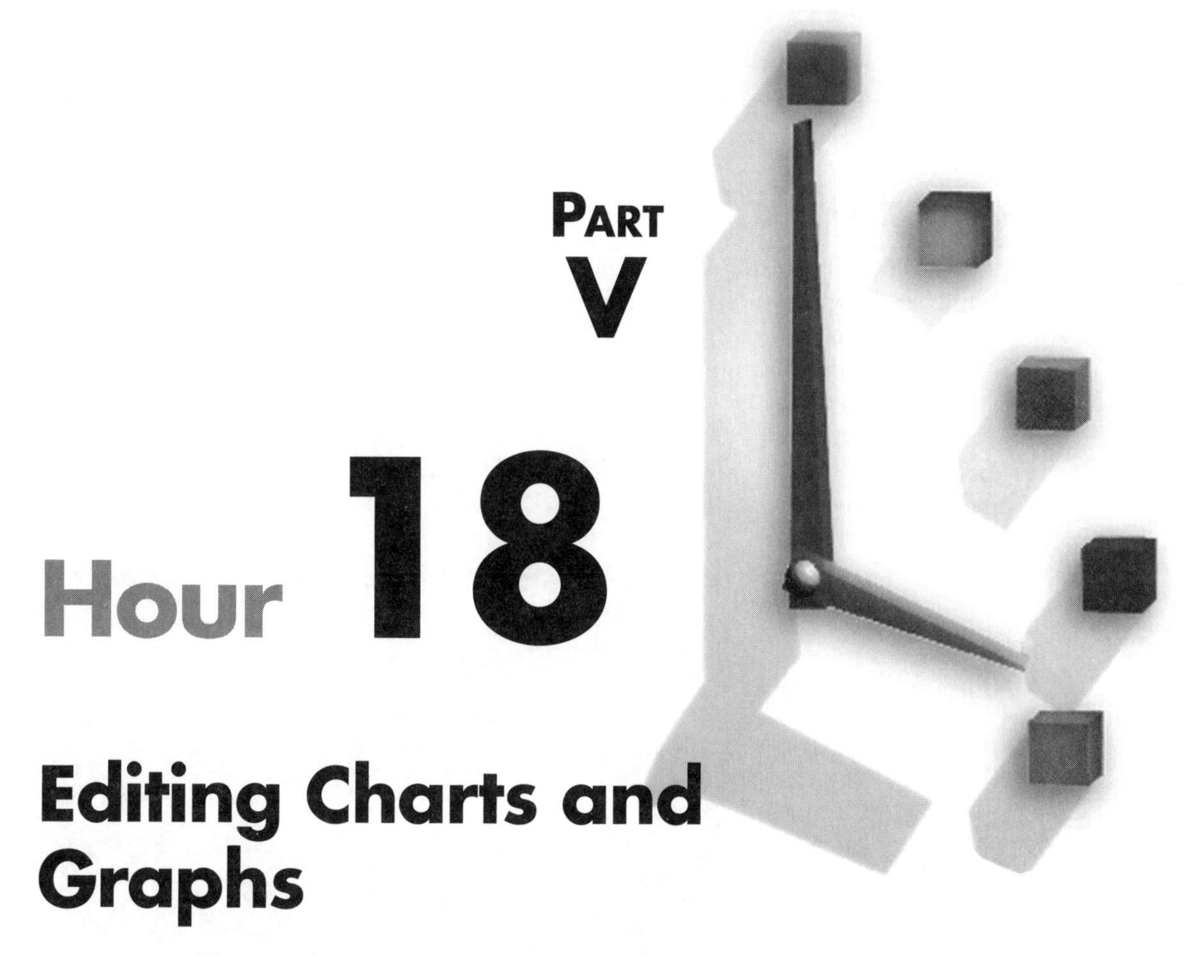

Part V

Hour 18

Editing Charts and Graphs

Now that you can insert and create a graph using the Microsoft Graph program, it's time to talk about editing the graph so that it looks just the way you (or Bob) want. Once a graph is successfully customized, there's no need to do all that hard work again next week. You can save extra effort by saving the graph as a custom chart type to reuse over, and over, and over again. With custom chart types, you not only get to take this Friday off, but next Friday as well.

In this hour, you learn the necessary basics for customizing a graph and creating a quality presentation. The basics to be covered give you the details for doing the following:

- Editing datasheet items
- Selecting chart objects
- Changing the attributes of the axis, legend, or a data series
- Plotting your chart by row (default) or by column

It's time to roll up those shirt sleeves and get started.

Editing Data Items

Sometimes the best work can be rendered useless. Bob came into your office, just as you'd finished the presentation for the board of directors, and told you the sales numbers (that he gave you) are all wrong. Just say "No problem, Bob." All you need to do is edit the information that Microsoft Graph 97 used to create your chart. You can do this task quickly and easily by editing the chart's datasheet, as shown in Figure 18.1.

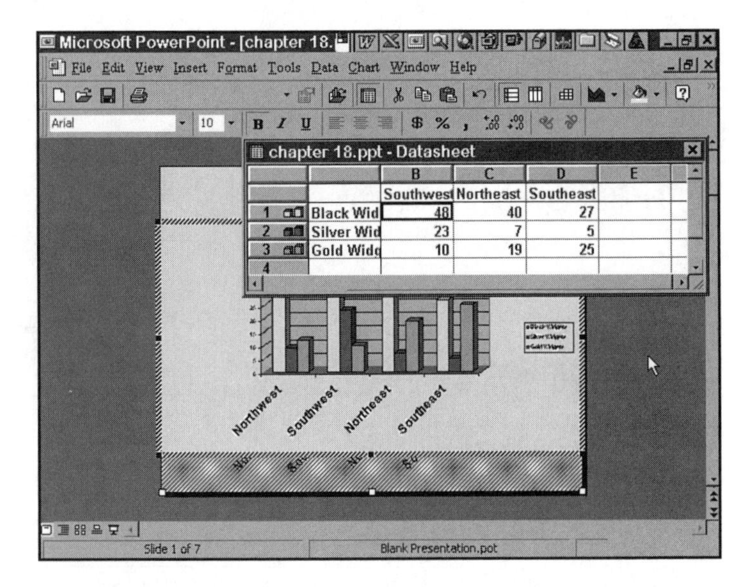

Figure 18.1.
Editing the Microsoft Graph datasheet.

Displaying the Datasheet

If you have already exited from Chart Edit Mode (or from PowerPoint for that matter), finding the datasheet is easy. Just double-click on your chart to return to Chart Edit Mode and bata-boom-bata-bing—the datasheet pops into view. You can also display a datasheet with one of these two methods:

- Choose View | Datasheet from the Microsoft Graph menu.

  or

- Click the View Datasheet button from the Microsoft Graph standard toolbar, as shown in Figure 18.2.

Once the datasheet has been displayed, you can easily change any information you want.

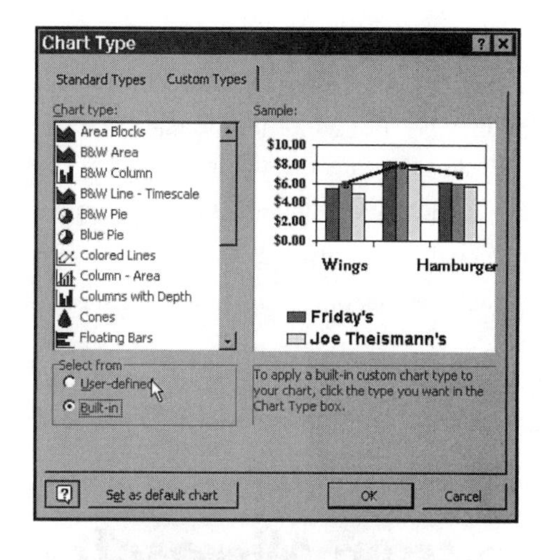

Figure 17.18.
The Custom tab for adding or selecting a custom chart type.

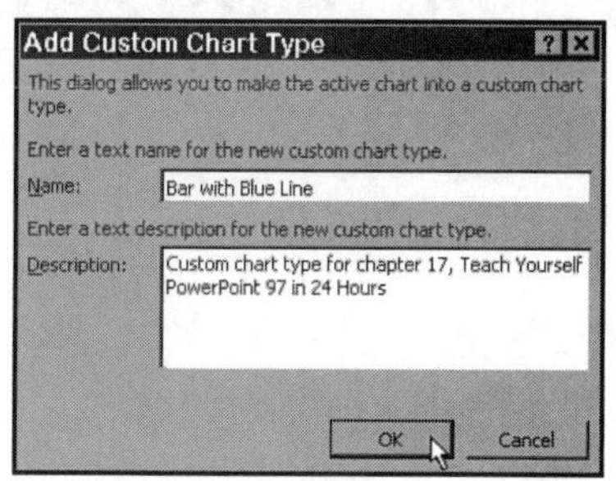

Figure 17.19.
Type a name and description for your custom chart type.

Whenever you want to apply your custom chart type (or one of Microsoft's), all you need to do is follow these steps:

1. Choose Chart | Chart Type from the menu.
2. Click the Custom tab.
3. Select either User-defined or Built-in.
4. Select a chart type from the list on the left.
5. Click the OK button to accept the new chart type.

Changing the Default Chart Type

To save time in the future, you might want to modify the default chart type. Microsoft Graph makes it easy to change the default chart type; simply follow these steps:

1. Choose Chart | Chart Type from the menu.
2. Click the Standard tab.

3. Select a chart type from the list.
4. Select a chart subtype from the samples at the right side of the window.
5. Click the "Press and hold to view sample" button to see a sample of your chart before accepting any changes.
6. Click the "Set as default chart" button.
7. Click the Yes button to accept the change to the default chart.
8. Click the OK button to accept the new chart type.

JUST A MINUTE

You also can set a custom chart type as the default chart.

Exiting from Microsoft Graph

As with all embedded objects, you can exit from Microsoft Graph by clicking outside the chart area. To get back into Chart Edit Mode and edit the chart, simply double-click the chart.

Summary

This hour has introduced you to the power available with Microsoft Graph 97. You can display any type of numeric information imaginable with a visual chart. There are several methods available for inserting a chart into your presentation, but the easiest is to use the Chart AutoLayout.

Every chart is derived from a base dataset. Entering data on the chart datasheet is easy. If you already have the information in an Excel or Lotus 1-2-3 worksheet, you can quickly copy or import the information into your chart datasheet. If you make a mistake, use the Undo feature right away, as Microsoft Graph remembers only the last thing you have done.

Microsoft Graph 97 has dozens of chart types available and also has many built-in custom chart types. If you still can't find just the right chart type, you have the option of creating your own custom chart type.

Stay tuned, because the next hour covers all the different formatting options to really make those charts stand out.

Workshop

In this hour's workshop, you create a chart to compare some of the dive depths available in the British Virgin Islands. This helps prepare you for your upcoming paid vacation that Bob will give you since you will soon be a true PowerPoint 97 wizard. Oh, yes—there are also a couple of questions after the short exercise.

Test What You've Learned

1. Start a new blank presentation with the Chart AutoLayout.
2. Type the Title `Dive Site Minimum & Maximum Depths.`
3. Double-click the chart placeholder.
4. Enter the data in Figure 17.20 in the datasheet.

Figure 17.20.
The data for your practice chart.

Chapter 17 TWYL.ppt - Datasheet

		A	B	C	D	E
		Caves	Indians	Angelfish	Spyglass Wall	
1	Minimum	10	15	15	20	
2	Maximum	40	45	40	55	

5. Change the chart type to the Standard 2-D Bar Chart.
6. Change the chart type to the Custom Built-in Tubes.
7. Save the file as `Hour 17 TWYL` (you will use this file for Hour 18's "Test What You've Learned" section.)
8. Close the file.

Q&A

Q I have all my chart information in an Excel worksheet as well as an Excel chart. Can't I just use the chart I have already created in Excel?

A By all means, please do. The charting features in Excel are actually better than those available with Microsoft Graph. If you know how to use the chart feature in Excel or have charts already created, the best thing to do is to select the chart in your Excel worksheet and copy it into your PowerPoint presentation slide. No need to do extra work if the job is already done (remember, you want to take Friday off).

17

Q When I change the chart type, I lose all the formatting that took me hours to do. Help!

A Whenever you change the chart type, Microsoft Graph will, by default, apply the formatting of the chart type to your chart. If you have made formatting changes to your chart, such as changing the font face, font size, color, background, or anything else, you might want to uncheck the "Default formatting" box under Options in the Chart Type dialog box.

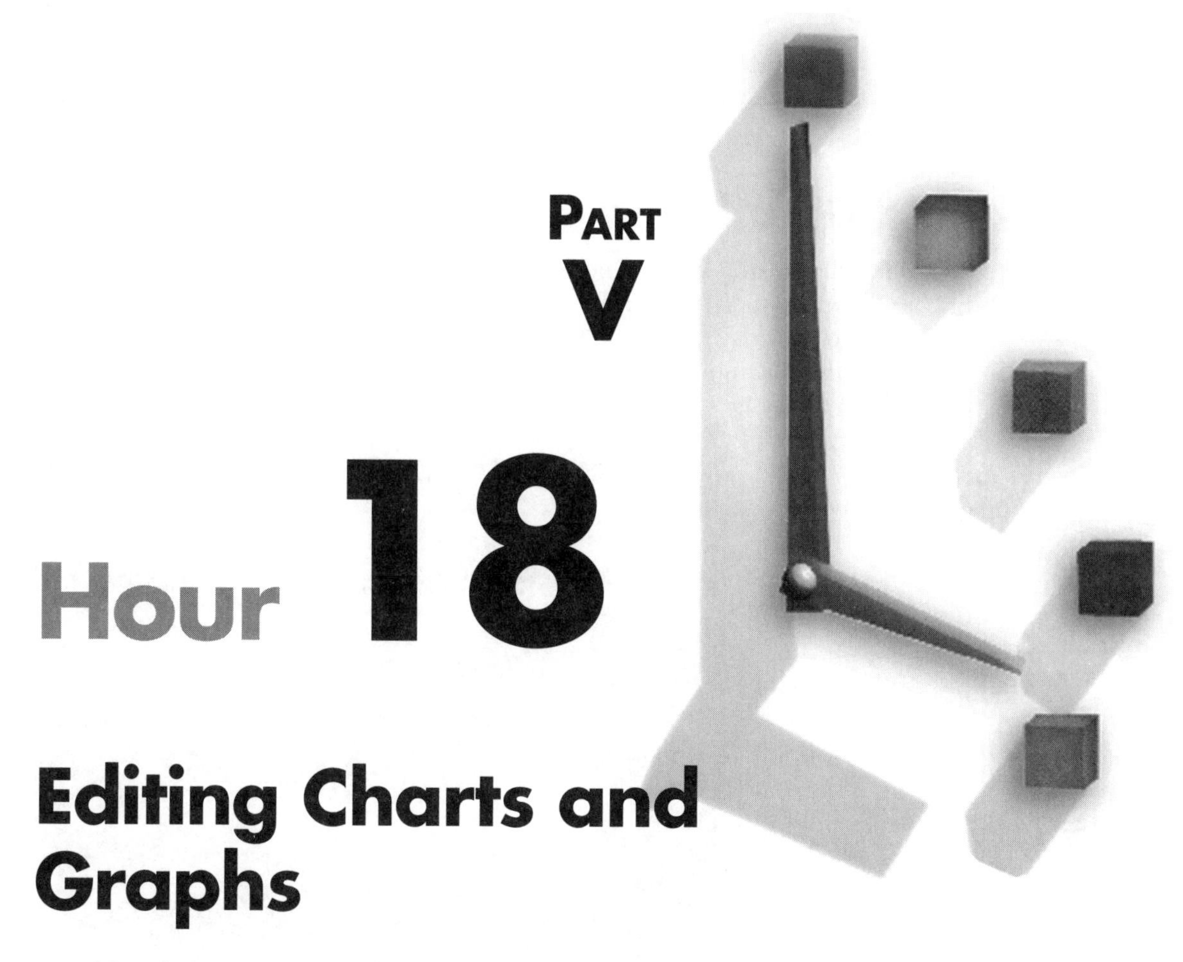

Part V

Hour 18

Editing Charts and Graphs

Now that you can insert and create a graph using the Microsoft Graph program, it's time to talk about editing the graph so that it looks just the way you (or Bob) want. Once a graph is successfully customized, there's no need to do all that hard work again next week. You can save extra effort by saving the graph as a custom chart type to reuse over, and over, and over again. With custom chart types, you not only get to take this Friday off, but next Friday as well.

In this hour, you learn the necessary basics for customizing a graph and creating a quality presentation. The basics to be covered give you the details for doing the following:

- Editing datasheet items
- Selecting chart objects
- Changing the attributes of the axis, legend, or a data series
- Plotting your chart by row (default) or by column

It's time to roll up those shirt sleeves and get started.

Editing Data Items

Sometimes the best work can be rendered useless. Bob came into your office, just as you'd finished the presentation for the board of directors, and told you the sales numbers (that he gave you) are all wrong. Just say "No problem, Bob." All you need to do is edit the information that Microsoft Graph 97 used to create your chart. You can do this task quickly and easily by editing the chart's datasheet, as shown in Figure 18.1.

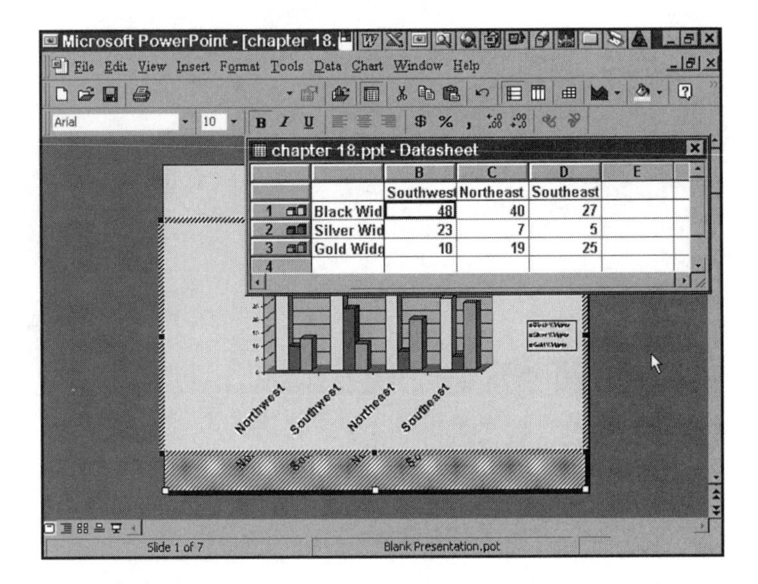

Figure 18.1.
Editing the Microsoft Graph datasheet.

Displaying the Datasheet

If you have already exited from Chart Edit Mode (or from PowerPoint for that matter), finding the datasheet is easy. Just double-click on your chart to return to Chart Edit Mode and bata-boom-bata-bing—the datasheet pops into view. You can also display a datasheet with one of these two methods:

- Choose View | Datasheet from the Microsoft Graph menu.

  or

- Click the View Datasheet button from the Microsoft Graph standard toolbar, as shown in Figure 18.2.

Once the datasheet has been displayed, you can easily change any information you want.

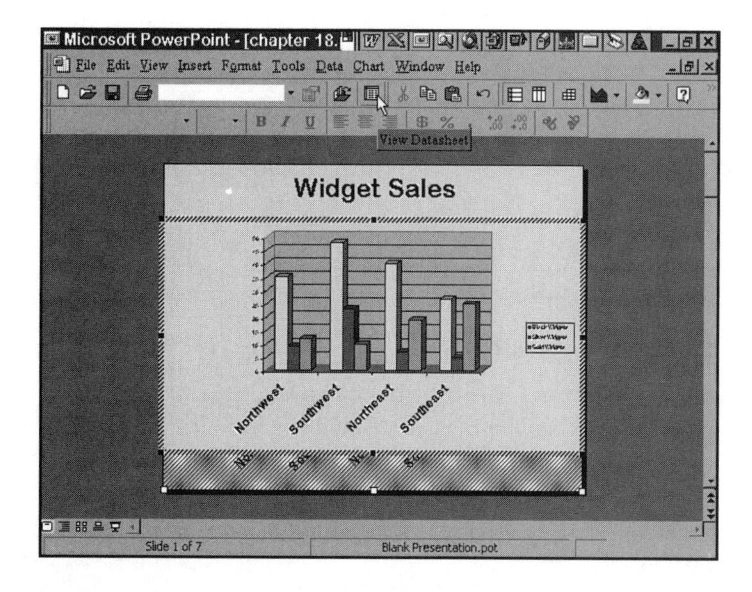

Figure 18.2.
Use the View Datasheet button to quickly display the Microsoft Graph datasheet.

Changing Information Using the Datasheet

When you need to change information in the Microsoft Graph datasheet, you might wonder: "Do I need to change the information entirely, or do I just need to edit the information?" Microsoft Graph gives you the option of either completely replacing the existing information or merely editing the existing information. To replace the existing information, follow these steps:

1. Click the cell you need to change.
2. Type in the new information.
3. Press Enter.

To edit existing information (if you misspelled a name, for example), use the following method:

1. Click the cell you need to edit.
2. Press the F2 key.
3. Position the blinking cursor where you need to edit, as shown in Figure 18.3.

Figure 18.3.
Editing information in the datasheet.

chapter 18.ppt - Datasheet

		B	C	D	E
		Southwest	Northeast	Southeast	
1	Black Wid	4	40	27	
2	Silver Wid	23	7	5	
3	Gold Wid	10	19	25	
4					

4. Edit the information.
5. Press Enter.

Dragging Data Markers in 2-D Charts

If your chart is two-dimensional, you can also change the value of a single data series item by dragging the data marker. This is a new feature in Microsoft Graph 97. Data marker dragging, shown in Figure 18.4, gives you a quick and easy way to edit a chart.

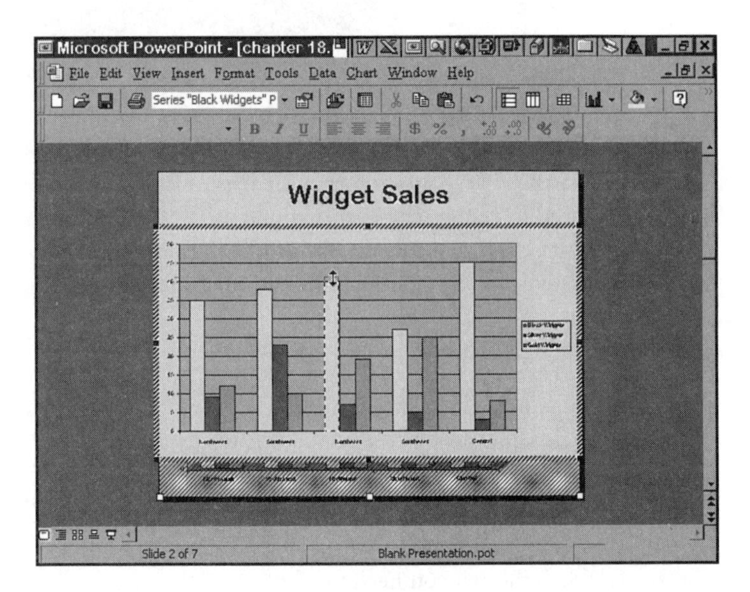

Figure 18.4.
Dragging a data marker.

NEW TERM A *data series* is the group(s) of related information on your chart. In a bar chart, each bar with the same color is part of the complete series, as in East, West, North, and so forth. A pie chart has only one data series. A *data marker* is a single item in a data series, such as the 1st Qtr information for the East.

To edit the value of a data marker by dragging, follow these steps:

1. Click once on any part of the data series.
2. Click once again on the data marker you want to edit.
3. Place the mouse on the top selection handle (for bar charts) and hold down the mouse button.
4. Drag the marker to the location you want.
5. Release the mouse button.

CAUTION

> Although dragging the data point can be an easy way to edit the value of a data marker, it's difficult to be accurate. If you need to enter accurate information, use the datasheet.

Plotting by Row or Column

Microsoft Graph usually plots the data series based on the information you enter in the datasheet rows. You can easily modify a chart's display by changing the graph's plot axis. The information is exactly the same, but you have a different view. For example, instead of comparing the sales figures of individual territories, you could compare how each product is selling. To change how Microsoft Graph plots the data series, do one of the following:

- Choose Data | Series in Rows (to plot by datasheet rows) or Data | Series in Columns (to plot by datasheet columns) from the menu.

  or

- Click the By Row (to plot by datasheet rows) or By Column (to plot by datasheet columns) button on the standard toolbar.

Figure 18.5 shows a chart that's plotted on the datasheet rows, and Figure 18.6 illustrates the same information plotted by using the datasheet columns.

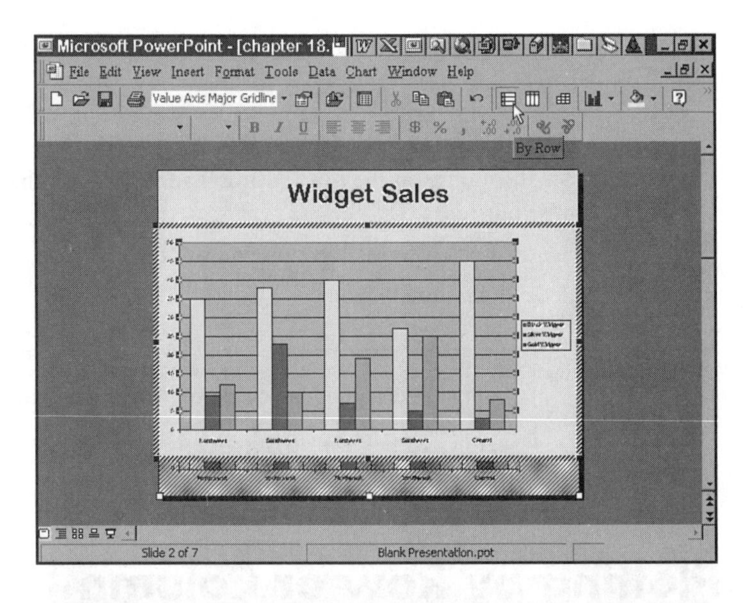

Figure 18.5.
Plotting on the datasheet rows.

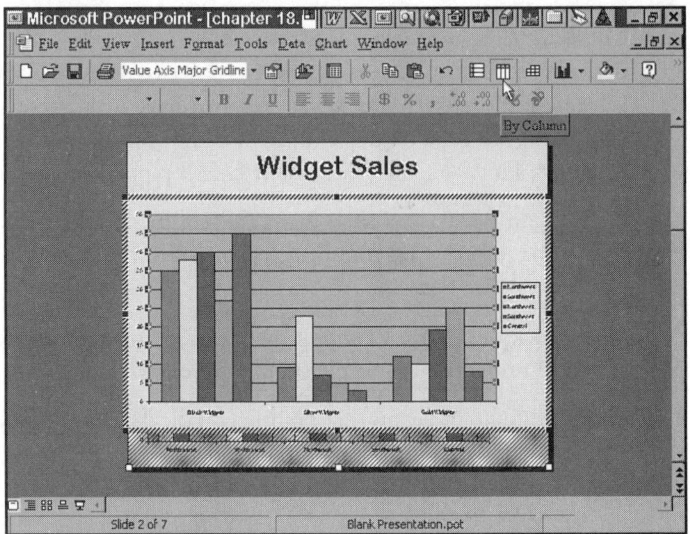

Figure 18.6.
Plotting on the datasheet columns.

Selecting Chart Objects

It's important to understand that when you're editing and customizing a chart, every single little piece of the chart can be changed. What do I mean by "every single little piece?" Well,

a chart consists of not only the data information, but also other items that make the chart readable. Some charts include the following pieces:

- Legend
- Chart floor
- Axis (X and Y)
- Description text
- Chart background and walls

There are even more chart items you can modify. How do you know which object piece you have selected? Look for the small, black, square selection handles on the chart. There should be one handle in each corner of the area you have selected. Also, take a look at the Chart Objects drop-down list on the standard toolbar. (See Figure 18.7.) The Chart Objects list tells you the name of the object that's currently selected.

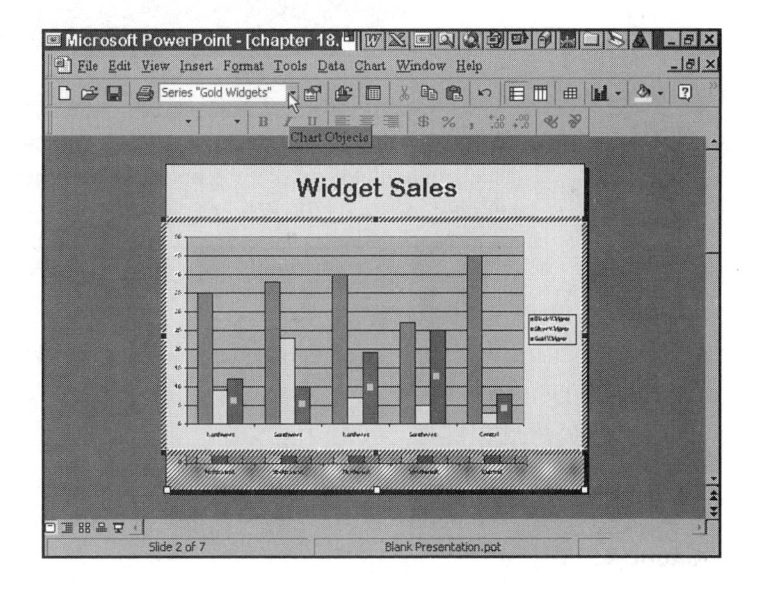

Figure 18.7.
The Chart Objects list lets you know what chart item is currently selected.

Using the Mouse

You can use the mouse to select any chart object. Simply click the object you want to select. Some objects, such as data series, data labels, and legend items, are grouped together. To select a single item in a group, you need to click once to select the group, and then click a second time to select the individual item. (See Figure 18.8.)

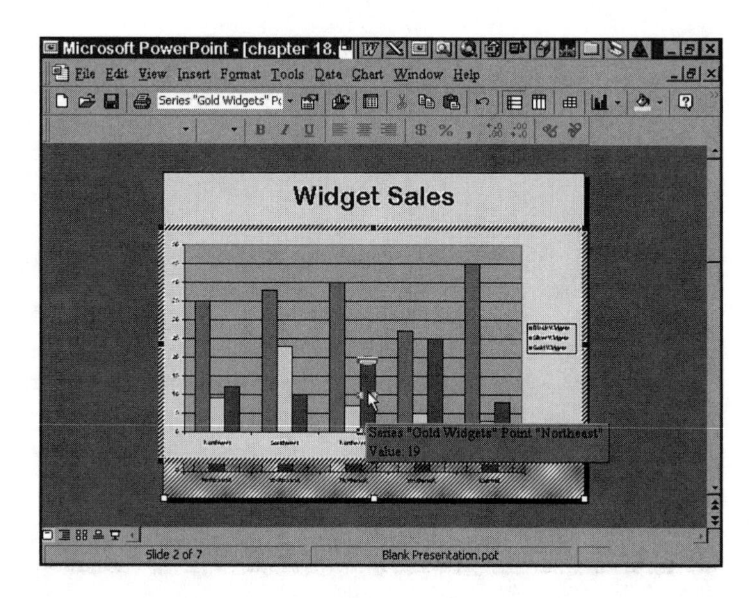

Figure 18.8.
Using the mouse to select a chart object.

CAUTION

Don't double-click. When you double-click an item, you jump directly into the Format dialog box for the particular item that was double-clicked. For this task, click, pause, and then click again on the item.

Using the Toolbar

Use the Chart Objects button on the standard toolbar to quickly select any main chart object, as shown in Figure 18.9.

CAUTION

The toolbar doesn't have options for selecting individual items from a data series, data label, or legend. Use the mouse selection method described previously to select these items.

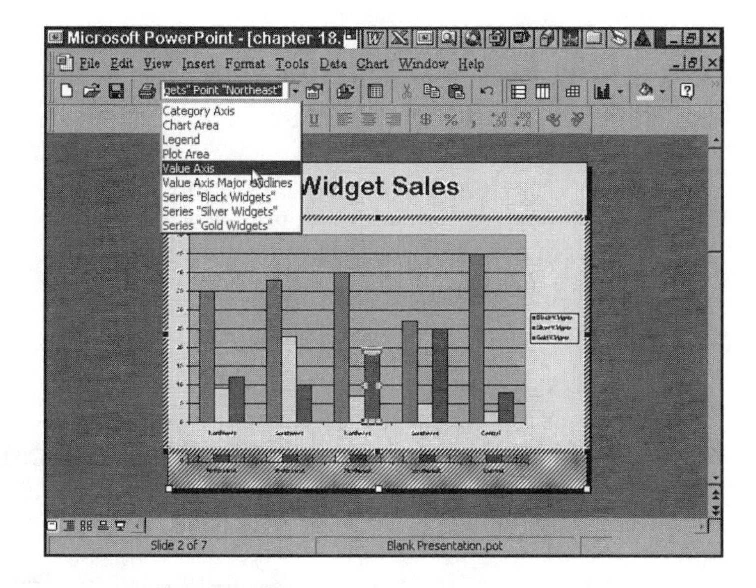

Figure 18.9.
Using the Chart Objects list on the standard toolbar to quickly select chart items.

Changing Chart Object Attributes

Every chart object attribute can be changed and customized to match your needs. The following sections cover the most frequently made changes for the axis, legend, and series objects. However, when you have time, experiment with each chart object to find how you can customize its attributes. To customize any chart item, perform the following steps:

1. Select the chart item you want to change.
2. Choose Format | Selected [*chart item name*] from the menu. (See Figure 18.10.)

   The [*chart item name*] changes depending on which item you have selected. In Figure 18.10, the chart item selected was Data Series.

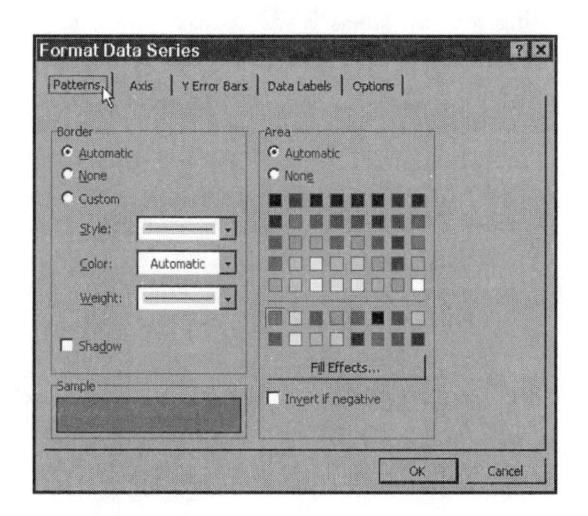

Figure 18.10.
The Patterns tab of the Format Data Series dialog box.

18

3. Make any changes you want from the Format dialog box.
4. Click the OK button when you're finished.

Axis Labels

The most popular items to change on a chart are the axis labels. Usually, people want to change the font, the font size, or the placement of the labels. Use the following instructions to format the axis label with different font attributes:

1. Select the axis you want to change.
2. Choose Format | Selected Axis from the menu.
3. Click the Font tab. (See Figure 18.11.)

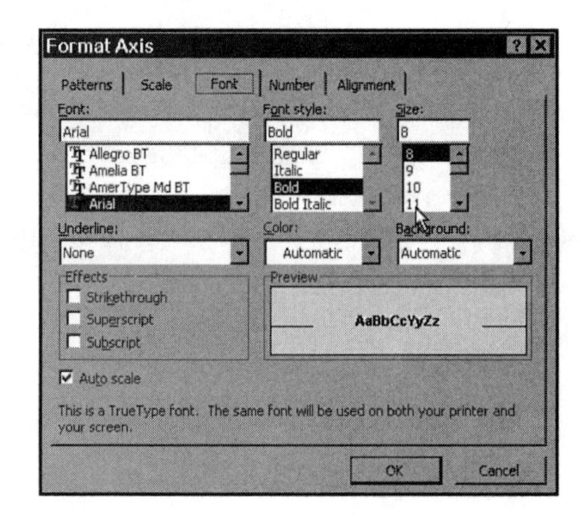

Figure 18.11.
The Font tab of the Format Axis dialog box.

4. Change the font.
5. Click the OK button.

Rotating the axis labels is just as easy and can help make them more readable. Use the following steps to rotate the axis labels:

1. Select the axis you want to change.
2. ChooseFormat | Selected Axis from the menu.
3. Click the Alignment tab. (See Figure 18.12.)

Figure 18.12.
The Alignment tab of the Format Axis dialog box.

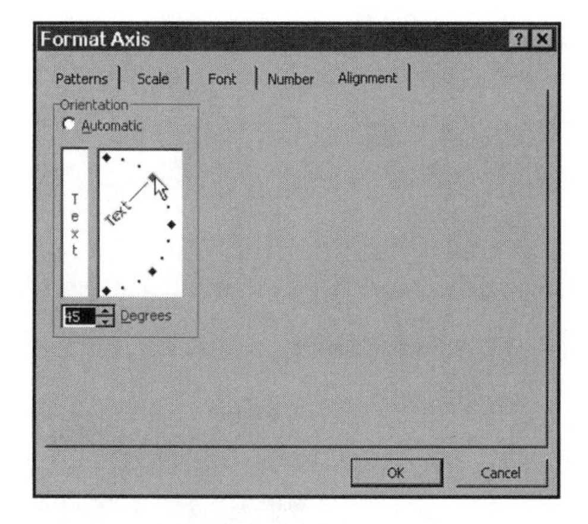

4. Under the Orientation section, click or drag the text rotation marker to the angle you want.

TIME SAVER

You also can enter a rotation angle, if you like, in the Degrees box. Type a positive number (up to 90) to rotate the text upward; use a negative number (up to –90) to rotate the text downward.

5. Click the OK button.

TIME SAVER

Microsoft Graph also allows you to quickly change the text orientation from horizontal to vertical by simply clicking the Vertical Text option in the Orientation section.

TIME SAVER

To quickly rotate text to a 45-degree angle, use the Angle Text Downward or Angle Text Upward buttons on the formatting toolbar.

Legends

You can also format the font attributes for legends. Their placement, for example, is frequently changed. The legend is typically displayed on the right of the chart. However, you can place the legend anywhere you want, as shown in Figure 18.13, by following these simple steps:

1. Select the legend.
2. Choose Format | Selected Legend from the menu.
3. Click the Placement tab.
4. Select the location you want for the legend. (See Figure 18.14.)
5. Click the OK button.

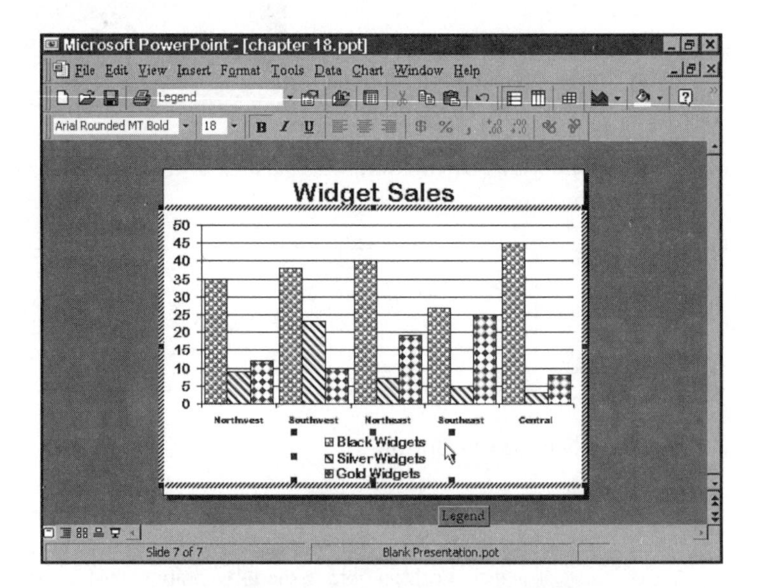

Figure 18.13.
The legend placed at the bottom of the chart.

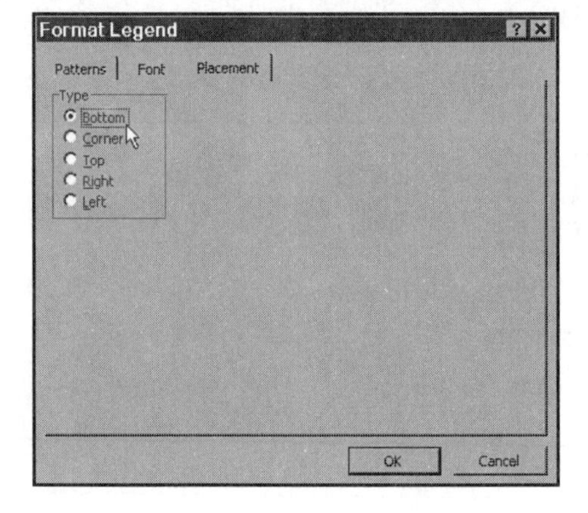

Figure 18.14.
The Placement tab of the Format Legend dialog box.

Data Series Colors and Patterns

The last item up for discussion this hour is the data series—specifically, how to change the color or pattern of the series. Figure 18.15 shows the sample chart that has been formatted to display a pattern for the data series.

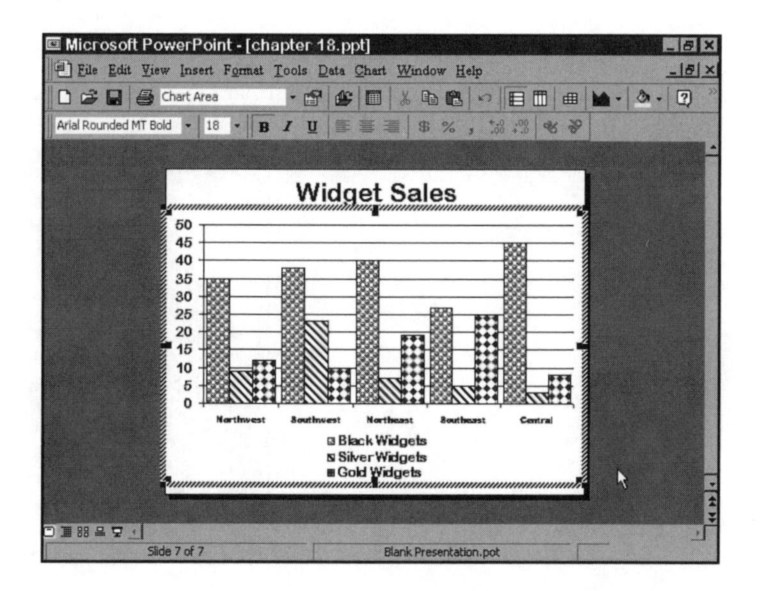

Figure 18.15.
A chart with each data series represented by a different pattern.

Using a pattern for the data series is great when you aren't giving a color presentation (as in this book). To change the color or pattern of a data series, follow these steps:

1. Select the data series you want to change.
2. Choose Format | Selected Data Series from the menu.
3. Click the Patterns tab.
4. Select the color you want for the series.

TIME SAVER

If you're going to use a pattern, pick a dark color. It contrasts better with the background.

1. For a pattern, click the Fill Effects button to open the Fill Effects dialog box.
2. In the Fill Effects dialog box, click the Pattern tab. (See Figure 18.16.)
3. Select a pattern.

Just a Minute

There are two things you should be aware of: First, choose a pattern that's easy to recognize onscreen, usually the simpler the better; second, make sure the background color is white, or the pattern might be hard to see.

4. Click the OK button in the Fill Effects dialog box.
5. Click the OK button in the Format Data Series dialog box.

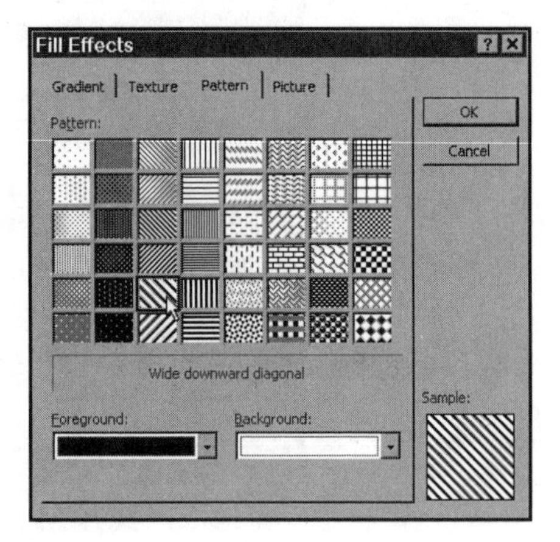

Figure 18.16.
The Pattern tab of the Fill Effects dialog box.

Summary

In this hour, you have learned how to edit information in the datasheet and have touched on a few of the formatting options available when using Microsoft Graph 97. Although you have seen only the options specific to the axis, legend, and data series objects, all the attribute changes mentioned apply to any chart object. There are so many options available when formatting a chart that the only way to learn every single option is to play (you remember how to play, don't you?), play, play. When your kids are bugging you for dinner, tell them that your spouse is making dinner tonight because you're having too much fun playing.

Workshop

In this hour's workshop, you will be enhancing the chart you started in Hour 17, "Creating Charts and Graphs with Microsoft Graph." Bob didn't like the style you chose for the dive chart, but he's so confident of your abilities that he has given you complete artistic freedom. Follow the instructions in the following section, but if you don't like the look, feel free to change the dive chart in any way you see fit. After all, it's your vacation.

Test What You've Learned

1. Open the TWYL file from Hour 17: Hour 17 TWYL.PPT.
2. Double-click the chart to go into Chart Edit Mode.
3. Edit the Caves Minimum to read 10.5 instead of 10 (use the editing method).
4. Change the Angelfish Minimum to read 27 instead of 15 (use the replace method).
5. Close the datasheet.

Time Saver

When you're working on charts, sometimes it's helpful to zoom in a bit to see the effects of your changes. As I was creating this exercise, I zoomed in to 66%. Choose View | Zoom from the menu, and click 66%.

6. Select the Y axis.
7. Format the Y axis font to Arial, Bold, 20 pts.
8. Use the Angle Text Upwards button to angle the Y axis labels.
9. Select the X axis.
10. Format the X axis font to Arial, Bold, 20 pts.
11. Angle the X axis text upward 90 degrees.
12. Select the legend.
13. Format the legend's placement so that it's on the right.
14. Select the Minimum Data Series.
15. Format the data series so that it has a bubble pattern, with dark blue as the foreground color and white as the background color.
16. Select the Maximum Data Series.
17. Format the data series so that it has a stripe pattern, with light blue as the foreground color and white as the background color.
18. Change the chart so that it's plotted by column.
19. Change the chart so that it's plotted by row.
20. Click outside the chart to exit Chart Edit Mode.
21. Save the presentation as `Chapter 18 TWYL`.
22. Close the presentation.

Q&A

Q How can I reproduce the cool background effect you have in the Test What You've Learned sample files?

A Hour 17 used a predesigned custom chart type called *tubes*. This chart type was created by selecting the Chart Area and formatting it so that it has a gradient fill effect, using the Horizon preset color.

Q I want my legend on the bottom of the chart, but in two rows instead of one. How can I do this?

A Format the legend so that it's placed on the bottom of the chart. Then you have to resize (I suggest using a corner handle) the legend so that it's shorter. You will see a ghost outline of the legend when you're resizing to let you know that the legend is going to be two rows of text.

Q I want to make the legend appear transparent. Can I do that?

A Yes. Simply format the legend using the following instructions:

1. Select the legend.
2. Choose Format | Selected Legend from the menu.
3. Click the Patterns tab.
4. Under Border, select None.
5. Under Area, select None.
6. Click the OK button.

This procedure simply turns off the border line and any fill for the legend. You should now have a transparent legend.

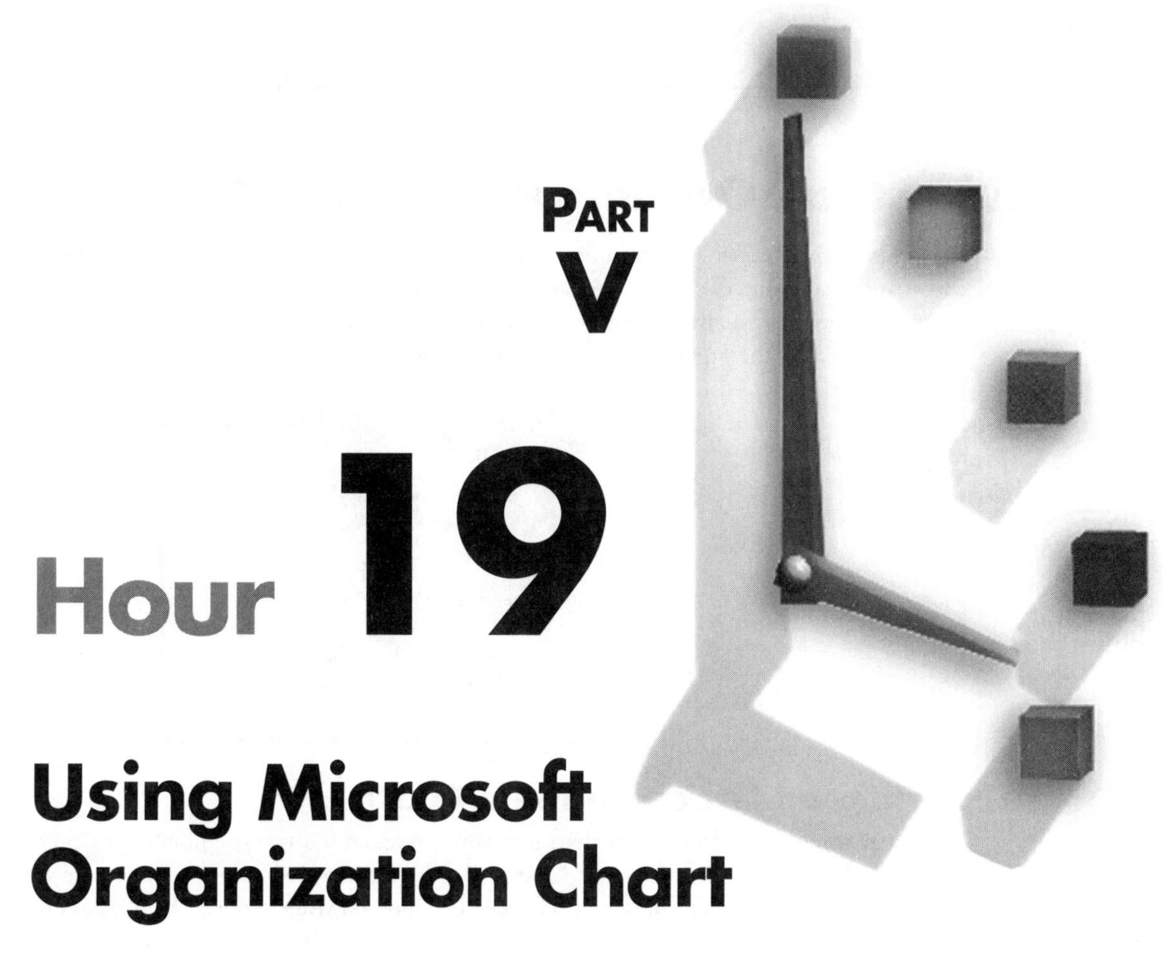

Part V

Hour 19

Using Microsoft Organization Chart

Most of us work with other people, and a lot of us work for companies that have five or more (many, many more) employees. How do the powers that be (in other words, the Human Resources Department) keep track of where everyone belongs, and who knows the corporate pecking order? How do you know that Bob is really your supervisor? Enter the Microsoft Organization Chart application.

In this hour, you will learn about the following topics:

- What an organizational chart is and why you might need one
- How to enter information into a Microsoft organizational chart
- How to add and delete a position

Organizational charts can be useful in a PowerPoint presentation. PowerPoint integrates closely with the Microsoft Organization Chart software to make creating and embedding organizational charts a simple task.

What Is an Organizational Chart?

An *organizational chart* is a graphical representation of the personnel structure for a corporation, committee, or any other collaborative team. Organizational charts are useful when you need to visually portray the team members and their respective relationships. Figure 19.1 shows the organizational structure of 100 Aker Woods.

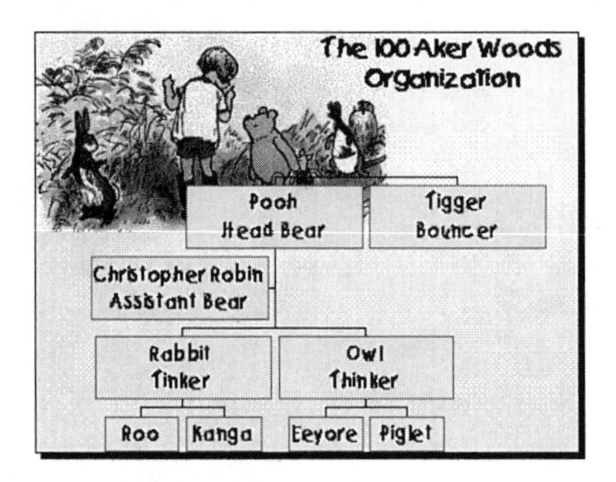

Figure 19.1.
The organization of Pooh and friends.

Inserting an Organizational Chart

When you insert an organizational chart into your presentation, you're embedding a chart created with Microsoft Organization Chart 2.0. There are two simple ways to insert an organization chart into your presentation slide. The method you choose is just a matter of personal preference. The easiest method (in my opinion) is outlined in the following steps:

1. Start a new slide.
2. Select the Organization Chart layout.
3. Double-click the organization chart placeholder.

Another method is using the Insert menu item, as follows:

1. Display the slide where you want to insert an organizational chart.
2. Choose Insert | Picture | Organization Chart from the menu.

Either method starts the Microsoft Organization Chart program (notice the button for it on your taskbar) and displays the screen shown in Figure 19.2. If you're not entering information right away, click outside the top box on any white area of the window.

Just a Minute

All the embedded objects covered so far have used the PowerPoint window for their operations. The toolbars and menu commands have changed to reflect that you have been working on an embedded object. Microsoft Organization Chart is a much older program, so it reacts

differently. When you embed an organizational chart, you're actually starting the Microsoft Organization Chart program in a separate window. You should notice that there's an additional button on the Windows 95 taskbar to represent Microsoft Organization Chart.

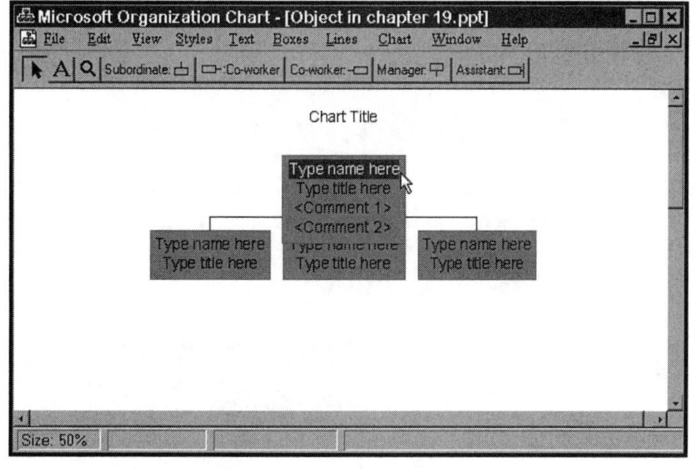

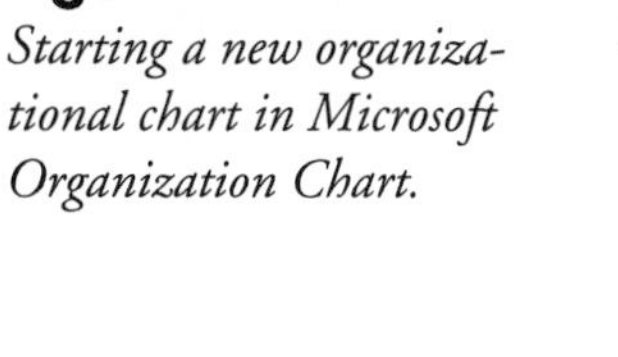
Figure 19.2.
Starting a new organizational chart in Microsoft Organization Chart.

CAUTION

Microsoft has been using the Microsoft Organization Chart 2.0 program since PowerPoint 4.0, and I have seen no indication that they have updated the program. Usually it works just fine, but on occasion I have had problems with my machine locking up or simply crashing when I use Microsoft Organization Chart. Although you should always save your work periodically, I know that most of us don't (including me, even though you would think I'd know better). However, if you're inserting an organizational chart into your presentation… then SAVE, SAVE, SAVE. If you don't heed my warning, be prepared for the "blue screen of death" (the blue Fatal Error screen).

Components of an Organizational Chart

An organizational chart is composed of boxes connected to each other by lines. Each of the boxes represents an individual in the organization. The lines that connect a box to other boxes illustrate the relationship of the individuals. There are four types of individual relationships—Managers, Co-workers, Subordinate, and Assistant.

In the 100 Aker Woods example, Pooh is the uppermost manager with Tigger as a Co-worker (or partner) and Christopher Robin as an Assistant. Rabbit and Owl are both Subordinates of Pooh. Rabbit is the Manager to both Kanga and Roo, and Owl is the Manager of Eeyore and Piglet.

You can format different attributes of organizational chart components, if you want. For example, you can change the font face or size, alter the fill color, modify the line style, or choose to have no line at all. Hour 20, "Editing an Organizational Chart," covers some of these formatting options.

Entering Information

When you first insert an organizational chart, you will probably see a sample chart containing four boxes. The top box should be the one that's selected and ready for you to start typing in the information. Once a box is selected, you can see that there are four field labels in each box, as shown in Figure 19.3.

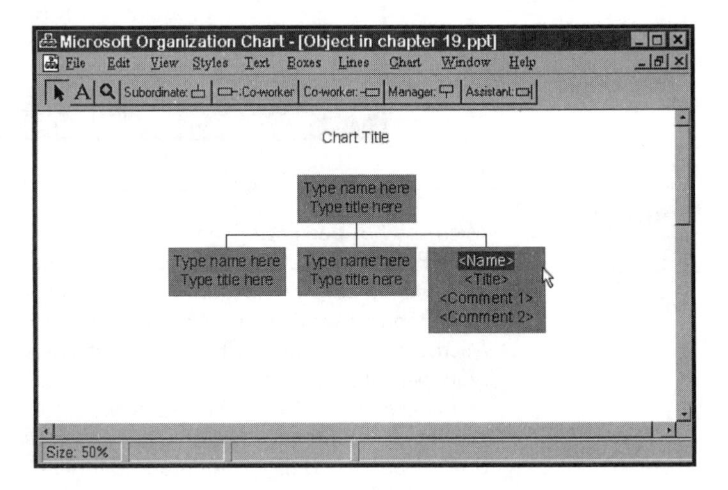

Figure 19.3.
A box with four field labels.

JUST A MINUTE

Sometimes you won't see the data entry space for the separate field labels on a box unless the box is selected. However, once the box is selected, you can type information spanning up to four short lines of text. If you don't use all the field labels, they won't be displayed in your organizational chart.

These field labels are simply placeholders that let you know where you can type in information. The labels also indicate the type of information you might want to include. To enter information, follow these steps:

1. Click once on the box to select it (if it's not already selected).
2. Click a second time on the box. The box should expand to display all the fields available for text entry, as shown in Figure 19.4.

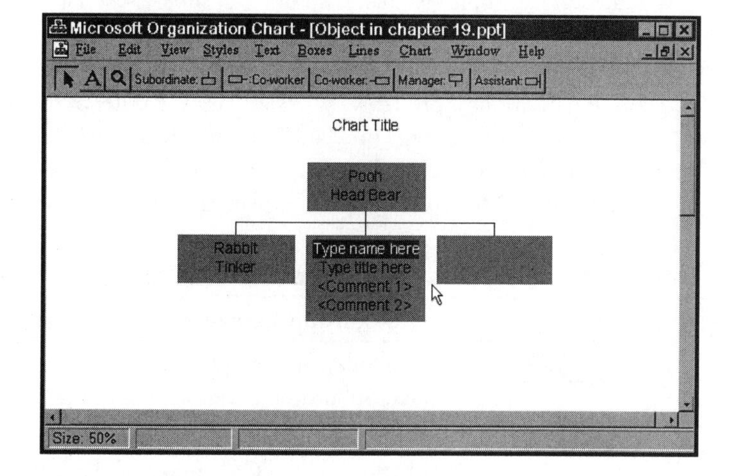

Figure 19.4.
A selected box in Microsoft Organization Chart, ready for data entry.

3. Press the Tab key until the field you want to enter information into is selected.
4. Type the information.
5. Press the Tab key to move to the next field.
6. Repeat steps 4 and 5 as necessary.
7. Click outside the box to deselect it.

JUST A MINUTE

If you make a mistake in Microsoft Organization Chart, you can use the Undo command.You have one only chance to undo your mistake, however, much like working in Microsoft Graph. So if you make a mistake, undo it right away. To undo a mistake, just choose Edit | Undo from the menu.

Adding, Deleting, and Moving Positions

All organizational charts are created with four default boxes for entering personnel information. Although these initial boxes are a great start, those nice folks at Microsoft realized that every organization would be different, so they've made it very easy to add, delete, or move boxes as you see fit. When I was initially putting together the Pooh example, I had to add, delete, and move boxes around. It was especially necessary when Tigger got promoted to the same level as Pooh. (Actually, no one can supervise a Tigger, so I had to let him just be.)

Adding Positions

Adding positions is probably the easiest task to master of the three box commands. You just need to decide what type of relationship to add and who you want to append the new box to. Table 19.1 shows the five types of relationship buttons available in Microsoft Organization Chart, with a corresponding explanation of the relationship.

Table 19.1. Organizational relationships.

Button	Relationship Explanation
Subordinate:	The Subordinate button attaches a new position box under another box. Subordinates report to a Manager box.
:Co-worker	The left Co-worker button attaches a new position box to the left of another box. Co-workers all have the same manager, and form a group.
Co-worker:	The right Co-worker button attaches a new position box to the right of another box as a Co-worker.
Manager:	The Manager button attaches a new position box above another box. Managers have other Subordinate boxes reporting to them.
Assistant:	The Assistant button attaches a new position box to another box. Assistant boxes can be used to represent a variety of positions, from secretarial to managerial assistance.

To insert a new position box into your organizational chart, follow these steps:

1. Click the Position Box button that represents the type of position you want to insert.
2. Click the existing box you want the new box to branch off from.

TIME SAVER

If you need to add several new position boxes to an existing box, you can click the Position Box button enough times to equal the number of boxes you need to add. For example, to add three subordinates to Tigger, click the Subordinate Position Box button three times, then click the Tigger box.

Using Zoom

After you have added new boxes, you might find it difficult to see the box text or the entire organizational structure. With Microsoft Organization Chart, you have several options available for zooming in or out of a document. Pick one of the zoom options outlined in Table 19.2 to zoom in to or out of organizational charts.

Table 19.2. Zoom options.

Size	Menu Choice	Keyboard
Fit in window	View | Size to Window	F9
50%	View | 50% of Actual	F10
Actual size	View | Actual Size	F11
200%	View | 200% of Actual	F12

JUST A MINUTE

You can also use the Reduce/Enlarge tool on the Microsoft Organization Chart toolbar to adjust the screen area. You can quickly magnify the screen area to actual size, or reduce the screen area to the size of the window. The tool changes to reflect which option is currently available; a magnifying glass indicates that you can magnify, and a chart means you can reduce. Simply click the tool, and then click your chart.

Selecting Boxes

Before I can talk about deleting boxes, I should first show you how to select a box. (Otherwise, how will Microsoft Organization Chart know which boxes you want to delete?) To select a box, just click once on it.

Wow, that was easy! A box is selected when it's highlighted in black, but not expanded.

TIME SAVER

You can select or deselect additional boxes by holding down the Shift key as you click each box you want to select.

Deleting Positions

Deleting positions in Microsoft Organization Chart is easier than it is in real life. Organizational charts don't show emotions or ask for termination pay. To delete a position, use this method:

1. Select the box(es) you want to delete.
2. Press the Delete or Backspace key.

CAUTION

Remember that the Microsoft Organization Chart program allows only one Undo operation. When you delete a position, you delete not only the box, but also the information inside the box. Use caution when you're deleting multiple boxes.

Moving Personnel Around

In the 100 Aker Woods example, Piglet and Owl have agreed to change places. You could simply delete the existing boxes and insert new ones, but that would take a lot of time and retyping effort. A quicker alternative is moving the boxes around a bit to get the layout you want.

In Figure 19.5, I moved Piglet up to the new position of co-worker with Owl. Next, you would move Owl to the position of subordinate to Piglet and Eeyore to the position of subordinate to Piglet.

Use the following steps to move a box to a new position.

1. Click and hold the mouse button on the box you want to move.
2. Drag the box to the new location.

JUST A MINUTE

The mouse pointer changes to reflect the type of position you're moving a box to. An arrow represents a co-worker, and a box with a line coming out of it represents a subordinate.

Figure 19.5.
Moving Piglet up to the new position.

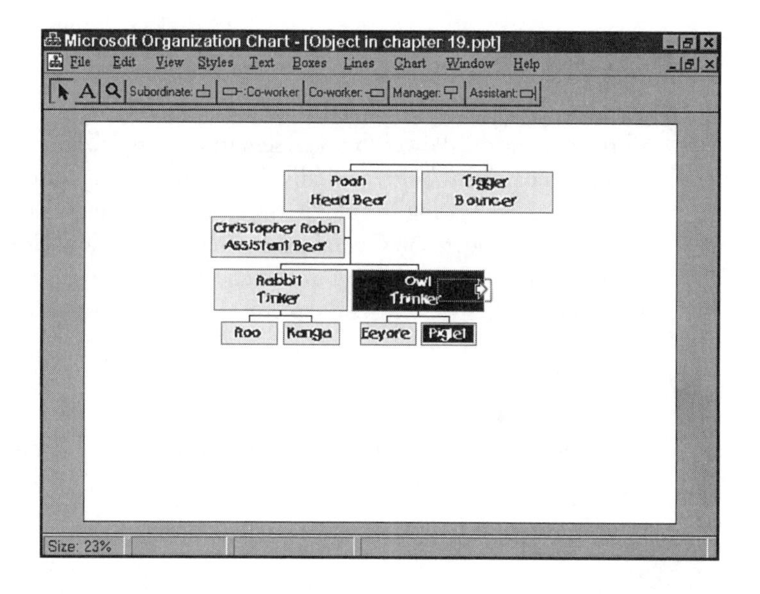

TIME SAVER

You can also use the Edit | Cut and Edit | Paste Boxes commands to move boxes around.

19

Exiting Microsoft Organization Chart

When you have finished the organizational chart, you exit Microsoft Organization Chart a little bit differently than you have with other embedded objects.

JUST A MINUTE

Remember that the Microsoft Organization Chart program is actually running in another window.

Here's how you exit Microsoft Organization Chart and return to PowerPoint:

1. Choose File | Exit and Return to [*PowerPoint filename*].
2. Click Yes to update and save the changes to your organizational chart.

TIME SAVER

If you make a really big mess of things and want to start over fresh, just exit without updating and saving the changes.

Summary

In this hour, you have learned how to create an organizational chart and embed the information into a PowerPoint presentation. Organizational charts are useful tools for outlining the responsibilities of individuals and defining the chain of command back to the eminent leader. Creating and modifying an organizational chart should be a quick task when you're using the Microsoft Organization Chart application. Go ahead and create some charts of your organization. The next hour teaches you how to customize the organizational chart display to seamlessly integrate the picture with your professional presentation.

Workshop

Because we all love Pooh, for this hour's workshop, try re-creating Pooh's organizational chart. Follow the step-by-step exercise to help reinforce all you have learned in this hour.

JUST A MINUTE

> Keeping with the theme of Winnie the Pooh, the sample slides shown throughout this chapter have all used a font called Kids. Hour 20 covers how to format the font in an organizational chart.

Psssstt...Don't forget about the questions and answers at the end of the section.

Test What You've Learned

1. Start PowerPoint, and start a new, blank presentation.
2. Select the Organization Chart layout.
3. Add a title, such as `The 100 Aker Woods Organization`.
4. Double-click the organizational chart placeholder.
5. In the first box, enter `Pooh` in the "Type name here" field. Then press the Tab key and enter `Head Bear` in the "Type title here" field.
6. Click on the first box on the left under Pooh to select it, and click once again on the box so you can enter information.
7. Press the Tab key until the "Type name here" field is selected and enter `Rabbit`. Next, press the Tab key and enter `Tinker` in the "Type title here" field.
8. Using the same method, enter the information for Owl in the middle box under Pooh. In the "Type name here" field, enter `Owl`, and in the "Type title here" field, enter `Thinker`.

9. Delete the last box on the right under Pooh.
10. Add a right Co-worker to the Pooh box.
11. Enter the following information: `Tigger` in the Name field and `Bouncer` in the Title field.
12. Add an Assistant box to Pooh.
13. Enter the following information: `Christopher Robin` in the Name field and `Assistant Bear` in the Title field.
14. Add two Subordinates to the Rabbit box.
15. In the first box, enter `Kanga` in the Name field.
16. In the second box, enter `Roo` in the Name field.
17. Add two Subordinates to the Owl box.
18. In the first box, enter `Eeyore` in the Name field.
19. In the second box, enter `Piglet` in the Name field.
20. Exit from Microsoft Organization Chart and update your presentation.
21. Save the presentation as `Hour 19 TWYL.PPT` (you will use this file for Hour 20's "Test What You've Learned" section).

Q&A

Q I want to format all the boxes to look the same. Is there an easy way to select all the boxes?

A Absolutely. Use the Edit | Select | All menu command or simply press Ctrl+A (my personal favorite). If you use the Edit | Select menu command, you can see several options besides selecting all the boxes. You can just as quickly select all the managers in a chart or all the co-workers.

Q Is there a way to move an entire group of boxes to a new location?

A Yes. You must select all the boxes you want to move first. Use the following steps to move several boxes to a new Manager position:

1. Select the boxes you want to move.
2. Choose Edit | Cut from the menu.
3. Click once on the Manager box they should be under.
4. Choose Edit | Paste Boxes from the menu.

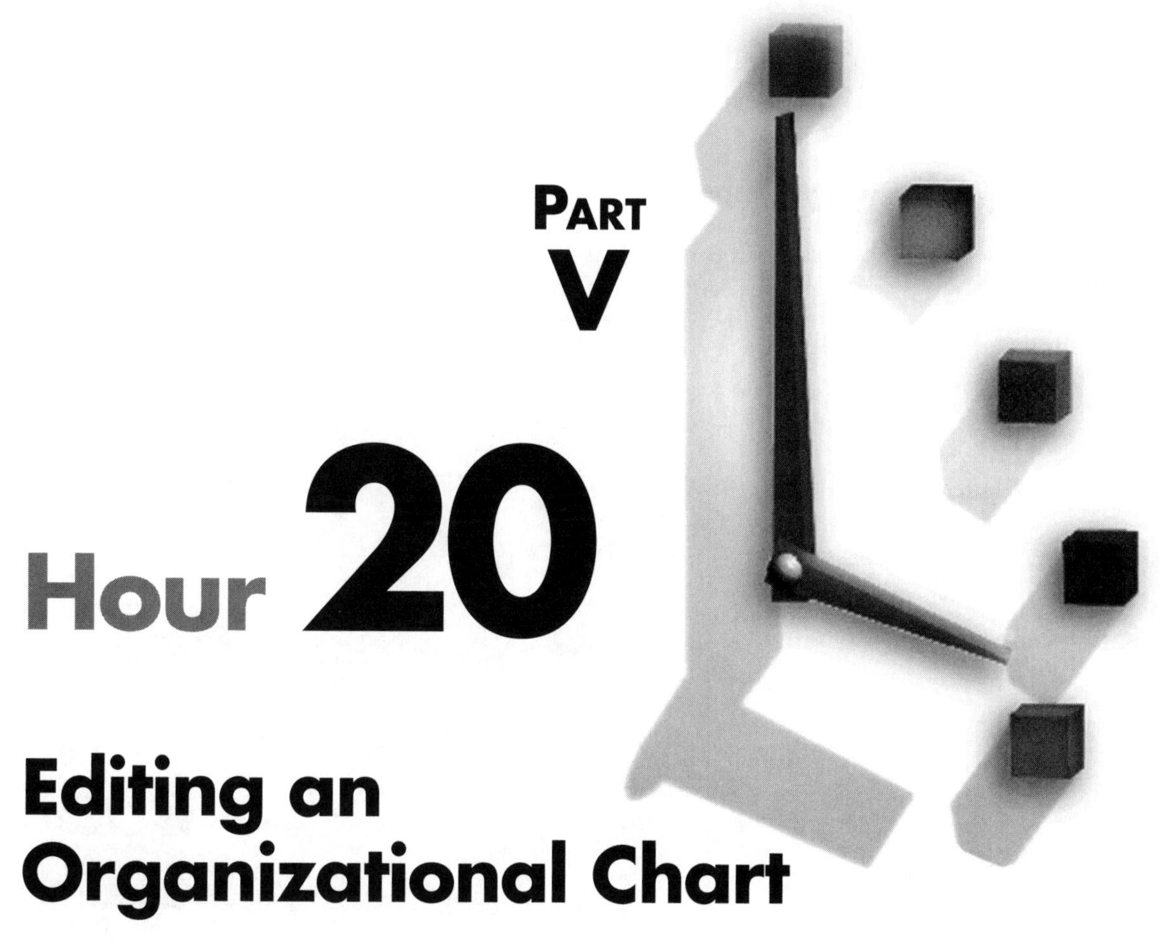

Hour 20

Editing an Organizational Chart

In the previous hour, you learned how to create a basic organizational chart. This hour focuses on how to edit and format the organizational chart to get just the right look for your presentation. Just as with the Microsoft Graph program, the Microsoft Organization Chart application lets you custom-format every element of an organizational chart. In this hour, you learn how to do the following:

- Change the chart style and add a title to the chart
- Change the text attributes
- Change the appearance of the boxes
- Format the connecting lines
- Format the chart background

Adding a Title

If your slide has other objects besides the organizational chart, you might want to add a title to the organizational chart object. Microsoft Organization Chart supplies a specific area for a chart title at the top center of the chart, above the first box. The phrase "Chart Title" serves as the placeholder for the chart title. (See Figure 20.1.) The title area is unique because it expands or contracts in relation to the size of your chart. However, the title's location always stays the same, and it never overlaps the chart itself.

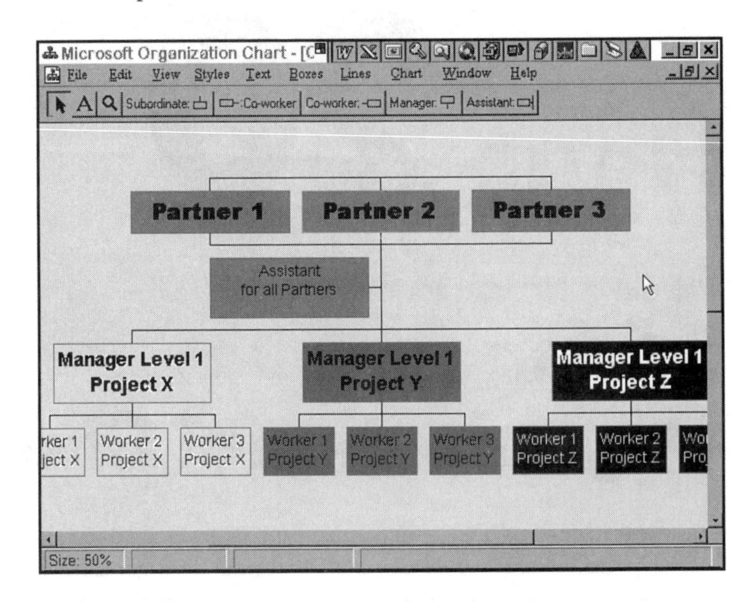

Figure 20.1.
The words `Chart Title` *act as a placeholder for the title.*

To add a title to an organizational chart, follow these steps:

1. Click once on the phrase `Chart Title` at the top of the organizational chart to position the cursor in the title area.
2. Delete the words `Chart Title`.
3. Type your organizational chart title.
4. Click anywhere off the organizational chart title to deselect it.

Time Saver

If you press the Tab key after clicking on the words `Chart Title`, that action selects the words. You can then start typing in the new organizational chart title.

Just a Minute

You can format the title by using any of the font formatting features discussed later in this hour.

Changing the Style of the Organizational Chart Boxes

Microsoft Organization Chart offers not only the traditional top-down style of chart, but also several other styles that might better represent the worker relationships in your organization. Although you can change the style of the entire organizational chart, folks usually change the style of either individual boxes or a selected group of boxes. Figure 20.2 shows an organizational chart in which the top level has three partners who are Co-managers. The project workers' style has also been changed to a vertical format to save space.

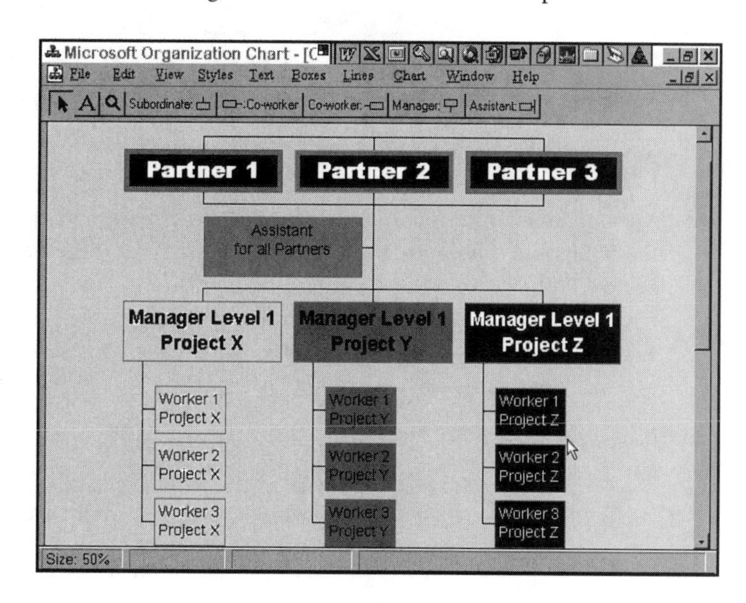

Figure 20.2.
An organizational chart using a vertical format.

To change the relationship style of boxes, follow these steps:

1. Select the boxes for which you want to change the style.
2. Choose Styles from the menu.
3. Select the box style that most closely matches your needs. (See Figure 20.3.)

20

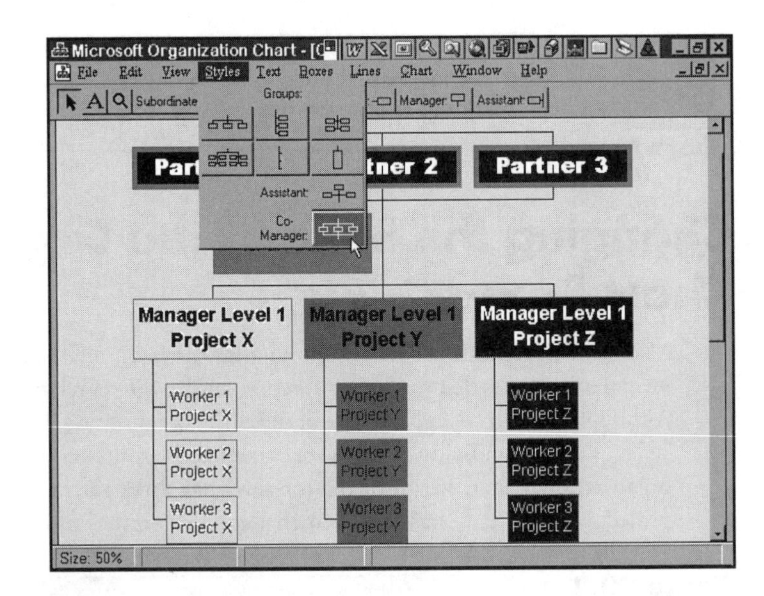

Figure 20.3.
Selecting a different relationship style.

Changing Attributes of Organizational Chart Objects

Most of an organizational chart's attributes can be formatted to give your presentation just the right look. You can format the text font face, size, and color as well as the alignment of any chart object. The boxes can be a different color or have a shadow; their borders can be customized to be thicker, a different color, or a dashed line. The connecting lines to each box can also be customized to fit your needs. Finally, you can also change the color of the organizational chart's background.

TIME SAVER

All the following instructions ask you to select a single box. However, if you have several boxes that should have identical formatting changes applied, you can quickly make these changes all at once. Simply select all the boxes that need to be modified by holding down the Shift key while clicking on each box.

Formatting Text

As mentioned earlier, you can format the text of any chart object with a different font face, size, color, and alignment. If you have a small chart, you might want to make the text bigger and bolder. In contrast, if your organizational chart is large, making the text smaller allows you to squeeze more information onto the page.

Font

You can use any font face, style, or size available on your PC for organizational chart text. Also, you can change the text appearance of an entire box or just portions of text in a box. To change the text appearance of an entire box, follow these steps:

1. Click on the box once to select it.
2. Choose Text | Font from the menu.
3. In the Font dialog box, select the font face, style, and size you want. (See Figure 20.4.)
4. Click the OK button.

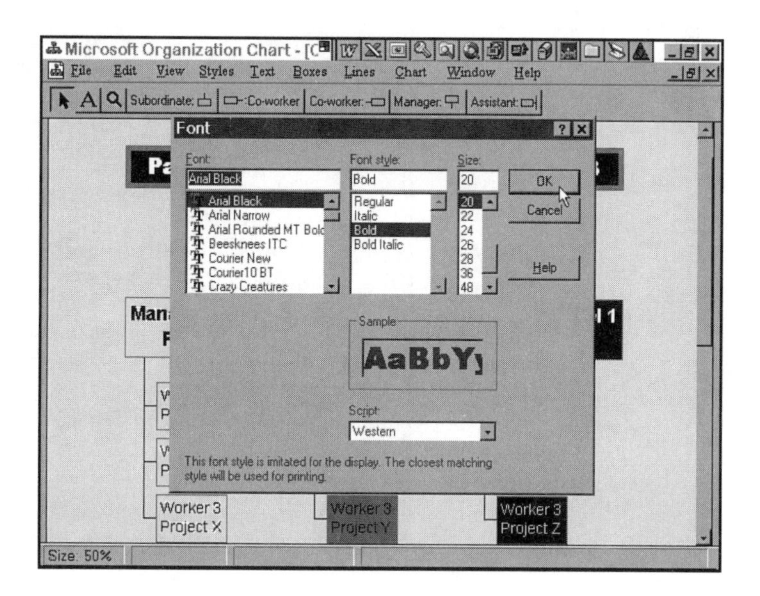

Figure 20.4.
Microsoft Organization Chart's Font dialog box.

To change the text appearance of just a portion of text in a box, follow these steps:

1. Click on the box once to select it.
2. Click again to view the text in the box.
3. Select the text you want to format.
4. Choose Text | Font from the menu.
5. In the Font dialog box, select the font face, style, and size you want.
6. Click the OK button.

Color

Microsoft Organization Chart offers 31 different colors to choose from for text. Select the color that best complements your chart's design. To change the text color of an entire box, use the following instructions:

1. Click once on the box to select it.
2. Choose Text | Color from the menu.
3. In the Color dialog box, select the color you want. (See Figure 20.5.)
4. Click the OK button.

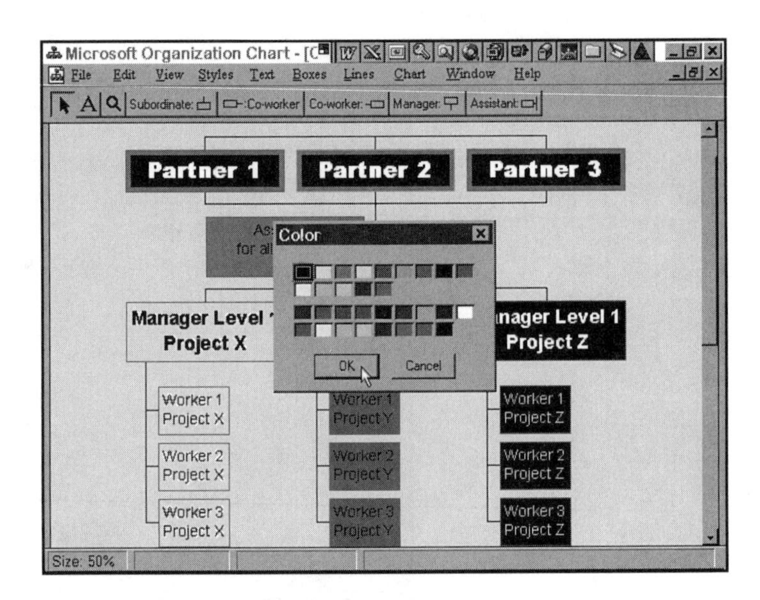

Figure 20.5.
Microsoft Organization Chart's Color dialog box.

To change the color of just a portion of text in a box, follow these steps:

1. Click on the box once to select it.
2. Click again to view the text in the box.
3. Select the text you want to format.
4. Choose Text | Color from the menu.
5. In the Color dialog box, select the color you want.
6. Click the OK button.

Alignment

As with the font attributes, you can change the text alignment of either an entire box or just a portion of text within the box. To change the text alignment of an entire box, follow these steps:

1. Click on the box once to select it.
2. Choose either Text | Left, Right, or Center from the menu. (See Figure 20.6.) Notice that the checkmark in the Text menu designates which alignment option is currently active.

Figure 20.6.
Selecting a text alignment.

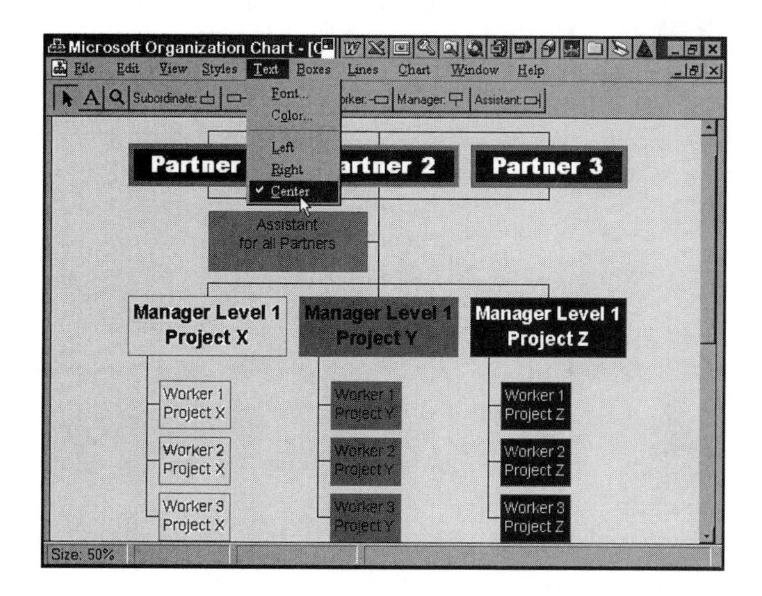

To change the text alignment of just one line of text within a box, follow these steps:

1. Click on the box once to select it.
2. Click again to view the text in the box.
3. Select the text you want to format.
4. Choose either Text | Left, Right, or Center from the menu.
5. Click outside the box to deselect it.

Customizing the Box's Appearance

As with most objects you have worked with so far, there are many options for when you want to add a bit of customization to your organizational chart. You can change the color of the box or add a shadow. The box border can be customized as well, with options for changing the line's thickness, style, and color.

Color

Color makes it easy for the presentation viewer to quickly identify organizational items. You can change the color of a box to emphasize a particular person or to help identify a team of people.

Just a Minute

When choosing a box color, keep the text color in mind. You wouldn't want a dark blue box with black text because no one would be able to read the text. If you use a dark color for the box, use a bright color or white for the text.

To change the box color, follow these steps:

1. Click once on the box to select it.
2. Choose Boxes | Color from the menu.
3. In the Color dialog box, select the color you want.
4. Click the OK button.

Just a Minute

Click the lower-right color box to create a transparent box—that is, a box with no color.

Shadow

Adding a shadow effect to the boxes in an organizational chart adds a professional design touch. Although you can certainly shadow just one or two boxes, this effect looks best when it's used consistently on either all or none of the items.

Just a Minute

Just a reminder: To quickly select all the boxes in an organizational chart, choose Edit | Select All from the menu.

To add a shadow effect to a box, follow these steps:

1. Click on the box once to select it.
2. Choose Boxes | Shadow from the menu.
3. Click on one of the eight shadow styles available. (See Figure 20.7.)

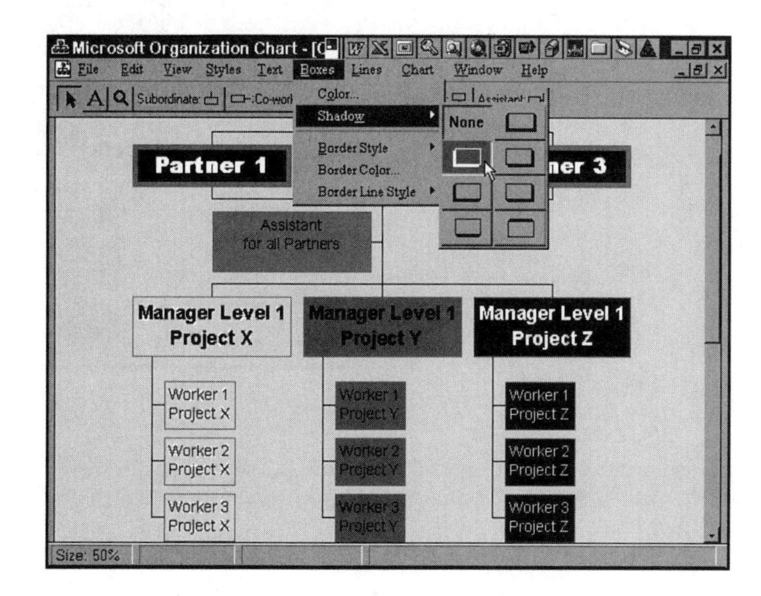

Figure 20.7.
Selecting a shadow option for a box.

Border Style

There are 12 border styles you can apply to a box. Style choices range from single lines to double lines, from thin to thick. To change the border style of a box, follow these steps:

1. Click once on the box to select it.
2. Choose Boxes | Border Style from the menu.
3. Select one of the 12 available border styles shown in Figure 20.8.

CAUTION

If you select None as the border style, you won't see a shadow.

20

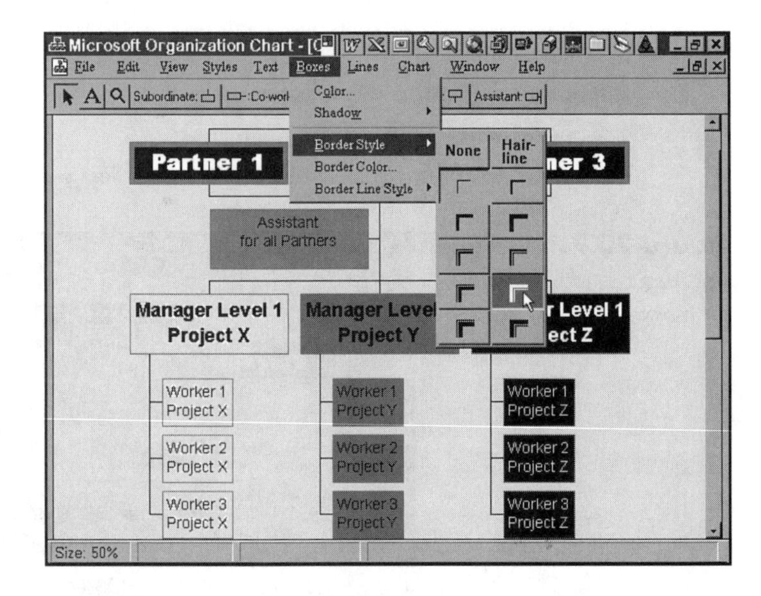

Figure 20.8.
Selecting a box border style.

Border Color

To create a frame around a box, you can select a contrasting color for the border. To change the box border color, follow these steps:

1. Click once on the box to select it.
2. Choose Boxes | Border Color from the menu.
3. Select a border color from the Color dialog box.
4. Click the OK button.

Border Line Style

Microsoft Organization Chart gives you three border line styles: solid, dotted, or dashed. When the border line styles are combined with the 12 border styles, you have several types of border lines available. I won't even mention that over 30 colors are available to enhance the border line. To change the box border line style, follow these steps:

1. Click on the box once to select it.
2. Choose Boxes | Border Line Style from the menu.
3. Select one of the three available border line styles, as shown in Figure 20.9.

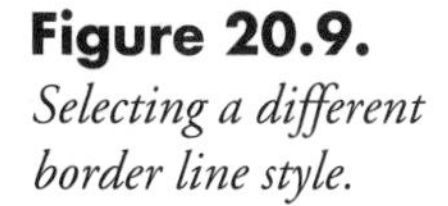

Figure 20.9.
Selecting a different border line style.

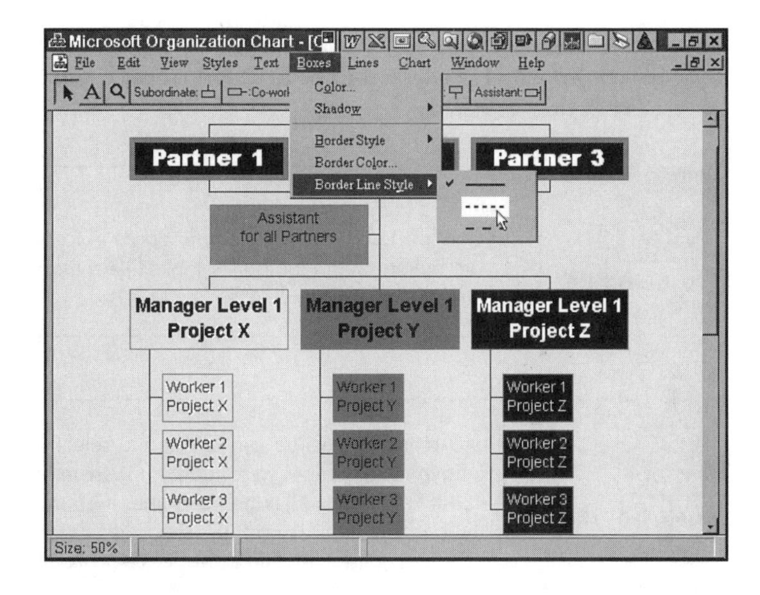

Changing the Connecting Lines

In Microsoft Organization Chart, you can also change the thickness, style, and color of the boxes' connecting lines. Notice in Figure 20.10, for example, that the connecting lines have been formatted to thick dashed lines. (You can also see the effects of using shadowed boxes and adding border styles.)

Figure 20.10.
Formatting connecting lines for the boxes.

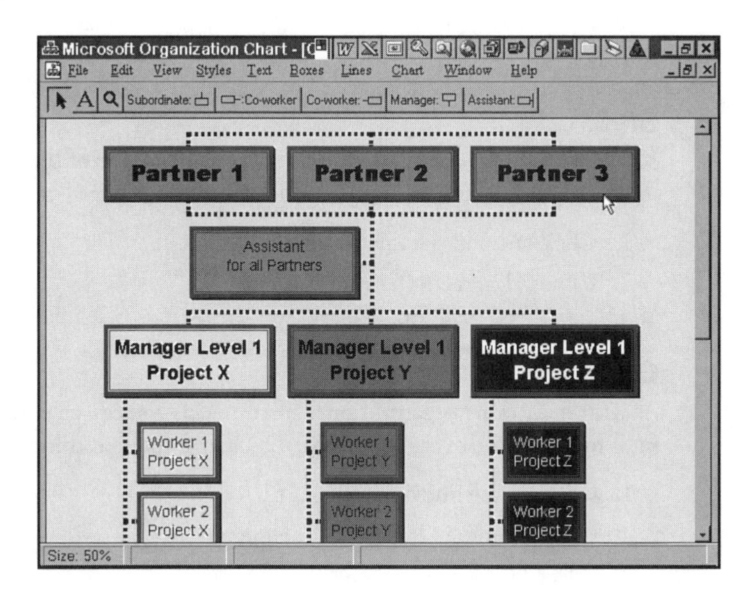

20

Before you can format any lines, however, you need to select the ones you want to change. To do this, simply click on the line to be formatted. It will be displayed in a dimmer color to show that it's selected.

JUST A MINUTE

> Selecting lines can be tricky if the chart is at 50 percent of the actual size or smaller. Use the View menu to zoom in to Actual Size, or click the Zoom button on the toolbar (it looks like a magnifying glass) to quickly zoom in on a specific line.

TIME SAVER

> All the following instructions ask you to select a single line. However, if you have multiple lines to format, you can select them by holding down the Shift key as you click on each line. If you want to change every line in the organizational chart, use the Edit | Select All command to select all the lines (and everything else) in your organizational chart.

Thickness

You have eight thickness options for the connection lines, ranging from none (no line) to very thick. To change the thickness of a line, follow these steps:

1. Click once on the line to select it.
2. Choose Lines | Thickness from the menu.
3. Select one of the eight line thickness options, as shown in Figure 20.11.

Style

Just as with the box borders, you can choose from one of three line styles: solid, dotted, or dashed. To change the line style, follow these steps:

1. Click once on the line to select it.
2. Choose Lines | Style from the menu.
3. Select one of the three line styles available.

Color

As with every other organizational chart object, you can change the color of the connection lines to one of the over 30 options. To change the line color, follow these steps:

1. Click on the line once to select it.
2. Choose Lines | Color from the menu.
3. Select the color you want.
4. Click the OK button.

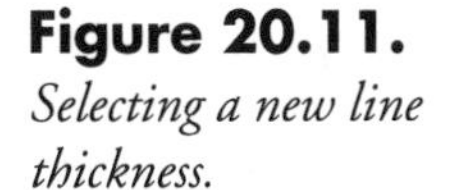

Figure 20.11.
Selecting a new line thickness.

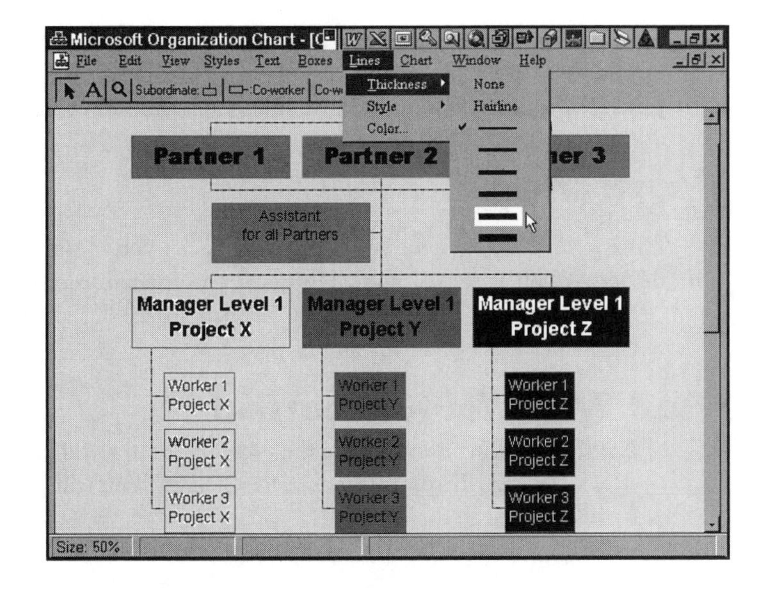

Recoloring the Chart Background

When you recolor the chart background, the chart object really stands out in your presentation slide as a separate object. To change the chart background, follow these steps:

1. Choose Chart | Background Color from the menu.
2. Select the color you want.
3. Click the OK button.

CAUTION

If you want the organizational chart to blend in with the slide background, don't change the color of the chart background. If you do change the background but don't like the results, you have two choices. You can undo the object formatting with the Edit | Undo command in PowerPoint (the Undo button or Ctrl+Z do the same thing). However, this action also undoes any other formatting changes you might have made to the organizational chart. If that would cause a problem, edit the organizational chart and change the background color to the transparent option in the Color dialog box (the color option in the lower-right corner).

Summary

That's a wrap for organizational charts. You now know how to professionally present your virtual organization to the venture capitalists who will fund it. In this hour, you have learned how to enhance a basic organizational chart by adding a title or modifying the style and attributes of the organizational chart boxes. Just like other presentation objects, organizational charts can be completely customized to reflect your creativity and organizational style.

Workshop

Once again, you're at the nifty workshop. I bet you're starting to feel like one of Pooh's helpers.☺ You will be editing and formatting the organization chart you created in last hour's "Test What You've Learned" section. So open up that file, and have some fun. Go ahead and bounce a bit; if a Tigger can, so can you.

Test What You've Learned

1. The following exercises use the presentation file you created and saved from Hour 19, "Using Microsoft Organization Chart." You will be using the skills you have just learned in this hour.
2. Open the file Hour 19 TWYL.PPT.
3. Select Pooh and Tigger and change the style to make them Co-managers.
4. Select Kanga and Roo and change the style to the vertical box style (first row, middle column).
5. Select Eeyore and Piglet and change the style to the vertical stacked box style (first row, last column).
6. Add a title to the organizational chart, such as `Revised as of [today's date]`.
7. Select all the boxes and change the text font face to Kids (or another appropriate font), using bold type and a larger size.
8. Change the title text to the same font face, bold, and a larger size than the boxes.
9. Change the title text color to red.
10. Select all the boxes and change the box color to yellow.
11. Format the boxes to have a shadow.
12. Format the box's border color to be yellow.
13. Format all the lines to be thick and dark blue.
14. Change the background color to light blue.
15. Exit from Microsoft Organization Chart and update the presentation.
16. Save the presentation as `Hour 20 TWYL`.

Q&A

Q I need more space for my organizational chart. How can I change the size of the boxes?

A Unfortunately, you can't change the size of the boxes. The boxes are a preset size, based on the text that's entered into them. They can get larger, if the need arises. If you need more space for the rest of your organizational chart, consider making the font size a little smaller.

Q Are there any other colors I can choose for the text and boxes?

A Unfortunately not. You're pretty much stuck with the 31 or 32 color choices in the Color dialog box.

Q I want to represent some people at the bottom of my organizational chart who don't really have any relationship to anyone. I can't delete the lines, so what should I do?

A I would add the boxes as normal subordinate boxes below the last row of boxes and then select all the lines and choose None as the thickness. This option gives the illusion of no lines, but the lines are actually still there. I have also used this little trick to add space between boxes. You can add a box and choose None for the box shadow and border style and the transparent color option for the box color. Once again, this gives the illusion of extra space between boxes, but there's really a box there.

Q I can't seem to start an organizational chart. Every time I double-click on the placeholder, PowerPoint gives me a message telling me I don't have enough memory to open Microsoft Organization Chart. I have plenty of memory, and I've tried rebooting. What am I doing wrong?

A You probably aren't doing anything wrong. Check out your fonts folder (usually found in C:\Windows\Fonts). If you have 600 or more fonts, you can't run the Microsoft Organization Chart program. You can either delete some fonts that you don't use, or move them to a new folder. Microsoft is working on a fix for this problem.

PART VI

Multimedia, the World Wide Web, and Other Cool Stuff

Hour

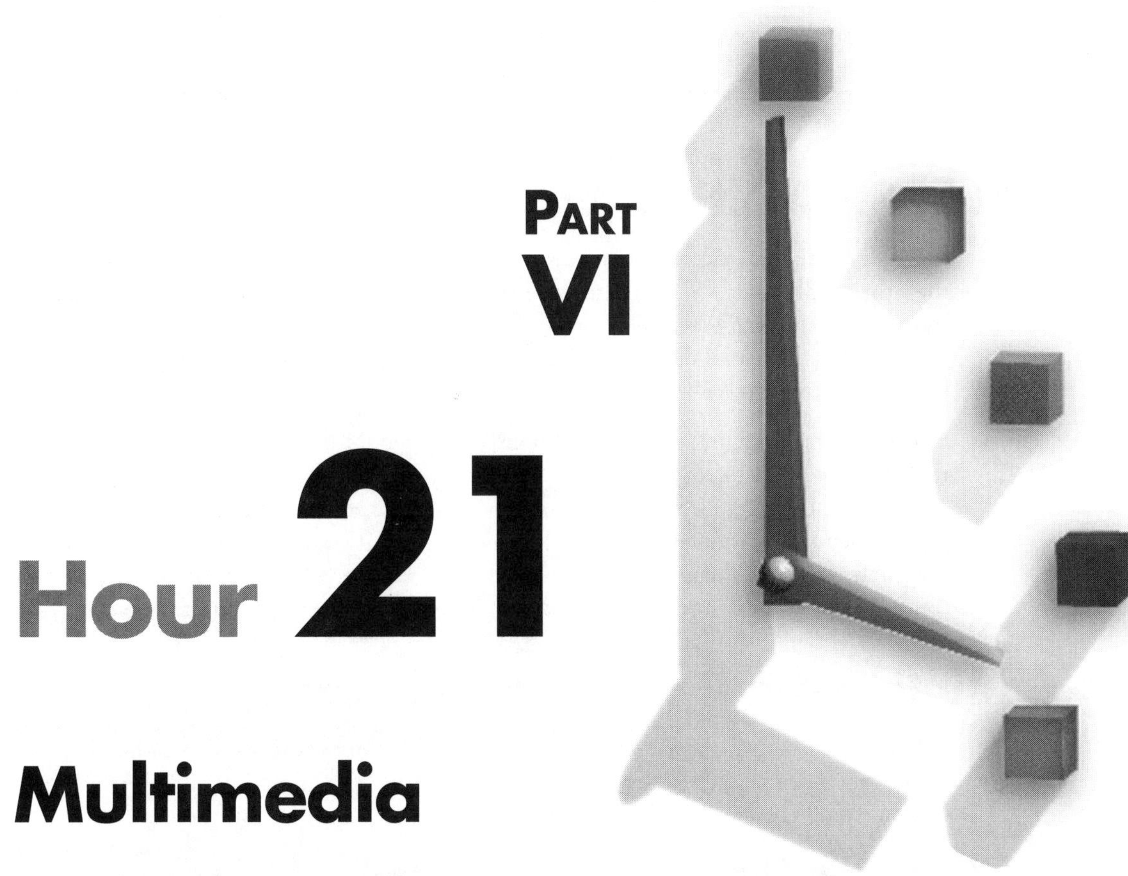

Part VI

Hour 21

Multimedia

by Ruel T. Hernandez

This is going to be a good solid hour where you will be learning about how to insert multimedia elements into your PowerPoint 97 presentations. This hour is really an expansion on Hour 6, "Working with Clip Art and Pictures," in which you learned the basics of handling clip art and pictures. In this hour, you will be expanding on what you learned in Hour 6 by seeing how you can enhance your PowerPoint 97 presentations with photos, sound, music, narration, and video.

As you work your way through this hour, you will learn about the following:

- ☐ Multimedia pictures and photos
- ☐ Sound files
- ☐ CD music
- ☐ Custom soundtracks
- ☐ Narration
- ☐ Adding video
- ☐ Finding multimedia files

What Is Multimedia?

Multimedia is sound, music, and pictures used to dazzle and entertain the senses. However, the term is really used to mean multimedia *objects*; the objects are clip art, photos and pictures, sound clips, music files, music from music CD tracks, custom soundtrack music, voice narration, and video—in other words, the things that make people say "ooh" and "aah" as you present your PowerPoint slide show.

Other than a gratifying audience response, why would you want to add these fancy multimedia objects to your PowerPoint 97 presentation? After all, you might already have some nice clip art built into your slide show. Well, you can add a little bit more pizzazz to your presentation by incorporating multimedia files. It's said that a picture is worth a thousand words, so imagine how much more you can say when you can add a photo of someone you know to your presentation or add music or video to your presentation!

Multimedia Pictures and Photos

Although you have already learned how to work with clip art and pictures in Hour 6, this section gives you a quick bare-bones review of inserting clip art and pictures. Later in this section, you'll move on to adding pictures that don't come with PowerPoint.

Using the Clip Gallery and Pictures

From the Clip Gallery, in addition to clip art, you can also select pictures, sounds, and videos to include in your PowerPoint 97 presentation. To see how to add clip art and pictures to your presentation, follow these steps:

1. Start with a new blank slide—no formatted template, just a blank slide. (For each section in this hour, you will use blank slides so you can see how to add multimedia objects to your PowerPoint slides.)
2. Choose Insert | Picture | ClipArt from the menu to open the Clip Gallery.
3. Click the Pictures tab to see the pictures portion of the Clip Gallery, shown in Figure 21.1.
4. Scroll through the different categories listed in the first column on the left. As you scroll up and down, notice that the selection of pictures changes as the category changes.
5. Pick a category you're interested in and then scroll through the selection of pictures. You can click the Clip Properties button to get more information about the file, such as what type of file it is.

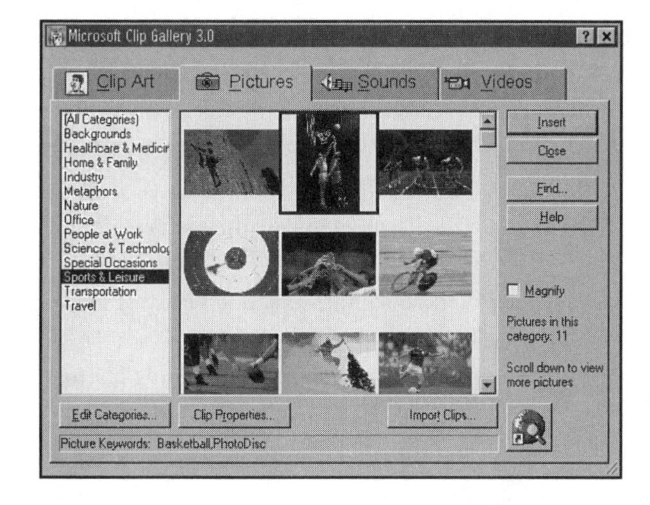

Figure 21.1.
In the Clip Gallery, you can pick clip art, pictures, sounds, and video to include in your presentation.

6. After you have picked the picture you want to use, click on that picture, and then click the Insert button. The picture is displayed on your slide, as shown in Figure 21.2.

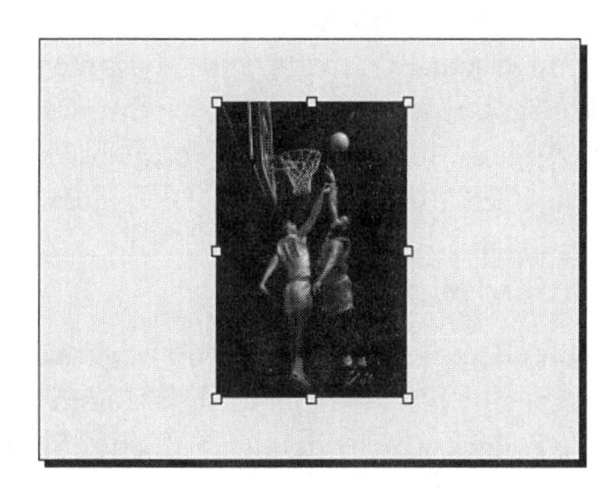

Figure 21.2.
Inserting pictures in your presentation.

As you learned in Hour 6, you can also resize the picture and move it to different areas on your slide. You can also use a floating picture toolbar, which is similar to the floating clip art toolbar you used with clip art. With the toolbar, you can manipulate the picture's brightness and color. If you aren't sure about what each button on the toolbar does, just move your mouse cursor over the button and a ScreenTip appears, telling you what the button does.

As you can see, inserting pictures in your PowerPoint 97 presentation is the same as the process for inserting clip art that you learned in Hour 6.

Scanning Pictures with Special Equipment

You might want to place a photograph in your presentation, too, but how do you do that? You might have only the printed photograph, which is certainly not in digital form on a disk. So how do you put a photograph on disk so you can add it to your PowerPoint presentation? You have the following options:

- Use a digital camera to take the picture and then directly transfer the picture to your computer by using a cable connection.
- Use a desktop scanner to scan an existing photograph or picture into your computer.
- Use a photo scanner to scan an existing photograph or picture into your computer.
- Use a photo-developing lab to develop your film and ask that your photographs be put on a disk or on a PhotoCD, so you can use them on your computer.

Digital cameras are handy to use because you don't have to wait for pictures to be developed. You can just take a picture, connect the camera to your computer, and put the picture on your computer.

Desktop scanners can scan documents and photos, but the smaller photo scanners can scan only photographs. Unfortunately, digital cameras, desktop scanners, and photo scanners require you to actually have this extra equipment. If you have the equipment, then just follow the instructions that came with it to determine how to transfer the pictures to your computer. However, please note that some inexpensive digital cameras suffer from image quality problems. If you don't have a digital camera and want to buy one, expect to pay several hundred dollars to get a good digital camera that gives you good quality images you can use in your PowerPoint presentations.

If you don't have the equipment, you might want to consider using a photo-developing lab to transfer your photographs to disk. PhotoWorks is one well-known photo developer; another is Konica, which offers its PC Picture Show. You can get your photographs developed by one of these—or similar—photo developers and have the pictures copied to a disk. With the Kodak CD, you can have your photographs stored on a CD-ROM, also known in the industry as a PhotoCD. The photo developer can often give you a program, such as a simple image-viewing program, to work with the photo on the disk or PhotoCD. You need to get a program like Photoshop or PhotoDeluxe to work with photos on PhotoCDs. In terms of cost, you might find that disks are cheaper than PhotoCDs (although PhotoCDs are supposed to last longer than regular disks), so you might want to shop around and do a cost comparison among the stores and photo developers in your area.

Whether you use a digital camera, desktop scanner, or photo scanner, or ask a photo developer to put your photos on disk or CD-ROM, you should use whatever program came

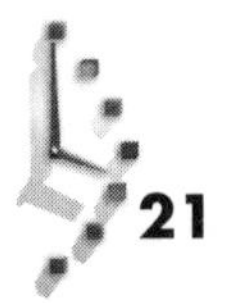

with the equipment or from the developer to transform your photos into file formats that PowerPoint can understand. For graphics files, which include clip art and pictures, the following file formats are compatible with PowerPoint:

.GIF	CompuServe GIF
.BMP	Windows Bitmap
.JPG	JPEG
PCX	Paintbrush
.TIF	Tagged Image File Format
.PMG	Portable Network Graphics
.PCD	Kodak PhotoCD
.TGA	True Vision Targa
.WMF	Windows Metafile
.EMF	Enhanced Windows Metafile
.DIB	Windows DIB
.CGM	Computer Graphics Metafile
.EPS	Encapsulated PostScript
.PCT	Macintosh PICT
.DRW	Micrografx Designer/Draw
.DXF	AutoCAD Format 2-D
.CDR	CorelDRAW!
.WPG	WordPerfect Graphics
.PIC	Lotus 1-2-3 Graphics
.HGL	HP Graphics Language

I would recommend that you refer to the instructions for whatever program came with your digital camera or scanner, or with the disk or CD-ROM from the film developer, to save or convert your photo files in either .JPG, .GIF, or .BMP formats. These are the most common formats you will use. You should also take note of which disk drive (A, B, C, and so forth) and directory the photo files are in.

Adding Scanned Pictures and Photos to Your PowerPoint Presentation

Once you've had your photos converted to file format, it's easy to add them to your PowerPoint presentation; just follow these steps:

1. Choose Insert | Picture | From File from the menu to open the Insert Picture dialog box. Here, you can search through your computer's drives and folders to retrieve a picture or photo file.
2. In the "File name" listbox toward the bottom of the dialog box, enter the letter of the drive, the folder name, and the filename to go to where your photo file is located.

For instance, say you want to find a photo file named SNAP.JPG, which you know is in the C:\MY DOCUMENTS directory. You could type in `C:\MY DOCUMENTS` in the "File name" listbox and press Enter to go to the directory and scroll down the list of files to find the one you're looking for, or you could type in `C:\MY DOCUMENTS\SNAP.JPG` to go directly to the file. (See Figure 21.3.)

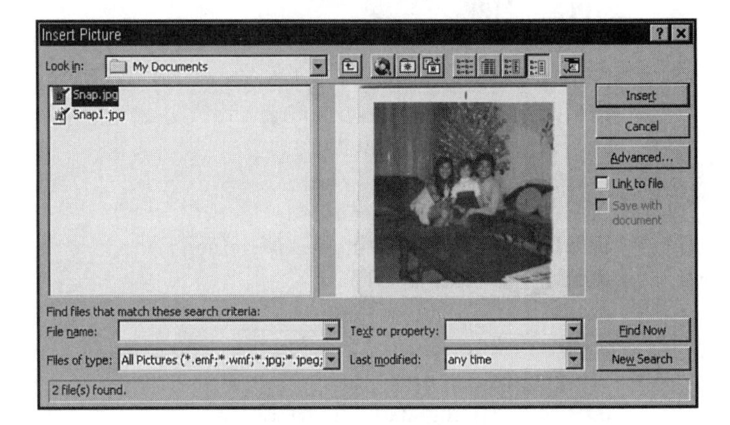

Figure 21.3.
Inserting photo files in your presentation.

3. Next, click the Insert button to insert the photo into your PowerPoint 97 presentation slide. You can then adjust the photo's color, brightness, and so forth, much as you modify clip art.

Working with Microsoft Photo Editor

If you selected the Typical option when you installed PowerPoint 97 or Office 97, you should also have Microsoft Photo Editor installed. You can run your scanner from PowerPoint 97 by choosing Insert | Picture | From Scanner from the menu. This action loads the Photo Editor program and then runs your scanner, using your scanner's software. Refer to your scanner's documentation for instructions on how to work the scanner and its software.

JUST A MINUTE

If you installed your scanner before installing PowerPoint 97 or Office 97, you might have to reinstall your scanner's software so PowerPoint 97 can determine that the scanner is installed. Refer to your scanner's instructions on how to install or reinstall the software.

After your scanner has scanned your photograph, you should see a Save button on your scanner's software for saving the photo to disk or a Transfer button to transfer the photo to Photo Editor (software for TWAIN-compliant devices, such as scanners, usually have these common commands). If you click the Transfer button, your scanned photo should be transferred to the Photo Editor program.

You can then use Photo Editor to select and copy certain sections of the photo so you can later paste them to use in PowerPoint. For instance, you might want to scan an old photo that has a white border you want to cut out. Here's how you would do that:

1. Click the Select button on Photo Editor's toolbar.
2. Then, using the dashed-line selection box, outline the portion of the photo you want to use. Start from one corner of the photo and drag the selection box to the other end of the area you're outlining.
3. After you have selected the area of the photo you want to use, click the Copy button to copy it.

If there's nothing you want to cut out, choose Edit | Select All from the menu to select the whole photo you scanned.

Before you select and copy a photo, you might want to look at Photo Editor's Effects menu. It includes functions to help you manipulate the photo, such as the useful Sharpen command. There are other commands in the Effects and Image menus that you can use to further modify the quality and look of the photo. After you have sharpened the photo, plus whatever other enhancements you've added, then you can go through the select and copy procedure. You might also want to save the changed photo to a file that you can later retrieve for use in PowerPoint.

After you have selected and copied the portion of the photo you want to use, switch back to PowerPoint and paste the photo into the slide. When you go back to PowerPoint, notice a closed box within the slide; it's similar to the selection box, but it's smaller and has little squares to designate its corners and sides. This box is where your photo will be pasted. Click the Paste button or choose Edit | Paste from the menu. It might take a few moments (so please wait), but either action pastes the scanned photo into your PowerPoint slide. After the scanned photo is pasted into your slide, you can then resize, move, and further fine-tune the photo for your PowerPoint presentation, just as you do with clip art and pictures from the Clip Gallery.

Sound Files, CD Music, Custom Soundtracks, and Narration

With slides of information, clip art, and pictures, PowerPoint presentations are effective by themselves, but they can be even more attention-grabbing with sound effects added to the presentation. These sound effects can come from playing sound files, a music track from a CD, a custom soundtrack, or narration of your presentation. To play sound files, custom soundtracks, or narration, however, you must have a sound card in your computer. Most newer computers and many laptop or notebook computers have sound cards built-in, so they should be able to play sound effects.

Recording the narration also depends on your sound card and on how much memory your computer has. If you have at least 16M of RAM, chances are you can record yourself narrating your PowerPoint slide show. However, not all computers are the same, so some with less RAM might be able to record your narration. And, of course, playing sound effects from a music CD requires a CD-ROM drive in your computer.

Using PowerPoint's Sound Clips

PowerPoint 97's Clip Gallery also includes a collection of sound clips. To select one, choose Insert | Movies and Sounds | Sound from Gallery from the menu. As shown in Figure 21.4, this opens the Sounds tab of the Clip Gallery.

Figure 21.4.
Choosing a sound clip from the Clip Gallery.

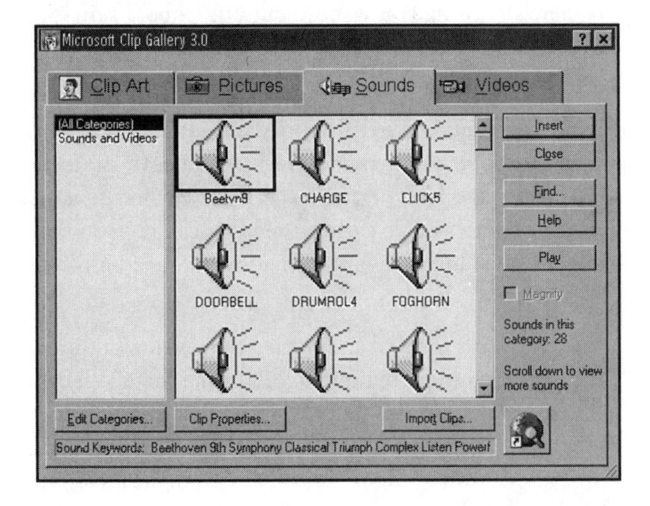

You can maneuver around the Clip Gallery to explore the different sound clips, designated by the speaker icons, the same way you browse through clip art and picture files. To hear a sound clip, just click the Play button. If you like the sound clip, then click the Insert button to add it to your presentation slide. After you have inserted the sound clip in your slide, you should see a tiny speaker icon, which you can move around, in the middle of your slide. If you plan to add another sound file to the slide, for example, you might want to move the speaker icon away from the middle of the slide. To hear the sound, double-click the speaker icon; in Slide Show View, just single-click. While you're in Slide Show View, you can also play all the sound clips at once. Note that the speaker icon only appears in the Slide View and the Slide Sorter View to remind you that there's a sound associated with the slide. The speaker icon doesn't show up when you present or print the slide.

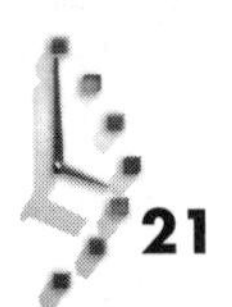

Adding Other Sound Files

PowerPoint 97 can play three different types of sound files: .WAV, .MID, and .RMI. The more popular ones are .WAV files, which are more like real recordings of actual sounds, and .MID files, which are MIDI music files that, depending on your computer's sound card, can sound like either an organ or a full-size orchestra.

In addition to the Clip Gallery, you might want to explore your Windows folders to see whether you can find any .WAV and .MID files. If you have Windows Plus! installed on your computer, you find more .WAV files in the Plus! Themes folder. Here are some folders to check for .WAV and .MID files:

C:\WINDOWS
C:\WINDOWS\MEDIA
C:\PROGRAM FILES\PLUS!\THEMES

To search for and select sound files from these folders, choose Insert | Movies and Sounds | Sound from File from the menu. As shown in Figure 21.5, this opens the Insert Sound dialog box, where you can search for sound files. Look for .WAV and .MID files, and select one to insert in your presentation. To place the .WAV or .MID file in your presentation, click the Insert button. A speaker icon shows up in the middle of your PowerPoint slide to designate the sound file. Again, you can move the icon around to another part of the slide.

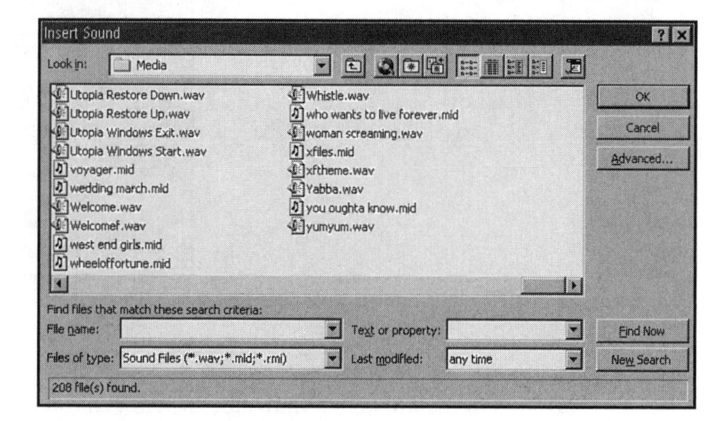

Figure 21.5.
Adding more sound clips to your PowerPoint presentation.

21

JUST A MINUTE

When you look for sound files outside the Clip Gallery, you can't play them from the Insert Sound dialog box. However, you can load the Windows Media Player program, which is built into Windows 95. Just click the Start button and choose Programs | Accessories | Multimedia. Use Media Player's File | Open command to search for a sound file. Once you have found it, load it and click the Play button (the button with the triangle pointing to the right) to hear what the file sounds like.

Playing Music from a CD Track

You can also play a track of music from a music CD, but you need a CD-ROM drive and a sound card in your computer. Most computers sold now, including many laptop and notebook computers, have these components built in.

To insert a track of music (you're really inserting an icon you can click so the music can be played from the CD), follow these steps:

1. Choose Insert | Movies and Sounds | Play CD Audio Track from the menu to open the Play Options dialog box. (See Figure 21.6.)

Figure 21.6.
Inserting music tracks from a music CD.

2. You need to know which track you want to play, as well its start and end times. After you have typed in those values, click the OK button. You should see a tiny CD icon in the middle of your slide, which you can move around the slide just as you did with the speaker icon.
3. To play the CD track, double-click the CD icon.

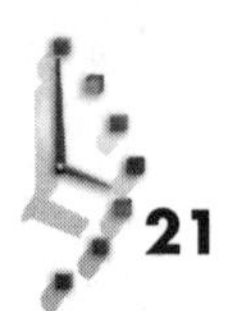

JUST A MINUTE

To determine the start and end times of a certain portion of a CD music track, use the Windows CD Player program built into Windows 95. Click the Start button, and then choose Programs | Accessories | Multimedia. The CD Player shows you the running time of a music track. Under the View menu, make sure Track Time Elapsed is checked so you can time the track from beginning to end.

CAUTION

If you're running Office 97 from the CD-ROM, you can't play a CD music track. And make sure you have right music CD in the drive when it's time to give your presentation so you don't accidentally play the wrong CD music track!

Recording Narration

To record narration for your PowerPoint presentation, you need a sound card with a microphone plugged in. You should also have a script prepared for whatever you want to say.

CAUTION

On some computers, the amount of RAM might affect whether you can record your narration; you will just have to try recording the narration to see if it works for you.

Also, note that the sound quality of your narration could be limited by the quality of your microphone and the amount of ambient noise. Ambient noise can be minimized (close the door or windows to the room you're in, turn off the radio or TV in the room, and so forth). You can use cheap microphones for informal presentations; however, you might want to buy a good quality microphone to get better quality sound for professional presentations.

Keep in mind, too, that if your microphone is built into your computer, it could pick up the buzzing sound of your computer's fan or the whirring sound of your computer's drives. Some monitors have microphones built in, but those microphones could pick up the hum of the monitor, even though they shouldn't. If your microphone is built into your keyboard, try to minimize your use of the keyboard when you record your narration.

Recording Narration for a Single Slide

To record narration for a single slide, follow these steps:

1. Choose Insert | Movies and Sound | Record Narration from the menu to open the Record Sound dialog box. (See Figure 21.7.)

Figure 21.7.
Recording the narration for your presentation.

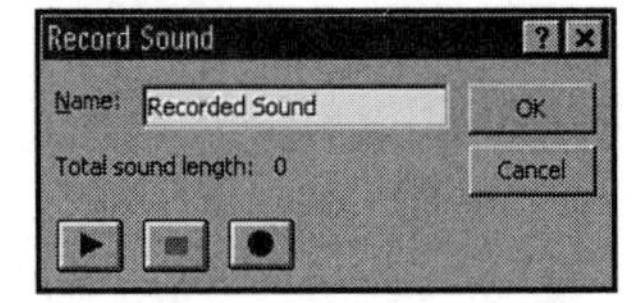

2. Enter the name of your narration in the Name field.
3. Below the Name field are three buttons. The first button, with the triangle pointing to the right, is the Play button. The next button, with the square box, is the Stop button. The last button, with the red dot, is the Record button. To start recording your narration, click the Record button and start talking into the microphone.
4. When you have finished your narration, click the Stop button. To check your recording, you can play it by clicking the Play button.
5. When you're finished recording, click the OK button; a speaker icon then appears in the middle of your slide. You might want to move the icon to another part of the slide.
6. If you want to play the narration, double-click the speaker icon.

Just a Minute

> You can also use the Sound Recorder program built into Windows 95 to record a slide narration. Click the Start button, and then choose Programs | Accessories | Multimedia. If you use Sound Recorder, you have to save your recording as a .WAV file that you insert as a sound file into your PowerPoint presentation.

Recording Narration While Viewing All Your Slides

A better way to record your narration is while viewing the slides for your presentation. To do this, choose Slide Show | Record Narration from the menu to open the Record Narration dialog box, shown in Figure 21.8.

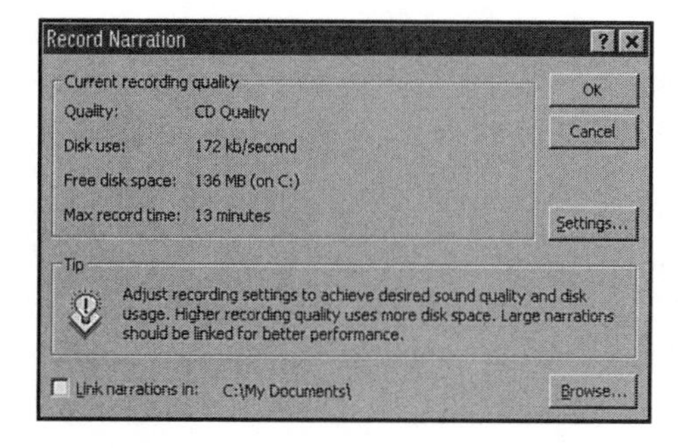

Figure 21.8.
Recording your narration while you view the slides for your presentation.

Click the Settings button to set the recording's sound quality, such as fine-tuning the CD quality. Note that the higher the sound quality, the more disk space you use. Once you have set the sound quality, click the OK button; your slide presentation begins, and you can read your narration into the microphone, moving from slide to slide and then ending the slide show as you normally would. When you end the slide show, you're asked whether you want the save the new timings (because of your added narration) and review them in Slide Sorter View.

Using Custom Soundtracks

Custom Soundtrack is a fun way to add music to your presentation, and you don't have to be a trained musician to use it. It's easy to install the Custom Soundtrack add-in program, which is on the PowerPoint 97 and Office 97 installation CD-ROM. First, go to the D:\VALUPAK\MUSICTRK directory (in this example, *D:* is your CD-ROM drive) on your Office 97 CD-ROM disk. Next, find and run the SETUP.EXE file to install Custom Soundtrack in PowerPoint.

To run Custom Soundtrack, choose Slide Show | Custom Soundtrack from the menu to open the Custom Soundtrack dialog box. (See Figure 21.9.)

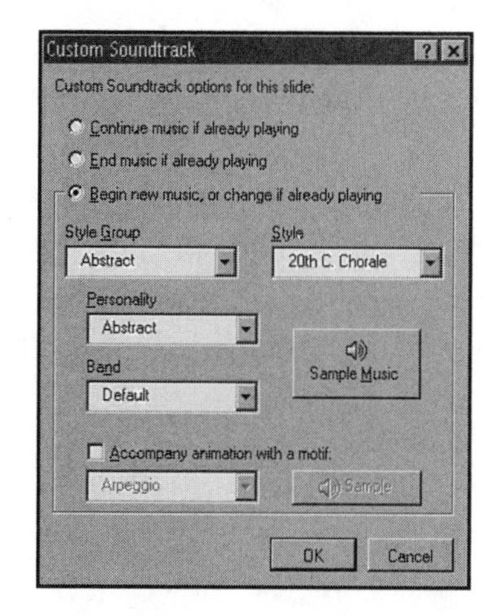

Figure 21.9.
Use Custom Soundtrack to add music to your PowerPoint presentation.

You can think of Custom Soundtrack as a way to add mood music to your presentation. It's somewhat like playing with an electronic organ that has special keys for different rhythms. In the Custom Soundtrack dialog box, notice the different settings for Style Group (from abstract to rock), Personality (from adventurous to upbeat), and Band (angel choir to synths). After you have set these options, click the Sample Music button to hear what the music sounds like. You can change the style, personality, and band even while the music is playing and hear the change instantaneously, and you can even add animation. When you advance to the next slide in your presentation, you can choose to continue the music, end the music, or start a new music track. After you have made all your selections, click the OK button.

With Custom Soundtrack, you don't have to deal with selecting and searching for sound files, knowing the correct beginning and end times of a CD music track, and other details. It's so easy to use and a lot of fun to play with.

Adding Video

Video is perhaps the ultimate multimedia object you can add to your PowerPoint presentation. You have a picture—in fact, a moving picture—as well as sound in a video clip, and they can combine to show some sort of dramatic action that people watch and pay attention to. A video clip, even a short one, can help you make a point in your presentation.

Just as with sound clips and photo files, you can get video clips by either using the PowerPoint Clip Gallery or finding other video files.

Using PowerPoint's Video Clips

As with clip art, pictures, and sound clips, you can also use PowerPoint's built-in Clip Gallery to browse through a selection of video clips; just follow these steps:

1. Choose Insert | Movies and Sounds | Movie from Gallery to open the Videos tab of the familiar Clip Gallery, shown in Figure 21.10.
2. Scroll through the selections and pick the one you want to use.
3. Click the Play button to play the video clip.
4. If you like the video clip, click the Insert button to place the video clip on your PowerPoint slide. You can then double-click the video clip icon to play the video clip (in Slide Show View, just single-click).

Before you double-click the video clip, it looks like a still picture, and you can resize and move the video clip just as you would with a still picture.

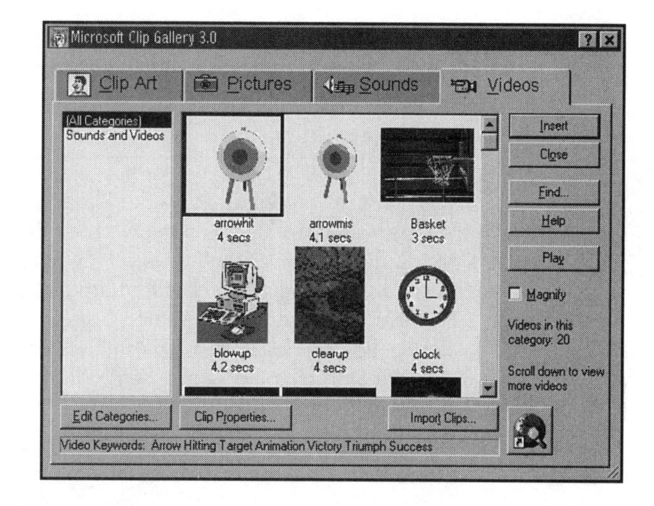

Figure 21.10.
Inserting a video clip into your PowerPoint presentation.

Adding Other Video Clips

If you have video clips that didn't come with PowerPoint, you can incorporate them, too, just as you can use picture and sound files from other folders on your hard drive. However, you probably don't have any other video clip files unless you created them or got them from the Internet.

The most common video file formats that work with PowerPoint are .AVI, .MPG, .FLC, and .FLI files. .AVI and .MPG files produce movie-like and television-like video clips, but these files tend to be rather large. A 30-second file can take up several megabytes. You can usually find .AVI and .MPG files at Web sites for movie and television studios; they offer these files as commercials or previews for their movies and television shows. .FLC and .FLI files produce animation-like video clips, such as cartoons. These files are much smaller, typically no more than a few hundred kilobytes. (There's also the popular .MOV video file, but it's not currently recognized by PowerPoint.)

To add one of these files to your PowerPoint presentation, follow these steps:

1. Choose Insert | Movies and Sounds | Movies from File to open the Insert Movie dialog box.
2. Use the Insert Movie dialog box to search your computer's drives and folders for a video clip file. When you find one and highlight it, click the Insert button to place it in your PowerPoint slide. This dialog box is similar to the File | Open dialog box and is different from the Clip Gallery. Unlike the Clip Gallery, the Insert Movie dialog box doesn't have a Play button you can click to play a video clip.

3. As with pictures and sound clips, you can resize the video clip and move it to anywhere on the slide. To play the video clip, double-click its icon on the slide (in Slide Show View, just single-click).

JUST A MINUTE

You can use the Windows Media Player program built into Windows 95 to play video clip files. You might prefer this program because the Insert Movie dialog box doesn't have a Play button. The Clip Gallery has a Play button for playing video clips that are already in the Clip Gallery. However, the Insert Movie dialog box, which is similar to the File | Open dialog, has no Play button. To use the Windows Media Player program, click the Start button and choose Programs | Accessories | Multimedia and then click Media Player.

There's also an Active Movie add-in program on the PowerPoint 97 and Office 97 CD-ROM that you might want to install. The file is AMOVIE.EXE in the D:\VALUPACK\AMOVIE directory. Run the AMOVIE.EXE file to install this add-in program.

JUST A MINUTE

If you have the right equipment, you can make your own video clips, but you need a video camera and at least a TV tuner card installed in your computer. In short, you hook up the video camera, or a VCR with the videotape made by the video camera, to your computer through the TV tuner card and run a video capture program to capture a portion of the videotape.

There is much fancier equipment you can use to do video-editing on a computer, but making your own video clips is beyond the scope of this book. Also, you need a computer with a great deal of RAM and hard drive space to make video clips. However, if you're interested in making your own video clips, you could visit my PC-TV Net Page at `http://www.ruel.net/pctv.html` for more information.

Finding Multimedia Files

You know you can find multimedia files from PowerPoint's Clip Gallery or search the folders on your hard drive for other multimedia files. But where else you can find multimedia files? Well, you can access PowerPoint Central from within PowerPoint and then open the Free Stuff tab to find files on your PowerPoint 97 or Office 97 CD-ROM. You can also look for clip art packages at your local computer software store or buy similar packages by mail order.

While you're in the Free Stuff tab in PowerPoint Central, if you're connected to the Internet, you can visit the Microsoft PowerPoint Web site for new graphics files (as well as PowerPoint templates). You can also visit Web sites like Shareware.com and Download.com (at `http://www.shareware.com` and `http://www.download.com`, respectively), and do a search using the keywords *clip art*, *multimedia*, *.WAV*, *midi*, *music*, and *pictures* to look for files. Most of the files are in .ZIP format that you have to unzip, so you need an "unzip" or "zip" program (which you can usually find on the Web, too, by doing a search). For music MIDI files (.MID), you can check out the MIDI collection at the Shout House Web site; it's at `http://shouthouse.com` (you don't need to type `www` in the address).

Summary

You have just had a solid hour of learning how to add multimedia object files to your PowerPoint 97 presentation. Since you already know how to insert and manipulate clip art files, you have a headstart on working with multimedia files. You now know that in addition to adding clip art to your PowerPoint presentation, you can insert pictures or photos from the Clip Gallery or from files outside PowerPoint. If you have the equipment, you can scan actual photographs to insert in your PowerPoint presentation slides.

You also know how to insert sound files, including .WAV and .MID files, and do a narration for your presentation. You have also learned how to work with Custom Soundtrack and insert video clips into your presentations. Finally, you know where to look for new multimedia files if you run out of ones you want to use.

Workshop

In this hour's workshop, you'll see whether you learned how to jazz up your PowerPoint presentations. This will be an easy test because there's so much you can do with multimedia. I'll be kind and not ask you to do a narration or to make a video clip!

This hour has barely scratched the surface in teaching you how to insert multimedia object files into your PowerPoint presentation, but the "Q&A" section includes some commonly asked questions to give you a little more detail.

Test What You've Learned

1. Start PowerPoint.
2. Select a blank presentation.
3. Select a blank slide.
4. Insert a picture on a blank slide, and then resize and move it around within the slide.

5. Add a sound clip to the slide with the picture.
6. Play the sound clip in both Slide View and in Slide Show View (don't forget how you're supposed to click the sound clip).
7. Make a new blank slide and insert a video clip; play the video clip when you're in the Clip Gallery or the Insert Movie dialog box.
8. As a bonus, if you haven't already done so, install the Custom Soundtrack add-in. (Hint: You might have to restart PowerPoint after you install the add-in program to get it to work.)
9. Add a custom soundtrack to your slide show.
10. If you're connected to the Internet, find a .WAV or .MID file and insert it into your slide show. (If you can do this last one, you deserve a standing ovation!) For those not connected to the Internet, you are hereby given extra time, beyond the hour allotted to this chapter, to find a multimedia file to add to your PowerPoint presentation.

Q&A

Q I have a "print shop" publishing program. Can I use the graphics files from that program with PowerPoint?

A Yes, you can, but only if those files are in a format that PowerPoint can understand or can be converted into a format compatible with PowerPoint.

Q This multimedia stuff is fun, but it seems to be too much for the presentation I want to do. Do I really have to insert multimedia files into each and every PowerPoint presentation I create?

A Ah, a content and design question. Well, it depends on what you're presenting and how you want to present it. Multimedia files are there to help you. If you're doing a straightforward presentation on a simple topic, then inserting a lot of multimedia files into your presentation might be overkill. Sometimes a simple photo can be enough, instead of going overboard with a video. So the answer is no, you don't have to insert multimedia files into your PowerPoint presentations all the time. Just use multimedia whenever you think it might be helpful to your presentation.

PART
VI

Hour 22

Creating Web Pages

A new feature in PowerPoint 97 lets you save presentations as World Wide Web documents, which can be posted on a Web site so that people from all over the globe can see your presentation. Although PowerPoint makes converting from a PowerPoint presentation to the standard Internet file format very easy, as a presentation designer, you must be aware of the benefits and limitations of the Internet.

First, the benefits. Your presentation can have active hyperlinks to dynamic content anywhere on the Internet. The presentation audience doesn't have to view your presentation in a linear format, but can quickly jump to topics they're interested in without raising their hands. As a special bonus, your audience can review your presentation at any time, even when the speaker is asleep.

Some of the more advanced PowerPoint features, however, shouldn't be incorporated into Internet presentations. You need to consider limitations on using special effects, large multimedia clips, and complex graphics.

In this hour, you learn how to do the following:

- Build a presentation and post its content on the Web
- Create a presentation home page

- Insert an Internet hyperlink
- Build presentation action buttons
- Save a presentation in the Internet format

Creating an Internet Presentation

For optimum results on the Web, you should design the presentation specifically for the Internet medium. PowerPoint offers special AutoContent Wizard dialog boxes and online PowerPoint templates to help you create Internet-ready presentations. You should then tailor the presentation to fit within the Internet's design limitations, yet take advantage of its benefits.

Using AutoContent Wizard's Internet Templates

The AutoContent Wizard has templates you can use to create Internet presentation files. To generate an Internet-ready presentation, follow these steps:

1. Choose File | New from the menu.
2. Click the Presentations tab.
3. Double-click the AutoContent Wizard icon to start the AutoContent Wizard.
4. Read the introduction screen, and click the Next button.
5. Select a presentation content type (such as Corporate Home Page) and click the Next button.
6. From the Output Options dialog box, select the "Internet, kiosk" option, and then click the Next button.
7. Select the presentation options you want to show on your Internet presentation. Click the Next button when finished.

   By setting the AutoContent Wizard's presentation options, you can customize the presentation pages with the following common Internet conventions. You can use the Internet Options dialog box shown in Figure 22.1 to include the following standard Web page items:

   - Copyright notice on each page and the copyright text
   - The date the presentation was last updated
   - Your e-mail address
8. Click the Finish button to generate your Internet presentation.

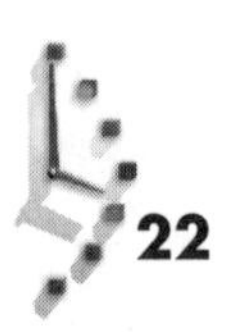

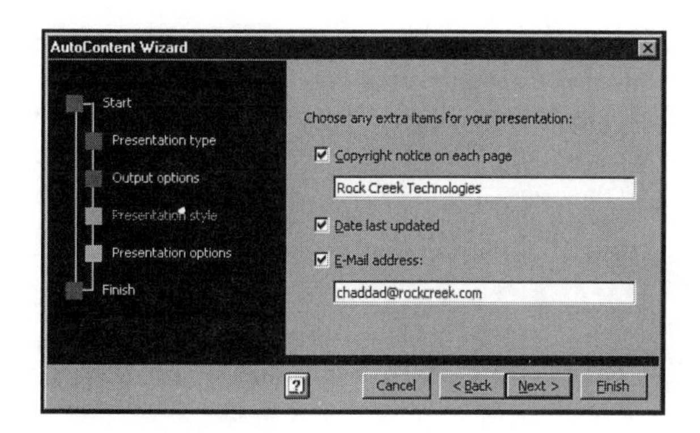

Figure 22.1.
The Internet Options dialog box.

Using the Web Page Templates

Another way to create an Internet presentation is with the template files. PowerPoint 97 includes presentation templates specifically designed to support Internet presentations.

To open an Internet-ready presentation template, follow this sequence:

1. Choose File | New from the menu.
2. Select the Presentations tab.
3. Select a template that has the word *online* as part of the description.
4. Click the OK button to create the presentation.

Reviewing Internet Presentation Basics

The Internet offers unique benefits and limitations for a presentation. For the best results, you should keep a few guidelines in mind when you're creating a presentation that will be viewed on the Internet. The next two sections outline the limitations and benefits you need to remember.

Internet Limitations

Unlike standard presentations that rely on a projection screen or printout, the Internet doesn't provide a consistent canvas for your presentation. You must pay attention to the typical hardware and connection limitations of your target audience. Does your average viewer have a 28.8 modem and 16-color screen display, or a T1 communication line and a true-color screen display? The impact of your presentation depends on how well you target the capabilities of your viewers' machines.

You should estimate the page download times and what presentation hardware is likely to be needed. Using animation, for example, means that your audience must install a special PowerPoint viewer to work with their Web browsers. Most of the time, audience participants don't want to change their machine configurations. Therefore, for most projects, you should stay away from animation and large multimedia files. The use of sound, another effective presentation component, depends on an active sound card. Sound cards are a rarity in the corporate and educational worlds, so you should avoid using sound in your Internet presentations.

JUST A MINUTE

Multimedia items make computer files larger, and the more multimedia, the larger the file. The larger the file, the longer the download time. Therefore, when creating Web pages, you should try to have some idea who your target audience is and how they will be accessing your Web page(s).

Are you targeting the computer-savvy folks who create games or graphics and have the most up-to-date equipment, including a fast modem or Internet connection? If so, go ahead and throw in some really cool multimedia stuff to attract their attention. They probably won't give your page a second look without it.

If, on the other hand, your target audience is Joe and Jane America, who might be connecting with a much slower modem, keep the graphics and other multimedia stuff to a minimum. If the page takes too long to download, Joe and Jane will just go somewhere else without ever seeing your cool Web page.

Internet Benefits

The most compelling benefit of the Internet is being able to gather knowledge from resources around the world. You can greatly enhance your presentation by supplying links to other relevant Internet resources. For example, a presentation on sports cars can have links to major car magazine reviews, company fact sheets, and where to find those hard-to-find parts.

Also, a Web presentation can be more dynamic than an auditorium demonstration because it's not constrained by the one-way dialogue usually associated with standard presentations. On the Internet, the audience is encouraged to interact with the presentation.You can also change the dynamics of the presentation experience; the slide order, for example, could be constructed in a tree hierarchy as opposed to a linear progression.

Adding Internet Features

With PowerPoint 97, you can quickly add features to your presentation that are unique to the Internet. Creating a home page, adding hyperlinks to Internet resources, and building action buttons to control the presentation are all tasks you need to learn to build an Internet-ready presentation.

22

Creating a Home Page

A *home page* is an introduction to your presentation. It serves as a table of contents for the presentation, providing navigation links to the important components. A home page should contain only the main items of interest, so try to keep the home page list of topics as short as possible. I'd suggest four or five main topic items, at most, so that the screen doesn't get too cluttered. To create a home page for your Internet presentation, follow these steps:

1. Click the Slide Sorter View button.
2. Select the slides you want to include on the home page (hold down the Ctrl key and click on the slides you're selecting).
3. Click the Summary Slide button on the Slide Sorter toolbar to create the summary slides. (See Figure 22.2.)
4. After the summary slides have been generated, customize the titles.

Figure 22.2.
Creating the summary slides.

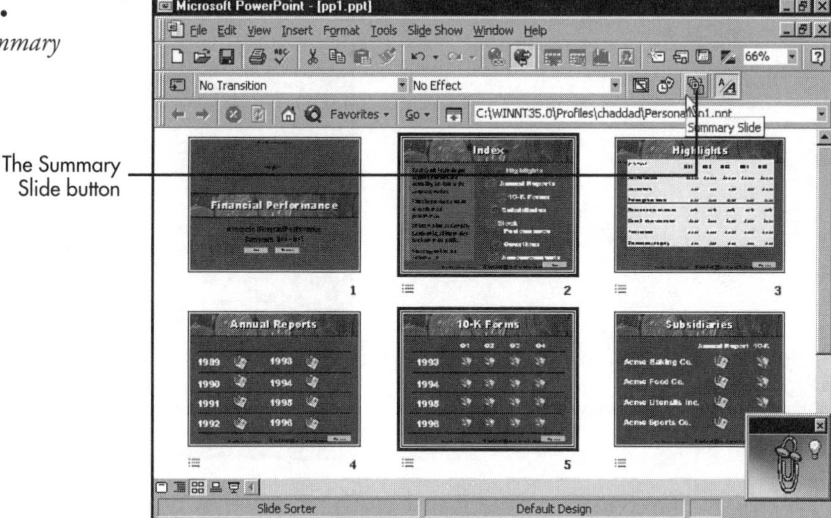

TIME SAVER

If you include information from several slides in the home page list, more than one summary slide might be generated. Because Internet browsers let viewers scroll the presentation screen, you might want to combine the separate summary screens into one long slide.

Hyperlinking to Presentation Resources

A *hyperlink* is a connection between two locations; your presentation audience can use hyperlinks to guide them to other resources, such as other presentation slides, Internet pages, or even computer files.

Creating a hyperlink is very simple; just follow these steps:

1. Select a presentation item to associate with the hyperlink.
2. Choose Slide Show | Action Settings from the menu or click the Insert Hyperlink button on the standard toolbar.
3. Select the "Hyperlink to" radio button.
4. Choose the type of resource that the hyperlink should point to. (See Figure 22.3.)
5. When you're finished creating hyperlinks, click OK.

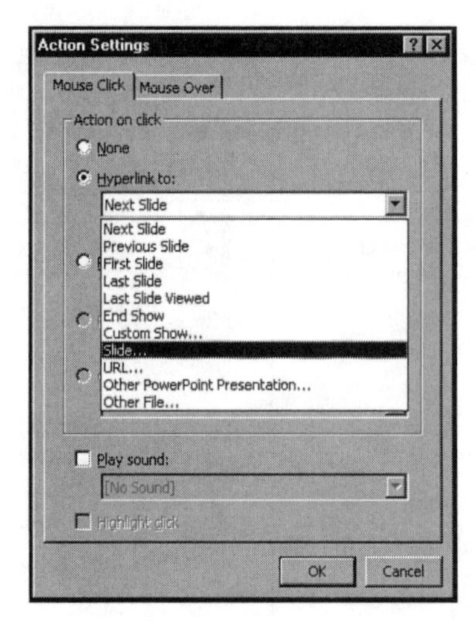

Figure 22.3.
The Action Settings dialog box.

The hyperlinks can point to three types of resources:

- Presentation slides
- Internet resources
- Office 97 files

Slides

A hyperlink can point to an existing presentation slide. In the Action Settings dialog box, you can select the self-explanatory Next Slide, Previous Slide, First Slide, Last Slide, and Last Slide Viewed options to supply basic navigation for your viewers.

TIME SAVER

Although you could incorporate basic navigation links in your presentation pages, don't. PowerPoint 97 automatically adds these basic navigation controls when the Internet HTML files are generated: First Slide, Previous Slide, Next Slide, and Last Slide.

NEW TERM *HTML*, which stands for *HyperText Markup Language*, is a way of marking a plain-text document so that it can be viewed on the Web, by any type of computer, anywhere in the world. All documents published on the Web must have an .HTM or .HTML extension.

Using the Slide option gives your viewers a hyperlink jump to any slide in the presentation. After choosing this option, the Hyperlink to Slide dialog box opens. Simply select the target slide, and click the OK button.

The Custom Show option, new to PowerPoint 97, lets you create a presentation within a presentation. Instead of creating several presentations that reproduce the same slides, you have the option of grouping slides into short segments so your viewers can jump between the grouped slides. Refer back to Hour 10, "Adding Pizzazz to a Slide Show," if you need a refresher on custom slide shows.

The powerful End Show option creates a hyperlink that terminates the slide show.

Internet Resources

The most common hyperlink destination added to Internet presentations is the URL hyperlink. A *URL* (*uniform resource locator*) is the unique address for an Internet resource. When possible, type the full path to the resource so that there are no name conflicts if the presentation is moved to another location. For example, `http://www.mcp.com/books` is the full path that points to the main index document for the books directory on Macmillan Computer Publishing's server.

NEW TERM Most directories have a main, or starting, document called INDEX.HTM that opens when you type in the directory address, as in the preceding example. Therefore, this document is typically referred to as the *index document.* If you want to see a different document, you can either click a link to the document or type in the document's name. For example, if I wanted to see the PowerPoint document in the books directory, I would type `http://www.mcp.com/books/PowerPoint.htm`.

To add an Internet resource, select the URL listbox option from the Action Settings dialog box.

If your hyperlink destination needs to be modified, PowerPoint 97 gives you an easy way to edit the information—just right-click on the hyperlink object and choose Hyperlink | Edit Hyperlink from the menu that pops up. Figure 22.4 shows the dialog box that's displayed.

You can then modify the resource name, resource location, and relative path option, or remove the link entirely.

TIME SAVER

The URL must be typed exactly as it appears in the address box for the page. URL addresses are also case sensitive, so here's one way to get the address absolutely correct:

1. Using your Web browser, go to the page you want to link to.
2. Click once in the address box (to select the entire address).
3. Press the Ctrl+C key combination to copy the address.
4. Switch to PowerPoint and open the Edit Hyperlink dialog box.
5. Click in the "Link to file or URL" box and press Ctrl+V to paste the address in.

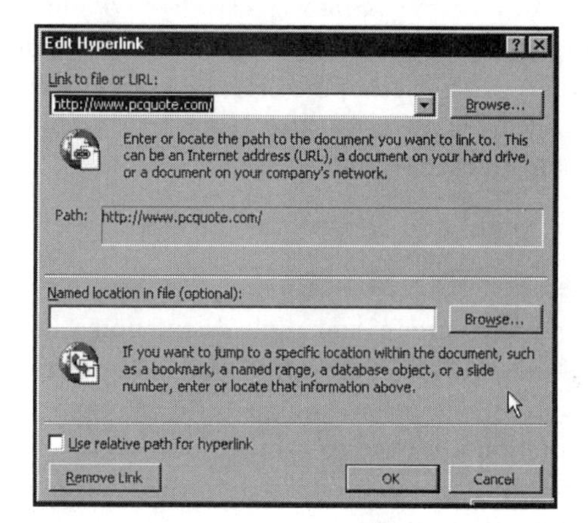

Figure 22.4.
The Edit Hyperlink dialog box.

Office 97 Files

PowerPoint 97 allows you to go outside the application and link to other Office 97 files. For example, a hyperlink to an Excel spreadsheet launches the Excel application and displays the spreadsheet document. To supply hyperlinks to Office 97 documents, select the Other File option in the Action Settings dialog box. This selection opens the Hyperlink to Other File dialog box, shown in Figure 22.5, so you can browse the file system and select the appropriate document.

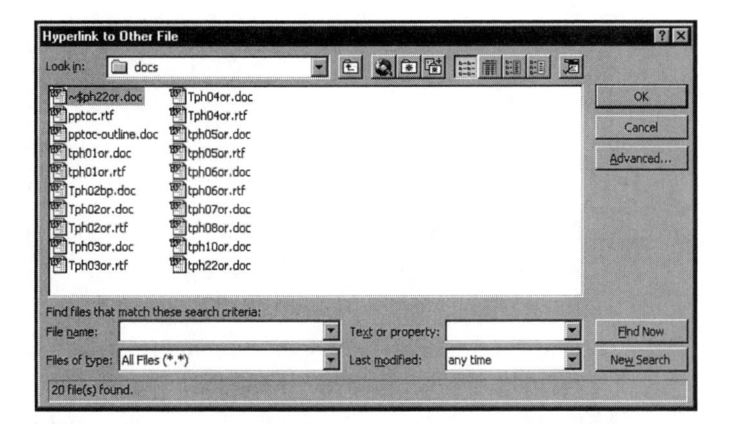

Figure 22.5.
Adding a file hyperlink.

TIME SAVER

Hyperlinks aren't restricted to just Office 97 files. Any document type that's registered with Windows can be chosen to successfully launch a helper application so you can view the document.

In PowerPoint, you can also "chain" presentations together by using the Other PowerPoint Presentation option. For example, you might have two presentations: Presentation A, which is in landscape orientation, and Presentation B, which is in portrait orientation. You could use the hyperlink options to go from slide 2 of Presentation A to slide 1 of Presentation B, and then move to slide 3 of Presentation A.

Using Action Buttons: Onscreen Controls

You can supply action buttons to help your viewers find useful features. When a user clicks an action button, PowerPoint performs a particular action. There are standard icon images that represent common functions or features, or you can create your own custom button image. Here's a list of some common action buttons:

Custom
Home
Help
Information
Back or Previous
Forward or Next
Beginning
End

Return
Document
Sound
Movie

To place an action button on your presentation slide, follow these steps:

1. Choose Slide Show | Action Buttons from the menu to open the button selection window shown in Figure 22.6.
2. Select the button you want to add.
3. Drag the mouse and create the button, just as though you were drawing an AutoShape.
4. Customize the Action Settings dialog box that pops up.
5. Click OK to finalize the action button.

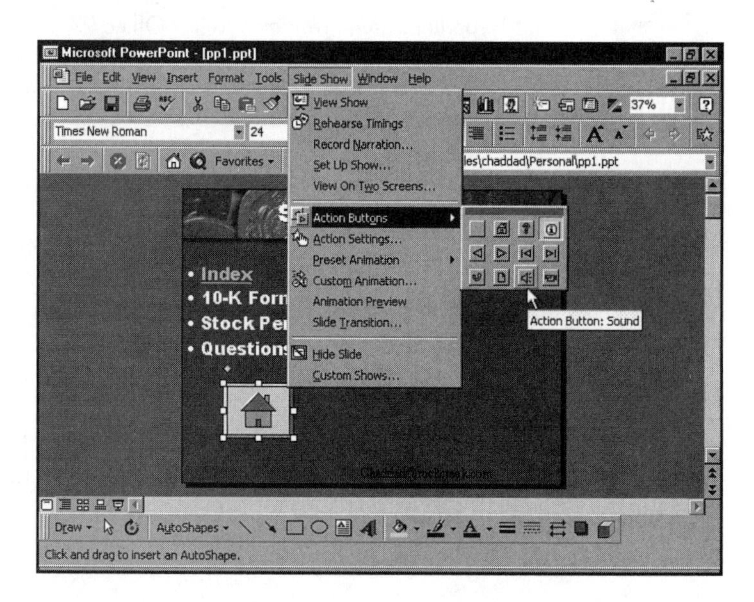

Figure 22.6.
Selecting action buttons.

The custom button usually requires some text to describe its function. Simply select the button after you have created it and type the text object to be overlaid on top of the button object. Refer to Hour 12, "Drawing Shapes in PowerPoint," for a refresher on working with AutoShapes.

JUST A MINUTE

Action buttons are AutoShapes and can be formatted and customized just like any of the other PowerPoint 97 AutoShapes.

Saving a Presentation in Internet Format

Before posting the presentation on the Internet, you must first convert the PowerPoint presentation file into the appropriate format. An Internet presentation is a set of HTML and graphics files that can be viewed by any graphical Web browser. PowerPoint 97 has an Internet Assistant that transforms the standard presentation into an Internet format.

Using the Internet Assistant

The Internet Assistant converts your presentation into Internet format. A series of Wizard windows are displayed so you can fine-tune your presentation. To generate Internet presentation files, just choose File | Save As HTML from the menu and follow the steps in the Wizard.

JUST A MINUTE

You must include the Web Page Authoring option during the installation of PowerPoint 97 to have access to these options.

These six options, explained in the following sections, must be defined to create an Internet presentation:

- Layout Selection
- Graphic Type
- Graphic Size
- Information Page
- Colors and Buttons
- Layout Options

Layout Selection

If you have previously generated an Internet presentation, you might want to reuse a saved layout. After you've selected the appropriate layout, the Wizard gives you the opportunity to review the options before generating the HTML files. The first decision is selecting a page style, either standard or browser frames.

Most Internet users prefer the standard format. Browser frames still aren't easy for most people to use.

Graphic Type

Use the Graphic Type dialog box to define the type of graphic files that the Internet Assistant creates. You have three choices in the Wizard:

- GIF—graphics interchange format
- JPEG—compressed file format
- PowerPoint animation

Choose GIF if the presentation contains mostly textual information and few images. For highly graphical presentations, choose JPEG to make the presentation run more quickly. With JPEG, you can select the compression value for the digital image files. Higher JPEG compression values result in high-quality images, but they take up a considerable amount of space. Lower compression values create smaller graphic files, but the images won't display with the same clarity.

If you select PowerPoint animation, the Internet presentation will include the full animation, transitions, and multimedia effects of the PC original.

CAUTION

> Using PowerPoint animation requires your audience members to install the PowerPoint Animation Player on their computers. Most users don't want to install the viewer. If the viewer is required, your audience might skip the presentation.

Graphic Size

The Graphic Size dialog box is used to indicate the size of the target monitor screen. You should set the values with your target audience in mind.

Selecting higher monitor resolution values creates larger graphical images that might not display properly on low-resolution machines. Higher resolution files are also larger in size and take more time to download. Choose 640×480 unless you're sure that all your audience members have better hardware.

The width of the graphic defines the amount of screen space the actual presentation display will take up. To get a good display, select three quarters or one half of the screen size. If you have small font sizes in your presentation, you should use the three quarters or full screen option, or the text won't be readable.

Information Page

Use the Wizard's information page to supply information for customizing your presentation *index page*, which is the entry point of the presentation. Think of the information page as the announcer for your presentation; typically, it has the contents listed in Table 22.1.

Table 22.1. Information page options.

Option	Description
E-Mail Address	The e-mail address of the presentation speaker
Home Page Address	The address of the home page for the site hosting the presentation.
Other Information	Other information that's relevant to the presentation contents
Download original presentation	A link to the original PowerPoint presentation file
Internet Explorer download button	A self-promoting button for Microsoft's Internet Explorer

Colors and Buttons

You can also use options in the Wizard to select page colors and button images. You can choose to either use the default browser values or override the values with a custom color scheme. Most of the time, you should use a custom scheme to preserve the unique "look" of your presentation. You can define custom colors for the following:

- Background
- Text
- Link
- Visited

Checking the Transparent Buttons option allows the button to be displayed in the screen's background color; otherwise, the button is displayed in gray.

The next window shows the button styles; you have four to choose from, shown in Figure 22.7. Pick a motif that's appropriate for your presentation.

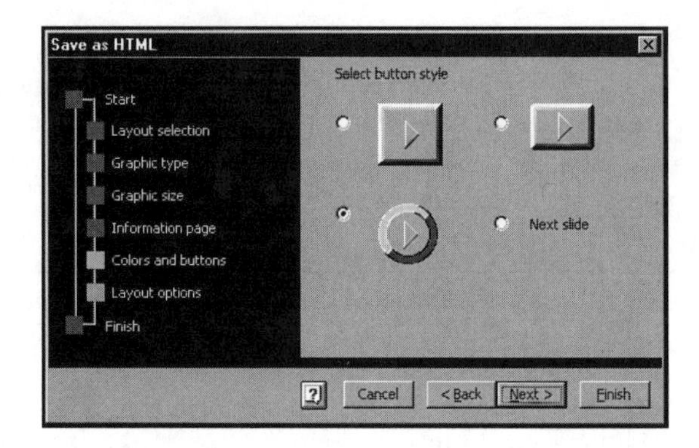

Figure 22.7.
Selecting a button style.

Layout Options

In the Layout Options dialog box, you choose the location for navigation buttons. You can specify that the navigation buttons should be located on the top, bottom, right, or left side of the presentation window. You can also indicate whether the speaker's notes should be included in the Internet presentation.

Last, the Internet Assistant asks for a location to store the generated PowerPoint presentation. Any available directory path is fine; you can always change it later.

CAUTION

The directory must exist before PowerPoint will create the Internet presentation. Click the Browse button and create a new folder if the target location directory doesn't currently exist.

After you click the Finish button, PowerPoint asks whether you want to permanently save the settings. Enter a layout template name and click Save to create a new layout, or click Don't Save to discard the settings. In both cases, the HTML presentation is generated. The Internet Assistant creates an index page for the presentation and an HTML document for every slide.

Checking Your Internet Presentation

Now that you've created your first Internet presentation, check out the results. You can open your Web browser directly from PowerPoint 97 and view the presentation. The PowerPoint Web toolbar has the basic commands to get you "wired." Accessing the Internet presentation is as easy as opening a regular presentation file.

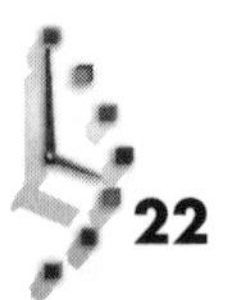

Just a Minute

It's always a good idea to test your presentation from a remote machine. Sometimes document and URL links work only if they're accessed from the local machine, so you need to find and fix improperly formatted links.

Using the Web Toolbar

The Web toolbar has the following basic commands for using the Web browser installed on your machine:

Back/Next
Stop
Reload
Home
Start Page
Search the Web
Favorites
Go
Show Only Web Toolbar
Location (URL)

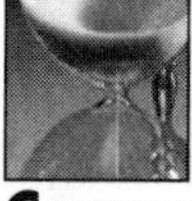

Caution

The Web toolbar works best with Internet Explorer 3.0. To start the Internet Explorer browser, the default application for HTML documents should be Internet Explorer.

Figure 22.8 shows an undocked Web toolbar.

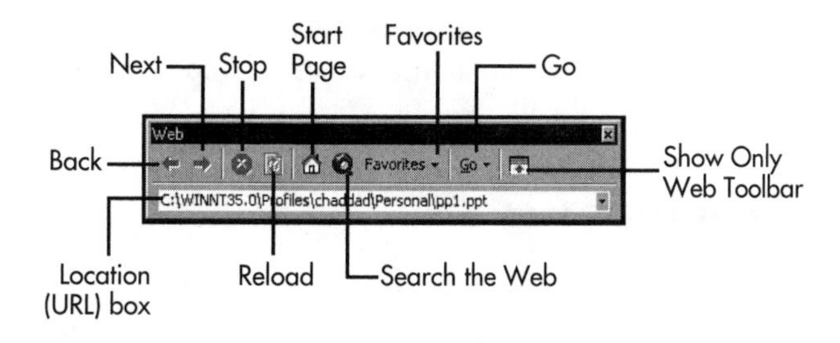

Figure 22.8.
The Web toolbar.

Accessing the Internet

Viewing an Internet presentation has never been easier. Once you have posted the presentation, simply enter the presentation address, and your presentation will be displayed in live HTML format. To view a presentation, follow these steps:

1. Click the Web Toolbar button on the standard toolbar or choose View | Toolbars | Web from the menu to display the Web toolbar.
2. On the Web toolbar, choose Go | Open to display the Open Internet Address dialog box.
3. Enter the Internet address for the presentation. If the presentation was saved to a local machine, you can simply browse to the destination directory. The filename to choose will be Index or Index.htm, depending on whether you've enabled file extension viewing.
4. Click the OK button.

JUST A MINUTE

Remote Internet addresses should begin with `http://`, and local addresses should begin with the drive designation, such as `C:\`.

Summary

With PowerPoint 97, you can display your presentation on the Internet. The presentation is converted into industry-standard HTML pages and graphics files that can be posted on the World Wide Web. Creating an Internet presentation is useful if the audience can't actually make it to the conference room or auditorium. Even though any presentation can be saved in HTML format, it's best to create one from scratch that will be Internet-ready from the start. After reading the material in this hour, you should be familiar with the steps for creating, saving, and viewing an Internet presentation. Test what you've learned, and let me know your presentation's address!

Workshop

Since there was so much information in this hour, you get a little break in the "Test What You've Learned" section. Just six easy steps, and you're on your way to the "Q&A" section. If all this discussion of Web page design has whetted your appetite for more information, check out *Laura Lemay's Teach Yourself HTML 3.2 in 7 Days* (Sams.net Publishing). This book is a fantastic reference and will get you well on your way to publishing superior Web pages.

Test What You've Learned

1. Create an Internet-ready presentation by using the AutoContent Wizard.
2. Add a home page.
3. Add a hyperlink from the home page to `http://www.mcp.com`.
4. Add an action button from the home page to an external document providing background information.
5. Save the presentation as `Hour 22 TWYL`.
6. View the presentation, and then close it.

Q&A

Q How do I post the presentation on my Web site?

A The process varies based on your particular Web server. You can usually post Web pages through your Internet Service Provider (ISP). Or, if you're creating a company Web page, ask your Web site administrator for details. Although exact procedures vary among the options, the general procedure is to copy all the files for the site to the Web space. If you're copying to a company server, you need rights to the network directories. Then, just use Windows Explorer to copy the files. If you're copying to an Internet Service Provider or some other remote computer, you usually use an FTP client to copy the files.

Q Can I move a PowerPoint Internet presentation after it's been generated?

A Yes. Just make sure that any external links use the full path to their location.

Q Can I find out who has viewed my presentation?

A You can't really see "who" has viewed your Web page, but you can find out what other computers have visited your site. Ask the Webmaster or Web site administrator to give you a report listing the visitors to the presentation pages. However, the report might supply only IP (Internet provider) addresses or machine names.

Q Can I post a quiz at the end of my presentation to check whether someone actually understood the material?

A Not by using just PowerPoint. You'll have to call in the experts to build an online data-entry form.

Q Can I add other program components to an Internet presentation?

A No, you can't directly add Java applets, JavaScript, VBScript, or ActiveX controls. You'll have to import the HTML presentation pages into an HTML editor to spruce them up.

PART VI

Hour 23

Using and Creating Macros to Automate Tasks

The true power of computers lies in their ability to automate work that would otherwise have to be done by people. Even though PowerPoint 97 embodies years of user feedback and incorporates many time-saving features, sometimes the developers at Microsoft didn't include a feature or shortcut that you'd find useful. What they did include with PowerPoint, however, is a powerful programming language. PowerPoint 97 contains Visual Basic for Applications (VBA), a subset of the Visual Basic programming language. With VBA, you can create macros that go way beyond mere keystroke recording. In fact, by using the language, macro programmers can now work with many of PowerPoint 97's internal components.

With VBA, you can teach PowerPoint 97 to automatically perform many routine tasks at the click of a toolbar button. Here are a few common operations that could be automated:

- Adding several new slides to a presentation
- Inserting a title slide and title text
- Turning bullets on and off
- Creating or deleting a custom show
- Manipulating command bars
- Copying slides between presentation
- Printing a presentation
- Naming a slide
- Opening a Web site

This hour covers the features available in the PowerPoint 97 Macro dialog box and also introduces you to the Visual Basic Editor (VBE). After you have successfully created your first macro scripts, you might want to learn more about the VBA programming capabilities by reading other books devoted solely to that topic.

Macro Command Central

The Macro dialog box is a centralized location for managing your presentation macros. You can view, run, edit, step into, create, or delete macros. To view all the macros in your presentation, open the Macro dialog box by choosing Tools | Macro | Macros from the main menu. Or, you can quickly open the Macro dialog box, shown in Figure 23.1, by pressing Alt+F8 while you're in any presentation view (Slide, Outline, Slide Sorter, or Notes Page).

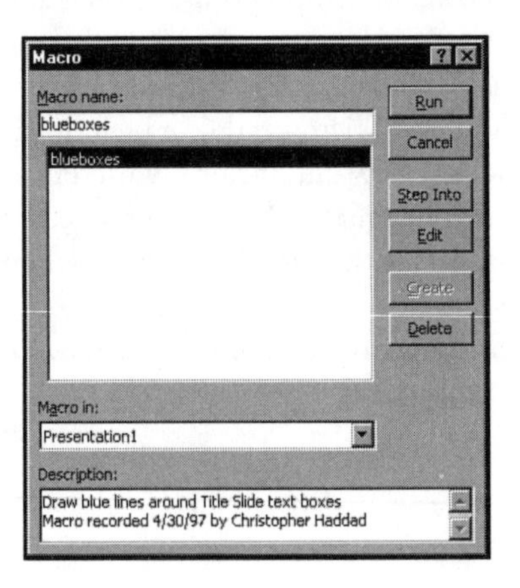

Figure 23.1.
The Macro dialog box.

Creating Macros

If you have opened a blank presentation without selecting any special templates, the Macro dialog box doesn't list any macros. PowerPoint 97 has three methods you can use to add macros to a presentation file:

- You can record a macro that contains keystroke, mouse movements, and menu commands.
- You can open a presentation from a macro template.
- You can directly code or copy VB macro subroutines.

Copying existing macros from sample code files is a quick way to become familiar with the power and flexibility of the Visual Basic for Applications language. The section "Finding More Macro Information" later in this chapter will teach you the steps for finding a wealth of sample code available from the Microsoft Web site. Also, rudimentary details about coding and testing VB macros are explained in the "Building Power Macros" section later in this chapter.

Macros can be stored in templates or presentation files and copied into your existing presentation. To use template macros in a presentation, you should create the presentation from the pre-existing template. Follow these steps to embed template macros in your presentation:

1. Choose File | New from the menu.
2. Select the template containing the macros you want to use.
3. Click OK.

If you have already built slides that you want to include in the new presentation, add them to the newly created presentation by choosing Insert | Slides from Files from the menu.

CAUTION

> When you apply a template to an existing presentation, the macros in the template aren't added to the presentation.

The easiest way to create a macro is to record the keystrokes as you replicate the task that should be automated. To record a new macro, follow these steps:

1. Choose Tools | Macro | Record New Macro from the menu to open the Record Macro dialog box. (See Figure 23.2.)

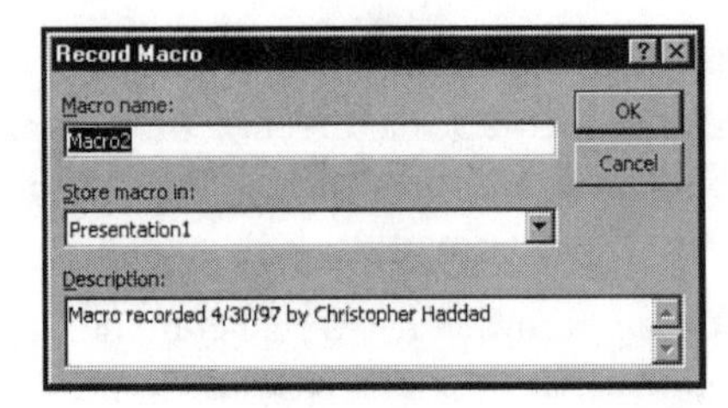

Figure 23.2.
The Record Macro dialog box.

2. Enter information in the "Macro name" and "Description" text boxes to name the macro and give a short explanation of its purpose.
3. The information in the "Store macro in" field should indicate which presentation file will contain the macro. You can select the current presentation or select "All open presentations" from the drop-down list to apply the macro to presentations that are currently open.
4. Click OK to start recording.
5. Execute the keystrokes or commands.
6. Click the Stop Recording button. (See Figure 23.3.)

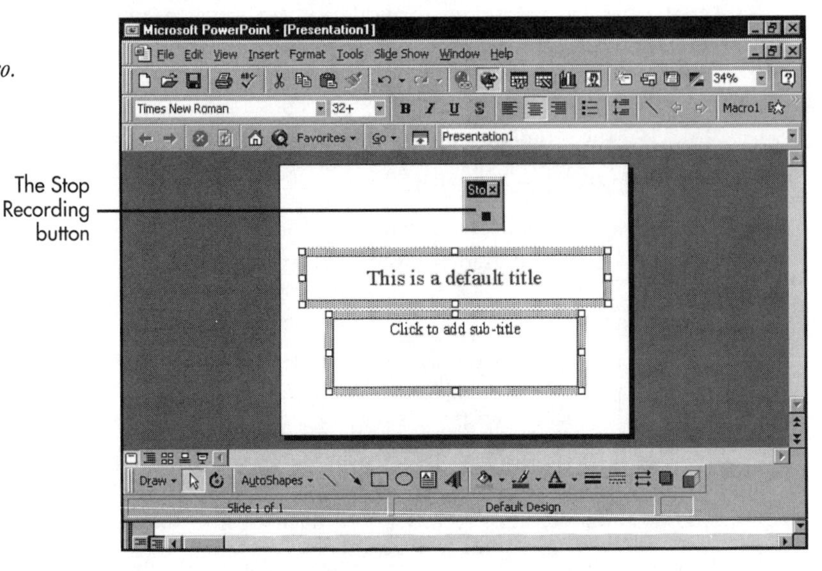

Figure 23.3.
Recording the macro.

CAUTION

PowerPoint doesn't actually record keystrokes in a macro. It analyzes the keystrokes and actions in an operation and converts them into the appropriate VBA commands. If there isn't a corresponding VBA command for the operation, the macro won't work as you intended. For example, you can't modify the Tools | Options dialog box by using a macro because there's no VBA command to do that.

Assigning Macros to Toolbars

To quickly access a PowerPoint macro, attach it to a button on either a built-in or custom toolbar. You can then run the macro by clicking the toolbar button. To add a macro to a toolbar, follow these steps:

1. Display the toolbar where you want to add the macro button.
2. Choose Tools | Customize to open the Customize dialog box.
3. Click the Commands tab and select the Macros category in the Categories box. (See Figure 23.4.)

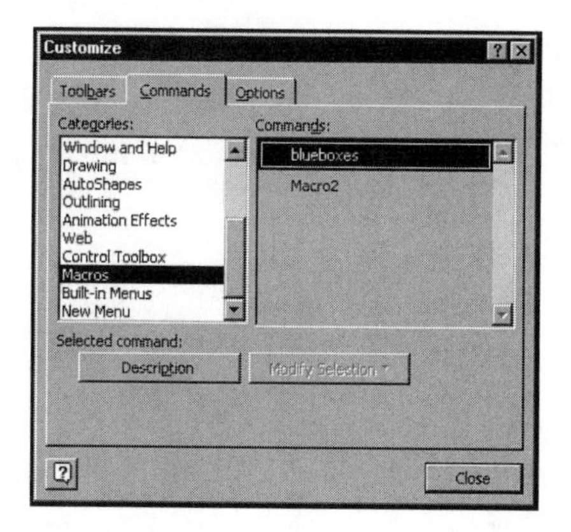

Figure 23.4.
Assigning a macro to a toolbar button.

4. Drag the macro name to the toolbar where you want the macro button.

Once you have created a button, you can customize its attributes by selecting Change Button Image from the Modify Selection drop-down list shown in Figure 23.5.

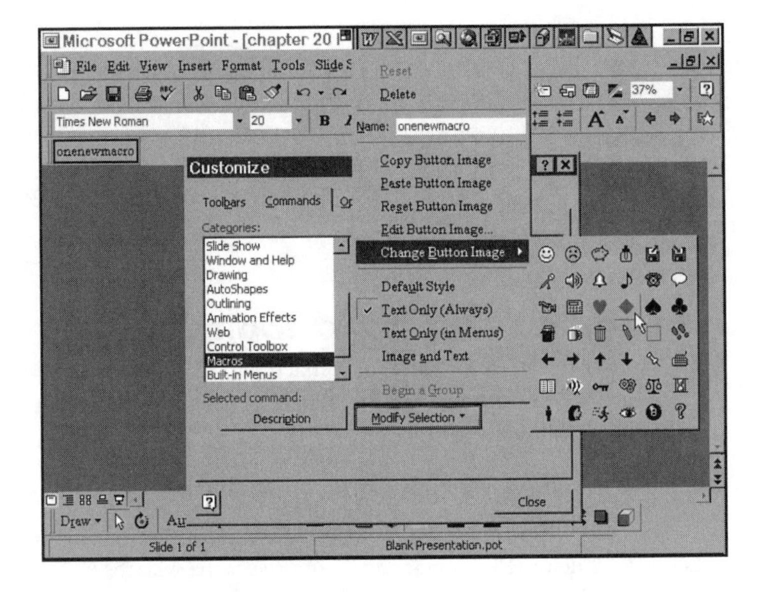

Figure 23.5.
Modifying a macro button's attributes.

To remove a macro toolbar button, follow these steps:

1. Right-click on the macro button.
2. Choose Customize from the properties list that pops up.
3. Drag the button off the toolbar into the presentation window to remove the button from the toolbar.

Running a Macro

After you have created a macro, you can run it at any time. *Running a macro* means executing the programming commands within the macro. To run a PowerPoint macro, click the macro's toolbar button or follow these steps:

1. Choose Tools | Macro | Macros from the main menu.
2. Enter the name of the macro you want to run in the "Macro name" box or select the macro from the list.
3. Click the Run button.

The macro then runs and performs its task.

TIME SAVER

To stop a macro that's running, press Ctrl+Break. This action interrupts the macro.

23

Editing Macros

After recording a macro, PowerPoint tries to reduce the sequence of recorded PowerPoint commands to a series of VBA commands that would have the same effect. However, sometimes this optimization can modify what the macro is meant to do. For example, I recorded a macro that had five Page Down keystrokes. PowerPoint 97 rewrote my macro to state that the macro should always jump to slide five. To create a macro that would move down five slides, you would have to use the Visual Basic Editor to edit the default macro and make it work the way you intended.

Follow these steps to edit a specific macro:

1. Choose Tools | Macro | Macros from the menu.
2. Enter the name of the macro to edit in the "Macro name" box.
3. Click Edit.

The Visual Basic Editor is then launched, with the edit cursor positioned at the macro you chose. You can now edit the macro commands to modify how it works.

To start the macro editor at any time and view the macro commands, you can also simply press Alt+F11. Follow these steps to edit a specific macro:

1. Choose View | Code from the VBA menu to open the VBA code window containing the macros.
2. Select the macro name from the drop-down list on the right in the code window.

TIME SAVER

The Visual Basic Editor has a different Help file than PowerPoint does. To view VBE's Help file, choose Help | Contents and Index from the Visual Basic menu.

Stepping into Macros

The Step Into button on the Macro dialog box runs the macro in debug mode. First, the Visual Basic Editor is launched, with the cursor placed at the first line of the macro. You can then walk through the code line-by-line by choosing Debug | Step Into from the menu or by pressing the F8 key. Become familiar with the Debug submenu commands because they will allow you to navigate through the VBA code quickly.

NEW TERM

Debug is a software development term that means you're watching the lines of code execute in an attempt to find programming errors.

Deleting Macros

In PowerPoint 97, you can also remove unused macros. If you frequently use pre-existing macro templates, you might want to delete the unused macros to conserve memory resources. Here's how to delete a macro:

1. Choose Tools | Macro | Macros from the menu.
2. Highlight the macro you want to delete.
3. Click the Delete button.

The macro is then deleted from the presentation file.

Building Power Macros: The Visual Basic Editor

By including the Visual Basic Editor (VBE), PowerPoint 97 gives you a built-in programming environment with a wealth of features. The editor is a subset of the popular Visual Basic language. Use the editor to write, debug, and manage macro script code. Also, the editor has many useful windows that help you explore the VBA language.

You can open the editor, shown in Figure 23.6, in one of two ways:

- Choose Tools | Macro | Visual Basic Editor from the main menu.

  or

- Press Alt+F11 while you're in any view.

Figure 23.6.
The Visual Basic Editor.

Microsoft Visual Basic - aaa.ppt [design] - [Module1 (Code)]

File Edit View Insert Format Debug Run Tools Window Help

(General) blueboxes

```
    ActiveWindow.Selection.ShapeRange.TextFrame.TextRange.Characters(Start
    With ActiveWindow.Selection.TextRange
        .Text = "This is a default title"
        With .Font
            .Name = "Times New Roman"
            .Size = 44
            .Bold = msoFalse
            .Italic = msoFalse
            .Underline = msoFalse
            .Shadow = msoFalse
            .Emboss = msoFalse
            .BaselineOffset = 0
            .AutoRotateNumbers = msoFalse
            .Color.SchemeColor = ppAccent1
        End With
    End With
End Sub
Sub Macro2()
'
' Macro recorded 4/30/97 by Christopher Haddad
'
End Sub
```

There are entire books that focus on Visual Basic's impressive capabilities, but in the following sections, I'll try to highlight just the basic features you need to create cool macros.

Adding Sample Macros

You can easily cut-and-paste or drag-and-drop sample code into a macro module. Open the Visual Basic Editor and choose View | Code from the menu or press F7 to display the code editor window. After you copy or add VBA code to the window, the macros are automatically displayed and available in PowerPoint's Macro dialog box.

Debugging Macros

As mentioned previously, the ability to debug a macro script is the lifeblood of the programming experience. Seeing the lines of executing script code lets you quickly spot the problem areas. To debug a macro, you must either step through the code from the beginning or set a *breakpoint*, which is a location in the macro where the script execution should stop. When you step through the code, each macro line is executed separately. When a line has finished running, control is returned to the VBE code window so that you can view the values of variables and determine where the problems are.

To set a breakpoint, follow these steps:

1. Open the code window by choosing View | Code from the menu.
2. Place the cursor on the line where the macro execution should stop.
3. Choose Debug | Toggle Breakpoint from the menu or press F9.

A code line with a breakpoint is displayed in a different color, and you can see a breakpoint "dot" to the left of the line. Figure 23.7 shows a breakpoint in a text-range `Select` statement.

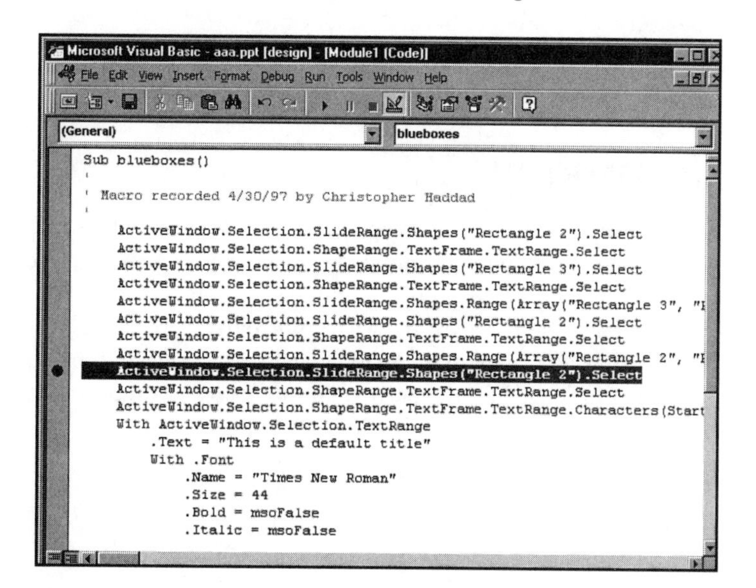

Figure 23.7.
A macro breakpoint.

When you run the macro, PowerPoint executes the lines until it reaches the breakpoint. When it does, the macro stops and the VBE window is displayed with the cursor at the breakpoint line. You can then step through the code and investigate the script's operation.

Finding More Macro Information

The Visual Basic Help files and Object Browser are useful reference sources; they can give you insight into the objects that macro subroutines can work with.

To find the latest information about using Visual Basic for Applications with PowerPoint 97, check out the Microsoft Knowledge Base on the Web. It has sample code for common automation tasks and useful tips and tricks that can save you time when programming macros. To find the Knowledge Base, just follow these steps:

1. Point your browser to `http://www.microsoft.com/kb`.
2. Set the search step options to Any Product and the number of matches to 100.
3. Select the "Search the article text" and "Show titles only" radio buttons.
4. Enter `PPT97 AND VBA` for the search phrase.
5. Click the Begin Search button.

At the time this chapter was written, the search returned 95 matches. Many items pointed to valuable sample code written by Microsoft experts.

The following are other useful keywords to search on:

- macros
- vbe
- kbmacro
- kbprg
- PowerPoint

Summary

PowerPoint 97 can be completely customized by adding macros written in the Visual Basic for Application programming language. You can create presentation macros to automate a wide variety of tasks. You might want to invest some time creating macros for tasks you perform often. Macros are also helpful for reducing complex command sequences to a simple button click. Exploring the VBA language and macro capabilities could keep you intellectually challenged for the next twenty-four hours or more.

Workshop

This hour's workshop walk you through creating a simple macro and cover a few commonly asked questions. After you've mastered macros and the Visual Basic Editor, there's no limit to the features you could add to your PowerPoint presentations.

Test What You've Learned

1. Open a blank presentation using the Title Slide AutoLayout.
2. Choose Tools | Macros | Record New Macro to open the Record Macro dialog box.
3. Enter `blueboxes` for the macro name and click OK.
4. Record a PowerPoint macro that uses the following commands in steps 5 and 6.
5. Hold down the Shift key and select both text boxes.
6. Set the border line color to blue.
7. Click the Stop Recording button to end the macro session.
8. Run the blueboxes PowerPoint macro.
9. View the blueboxes VBA source code.
10. Set a breakpoint in the source code.
11. Run the macro again and note that it stops at the breakpoint line.

Q&A

Q I applied a template to my presentation, but no macros are available. What happened?

A Simple—when you apply a template to an existing presentation, the macros in the template aren't added to the presentation. You should open a presentation using the template file, and then insert the slides in the newly created presentation.

Q While recording a macro, I entered the keystrokes out of order. Is there a way to reverse the key after it's typed?

A You must either delete the macro and then record it again, or try to edit the macro in the Visual Basic Editor after the keystroke recording has stopped.

Q My macro doesn't always run properly. What could be wrong?

A The macro might depend on the particular view or active settings to work correctly. The Visual Basic Help files have pages that explain the error message returned by PowerPoint. To consult them, choose Help | Contents and Index from the Visual Basic menu.

Part VI

Hour 24

PowerPoint Power Hour

Whew, you've made it through 23 hours of PowerPoint. What, you haven't had enough yet? Well, during this last hour, you touch on a few of PowerPoint's neat features and learn how to really tweak PowerPoint to work for you. This last hour covers the followings topics:

- AutoCorrect: What it is and how to make it work for you
- Toolbars: How to create your very own special toolbar with only your favorite buttons
- Options: How to get the most from PowerPoint 97
- Hyperlinks: How you can use them in a slide show
- Presentation designs: Some ideas for creating your own custom template

Relax, and go get an espresso (decaf is okay, but just this once). You've come so far—now it's time to put the power into PowerPoint 97.

Using AutoCorrect

You might have noticed something strange happening while you have been creating the slide presentations in the "Test What You've Learned" sections (or maybe not). If you forget to capitalize the first letter of a sentence, it has magically been capitalized for you. If you type *adn*, it magically changes to *and*. Try to type (c) or :) and you get © or ☺ instead. Or have you ever accidentally left the Caps Lock key on and had to go back and retype all the text again? Well, now there's no need to.

PowerPoint now automatically corrects all these common mistakes and more with the IntelliSense of AutoCorrect. Want to know more about this fabulous feature, and all that it will do for you? Just use the following instructions to take a peek at what's going on behind the scenes:

1. Choose Tools | AutoCorrect from the menu to open the AutoCorrect dialog box.
2. Scroll through the "Replace text as you type" list to see everything that can and will be corrected for you as you type. (See Figure 24.1.)
3. Click the OK button when you're finished.

Just a Minute

You're just taking a look right now; you'll be back to customize AutoCorrect in a few moments.

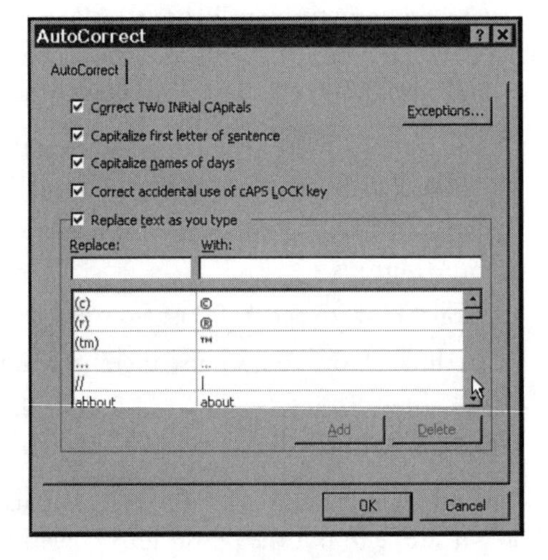

Figure 24.1.
The AutoCorrect dialog box.

You can add entries to AutoCorrect for those frequent typographical mistakes that only you make. I also use the AutoCorrect feature as a kind of typing shorthand to help save time. This

feature comes in handy for me, especially when writing these "Teach Yourself Whatever in 24 Hour" books. I have added unique abbreviations for lengthy or odd words that I need to type over and over again. Figure 24.2 shows me adding my initials that will be replaced with my name in the AutoCorrect dialog box. To add your own AutoCorrect items to the AutoCorrect list, follow these steps:

1. Choose Tools | AutoCorrect from the menu.
2. In the Replace box, type the text you want to replace, such as your initials.
3. In the With box, type the correct text.
4. Click the Add button.
5. Repeat steps 2–4 for each entry you want to add.
6. Click the OK button when you're finished.

24

Figure 24.2.
Adding a personal entry to the AutoCorrect list.

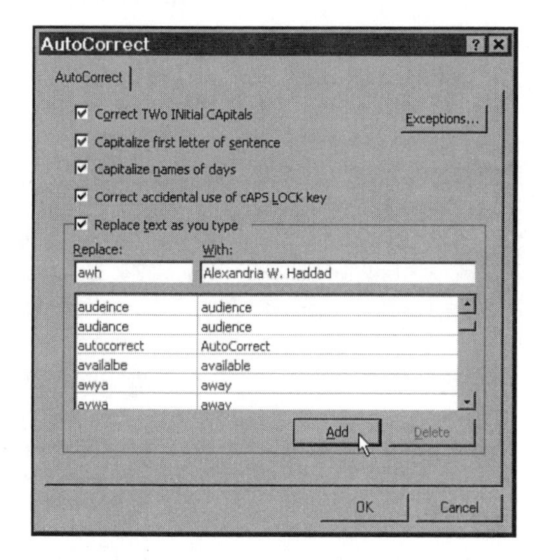

TIME SAVER

When using AutoCorrect as a shorthand tool, make sure you think of unique entries for the Replace option. For example, if your company's name is "Anderson's Naughty Desserts," you wouldn't want the AutoCorrect Replace entry to be `and` because that would be more hindrance than help. A better Replace entry might be `/and/` or something else just as unique that you wouldn't otherwise type.

Although AutoCorrect entries are helpful, there might be a few you don't want to have around. Maybe you type (c) on a daily basis, and don't want the © symbol to keep popping up. To delete an AutoCorrect entry, follow these steps:

1. Choose Tools | AutoCorrect from the menu.
2. Select the entry you want to delete from the "Replace text as you type" list.
3. Click the Delete button.
4. Repeat steps 2 and 3 for each entry you want to delect.
5. Click the OK button when you're done.

You can also turn off any of the other AutoCorrect features, like the "Correct accidental use of cAPS LOCK key" option. To turn off any automatic corrections, follow these steps:

1. Choose Tools | AutoCorrect from the menu.
2. Uncheck any checkboxes you need to.
3. Click the OK button.

JUST A MINUTE

There are some exceptions to the Correct TWo INitial CApitals and the Capitalize First Letter of Sentences options. To see a list of these exceptions, click the Exceptions button. In the AutoCorrect Exceptions dialog box, as shown in Figure 24.3, you can even add your own exceptions.

Figure 24.3.
The AutoCorrect Exceptions dialog box.

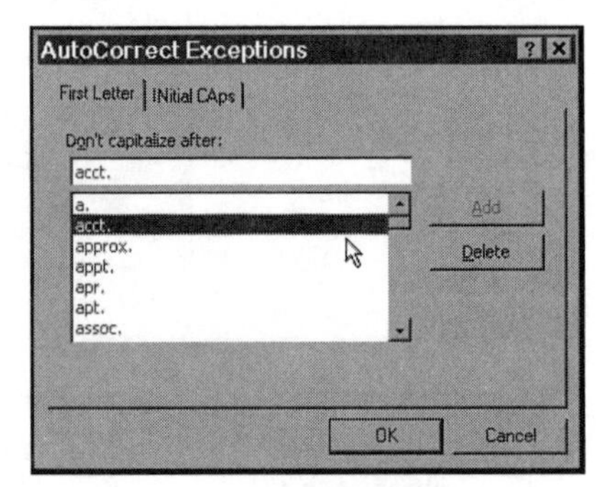

Customizing and Creating Toolbars

So many toolbars, so little screen space. Although PowerPoint comes with several toolbars to choose from, ever wish there was just one toolbar with all your favorite tools on it? Well,

welcome to the wonderful world of PowerPoint. You can create your own toolbar with only those items you use most often, and therefore free up some of that valuable screen space. You can now add menus to toolbars, too! You can even customize any of the existing toolbars (or even the menu bar), if you want.

To create a new custom toolbar, follow these steps:

1. Choose View | Toolbars | Customize from the menu.
2. Click the Toolbars tab of the Customize dialog box.
3. Click the New button.
4. Type a name for the toolbar, such as `My Favorite Tools`, in the New Toolbar dialog box.
5. Click the OK button in the New Toolbar dialog box. The new toolbar is then displayed as a very small floating toolbar.
6. Double-click the title bar of the new toolbar to dock it on the top of the screen, as shown in Figure 24.4. It will be blank, but you'll fill it up with commands soon enough.

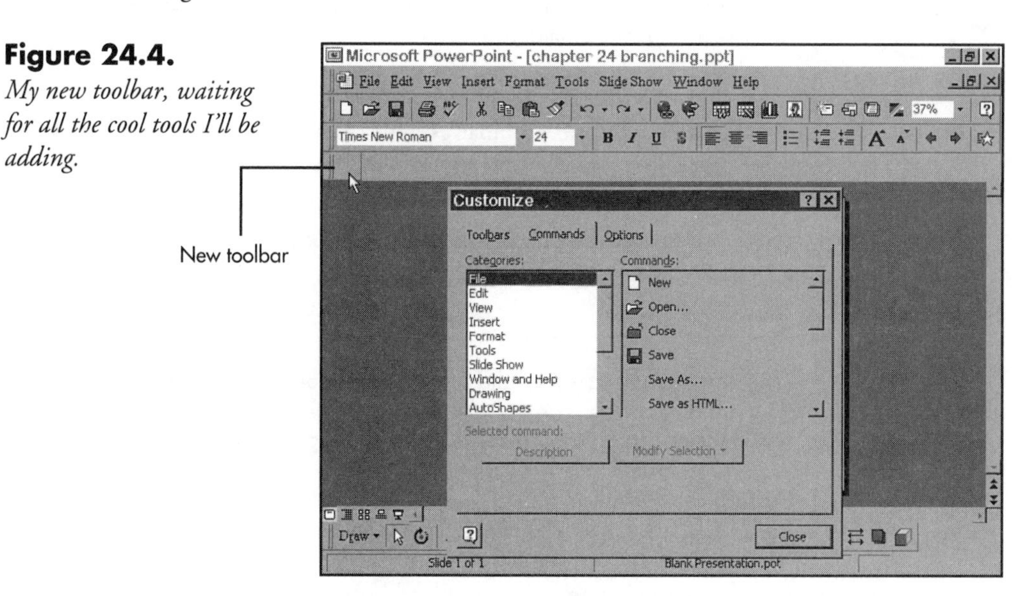

Figure 24.4.
My new toolbar, waiting for all the cool tools I'll be adding.

7. Click the Commands tab. (See Figure 24.5.)

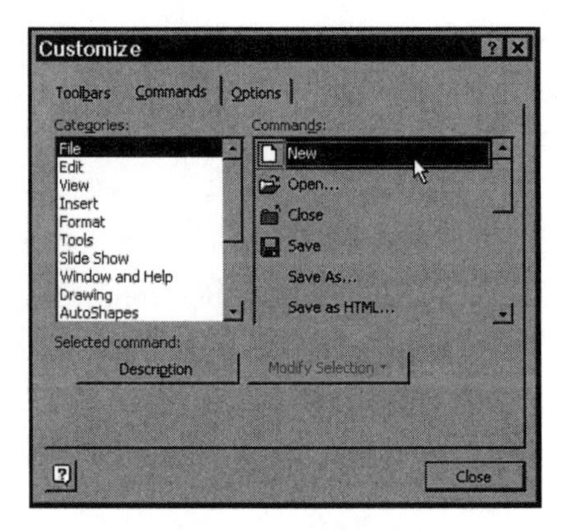

Figure 24.5.
The Commands tab of the Customize dialog box.

8. Select a category from the Categories list.
9. Select a command from the Commands list.

TIME SAVER

If you're not sure what the command does, click the Description button after selecting the command.

10. Drag the command to your new toolbar. A dark I-beam shows where the button will be placed. Release the mouse button when the I-beam is in the position you want.
11. Repeat steps 8–10 to add any other tools you want to the toolbar.
12. Click the Close button when you're finished.

JUST A MINUTE

You can use any category and add as many command buttons as needed to a toolbar. However, keep in mind that a toolbar is supposed to make tasks easier and quicker to perform. If you're spending a lot of time searching through all the buttons on a toolbar, then the toolbar isn't serving its purpose.

To customize an existing toolbar and add command buttons, follow these steps:

1. Choose View | Toolbars | Customize from the menu.
2. Click the Toolbars tab.

3. If the toolbar you want to customize isn't currently displayed, click the checkbox next to the toolbar name to display the appropriate one. A toolbar must be displayed to customize it.
4. Click the Commands tab.
5. Select a category from the Categories list.
6. Select a command from the Commands list.
7. Drag the command to the desired toolbar. A dark I-beam shows where the button will be placed. Release the mouse button when the I-beam is in the position you want.
8. Click the Close button.

To customize an existing toolbar and delete command buttons, follow these steps:

1. Choose View | Toolbars | Customize from the menu.
2. Click the Toolbars tab.
3. If the toolbar you want to customize isn't currently displayed, click the checkbox next to the toolbar name to display the appropriate one.
4. Drag the command button you want to delete off the toolbar. When the mouse pointer has a little × in the lower-right corner, as shown in Figure 24.6, release the mouse to delete the command button.
5. Click the Close button.

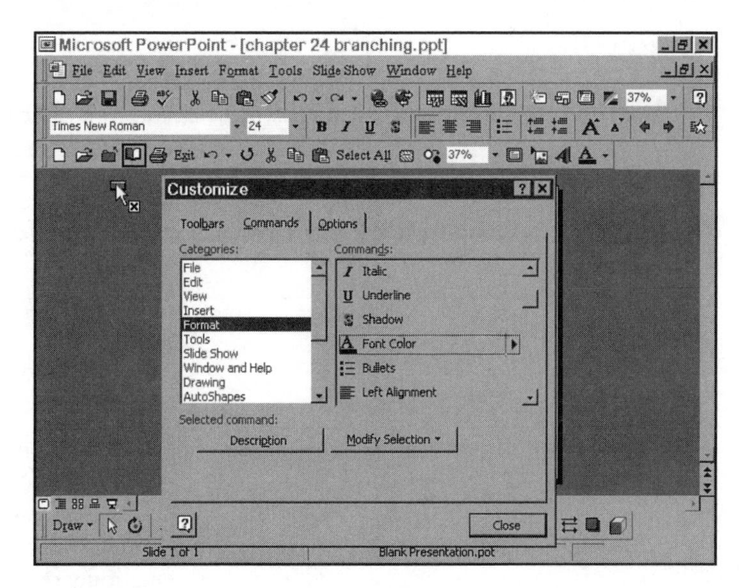

Figure 24.6.
Deleting a toolbar command button.

CAUTION

I strongly suggest just creating your own toolbar and leaving the ones that came with PowerPoint alone (this especially applies to the menu bar). I was recently playing around and accidentally deleted the Edit menu from my menu bar. If this happens to you, fear not; just click the Reset button, and click Yes to reset the selected bar. The reset message is a little cryptic, but it does reset the bar to the original settings.

Setting Options

There are many options you can change to customize PowerPoint 97 to work with you in the best way possible. For example, when you save a file, is there a specific folder you're always switching to? You might want to change the File option in PowerPoint to always point to that folder. Or how often do you want PowerPoint to save your work in case of a power outage? These options and more can all be customized in the Tools | Options dialog box. To help you on your way, Table 24.1 lists all the options available, explains what they do, and offers some suggestions.

JUST A MINUTE

A checkmark next to an option indicates that the option is active.

JUST A MINUTE

The following table lists the tab of the Options dialog box in boldface type before explaining each of the options you can customize in that tab.

Table 24.1. Description of the options available for customization.

Option	Description
	View
Startup dialog box	Shows the PowerPoint dialog box when you first start PowerPoint.
New slide dialog box	When you insert a new slide, PowerPoint displays the New Slide dialog box so you can select a layout for the slide. If this option is not checked, you won't automatically see this box.

Option	Description
	View
Status bar	Displays the status bar at the bottom of the screen.
Vertical ruler	Displays a vertical ruler on the left of the screen.
Pop-up menu on right mouse click	Allows using the right mouse button to quickly perform certain tasks during a slide show.
Show pop-up menu button	During a slide show, displays the very dim menu button (in the lower-left corner of the slide) for selecting slide show commands.
End with black slide	Ends a slide show with a black screen.
	General
Provide feedback with sound to screen elements	Plays a sound when certain actions are performed. Requires sound capabilities with your machine.
Recently used file list: *xx* entries	Determines whether (and how many) recently used files show up at the bottom of the File menu.
Macro virus protection	Displays a warning when opening any file that has a macro, good or bad, in it.
Link sounds with file size greater than *xxx* Kb	PowerPoint automatically creates a link to sound files bigger than the amount specified.
Name	The name that automatically appears in the properties sheet for the presentation.
Initials	The initials that automatically appear in the properties sheet for the presentation.
	Edit
Replace straight quotes with smart quotes	Automatically replaces plain old straight quotes, " ", with pretty curly quotes, “ ”.

continues

Table 24.1. continued

Option	Description
	Edit
Automatic word selection	Automatically selects whole words when dragging with the mouse.
Use smart cut and paste	Adds or removes extra spaces or returns when you cut and paste.
Drag-and-drop text editing	Allows using the mouse to cut or copy selected text by dragging.
New charts take on PowerPoint font	All new charts start with 18-point Arial font.
Maximum number of undos: *xx*	How many actions PowerPoint remembers to undo.
	Print
Background printing	Allows printing to be done in the background so you can continue working.
Print TrueType fonts as graphics	Prints Windows TrueType fonts as graphics rather than text.
Print inserted objects at printer resolution	Uses the printer's default resolution.
When printing Presentation1 via toolbar button or binder...	You have two choices when you click the Print button: 1. Print using the most recent print settings (those you used the last time you chose File | Print from the menu. 2. Print using the default settings.
	Save
Allow fast saves	Fast saves speed up saving a file, but increase the file size.
Prompt for file properties	When you save a file, displays the File Properties dialog box.
Full text search information	Keeps the full text search information with the presentation.

Option	Description
	Save
Save AutoRecover info every *xx* minutes	How often PowerPoint saves your work in case of a power outage.
Save PowerPoint files as:	Default file type that PowerPoint saves files as.
	Spelling
Spelling	Displays red squiggly underlines under misspelled words.
Hide spelling errors	Hides the red squiggly underlines under misspelled words.
Always	Always suggest possible correct spelling during a spellcheck.
Words in UPPERCASE	Ignore UPPERCASE words during a spellcheck.
Words with numbers	Ignore words with numbers during a spellcheck.
	Advanced
Render 24-bit bitmaps at highest quality	Shows pictures at the highest screen quality available, but might slow down the display.
Export pictures:	You have two choices: 1. Export pictures in the best quality for printing. 2. Export pictures in the best quality for viewing onscreen.
Default file location:	The folder PowerPoint looks in first when you choose either Save or Open from the menu.

To change any PowerPoint options, follow these steps:

1. Choose Tool | Options from the menu.
2. Change any settings you want.
3. Click the OK button.

Branching to Another Presentation with Hyperlinks

You can have an onscreen presentation branch to other presentations or other slides during the slide show. This nifty new feature is great when you want some slides in a presentation to have different Page Setup options, such as the page orientation. To branch to another presentation (or a single slide in a presentation), just place a link on each slide to branch first to the second presentation, and then back.

For example, suppose you have a presentation (call it the Summer presentation) with eight slides. After Summer slide 5, you want to view Pooh slide 4, then come back to Summer slide 6 and finish the Summer presentation. To do that, place a link on Summer slide 5 to Pooh slide 4, and a link on Pooh slide 4 to Summer slide 6. (See Figure 24.7.)

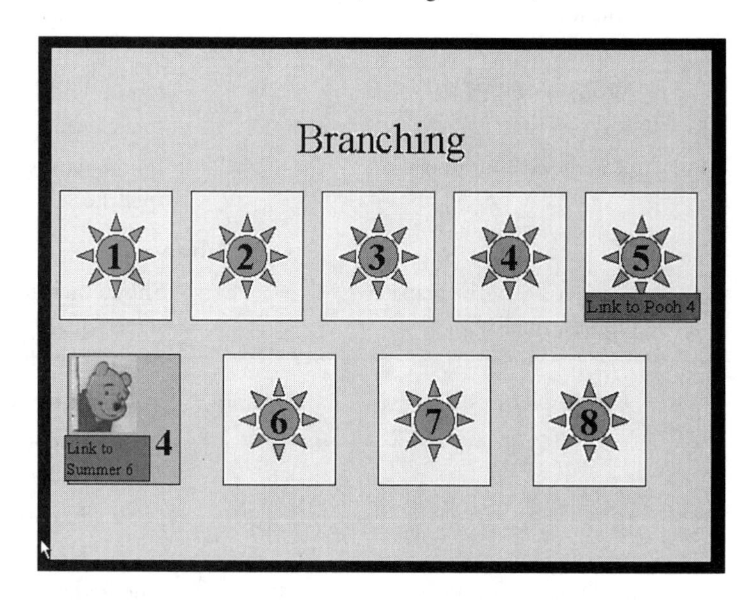

Figure 24.7.
Branching to Pooh slide 4 and back again.

To add a hyperlink to a presentation slide, follow these steps:

1. Make sure the presentations you're linking have been saved.
2. Select the text or object that will serve as the link (create one if needed).
3. Choose Slide Show | Action Settings from the menu.
4. Select the Mouse Click tab.
5. Select the "Hyperlink to" option.
6. From the "Hyperlink to" drop-down list, select Other PowerPoint Presentation.

7. In the Hyperlink to Other PowerPoint Presentation dialog box, select the folder and file you want to link to.
8. If there's more than one slide in the presentation, PowerPoint shows the Hyperlink to Slide dialog box. Simply select the slide you want to link to and click the OK button.
9. Click the OK button.
10. Open the second presentation.
11. View the slide where you will link back to the original presentation.
12. Repeat steps 2–9.
13. View the first presentation using your links to test everything out.

Creating Your Own Presentation Design

If you have created a custom look for presentations that you would like to use over and over again, you can save your presentation as a presentation design template. To do that, follow these steps:

1. Open the presentation you want to base the template on.
2. Delete all the slides, text, and other objects that you don't want to appear on every new presentation you create when you use this template.
3. Choose File | Save As from the menu.
4. Type a name for the template, such as `XYZ Corp`.
5. Select "Presentation templates" from the "Save as type" drop-down list.
6. Click the Save button.

Summary

In this final hour of PowerPoint 97, you have learned about some of the features that will really show Bob what a power user you have become. You can save lots of typing time by using AutoCorrect, and you can now customize or create toolbars. PowerPoint 97 has many options you can change so that it works better for you. The sections on hyperlinks and presentation designs had several ideas to help you on your way to complete customization of PowerPoint 97.

We hope you have as much fun learning about PowerPoint 97 as we have had writing about it. You've been a great audience. Let us know what you thought—we're always looking for ways to improve.

Workshop

Just one last "Test What You've Learned" section, and then you're outta here, Alice. Please be sure to read the last "Q&A" section.

Test What You've Learned

1. Open a new, blank presentation.
2. Add your initials to the AutoCorrect dialog box so that your full name will be replaced.
3. Create a custom toolbar.
4. Open the Options dialog box and change the options to your liking.
5. Save the presentation as `Hour 24 TWYL`.
6. Create a branch to the Pooh presentation (from Hour 19's "Test What You've Learned") and branch back to this presentation.
7. Save the presentation as a presentation design template. Call it `TWYL Template`.
8. Close the presentation.
9. Exit from PowerPoint.
10. Shut down the computer.
11. Turn off the computer.
12. Go on vacation (or write another book).

Q&A

Q Mommy, are you done yet?

A Yes.

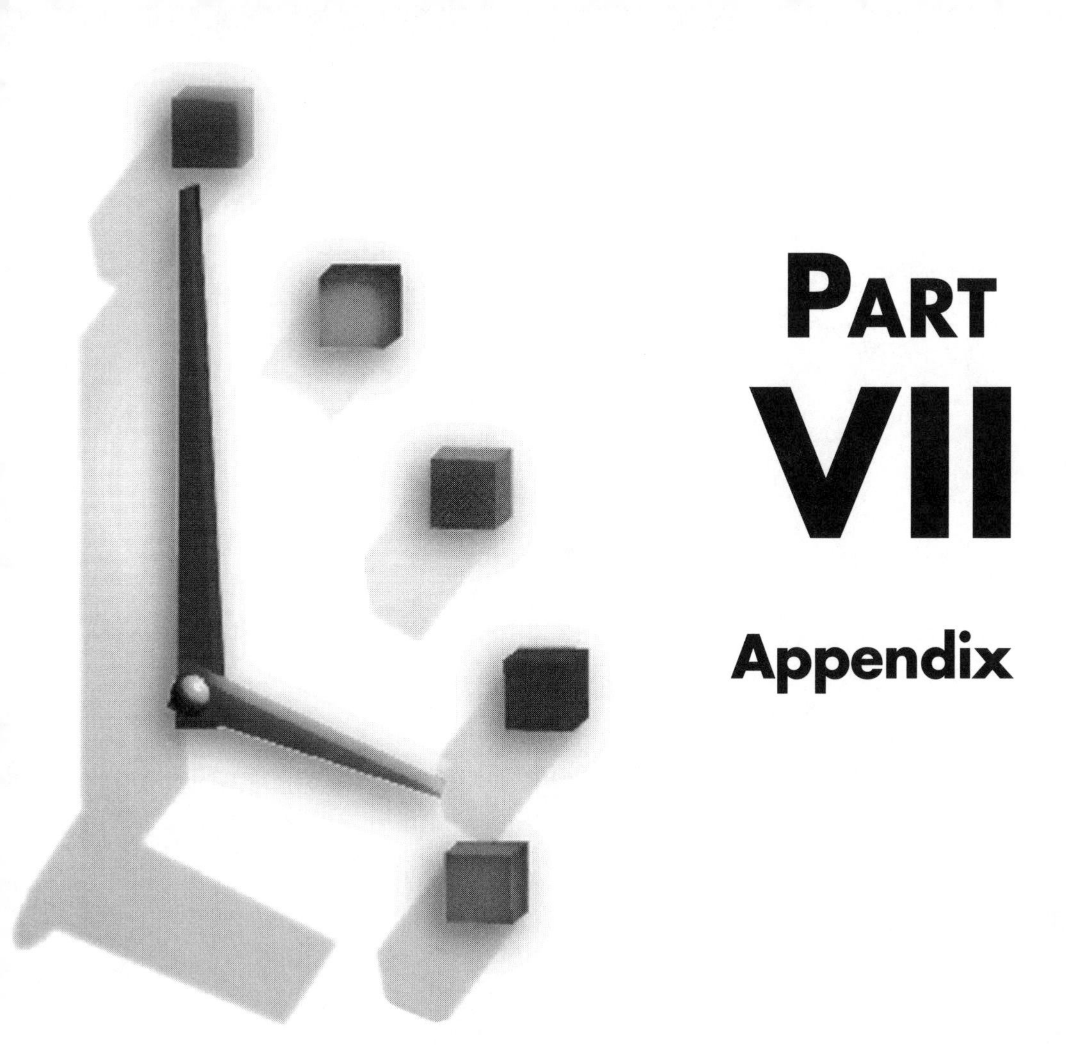

PART VII

Appendix

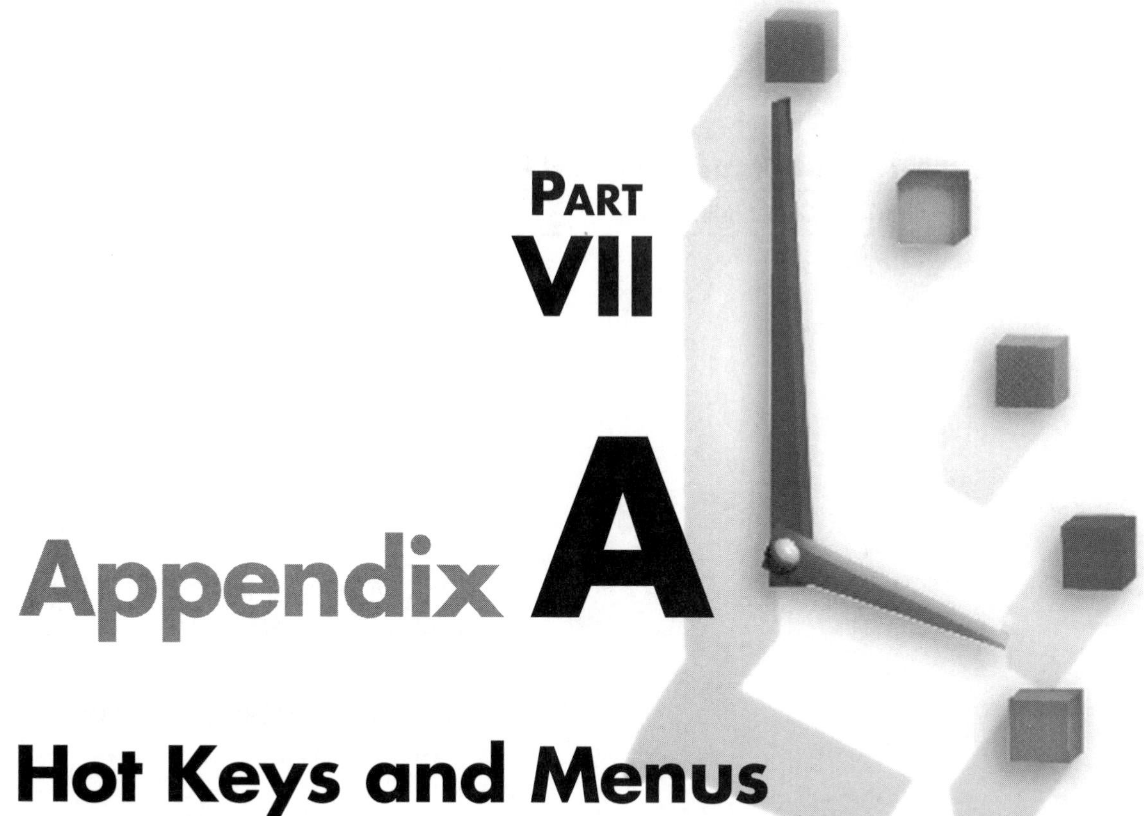

PART VII

Appendix A

Hot Keys and Menus

The following tables outline most of the shortcut keys available in PowerPoint, but PowerPoint lists many other shortcut keys in the Help Index, too.

Table A.1 lists, in alphabetical order, the shortcut key combinations that use the Ctrl key.

Table A.1. Shortcuts using the Ctrl key.

Shortcut Key Combination	Action Performed
Ctrl+A	Slide View: Select all objects
	Outline View: Select all text
	Slide Sorter View: Select all slides
Ctrl+B	Bold
Ctrl+C	Copy
Ctrl+D	Duplicates selected object
Ctrl+E	Center align
Ctrl+F	Find
Ctrl+G	Turn guides on or off
Ctrl+H	Replace
Ctrl+I	Italics
Ctrl+J	Justify align (or left and right align)
Ctrl+K	Insert a hyperlink
Ctrl+L	Left align
Ctrl+M	Insert a new slide
Ctrl+N	Start a new presentation
Ctrl+O	Open a presentation
Ctrl+P	Print a presentation
Ctrl+Q	Exit from PowerPoint
Ctrl+R	Right align
Ctrl+S	Save a presentation
Ctrl+T	Format the font
Ctrl+U	Underline
Ctrl+V	Paste
Ctrl+W	Close the presentation
Ctrl+X	Cut
Ctrl+Y	Repeat the last action (or command)
Ctrl+Z	Undo last action (or command)

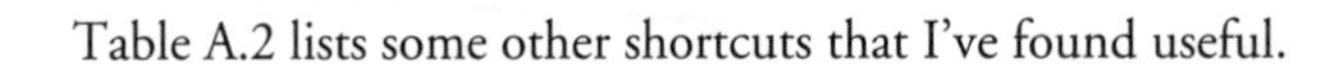
Table A.2 lists some other shortcuts that I've found useful.

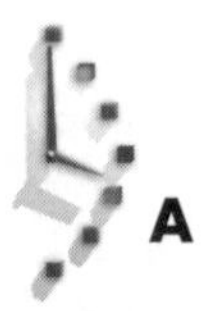

Table A.2. Other shortcuts with the keyboard and function keys.

Shortcut Key Combination	Action Performed
Cursor movement using the keyboard	
Ctrl+Left Arrow	Move one word to the left
Ctrl+Right Arrow	Move one word to the right
End	Move to the end of the line
Home	Move to the beginning of the line
Ctrl+Up Arrow	Move up one paragraph
Ctrl+Down Arrow	Move down one paragraph
Ctrl+Home	Go to the first slide (if no object is selected), or go to the beginning of all text (if object is selected)
Ctrl+End	Go to the last slide (if no object is selected), or go to the end of all text (if object is selected)
Selection options using the keyboard	
Shift+Right Arrow	Select one character to the right
Shift+Left Arrow	Select one character to the left
Ctrl+Shift+Right Arrow	Select one word to the right
Ctrl+Shift+Left Arrow	Select one word to the right
Shift+Up Arrow	Select one paragraph up
Shift+Down Arrow	Select one paragraph down
Tab (with nothing selected)	Select an object on a slide
Other shortcuts and function keys	
Ctrl+Backspace	Delete one word to the left (going back) of the cursor
Ctrl+Delete	Delete one word to the right (going forward) of the cursor
Ctrl+F9	Minimize the presentation window
Ctrl+F10	Maximize the presentation window
F1	Help
F2	Toggle between selecting all the text in an object or selecting the object
F7	Spelling

Menus

As with any Windows program, you can choose any menu command by using the keyboard. Press the Alt key followed by the underlined letter in the main menu (for example, pressing Alt+F opens the File menu). Pressing any underlined letter in a menu, without using the Alt key, chooses the menu command. For example, to print a presentation, use the following keystrokes:

1. Alt
2. F
3. P

If you like this method of choosing menu commands, you will find that the more you use it, the faster you get. Christopher almost always uses the keyboard to perform menu commands.

You can customize any menu by using the following instructions. First, to add a command to a menu, follow these steps:

1. Choose View | Toolbars | Customize from the menu.
2. Click the Toolbars tab.
3. Select Menu Bar from the list of toolbars.
4. Click the Commands tab.
5. Select a category from the Categories list.
6. Click the menu heading you want to edit to open the menu.
7. Drag the command to the menu.
8. Repeat the above steps, if needed.

Here's how you can delete a command from a menu:

1. Choose View | Toolbars | Customize from the menu.
2. Click the Toolbars tab.
3. Select Menu Bar from the list of toolbars.
4. Click the menu heading you want to edit to open the menu.
5. Drag the command off the menu.
6. Repeat the above steps, if needed.

CAUTION

Don't customize your menu so much that you (or someone else who shares your machine) can't get your work done. If you accidentally get carried away with all this cool customization stuff, and you fall off the wall, you can put everything back together (unlike Humpty Dumpty). To reset your menu to the original settings, follow these steps:

1. Choose View | Toolbars | Customize from the menu.
2. Click the Toolbars tab of the Customize dialog box.
3. Select Menu Bar from the list of toolbars.
4. Click the Reset button; the Reset Toolbar dialog box pops up.
5. Click the OK button in the Reset Toolbar dialog box.
6. Click the Close button in the Customize dialog box.

Only ten seconds, and you have put Humpty Dumpty back together again.

INDEX

B

C

D

E

F

G

H

I

J-L

M

N

O

P-Q

R

S

T

U

V

W

Z

Technical Support:

If you need assistance with the information in this book or with a CD/Disk accompanying the book, please access the Knowledge Base on our Web site at **http://www.superlibrary.com/general/support**. Our most Frequently Asked Questions are answered there. If you do not find the answer to your questions on our Web site, you may contact Macmillan Technical Support **(317) 581-3833** or e-mail us at **support@mcp.com**.

Teach Yourself Microsoft Word 97 in 24 Hours

Linda Jones

Written in a straightforward, easy-to-read manner, this book allows you to quickly become productive with Word 97. From basic concepts, such as opening new and existing documents, to more complex features like using styles and macros, even beginning users can learn how to use the new features of the most popular word processing application.

Includes coverage the Microsoft Office 97 suite—how applications relate to each other and how to access online resources.

$19.99 USA; $28.95 CAN   0-672-31115-1   400 pp.   7/1/97
New—Casual   Word Processing

Teach Yourself Microsoft Excel 97 in 24 Hours

Lois Patterson

This book uses a task-oriented format to help you become productive in this spreadsheet application with just 24 one-hour lessons. Many new features of Excel 97, including increased connectivity and the enhanced Chart Wizard, are covered, so it's also a tutorial for those upgrading from previous versions of Excel. Accomplished users will find many tips to help increase their productivity.

Includes many illustrations and figures that show how to operate Excel's key features and more mathematical and scientific examples than many other texts have.

$19.99 USA; $28.95 CAN   0-672-31116-x   400 pp.   7/1/97
New—Casual   Spreadsheets

Teach Yourself Access 97 in 24 Hours

Timothy Buchanan, Craig Eddy, and Rob Newman

As organizations and users continue to upgrade to NT Workstation and Windows 95, a surge in 32-bit productivity applications, including Microsoft Office 97, is expected. Using an easy-to-follow approach, this book teaches the fundamentals of a key component in the Microsoft Office 97 package: Access 97. You will learn how to work with existing databases, create database with wizards, and build databases from scratch in 24 one-hour lessons.

$19.99 USA; $28.95 CAN   0-672-31027-9   400 pp.   02/01/97
New—Casual   Databases

Paul McFedries' Windows 95 Unleashed, Professional Reference Edition

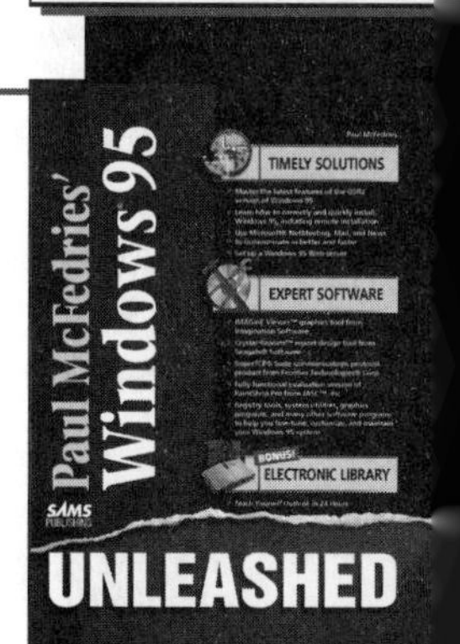

Paul McFedries

Essential for all Windows users, this book takes you beyond the basics, exploring all facets of this operating system, including installation, the Internet, customization, optimization, networking multimedia, Plug-and-Play, and the new features of Windows Messaging System for communications.

- Updated with additional reference material
- Covers the enhancements since the initial release of Windows 95
- Includes coverage of Internet Explorer 4.0, bringing the "active desktop" to Windows 95

CD-ROM contains 32-bit software designed for Windows 95 and an easy-to-search online chapter on troubleshooting for Windows 95.

$59.99 USA; $84.95 CAN   0-672-31039-2   1,750 pp.   7/1/97
Accomplished—Expert   Operating Systems

Microsoft Office 97 Unleashed, Second Edition

Paul McFedries

Microsoft has brought the Web to its Office suite of products. Hyperlinking, Office Assistants, and Active Document Support let you publish documents to the Web or an intranet site. Office 97 also completely integrates with Microsoft FrontPage, making it possible to point-and-click a Web page into existence. This book covers each of the Office products—Excel, Access, PowerPoint, Word, and Outlook—and shows the estimated 22 million registered users how to create presentations and Web documents.

- Shows how to extend Office to work on a network
- Describes the different Office Solution Kits and how to use them

CD-ROM includes powerful utilities and two best-selling books in HTML format.

$39.99 USA; $56.95 CAN 0-672-31010-4 1,200 pp. 12/01/96
Accomplished—Expert

Teach Yourself Web Publishing with Microsoft Office 97 in a Week

Michael Larson

As the best-selling office suite in the business world with over 22 million users, Microsoft Office is taking the market by storm. By following a clear, step-by-step approach and practical examples, you will learn how to effectively use Office components to publish attractive, well-designed documents for the World Wide Web or an intranet.

- Focuses on the Web publishing features of the latest versions of Microsoft Word, Excel, Access, and PowerPoint
- Explains the basics of Internet/intranet technology, the Microsoft Internet Explorer browser, and HTML

CD-ROM is loaded with Microsoft Internet Explorer 3.0 and an extensive selection of additional graphics, templates, scripts, ActiveX controls, and multimedia clips to enhance Web pages.

$39.99 USA; $56.95 CAN 1-57521-232-3 464 pp. 02/01/97
New—Casual—Accomplished

Teach Yourself Microsoft FrontPage 97 in a Week

Donald Doherty and John Jung

FrontPage is the number-one Web site–creating program in the market, and this book explains how to use it. Everything from adding Office 97 documents to a Web site to using Java, HTML, wizards, Visual Basic Script, and JavaScript in a Web page is covered. With this book, you learn all the nuances of Web design. By following the step-by-step examples, you create an entire Web site using FrontPage 97.

CD-ROM includes Microsoft Internet Explorer 3.0, ActiveX and HTML development tools, plus ready-to-use templates, graphics, scripts, Java applets, and more.

$29.99 USA; $42.95 CAN 1-57521-225-0 500 pp. 01/01/97
New—Casual Internet/Web Publishing

Teach Yourself Microsoft Outlook 97 in 24 Hours

Brian Proffitt and Kim Spilker

Microsoft Office is the leading application-productivity suite available; in its next version, it will have Outlook as a personal information manager. Using step-by-step instructions and real-world examples, you explore Outlook's new features and learn how to successfully and painlessly integrate it with other Office 97 applications.

Each day focuses on working with Outlook as a single user and in a group setting.

$19.99 USA; $28.95 CAN 0-672-31044-9 400 pp. 04/01/97
New—Casual Integrated Software/Suites

Book ISBN 0-672-31117-8